The Cutting Edge of the Poet's Sword

The Muslim World in the Age of the Crusades

STUDIES AND TEXTS

Edited by

Suleiman A. Mourad (*Smith College*)
Paul M. Cobb (*University of Pennsylvania*)
Konrad Hirschler (*SOAS University of London*)

Advisory Board

Anne-Marie Eddé (*Université Paris I – Panthéon-Sorbonne*)
Carole Hillenbrand (*Edinburgh University*)
Adam J. Kosto (*Columbia University*)
Christopher H. MacEvitt (*Dartmouth College*)
Stephennie Mulder (*University of Texas – Austin*)
Jonathan Phillips (*University of London – Royal Holloway*)
Daniella Talmon-Heller (*Ben-Gurion University of the Negev*)

VOLUME 3

The titles published in this series are listed at *brill.com/mwac*

The Cutting Edge of the Poet's Sword

Muslim Poetic Responses to the Crusades

By

Osman Latiff

BRILL

LEIDEN | BOSTON

Cover illustration: Image from an eighth-/fourteenth-century Mamluk manuscript from the British Library's collection of Arabic manuscripts: *Nihāyat al-sūʾl wa-l-umniyya fī taʿallum aʿmāl al-furūsiyya* ("An end of questioning and desiring [further knowledge] concerning learning of the different exercises of horsemanship"). The Arabic text to the right of the image states that it is an 'Illustration of a horseman with the edge of the sword under his right arm, the hilt in his left with the reins.' (Add. MS. 18866, fol. 127r).

The Library of Congress Cataloging-in-Publication Data is available online at http://catalog.loc.gov
LC record available at https://lccn.loc.gov/2017037316

Typeface for the Latin, Greek, and Cyrillic scripts: "Brill". See and download: brill.com/brill-typeface.

ISSN 2213-1043
ISBN 978-90-04-34521-8 (hardback)
ISBN 978-90-04-34522-5 (e-book)

This book is printed on acid-free paper and produced in a sustainable manner.

Contents

Acknowledgements VII
A Note on Transliteration IX
Abbreviations X
Chronology XI

1 **Introduction: Setting the Scene** 1
The Historical and Historiographical Context – Ideas and Definitions 2
Sanctities of Space 4
Sources 9
Ideological Pursuits: Nūr al-Dīn, Ṣalāḥ al-Dīn, and Political Patronage: An Overview 17
Al-Ghazālī and the New Sunnism of the Saljūq Period 27
Faḍā'il al-Quds (Merits of Jerusalem): Historiography and Relevance 30

2 **Poetry and Poetics in Medieval Arabic Discourse** 40
Historiographical Considerations 40
The Place of Poetry and Modern Perspectives 48

3 **Theories and Principles of *Jihād* and the Quest for Martyrdom** 55
Yūsuf al-Findalāwī and the Pursuit of Martyrdom 61

4 **Formative Muslim Responses: Franks (Faranj), Christians (Rūm), and the Making of a Christian Enemy** 67
The First Crusade 488–93/1095–99: Syria and Internal Reform 67
Verses in al-Sulamī's *Kitāb al-Jihād* 78
The Proximity of an Islamic Jerusalem: The Fall of Edessa, Banū Aṣfar, and the Revival of *Jihād* 82
Images of the Franks in Muslim Poetry 89
The Merging of Sacred Designations 93

5 **Poeticising the Reconquest and Future Expectations** 99
The Reconquest of Jerusalem and Popular Piety 99
The Sanctification of Spaces 106
Constantinople and its Relation to Jerusalem 115
Ibn Jubayr: Pilgrimage, Poetry, and Social Accountability 121

6 **Literary Underpinnings of the Anti-Frankish *Jihād*** 129
Steering an Image: The Figure of the Christian 'Other' in Muslim Poetry 130
Nūr al-Dīn and the Creation of a Pious Warrior Ethos 150
The Inspiration of the Qur'ān in *Jihād* Poetry 166
Heightened Fears and Eschatological Undercurrents in Muslim Poetry 172
Gendering the Anti-Frankish *Jihād* 183

7 **The Place of Egypt in Poetic Discourse** 192
Egypt and the Language of Realpolitik 193
Poetry in Diplomacy and Calls for Unity 199

8 **Shattered Dreams: Jerusalem, the *Umma*, and New Enemies** 209
Post-Reconquest Poetry 209
Dismantling the Walls 214

Conclusion 219

Appendix: Arabic Poems 227
Bibliography 248
Primary Sources 248
Primary Sources in Translation 251
Secondary Material 252
Index of Names and Places 269
Index of Subjects 278

Acknowledgements

All credit goes firstly to God for His enabling me to complete this task, for His Mercy and Kindness in times of ease and difficulty. In line with the prophetic tradition,

من لا يشكر الناس لا يشكر الله

He who does not thank the people has not thanked God,

I would like to express my heartfelt love and appreciation to my dear parents, Zarina and Mohamed Latiff, for their unconditional love, for inspiring me to follow my dreams, and for maintaining the ease which has allowed me to complete this, and so many other tasks, in an environment of peace and comfort. They have my enduring gratitude and admiration, and to them I am indebted.

I am very grateful to my PhD supervisor, Professor Jonathan Phillips, for his support, trust in me, and genuine goodwill during my undergraduate and postgraduate tenures. A special thanks to my wife Razan for her love, untiring support and patience, and belief in me. I thank my sons Mujahid and Hudhaifa and my daughter Maryam, for their beauty and innocence, and for their pleasant distractions.

I owe a huge thanks to the many others who have helped me in so many ways, particularly to Musaab al-Barghash for his suggestions and crucial input; to Irfan Shahzad, Ghazi al-Mannai, Abdul Basith Awan, Umar Ansari; to my beloved aunts, Samina Butt and Shahpara Shah, with whom I share so many fond memories, for their kindness and love; and to my ever-supportive brothers Omar and Akbar who have stood by me throughout the years; and to other family members and friends, each of whom played an invaluable part in helping with this research. Even though memories may have subsided, special and warm thanks must go to my secondary school history teacher, Mr. R. Grimes for his charisma and wit in the classroom and for his passion for history, which was a great source of inspiration.

I am very grateful to the Arts and Humanities Research Council (AHRC) for the grant they awarded me during the first three years of my PhD research, and to the Institute of Historical Research (IHR) for the Isobel Thornley Fellowship I was awarded during my final year.

I wish to thank those many people who attended papers I have presented, for their questions and insightful comments that have sometimes made me rethink my arguments. I am grateful to Brill's MWAC editorial board and to

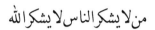

Valerie Joy Turner whose positive guidance and assistance at the last stages of the book's publication have been much appreciated. A thank you to Professor Carole Hillenbrand for inspiring me with her work on the crusades and for advising me about the fomat of this book. Finally, I wish to thank the 'Crusades and the Latin East' Seminar community at the IHR for the many presentations and discussions from which I greatly benefited.

A Note on Transliteration

To facilitate the book for those who are not familiar with Arabic terms, I have occasionally opted to use the singular form with an English plural instead of the pluralised Arabic form where obvious confusion may arise, for example, *ḥadīth*s rather than the correct plural, *aḥadīth*.

I have opted for 'Syria' as opposed to 'al-Shām' or 'Bilād al-Shām' (Greater Syria) to denote the geographical area of Syria, Jordan, Lebanon, and Palestine. All translations in the book are my own, unless otherwise noted. The numbers at the beginning of lines of verse refer to the verse numbers in the Arabic poems, whenever these are given in the various Arabic references. The numbers in parentheses following the lines of verse correspond to that verse in the appendix, where the poetry appears in Arabic in full.

Date Conversions

The references to Islamic sources are dated according to the Hijri and Gregorian calendars. For conversion from Hijri to Gregorian dates I have relied on the 'Conversion of Islamic and Christian dates' by J. Thomann, available online: http://mela.us/hegira.html.

Abbreviations

BSOAS	*Bulletin of the School of Oriental and African Studies*
EI[2]	*Encyclopaedia of Islam*, new edition, ed. P. J. Bearman, Th. Bianquis, C. E. Bosworth, E. van Donzel, and W. P. Heinrichs et al., 12 vols (Leiden: Brill, 1960–2005).
IJMES	*International Journal of Middle East Studies*
IOS	*Israel Oriental Studies*
JAOS	*Journal of the American Oriental Society*
JSAI	*Jerusalem Studies in Arabic and Islam*
SI	*Studia Islamica*

Chronology[1]

1009	The Fāṭimid caliph al-Ḥākim bi-Amr-Allāh destroys a part of the Church of the Holy Sepulchre
1071	Alp Arslān defeats Romanus Diogenes at Manzikert
1095	Pope Urban II preaches the First Crusade
1097	Crusaders take Nicaea
1098	Baldwin of Boulogne seizes control of Edessa
1098	Crusaders take control of Antioch
1098	Fāṭimids wrestle control of Jerusalem from the Saljūqs
1099	Crusaders capture the city of Jerusalem
1099	Crusaders defeat Fāṭimids at Ascalon
1099–1111	Muslim contingents from Syria arrive in Baghdad calling on assistance against the crusaders
1099-1123	Around this time poets such as Abū Muẓaffar al-Abīwardī and Ibn al-Khayyāṭ compose poetic verses denouncing the crusade
1105	ʿAli ibn Ṭāhir al-Sulamī composes his *Kitāb al-Jihād* (Book of Jihād) at Damascus
1119	Īl-Ghāzī defeats crusaders at the Battle of the Field of Blood/ Battle of Balat
1128	ʿImād al-Dīn Zangī becomes ruler of Aleppo
1144	ʿImād al-Dīn Zangī captures the Crusader state of Edessa
1146	Death of Zangī. His son Nūr al-Dīn takes power in Aleppo.
1147	Agreement of diplomacy between Nūr al-Dīn of Aleppo and Muʿīn al-Dīn of Damascus
1148	The launch of the Second Crusade. Crusaders attack Damascus and the attack fails.
1154	Nūr al-Dīn takes Damascus
1168	Shirkūh sets out for Egypt
1169	Franks withdraw from Egypt. Shāwār is executed and Shirkūh is made vizier
1169	Shirkūh dies. Ṣalāḥ al-Dīn becomes the Fāṭimid vizier
1171	Ṣalāḥ al-Dīn abolishes the Fāṭimid caliphate
1174	Death of Nūr al-Dīn
1174	Ṣalāḥ al-Dīn takes Damascus
1176	Peace treaty is established between Ṣalāḥ al-Dīn and the Zangids

1 This chronology covers the dates that have a direct bearing on the events described in this book.

1177	Ṣalāḥ al-Dīn suffers defeat by Franks at Montgisard
1183	Reynald of Chatillon's Red Sea incursion is thwarted
1183	Ṣalāḥ al-Dīn takes Aleppo
1183–1184	Ṣalāḥ al-Dīn attacks Kerak
1185	Ṣalāḥ al-Dīn makes a truce with the Franks
1187	Reynald of Chatillon attacks a Muslim caravan
1187	Ṣalāḥ al-Dīn takes Tiberias
1187	Ṣalāḥ al-Dīn defeats the crusader at Hattin
1187	Ṣalāḥ al-Dīn recaptures Jerusalem
1189	Third Crusade is launched
1191	King Richard I defeats Ṣalāḥ al-Dīn at Arsuf
1192	Richard I attempts to march on Jerusalem but is forced to turn back
1192	Peace treaty is established between Ṣalāḥ al-Dīn and Richard I
1193	Death of Ṣalāḥ al-Dīn. He is succeeded by his sons and relatives
1204	The Fourth Crusade and the Sack of Constantinople
1217–1221	The Fifth Crusade
1218	Crusaders attack Damietta
1219	Damietta captured by crusaders
1219	al-Muʿaẓẓam begins pre-emptive destruction of the walls and towers of Jerusalem

CHAPTER 1

Introduction: Setting the Scene

The study of the crusades has long fascinated European and Middle Eastern historians. Shaped by many attitudes over a good part of two centuries, the crusades involved peoples of many races and from many lands, of various theological leanings, and motivated by different reasons. The conflict significantly affected the development of medieval Europe and had a lasting impact on the peoples against whom they were waged. While the translation and edition of Latin sources continues to provide fresh insight into the dynamics of the crusades and the life and settlement of Christians in the Latin Kingdom of Jerusalem, our Western understanding of the anti-Frankish *jihād* is not as complete. The purpose behind this book is to allow the European reader to see and appreciate the impact of the crusades from 'the other side,' in particular from the perspective of Muslim poets. These lyricists composed verses at times of victory and at times of loss, about crusading invaders and beautiful Frankish women. Their compositions were motivated by both secular and religious influences and provide an insightful outlook into the sentiments of propagandists who used the medium of ornate verse as a powerful motivational and recruiting tool during the crusades.

While narrative texts are the main historical source for the events of the crusades, the historical value of other source material, including books of *faḍāʾil* (the merits of Jerusalem/Greater Syria), inscriptions, sermons, and poetry should not go unnoticed. Such sources not only complement what is already known, but also provide us with an understanding of purpose and expressions of important sentiments, and allude to changing attitudes. Sometimes by closely reading existing texts and taking nuanced approaches toward sources that have been deemed of little worth in providing 'historical truth,' we can reveal attitudes that may have gone unnoticed.

This book does not attempt to present a holistic examination of the political, religious, economic, and social influences that shaped the Muslim experience we know of as the 'anti-Frankish *jihād*.' Although modern scholarship on the crusades and *jihād* covers a wide variety of subjects, this new contribution does not narrate the history of the conflict, as other works have done successfully, rather it provides new insights into the workings of poetry as an ideological and political vehicle, an important part of *jihād* preaching in this period.

Since Arabic poetry is a source material hitherto neglected or inadequately treated by modern historians of the crusades, in this book my aim is to bring to

 | DOI 10.1163/9789004345225_002

the fore a range of themes that emerged in the poetry of the sixth/twelfth and seventh/thirteenth centuries. These poems served as a stimulus for the anti-Frankish *jihād*; some were intended to lampoon the enemy; others were fused with religious imagery and aimed to show the superiority of Islam; others reflected cultural attitudes during encounters between Muslims and Christians. This book reveals how poetry brings to light new considerations of the way Muslims perceived themselves, the crusaders, and their time.

The Historical and Historiographical Context – Ideas and Definitions

It is important to begin by outlining the historical context that shaped the focus of this book. The initial Muslim reaction following the capture of Jerusalem on 23 Shaʿbān 492/15 July 1099 has been described as one of apathy; the internal divisions that existed during the crusader onslaught continued to worsen during the early decades of the occupation, and instead of a united political response from the Muslim world, the rulers of Syria made alliances and social contracts with the Franks and continued their territorial infighting.[1] Although many *khaṭībs* and scholars were killed in the First Crusade, the religious outrage from neighbouring regions was surprisingly small; similarly, Muslim efforts to engage the Franks in battle during the early decades of the sixth/twelfth century were also intermittent.[2] The *Kitāb al-Jihād* [Book of *jihād*] of

1 D. Ephrat and M. D. Kabha, 'Muslim Reactions to the Frankish Presence in Bilād al-Shām: Intensifying Religious Fidelity within the Masses,' *Al-Masāq* 15 (March 2003), 47; C. Hillenbrand, *The Crusades: Islamic Perspectives* (Edinburgh: Edinburgh University Press, 1999), 329–430. Hadia Dajani-Shakeel cites the treaty between Ṭughtikin and the ruler of Tripoli on Rafaniya in 503/1110, the concord between Ṭughtikin and King Baldwin I at al-Sanamayn in 504/1111, and other examples. See H. Dajani-Shakeel, 'Diplomatic Relations between Muslim and Frankish Rulers,' *Crusaders and Muslims in Twelfth-Century Syria*, ed. M. Shatzmiller (Leiden: Brill, 1993), 190–215.

2 The killing of religious scholars and devout worshippers was a particular focus, for example, of Ibn al-Athīr in his, albeit much later, description of the capture of Jerusalem (492/1099): "In al-Aqṣā Mosque the Franks killed more than 70,000, a large number of them being *imāms*, scholars, pious men, and ascetics, Muslims who had left their native lands and come to live a holy life in this venerated place." Ibn al-Athīr, *al-Kāmil fī al-tārīkh*, ed. ʿUmar ʿAbd al-Salām al-Tadmurī (Beirut: Dār al-Kutub al-ʿArabī, 2006), 9:425. It must be pointed out, however, that Ibn al-Athīr's description of the religious classes bearing the brunt of crusader violence cannot be corroborated from contemporary historical accounts, although it is likely that many from the religious classes would have been killed during the capture of Jerusalem. B. Kedar

ʿAlī b. Ṭāhir al-Sulamī that he preached in 498/1105 is a unique early example of a theologically-motivated response to the occupation.[3] Muslim poets such as Aḥmad b. Muḥammad b. al-Khayyāṭ (450–517/1058–1123) and Abū l-Muẓaffar al-Abīwardī (d. 507/1113) also expressed outrage at the First Crusade, highlighted the plight of the Muslims of Syria, and called for Muslim unity.[4] Yet for almost half a century there was no widespread surge of religious fervour and organised response to the occupation.

The reasons for the slow Muslim response have been a subject of much historical debate, particularly given Jerusalem's esteemed position in Islam. The Holy City is held to be the third most important city in Islam after Mecca and Medina. Al-Aqṣā Mosque is specifically mentioned in the Qur'ān in relation to the Prophet's ascension (*miʿrāj*),[5] Jerusalem was a regular place of pilgrimage (*ziyāra*) and the city also holds a venerated position in Islamic eschatological thought. The lack of military action however, particularly from the Sunnī ʿAbbāsid caliph in Baghdad, al-Mustaẓhir (r. 487–512/1094–1118), should not be read as overwhelming Muslim disinterest in the *jihād*; although aspirations to promote the *jihād* were certainly extant in religious classes during the early decades of the sixth/twelfth century, the political make-up of Syria in the early decades was not conducive to Muslim unity. Furthermore, like the Sunnīs, the Fāṭimid Shīʿīs were unable to legally prosecute a *jihād* without the sanction of their caliph. The precarious political rivalries that had engulfed the Fāṭimid leadership with the weakening of the caliph through the establishment of the

---

and K. Hirschler have reassessed the view of widespread massacres in their respective works. On the basis of mostly Latin sources Kedar concludes that the massacre was more extensive in Jerusalem than in other towns. Hirschler argues that though the Arabic sources do describe a massacre taking place, it is unlikely that the conquest of Jerusalem was met with a massacre of the entire population. See B. Kedar, 'The Jerusalem Massacre of July 1099 in the Western Historiography of the Crusades,' *Crusades* 3 (2004), 15–75; K. Hirschler, 'The Jerusalem Conquest of 492/1099 in the Medieval Arabic Historiography of the Crusades: From Regional Plurality to Islamic Narrative,' *Crusades*, 13 (2014), 37–76.

3 For more information see N. Christie, *The Book of the Jihad of ʿAli ibn Tahir al-Sulami (d. 1106): Text, Translation and Commentary* (Farnham: Ashgate, 2015); N. Christie, 'Motivating Listeners in the *Kitāb al-Jihād* of ʿAlī ibn Ṭāhir al-Sulamī (d. 1106),' *Crusades* 6 (2007), 1–14.

4 Ibn al-Jawzī, *al-Muntaẓam fī tārīkh al-mulūk wa-l-umam* (Hyderabad: Maṭbaʿat Dā'irat al-Maʿārif al-ʿUthmāniyya, 1940), 9:108; F. Gabrieli, *Arab Historians of the Crusades* (Berkeley and Los Angeles: University of California Press, 1969), 12; H. Dajani-Shakeel, '*Jihād* in Twelfth-Century Arabic Poetry: A Moral and Religious Force to Counter the Crusades,' *Muslim World* 66 (1976), 96–113; Ibn al-Khayyāṭ, *Dīwān*, ed. Khalil Mardam Beg (Beirut: Dār Ṣādir, 1994), 182–187; Ibn Taghrībirdī, *al-Nujūm al-zāhira fī mulūk Miṣr wa-l-Qāhira* (Cairo: Dār al-Kutub wa-l-Wathā'iq al-Qawmiyya, 2005), 5:151–152.

5 Qur'ān, 17:1.

'Jamālī' dynasty[6] meant that the latter's use of *jihād* propaganda was not conducive to its own legitimacy, and instead might lead the Shīʿī population back to the authority of the caliph.[7]

It was ʿImād al-Dīn Zangī's taking of Edessa in 538/1144 and the Second Crusade of 541–43/1147–48 that focused the attention of the inhabitants of Syria on the Franks and the liberation of Jerusalem. Zangī's capture of Edessa and the crusaders' later failed siege of Damascus in 543/1148 were instrumental in raising Muslim hopes and inspiring confidence in Islam's military leaders. There was a new-found attention on the sacred space of Jerusalem and books of *faḍā'il* began to proliferate from the time of Zangī's conquest and especially during the reign of his son Nūr al-Dīn, though one must not disregard Zangī, who also made use of *jihād* slogans during his rule. There may be more than one reason why this was the case; the population may have had a new-found confidence in the military leaders after the Second Crusade, or the Muslim victories may have encouraged the leaders to look to their religious communities. Furthermore, the clearer focus on *jihād* and *faḍā'il* in these years may have been influenced by Nūr al-Dīn's public and private displays of piety. Or the situation may reflect a combination of these factors.

Sanctities of Space

In the crusades and anti-Frankish *jihād*, the city of Jerusalem held a central role for Muslims and Christians. Jerusalem constitutes not only a temporal sacred space, but also an everlasting space for all three monotheistic religions. For medieval Christians Jerusalem was seen as a physical relic of Christ's life, sanctified by his presence, his resurrection, and his expected return; a spiritual connection to the city of Jerusalem represented not an abstract fixation but a permanent one born out of a clearly established link between the person of Jesus and the physical space he occupied.[8] Jerusalem therefore had heavenly

6 The lineage of powerful Fāṭimid viziers established by Badr al-Jamālī (467–87/1074–94).

7 For more information see W. Hamblin, 'To Wage *Jihād* or Not: Fāṭimid Egypt during the Early Crusades,' in *The Jihād and its Times*, ed. H. Dajani-Shakeel and R. A. Messier (Ann Arbor: University of Michigan Press, 1991), 31–40.

8 A central theme in the preaching of the crusades was the idea of violation of the sacred; this emerged from the inception of the crusades with Pope Urban II, when he preached (in the First Crusade) that the Muslims have "razed the churches of God to the ground ... Take the road to the Holy Sepulchre, rescue that land ..." Robert of Rheims in his account of Urban II's speech at Clermont, from L. and J. S. C. Riley Smith, *The Crusades: Idea and Reality, 1095–1274* (London, 1981), 42–45; furthermore, in Abbot Bernard of Clairvaux's letter

importance, an idea echoed by Gilbert of Aalst, who in 489/1096 founded the nunnery of Merhem for his sister Lietgard, "so that he should find a better inheritance in the heavenly Jerusalem."[9] Furthermore, by the time of the reconquest, Muslims grew to realise that it was the site that was sacred to Christians, not the structures. Though the loss of structures would infuriate the Christians, the location and site would still remain intrinsically important.

Judaism has an inseparable connection to the city of Jerusalem, which was accorded a place of superiority and prestige in the various genres of Jewish literature. Its position in Jewish apocalyptic literature, however, was of particular importance.[10] The contentions in the conflicts between Muslims and Christians sparked an increase in apocalyptic literature in which the notion of a future redemption preceded by social turmoil and wars was a feature of Biblical eschatology; this was further emphasised in rabbinical literature.[11] One of the apocalyptic texts written during the period of the crusades was the *Tefillat Rabbi Shim'on ben Yohai* [Prayer of Rabbi Simeon ben Yohai], that describes the killing of Muslim and Jewish residents of Jerusalem. It equates the Christian slaughter in the name of Jesus with Pharaoh's decree ordering Jewish male infants to be thrown into the Nile, and connects the suffering to the expected redemption preceded by various divine signs.[12]

---

to the English people during the Second Crusade 1145–49, of which at least nine copies were sent out, Bernard used very strong imagery to call on the faithful: "ad ipsum, proh dolor, religionis christianae sacrarium inhiant ore sacrilego, lectumque invadere et conculcare conantur, in quo propter nos Vita nostra obdormivit in morte." [Alas! they rage against the very shrine of the Christian faith with blasphemous mouths, and would violate that very couch on which, for our sake, the Lord of life fell sleep in death.] 'That very couch' is certainly a reference to the Holy Sepulchre, and the thought of it being violated would have ignited the fury of Christians. Bernard of Clairvaux, 'Epistolae,' in *Sancti Bernardi Opera*, (No. 363), ed. J. Leclercq and H. Rochais (Rome, 1955–77), 8:312.

9 J. S. C. Riley-Smith, *The First Crusaders 1095–1131* (Cambridge: Cambridge University Press, 1998), 120.

10 A. Grossman, 'Jerusalem in Jewish Apocalyptic Literature,' in *The History of Jerusalem: The Early Muslim Period 638–1099*, ed. J. Prawer and H. Ben-Shammai (New York: New York University Press, 1996), 295.

11 "Major turning points, especially turning of centuries, and human and natural catastrophes provide fertile grounds for nourishing old apocalypses which are adjusted to address the new situations, as well as 'coining' new ones, in the sense of acquiring for them a sublime, prophetical level and authority." S. Bashear, 'Muslim Apocalypses and the Hour: A Case-Study in Traditional Reinterpretation,' *IOS* 13, ed. Joel L. Kraemer (Leiden, 1993), 98.

12 A. Grossman, 'Jerusalem in Jewish Apocalyptic Literature,' 305.

In the Islamic tradition, the sanctity of the city arose from the *baraka* (blessing) that emanates from the religious personages who have been present, the spiritual effect of religious learning, and the sanctity created by the soteriological role of the locality. Yet more compelling and even more significant religiously, is the cosmological sanctity assigned to the city. Jerusalem, furthermore, is intricately connected to eschatology in Judaism, Christianity, and Islam, and these ideas have played a pivotal role in shaping a framework of religious cosmology in which humanity's role in the universe is understood. Muslims did not express a consistent conception of 'sacredness,' and problems can arise when new terminologies, such as those related to 'blessing' and 'sanctity,' were unconnected to boundaries of the cities in geographical sources and were instead attached to geographical regions, but the idea of *baraka* can take on a physical as well as a moral nature. Though the idea of a city's physical 'blessedness' may emanate from its geographical location and features, it is the moral 'blessedness,' formed by religious, spiritual, and eschatological attribution to the city that transforms the land into a "land for sacred struggle for God's cause, a land of promise, the centre for the future Islamic Caliphate, and the place where people will be raised from the dead and assembled on the Day of Judgement."[13] Ibn ʿAsākir cites a tradition that elaborates upon this idea:

> If the world is in catastrophe and drought, then Syria will be in ease and well being, and if Syria is in catastrophe and drought then Palestine will be in ease and well being, and if Palestine is in catastrophe and drought then Jerusalem will be in ease and well being. And he said: Shām is *mubāraka* [blessed], Palestine is *muqaddasa* [holy], and Jerusalem is *quds al-quds* [holy of holies].[14]

13 A. F. El-Awaisi, 'The Significance of Jerusalem in Islam: An Islamic Reference,' *Journal of Islamic Jerusalem Studies* 1 (1998), 50–51; here one may compare the Christian and Muslim conception of blessedness by noting the religious perspicacity of the majority of Ṣalāḥ al-Dīn's advisers, who argued, following a discussion about the closure or demolition of the Holy Sepulchre, that, "Those who come to visit it come to worship at the location of the cross and the grave rather than at the building itself. Christians will never stop making pilgrimages to this location, even if it has been totally uprooted. And when the leader of the believers ʿUmar, may God be pleased with him, captured Jerusalem during the early Islamic period, he granted this place to them, and did not order that the building should be destroyed." ʿImād al-Dīn al-Iṣfahānī, *al-Fatḥ al-qussī fī l-fatḥ al-qudsī*, ed. Muḥammad Ṣubḥ (Cairo: al-Dār al-Qawmiyya lil-Ṭibāʿa wa-l-Nashr, 1965), 146.

14 Ibn ʿAsākir, *Tārīkh Madinat Dimashq*, ed. Muḥibb al-Dīn al-ʿAmrawī (Beirut: Dār al-Fikr, 1995), 1:145.

Such descriptions denoting the idea of holiness were used interchangeably, particularly in relation to land.

Nāṣir-i Khusraw's account of the time he spent in Jerusalem in 438/1047 while en route to Mecca, passing through the Caspian coast of Iran, eastern Anatolia, and into Syria and Palestine provides an eschatological outlook. He describes

> a large, expansive, and flat plain called Sahira. They say that this is where the Resurrection will take place, where all people will be gathered together. For this reason many people have come there from all over the world and taken up residence in order to die in that city. When God's appointed time comes, they will already be in the stipulated place.[15]

Khusraw's observation not only reveals the pre-crusade eschatological relevance of the Holy City, but also suggests that the faithful believed that the Last Hour was closer than expected. The idea of placing oneself in a position to induce the events of the end time is akin to the kind of arguments made by the First Crusaders. For Guibert of Nogent, Jerusalem was, of course, the centre stage for the apocalypse. Although Guibert admitted that what he wrote did not reflect Urban's exact words, he did believe that this was Urban's intention. According to Guibert,

> Ponamus modo in Iherusalem Christum neque mortuum nec sepultum nec ibidem aliquando vixisse. Certe, si haec deessent omnia, solum illud ad subveniendum terrae et civitati vos excitare debuerat quia de Syon exierit lex et verbum domini de Iherusalem.[16]

[If Christ had never died, nor had been buried, nor had lived at any time in Jerusalem … If none of these things had in fact occurred you ought still to be moved to help the land and the city by this thought alone: that the law will come out of Zion and the Word of the Lord from Jerusalem.]

Guibert thought it was imperative for Christians to be present in Jerusalem, since "if Antichrist finds there no Christian (just as at present when scarcely any dwell there), no one will be there to oppose him, or whom he may rightly

---

15 There is a Qur'ānic association with the place: "[But,] then, that [Last Hour] will be [upon them of a sudden, as if it were] but a single accusing cry – and then, lo, they will be *Sāhira* (fully awakened [to the truth])! (79:13–14); Nāṣir-i Khusraw, *Book of Travels*, ed. and trans. Wheeler M. Thackston Jr. (Costa Mesa, CA: Mazda Publishers, 2001), 28.

16 Guibert of Nogent, *Dei Gesta Per Francos*, ed. R. B. C. Huygens, Corpus Christianorum, Continuatio Mediaevalis 127A (Turnhout, 1996), 113.

overcome."[17] The crusade was therefore a way of setting the scene for the final battle, a way of mobilising the Christians to be in their appropriate place, since what has been foretold "cannot possibly come to pass unless Christianity will take the place of paganism."[18]

It is essential to note, therefore, that the city of Jerusalem, al-Aqṣā Mosque, and other sacred designations in and around Palestine are not geographically exclusive; authors of *faḍāʾil* works on Syria generally included references extolling the virtues of Jerusalem. It is thus significant to point out the inclusion of Jerusalem in the geographical consideration of the Syrian region. Unlike the cities of Mecca and Medina, which have specific sacred designations, Shām is inclusive of Syria, Jordan, and Palestine. Books of *faḍāʾil al-Shām* thus contain sections on *faḍāʾil al-Quds* and its precincts. Maḥmūd Ibrāhīm's critical analysis of *faḍāʾil al-Quds* manuscripts includes the *Faḍāʾil al-Shām wa-faḍl Dimashq* of Abū l-Ḥasan ʿAlī b. Muḥammad al-Rabaʿī (d. 444/1052); he argues that many, if not most, books extolling the virtues of Jerusalem elucidate the merits of other cities in Syria and not solely Jerusalem.[19] And as Cobb pertinently notes, "given the pre-eminence of Jerusalem in the *Faḍāʾil* genre, most scholarship has focused on traditions dealing with that city and have ignored the fact that such traditions were part of, or were at least conversant with a wider body of discourse extolling the virtues of Syria in general."[20]

---

17 E. Peters (ed.), *The First Crusade: the Chronicle of Fulcher of Chartres and other Source Materials*, 2nd edition (Philadelphia: University of Pennsylvania Press, 1998), 35.

18 L. and J. S. C. Riley-Smith, *The Crusades: Idea and Reality, 1095–1274* (London: Edward Arnold, 1981), 45–49.

19 M. Ibrāhīm, *Faḍāʾil Bayt al-Maqdis fī makhṭūṭāt ʿarabiyya qadīma* [The Virtues of Jerusalem in Old Arabic Manuscripts] (Kuwait, 1985), 85; in this context K. al-Asali also includes al-Rabaʿī's treatise in an article intended to highlight books of *faḍāʾil al-Quds* in the fifth century AH/eleventh centrury CE, and further notes the *faḍāʾil al-Shām* of al-Samʿānī and several other texts on Syria that elucidate the merits of Jerusalem. K. J. al-Asali, 'Kutub al-qarn al-khāmis al-hijrī fi faḍāʾil bayt al-maqdis' [The books of the fifth century hijri on the merits of Jerusalem: A study and bibliography], *Risalat al-Maktaba* 16 (1981), 8–10.

20 P. M. Cobb, *White Banners: Contention in ʿAbbasid Syria*, 750–880 (Albany: State University of New York Press, 2001), 52–53. What is a theological belief for Muslims must be qualified however around a broader discussion pertaining to the 'development' of Jerusalem's sanctity. According to Tibawi the Umayyad construction of al-Aqṣā Mosque in 96/715 "gave reality to the figurative name used in Koran." A. L. Tibawi, *Jerusalem: Its Place in Islam and Arab History* (Beirut: Institute for Palestine Studies, 1969), 9. Furthermore, J. Wansbrough holds that '*asrā bi-ʿabdihī laylan*' (17:1) resembles *fa-asri bi-ʿibādī laylan* (44:23) in connection to the flight of Moses from Pharaoh, and could therefore allude to Moses and not the Prophet Muḥammad. J. Wansbrough, *Quranic Studies* (Oxford: Oxford University Press, 1977), 68. Also see A. Guillaume, 'Where was al-Masjid al-Aqsa?' *Al-Andalus* 18 (1953),

Sources

Although most of the authors I discuss in this book are poets themselves, several other writers appear regularly, and while I do not propose anything strikingly new about their careers, this section provides brief details pertaining to these authors and the relevance of their sources to this study.[21]

ʿAlī b. Ṭāhir al-Sulamī (430–1/1039 to 499–500/1106): Al-Sulamī was a Shāfiʿī Damascene grammarian who taught in the Umayyad Mosque of Damascus. His *Kitab al-Jihād* [Book of *jihād*] (498/1105) is believed to be the first treatise on *jihād* to be produced after the arrival of the Franks in the Near East. He was a source of much discussion because of his rapid assimilation of the aims of the crusaders. Unlike some contemporaries, he did not confuse the crusaders with Byzantines, rather he described the assault on Jerusalem and the crusader expansion as a Christian '*jihād*.' For al-Sulamī, the capture of Jerusalem was part of a wider Christian military scheme that began with conflicts in Sicily and Spain. Al-Sulamī's treatise is of immense significance for the information it provides about the Muslims' moral condition and political weakness, which he saw as reasons for the crusader victories. Only two incomplete manuscripts of al-Sulamī's treatise exist, both are in the Asad Library in Damascus.[22]

323–336. According to Goitein, however, there is considerable evidence to demonstrate that what is intended by 17:1 is in fact Jerusalem. The verses that follow (17:5–6) refer to the destruction of the Temple in Jerusalem, called *masjid* in verse 7. When read together in context, the idea that the earthly Jerusalem is being denoted is entirely plausible although the image of 'heavenly Jerusalem' may have been connected to it in one way or another. O. Grabar, 'al-Ḳuds,' *EI*², 5:322–344. Aside from Muslim scriptural interpretations of 'Masjid al-Aqṣā' in 17:1 we might also consider the significance of *alladhī bāraknā ḥawlahū* (whose precincts We did bless) in the same verse. According to al-Qurṭubī, the precincts are "Shām ... and because of the prophets and righteous ones buried there it became *muqaddasā* (sanctified)." Al-Qurṭubī, *Mukhtaṣar tafsīr al-Qurṭubī* (Beirut: Dār al-Kutub al-ʿIlmiyya, 2001), 2:617. According to al-Rāzī it is blessed because of the presence of "fruits and flowers, and because it is the dwelling place of prophets and the place where angels descend." Al-Rāzī, *Tafsīr al-kabīr*, vol. 10, part 20 (Beirut: Dār al-Kutub al-ʿIlmiyya, 2004), 10:117.

21 Mallett's recent collection of articles is a valuable addition: *Medieval Muslim Historians and the Franks in the Levant* (Leiden: Brill, 2014) introduces seven studies, each of which assesses the significance of one Muslim historian relevant to the crusading period.

22 ʿAlī b. Ṭāhir b. Jaʿfar al-Sulamī, 'Kitāb al-Jihād,' in *Arbaʿa kutub fī l-jihād min ʿaṣr al-ḥurūb al-ṣalībiyya*, ed. S. Zakkār (Damascus: Dār al-Takwīn, 2007); Christie, *The Book of the Jihad*; N. Christie, 'Motivating Listeners'; N. Christie, 'Jerusalem in the Kitāb al-Jihād of ʿAlī ibn Ṭāhir al-Sulamī,' *Medieval Encounters* 13, no. 2 (2007), 209–221.

Thiqat al-Dīn Abū l-Qāsim ʿAlī b. al-Ḥasan b. ʿAsākir (499–571/1106–1175): Ibn ʿAsākir was one of the most important scholarly figures of the sixth/twelfth century. He was from a prominent line of Shāfiʿī scholars of Damascus and lived in the city under the patronage of Nūr al-Dīn, who, in 549/1154, commissioned him to continue his *Tārīkh madinat Dimashq* [History of the city of Damascus] – a voluminous biographical dictionary of all the personalities who settled in, or visited, Damascus and other Syrian cities.[23]

The ***Baḥr al-fawāʾid*** is an anonymous treatise written in Persian in the middle of the sixth/twelfth century. It belongs to the 'mirrors for princes' genre that was popular in the medieval Islamic period. These texts were compiled to provide indispensable Islamic instructions for those invested with political authority. Mostly written in Persian, they make use of anecdotes, maxims, and prophetic traditions attributed to kings and saints. Although many of these texts, mainly those composed in Arabic, served largely literary functions, some of those written in Persian emanated from the period of Saljūq political ascendancy and are particularly relevant to understanding how ideas about governance may have filtered through to *jihād* leaders of the sixth/twelfth and seventh/thirteenth centuries. In light of the date of the text's composition – which coincides with the promotion of Nūr al-Dīn's *jihād* programme – it is particularly relevant for its sections on *jihād* and *taṣawwuf* (Sufism). The author of the *Baḥr al-fawāʾid* states that the text was composed for Alp Qutlugh Jabūghā Ulugh Atābak, a Sunnī identified by Meisami as the son of Āq Sunqur Aḥmadīlī who ruled Marāgha and Mosul until he was murdered in 527/1133 and then succeeded by his son. According to Meisami the text was completed some time between 554/1159 and 557/1162.[24]

Usāma b. Munqidh (d. 588/1188): Usāma was known as a man of action and adventure, as a huntsman and writer. He served under the Fāṭimids, Zangī, Nūr al-Dīn, and Ṣalāḥ al-Dīn, and spent much of his long life in contact with the

23 Ibn ʿAsākir, *Tārīkh Madinat Dimashq*; Suleiman A. Mourad and James E. Lindsay, *The Intensification and Reorientation of Sunni Jihad Ideology in the Crusader Period: Ibn ʿAsākir of Damascus (1105–1176) and His Age, with an Edition and Translation of Ibn ʿAsākir's* 'The Forty Hadiths for Inciting Jihad' (Leiden: Brill, 2013); S. Mourad, 'Ibn 'Asakir,' in *Medieval Islamic Civilization: An Encyclopedia*, ed. J. W. Meri (Abingdon: Routledge, 2006), 1:351–352; C. E. Bosworth, 'Ibn ʿAsākir,' *Encyclopedia of Arabic Literature*, ed. J. S. Meisami and P. Starkey (London: Routledge, 1998), 1:313.

24 J. S. Meisami (trans. and ed.), *The Sea of Precious Virtues (Baḥr al-fawāʾid): A Medieval Islamic Mirror for Princes* (Salt Lake City: University of Utah Press, 1991); Geert Jan van Gelder, 'Mirror for Princes or Vizor for Viziers: The Twelfth-Century Arabic Popular Encyclopedia Mufid al-ʿulum and its Relationship with the Anonymous Persian *Bahr al-fawaʾid*,' BSOAS, 64, no. 3 (2001), 313–338.

Franks and the Ayyūbid and Fāṭimid civilian elite. His autobiography, *Kitāb al-I'tibār*, is a reflection on the inevitability of fate in human affairs; the work uses examples drawn from his adventurous life and is filled with details of daily life, politics, and observations of public life. It is also valuable for what it reveals of cultural friction and accord between the Muslims and Franks during the sixth/twelfth century. Usāma also composed his own *dīwān* (anthology of poetry) and was much admired for his poetic skills.[25]

'Imād al-Dīn al-Iṣfahānī (d. 579/1201): Born in the town of Isfahan in Persia, 'Imād al-Dīn worked as a secretary to Nūr al-Dīn until his patron's death in 569/1174. 'Imād al-Dīn then transferred his services to Ṣalāḥ al-Dīn and worked as his chancellor under the latter's chief secretary al-Qāḍī l-Fāḍil. He remained with Ṣalāḥ al-Dīn until his death in 589/193. 'Imād al-Dīn was also a traditional scholar and poet, and compiled a vast anthology of sixth-/twelfth-century poetry entitled *Kharīdat al-qaṣr wa-jarīdat al-'aṣr*. He received a full Islamic education in Isfahan, within which the study of poetry was a core subject of primary education. In terms of his historical works, 'Imād al-Dīn composed an eyewitness account of Ṣalāḥ al-Dīn's reconquest of Jerusalem, entitled *al-Fatḥ al-qussī fī l-fatḥ al-qudsī*, and an account of Ṣalāḥ al-Dīn's other feats, entitled *al-Barq al-Shāmī* which is still in manuscript form in the Bodleian Library and survives only in part.[26]

Abū l-Ḥusayn Muḥammad b. Aḥmad Ibn Jubayr (539–613/1145–1217): Ibn Jubayr was an Andalusian traveller, author, and *muḥaddith* (scholar of *ḥadīth*). His account of his travels between the years 578/1183 and 581/1185, entitled the

25 Usāma b. Munqidh, *Kitāb al-I'tibār*, ed. Philip K. Hitti (Princeton, NJ: Princeton University Press, 1930); Usāma b. Munqidh, *The Book of Contemplation: Islam and the Crusades*, trans. Paul M. Cobb (London: Penguin Classics, 2008); An earlier outdated translation is by P. K. Hitti: Usāma b. Munqidh, *An Arab-Syrian Gentleman and Warrior in the Period of the Crusades* (New York: Columbia University Press, 2000); R. Irwin, 'Usamah ibn Munqidh: An Arab-Syrian Gentleman at the Time of the Crusades Reconsidered' in *The Crusades and their Sources: Essays Presented to Bernard Hamilton*, ed. J. France and W. G. Zajac (Aldershot: Ashgate, 1998).

26 'Imād al-Dīn al-Iṣfahānī, *al-Fatḥ al-qussī*; 'Imād al-Dīn al-Iṣfahānī, *Kharīdat al-qaṣr wa-jarīdat al-'aṣr: qism shu'arā' al-Shām*, vol. 1, ed. Shukri Faisal (Damascus: Dār al-Kutub wa-l-Wathā'iq al-Qawmiyya, 1955); Lutz Richter-Bernburg, ''Imād al-Dīn al-Iṣfahānī,' in *Medieval Muslim Historians and the Franks in the Levant*, ed. Alex Mallett (Leiden: Brill, 2014), 29–51. D. S. Richards, ''Imād al-Dīn al-Iṣfahānī: Administrator, Litterateur and Historian,' in *Crusaders and Muslims in Twelfth-Century Syria*, ed. M. Shatzmiller (Leiden: Brill, 1993), 133–146; H. A. R. Gibb, 'Al-Barq al-Shāmī: The History of Saladin by the Katib 'Imād al-Dīn al-Iṣfahānī,' *Wiener Zeitschrift für die Kunde des Morgenlandes* 52 (1953–55), 93–115.

Riḥla, provides some vital examples of Muslim life in the Levant. On his pilgrimage journey he passed through Egypt on his way to Mecca. On his return he crossed to Kufa in Iraq and then travelled north to Baghdad and Mosul, and then on to Aleppo in Syria. He finally travelled south to Damascus from where he journeyed to Acre and Tyre. His description of these two cities provides us with an indispensable contemporary view of life for Muslims in Frankish Palestine and the cross-cultural relations between the Muslims and Franks. Ibn Jubayr's *Riḥla* is also significant for its description of Damascus; it serves as the fullest contemporary account that we have of the medieval city.[27] In this book (cited in chapter 4) we find a lengthy poem Ibn Jubayr composed for Ṣalāḥ al-Dīn particularly relevant.[28]

ʿAlī ʿIzz al-Dīn b. al-Athīr (d. 630/1233): Ibn al-Athīr is most renowned for his universal history, *al-Kāmil fī l-tārīkh*, which extends to the year 628/1231. Although he visited Baghdad, Jerusalem, Aleppo, and Damascus, it was in Mosul that he spent most of his career. In Mosul Ibn al-Athīr enjoyed the patronage of members of the Zangid dynasty, and their later successor, Badr al-Dīn Luʾluʾ (r. 619–657/1222–1259); it is likely that the *Tārīkh* was commissioned under his patronage. In a famous passage of the *Tārīkh*, Ibn al-Athīr connected the First Crusade to Christian advances in Spain and Sicily, an insight akin to that of ʿAlī b. Ṭāhir al-Sulamī a century before.[29]

Bahāʾ al-Dīn b. Shaddād (d. 631/1234): Ibn Shaddād was the *qāḍī* of Ṣalāḥ al-Dīn's army and his royal biographer from 585/1189 until his patron's death in 589/1193. During the time he accompanied Ṣalāḥ al-Dīn on his campaigns, Ibn Shaddād was a valuable eyewitness; his account provides a firsthand experience of Ṣalāḥ al-Dīn's life and career. For Ṣalāḥ al-Dīn's early career Ibn Shaddād relied on other sources of information. His biography, *al-Nawādir al-sulṭāniyya wa-l-maḥāsin al-Yūsufiyya*, is divided into two parts; the first draws attention to Ṣalāḥ al-Dīn's virtues and his Sunnī orthodoxy and the second part is a chronicle of his life. Since Ibn Shaddād began his work after Ṣalāḥ al-Dīn's

27 Ibn Jubayr, *The Travels of Ibn Jubayr*, trans. Roland Broadhurst (London: J. Cape, 1952), 271–312.

28 Ibn Jubayr, *Travels*; Ibn Jubayr, *Tadhkira al-akhbār ʿan ittifāqāt al-asfār*, ed. ʿAlī Aḥmad Kanʿān (Beirut, 2001); J. Phillips, 'The Travels of Ibn Jubayr and his View of Saladin,' in *Cultural Encounters during the Crusades*, ed. K. V. Jensen, K. Salomen, and H. Vogt (Odense: University Press of Southern Denmark, 2013), 75–90.

29 Ibn al-Athīr, *al-Kāmil fī l-tārīkh*, 8:415; Ibn al-Athīr, *The Chronicle of Ibn al-Athīr for the Crusading Period from al-Kāmil fī'l-Tārīkh*, parts 1–3 (Aldershot: Ashgate 2006–08); Ibn al-Athīr, *al-Tārīkh al-bāhir fī l-dawla al-Atābikiyya* (Cairo: Dār al-Kutub al-Ḥadītha, 1963); Ibn al-Athīr, *al-Kāmil fī l-tārīkh*.

most celebrated achievements – his victory at Ḥaṭṭīn and the reconquest of Jerusalem – the text was shaped around the legacy of these victories.[30]

Abū l-Muẓaffar Sibṭ b. al-Jawzī (d. 654/1256): Sibṭ b. al-Jawzī was brought up in the scholarly community of Damascus in the first half of the seventh/thirteenth century. His father was a slave of the celebrated Ibn Hubayra, the vizier (*wazīr*) of Baghdad who freed him and arranged for his marriage to the daughter of the Baghdad-based Ḥanbalī jurist Ibn al-Jawzī. A hugely influential teacher and preacher in the mosques of Damascus, and particularly in his *majālis al-waʿẓ* (assemblies of exhortation), Sibṭ b. al-Jawzī's most noted work is the *Mirʾāt al-zamān fī tārīkh al-aʿyān* [The mirror of the age in the history of the elites], a universal history ending in the year 654/1256. For information pertaining to the sixth/twelfth century, his grandfather was an important source for events he witnessed in Iraq and Syria.[31]

Ibn Khallikān (d. 681/1282): Ibn Khallikān was known as a reputable jurist and grammarian who worked as a judge in Damascus from 659/1261 to 669/1271, and then from 676/1278 until 679/1281. His most famous work is his biographical dictionary of scholars and political figures, *Wafayāt al-aʿyān wa-anbā abnāʾ al-zamān*. He began his work in 654/1256 and completed it in 672/1274.

Jamāl al-Dīn Muḥammad b. Wāṣil (d. 697/1298): For the history of the Ayyūbid dynasty generally, by far the most complete and reliable chronicle is the *Mufarrij al-kurūb fī akhbār Banī Ayyūb* of Ibn Wāṣil. In 663/1264–5 Ibn Wāṣil was appointed chief *qāḍī* in his hometown of Hama; it was then that he wrote the chronicle under the patronage of the late Ayyūbids. The text, which is mostly concerned with the history of the Zangids, the career of Ṣalāḥ al-Dīn and the Ayyūbid dynasty, and the early Mamlūks, provides valuable insights in particular into the Fifth Crusade to Egypt, the crusade of Frederick II, and the crusade of Louis IX to Egypt. It thus also serves as a very valuable source for the seventh-/thirteenth-century crusades.[32]

---

30 Ibn Shaddād, *Min kitāb al-nawādir al-sulṭāniyya wa-l-maḥāsin al-yūsufiyya*, selected by Muḥammad Darwīsh (Damascus: Dār al-Takwīn, 1979); Ibn Shaddād, *The Rare and Excellent History of Saladin*, trans. D. S. Richards (Aldershot: Ashgate, 2002); El-Shayyal, G., 'Ibn Shaddād,' *EI*², 3:933–934; Ibn Shaddād, Kitāb Faḍāʾil al-jihād,' in *Arbaʿa kutub fī l-jihād min ʿasr al-ḥurūb al-Ṣalībiyya*, ed. Suhayl Zakkār (Damascus: Dār al-Takwīn, 2007), 183–273.

31 Sibṭ b. al-Jawzī, *Mirʾāt al-zamān fī tārīkh al-aʿyān*, vol. 8, parts 1 and 2 (Hyderabad, 1952); Alex Mallett, 'Sibṭ Ibn al-Jawzī,' in *Medieval Muslim Historians and the Franks in the Levant* (Leiden: Brill, 2014), 84–108; C. Cahen, 'Sibṭ,' *EI*², 3:752–753.

32 Ibn Wāṣil, *Mufarrij al-kurūb fī akhbār Banī Ayyūb*, vols. 1 and 2, ed. Jamāl al-Dīn al-Shayyāl (Cairo: Dār al-Kutub, 1953); Ibn Wāṣil, *Mufarrij al-kurūb fī akhbār Banī Ayyūb*, vol. 4, ed. Ḥusayn Muḥammad Rabiʿ (Cairo: Dār al-Kutub, 1977); Konrad Hirschler, 'Ibn Wāṣil: An

ʿImād al-Dīn Ismāʿīl b. ʿUmar b. Kathīr (d. 774/1373): Ibn Kathīr was a leading intellectual figure of eighth-/fourteenth-century Syria. He was educated in the scholarly circles of Damascus and gained his first teaching appointment in 742/1341. He was later granted a senior position at the Umayyad Mosque in 767/1366. Ibn Kathīr is best known for his *Tafsīr al-Qurʾān al-ʿaẓīm* and his voluminous universal history *al-Bidāya wa-l-nihāya*. His relevance in this study stems from a treatise he authored in the wake of the crusaders' sack of Alexandria in 767/1365, *Ijtihād fī ṭalab al-jihād*. The author states that he wrote the treatise at the behest of the Mamlūk *amīr* Sayf al-Dīn Manjak (d. 776/1374).[33]

Ibn al-Qaysarānī (d. 547–48/1153–54): Abū ʿAbdallāh Muḥammad al-Ḥalabī b. al-Qaysarānī was born in the port city of Acre in 478/1085–86 and grew up in Caesarea, which was captured by the crusaders in 494/1101 when the poet was sixteen years old. Acre in turn was captured in 497/1104. Aside from his interest in poetry, Ibn al-Qaysarānī was also well versed in astronomy and philology. He later moved to Damascus and then Aleppo and found favour and fortune in the patronage of ʿImād al-Dīn Zangī and later his son, Nūr al-Dīn. He was a man of great repute and learning, and together with Ibn al-Munīr was one of the greatest poets of his time.[34]

ʿAbd al-Munʿim b. ʿUmar b. ʿAbdallāh al-Jilyānī l-Ghassānī l-Andalūsī (d. 602/1205–06): Al-Jilyānī was a skilled litterateur (*adīb*), poet, doctor, and someone who was inclined to the Sufi path, which had become popular by this time by ascetic jurists such as Abū Ḥāmid al-Ghazālī and al-Jilānī. Known as

---

Ayyubid Perspective on Frankish Lordships and Crusades,' in *Medieval Muslim Historians and the Franks in the Levant*, ed. A. Mallett (Leiden: Brill, 2014), 136–160; D. S. Richards, 'Ibn Wasil, Historian of the Ayyubids,' in *Ayyubid Jerusalem*, ed. R. Hillenbrand and S. Auld (London: al-Tajir Trust, 2009), 456–459; K. Hirschler, 'Social Contexts of Medieval Arabic Historical Writing: Court Scholars Versus Ideal/Withdrawn Scholars – Ibn Wāṣil and Abu Šāma,' in *Egypt and Syria in the Fatimid, Ayyubid and Mamluk Eras IV*, ed. U. Vermeulen and J. Van Steenbergen (Leuven: Peeters, 2005), 311–331; Gamal el-Din el-Shayyal, 'Ibn Wāṣil,' EI², 3:967; K. Hirschler, *Medieval Arabic Historiography* (London: Routledge, 2006).

33 See H. Laoust, 'Ibn Kathīr,' EI², 3:817–818; Ibn Kathīr, *al-Bidāya wa-l-nihāya*, vol. 12 (Cairo: Dār al-Taqwa, 2004); Ibn Kathīr, *al-Bidāya wa-l-nihāya*, vol. 13 (Cairo: Dār al-Taqwa, 2004); Ibn Kathīr, 'Kitāb al-ijtihād fī ṭalab al-jihād,' in *Arbaʿa kutub fī l-jihād min ʿaṣr al-ḥurūb al-ṣalībiyya*, ed. S. Zakkār (Damascus: Dār al-Takwīn, 2007).

34 See C. Hillenbrand, 'Ibn al-Qaysarānī,' in *Encyclopedia of Arabic Literature*, vol. 1, ed. J. S. Meisami and P. Starkey (London: Routledge, 1998), 359; Ibn al-Qaysarānī, *Dīwān Muḥammad b. Naṣr b. Ṣaghīr al-Qaysarānī* MS no. 1484 (Cairo: Dār al-Kutub al-Miṣriyya), see Maḥmūd Ibrāhīm, *Ṣida al-ghazwu al-salībiyy fī shiʿr ibn al-Qaysarānī* (Amman: Dār al-Bashīr, 1988).

Ḥakīm al-zamān (lit., 'the wise one of his time'), al-Jilyānī, from the precinct of Jilana in al-Andalus, moved to Damascus and was known to have met the Syrian geographer Yāqūt al-Hamawī during his time in Damascus. He may have encountered other notables when he visited Baghdad in 601/1204, a year before his death. Al-Jilyānī found favour with Ṣalāḥ al-Dīn and composed many verses in his praise, the most noted being his *Dīwān al-tadbīj*, known also for its attractive form and structure, and its adoption of floral designs and geometric patterns. He completed his anthology in 568/1172, some years before the reconquest of Jerusalem.[35]

'Abd al-Raḥman b. Ismā'īl Abū Shāma (599–655/1203–68): The majority of the poetry used in this book was extracted from Abū Shāma's *Kitāb al-Rawḍatayn* [Book of the two gardens], and thus I pay particular attention to him in this section. The author, from Jerusalem, wrote his text as an instructive history of what he deemed to be two exemplary eras, the 'two gardens' of Zangid and Ayyūbid Muslim rule. His selection of material was shaped by his desire to acclaim Nūr al-Dīn and Ṣalāḥ al-Dīn for their commitment to Islam and their successful pursuit of the *jihād*; his composition was further born out of an antipathy toward the power holders of his day, judges, and even scholars who he believed, by taking prestigious and influential positions in towns, had become too close to those in power.[36] Therefore the author does not include material critical of his protagonists, like the work of the Damascene poet Ibn 'Unayn (d. 630/1233), who was banished from Damascus by Ṣalāḥ al-Dīn for a harsh invective against him. The melancholy of some of Abū Shāma's poetry in exile is, however, praised for its genuine expression of homesickness. What makes his work so impressive is the inclusion of a wide corpus of texts, including the historical works of Ibn al-Qalānisī (d. 555/1160); the work of Nūr al-Dīn's and Ṣalāḥ al-Dīn's secretary 'Imād al-Dīn al-Iṣfahānī – both his *al-Fatḥ al-qussī fī l-fatḥ al-qudsī* and *al-Barq al-Shāmī*; the jurist and judge of Ṣalāḥ al-Dīn's army Bahā' al-Dīn b. Shaddād; the Mosuli historian Ibn al-Athīr and the lost historical work of Ibn Abī Ṭayy (d. 633/1233). The author's material includes narratives, anecdotes, poetry, quotations, and letters; he made it a rule to cite each author that he quoted although he did not comment on the veracity of those accounts. His distance in time, writing some fifty years after the death of Ṣalāḥ al-Dīn, as well as his lack of involvement in the events he describes explains his uncritical approach, although sometimes he makes clear his own views, marked by the statement 'qultu' (I say). It was from 1289/1872 onwards that

35 'Abd al-Mun'im al-Jilyānī al-Andalusī, *Dīwān al-tadbīj*, ed. Kamāl Abū Dīb (Beirut: Dār al-Sāqī, 2010).

36 Hirschler, *Medieval Arabic Historiography*, 28–42.

translations of sections of Abū Shāma's *Kitāb al-Rawḍatayn* began to appear in the *Recueil des Historiens des Croisades* although none of his large selections of poetry was translated. Thus, as Irwin highlights, "the omission, for example, of all of Abū Shāma's poetry to be found in his chronicle meant that some rather important political messages couched as poems had been ignored."[37]

The popularity of the *Kitab al-Rawḍatayn* is revealed through the extent of its transmission; there are about twenty surviving manuscripts of the work and the dates of copying of the manuscripts show an even distribution of copies until the present day. During the seventh/thirteenth century more manuscripts were copied than at any other time following the death of the author, perhaps this was for eulogistic as well as practical reasons, following the Mongol invasion. Abū Shāma's central question of ideal rule of course had ongoing relevance insofar as Muslim society was continually troubled by internal conflict and external threat. The extent to which it came to be seen, in twentieth-century publications, as a prominent anti-crusader text does not negate the same appeal in earlier times. The plethora of poetry cited by Abū Shāma sheds crucial light on an active social apparatus; the author perhaps wished to make the point that poetry was both timely and relevant and that poets were extremely significant. According to Gabrieli, "an Arabic religious poetry was born with Islam, presupposing it and nurtured by it,"[38] and Abū Shāma wished to work within these obvious literary-conventional parameters in his main work – although toward the end of his life he abridged the *Rawḍatayn* into a smaller volume entitled *'Uyūn al-rawḍatayn* [The essence of the two gardens]; this work lacks most of the poetry in his main work. His yearning to promote *jihād*, unity, and the ethics of just rule in the highly charged religious atmosphere of his age make his inclusion of poetry in celebration of the feats of his protagonists (and the abasement of their rivals), an indispensable feature that also reflects the prominent place of poets in the retinues of sultans and local rulers such as Nūr al-Dīn and Ṣalāḥ al-Dīn.

The literary make-up of Abū Shāma's text is conventional in that it was not uncommon for a prose text to include poetry, even in substantial amounts. The interaction of prose and poetry in Arabic literature had a significant and meaningful purpose. Abū Shāma's text is primarily concerned with political

37 R. Irwin, 'Orientalism and the Early Development of Crusader Studies,' in *The Experience of Crusading: Defining the Crusader Kingdom*, vol. 2, ed. P. W. Edbury and J. P. Phillips (Cambridge: Cambridge University Press, 2003), 226. For more information on Abū Shāma see Hilmy Ahmad, 'Abū Shāma,' *EI*^{2}, 1:150–151.

38 F. Gabrieli, 'Religious Poetry in Early Islam,' in *Arabic Poetry: Theory and Development*, ed. G. E. von Grunebaum (Wiesbaden: Otto Harrassowitz, 1973), 6.

matters of the Fāṭimids, Ayyūbids, and Zangids. The dynastic transitions from the Fāṭimids and Zangids to the Ayyūbids of course had implications for notables who shifted alliances from one patron to the next. Much of the poetry is therefore concerned with these political developments. The socio-economic condition of the Muslim Near East shaped the poetry around events that had a bearing on the bulk of society. Although the method of poets was in some ways homogeneous with that of pre-crusade poetry, it was obviously not entirely so. The particular socio-political climates of the sixth/twelfth and seventh/thirteenth centuries had not been witnessed before. Therefore we are able to differentiate the various trends of poetry in this period and discern the specifics and specialities of anti-Frankish poetry from other types of poetry.

Ideological Pursuits: Nūr al-Dīn, Ṣalāḥ al-Dīn, and Political Patronage: An Overview

> The worst kings are those who keep themselves distant from the *ʿulamāʾ*, and the worst *ʿulamāʾ* are those who seek closeness to kings.[39]

Nūr al-Dīn and Ṣalāḥ al-Dīn feature prominently in this book; this fact, along with the role of the civilian elite in their *jihād* programme, means that it is vital to ascertain their place as religious and political patrons in order to contextualise the *jihād* initiatives that emerged within the framework of a strong religious milieu, and one that sought to give credence to their political and military objectives. In this section I outline some of the components of patronage that made provisions for the religious communities in Syria and, most significantly, contributed to the legitimacy of their patrons' political policies.

The dictum cited above from the *Baḥr al-fawāʾid* suggests that the integration of the scholarly society with the political was generally approved of. Maintaining close ties to the *ʿulamāʾ* served not only to generate a sense of divine *baraka* for the ruler and his subjects, but in material terms served as a way to gain recognition for the ruler's political authority and actions. In Ibn al-Jawzī's *naṣīḥa* (advisory) text, the picture is distinct; the inherent "danger" in authority, temporal or religious, should guide toward a keener religiosity. The *naṣīḥa* genre served as instruction manuals for the ruling class and princes, and comprised anecdotes and religious maxims of practical ethics for the ruling elite to adhere to. Ibn al-Jawzī begins his work by asking, "Do you not see that winning is by [achieved by] riding into the sea and that this involves

39 Meisami (trans. and ed.), *The Sea of Precious Virtues*, 297.

danger, that issuing a *fatwā* is the goal of knowledge and that in it is danger? And so too is the sultanate ..."[40] And a statement from Sufyān al-Thawrī follows: "There are two groups of people, if they are good the rest of the people will be good: the sultans and the *ʿulamāʾ*."[41]

The closeness of Nūr al-Dīn and Ṣalāḥ al-Dīn to the *ʿulamāʾ* and their bestowing of endowments (*waqf*, pl. *awqāf*) to the religious classes helped to shape their images as 'holy' warriors, as opposed to mere political and military opportunists. In return, the religious classes became actively involved in the *jihād* effort as soldiers, but even before military engagements, they served as preachers, Qur'ān reciters, and participants in public readings. In this respect, the religious classes were not doing something entirely novel; the Qur'ānic injunction to "Go forth [to war] lightly or heavily ..."[42] was understood to suggest an inclusive contribution to the *jihād* effort. Yet their patrons also pursued initiatives that may have been aimed at dynastic expansion, an approach that highlighted the need for religious patronage as a means to justify their 'secular' agendas – otherwise, of course, detractors might see them as manipulating Islam for personal gains. We should not, however, discount the possibility of pious motives in their actions. The consideration must be counterbalanced by the need both men felt to revitalise Sunnī Islam, to suppress Shīʿī "heresy", to raise Muslim consciousness, and counter the crusader threat.

The vibrancy of learning the traditional sciences in sixth-/twelfth- and seventh-/thirteenth-century Damascus was unparalleled. Nūr al-Dīn's commitment to overseeing the expansion of new centres of learning meant that his anti-Frankish focus fell within the framework of the existing scholarly standing of the city. By the end of his rule in 569/1174 Damascus boasted a total of twenty-two *madrasas* compared to eleven when he entered the city in 548/1154. During the reign of Ṣalāḥ al-Dīn and his Ayyūbid successors and until the Mongol invasion of 658/1260 that number increased to ninety-two *madrasas*. The new salaried posts available for teachers, the travels of students to further their studies, and the migration of scholars from other lands to Damascus to teach in these new religious institutions made the city a focal point for the widespread teaching of the religious sciences. The mechanics of the religious establishment were geared, in part, toward the expulsion of the crusaders

40 Ibn al-Jawzī, *al-Shifāʾ fī mawāʿiẓ al-mulūk wa-l-khulafāʾ*, ed. Fuʾād ʿAbd al-Munʿim Aḥmad (Mecca, 1991), 45; for information on the author, see H. Laoust, 'Ibn al-Djawzī,' *EI*², 3:751–752.

41 Ibn al-Jawzī, *al-Shifāʾ fī mawāʿiẓ*, 45.

42 Qur'ān 9:41. See Ibn Kathīr, *Tafsīr al-Qurʾān al-ʿaẓīm* (Beirut: Dār al-Maʿrifa, 2003), 727; al-Bayḍāwī, *Tafsīr al-Bayḍāwī* (Beirut: Dār al-Kutub al-ʿIlmiyya, 2001), 1:407.

from Muslim lands and in this the *madrasas* played a part. Though this was not the only role they played. The *madrasas* were scholarly hubs and the fact that *ʿulamāʾ* could be experts in religious fields and air their political concerns, or write chronicles, or compose poetry, and even fight in battle meant that a broad array of influences guided particular studies, the selection of texts, and the appointments to posts of learning. As Tibawi maintains, teaching in the *madrasa* "was on the whole free and subject only to mutual checks and balances within the learned community."[43]

Furthermore, there was a good degree of homogeneity in medieval Islamic education in which scholars and students from Khurasan, Baghdad, and Damascus travelled to study with one another, and teach the books of one another in distant lands.[44] Yet the creation of an influential civilian elite was not simply the result of the exchange of religious education. On the contrary, *ʿulamāʾ* could be historians, grammarians and, very often, poets, and the *baraka* (blessing) of their teachers and even their *ḥubb* (love) for them meant that intellectual esteem was not always the underlying feature of the transfer of knowledge.[45] Poets were thus known to have made use of the verses of others without censure; the benefit they might have seen in the dissemination of knowledge and ideas was sometimes of greater concern than individual prestige.[46]

It was the endowment (*waqf*) policy of rulers like Nūr al-Dīn and Ṣalāḥ al-Dīn that helped to make the transformation of cities into religious centres possible. In subsequent chapters we see that Ṣalāḥ al-Dīn's appointment of Ibn al-Zakī as *khaṭīb* in al-Aqṣā Mosque and Ibn Barrajān as a teacher in the Dome of the Rock served an indispensable purpose; the promotion of well-known scholars elicited a sense of authenticity and orthodoxy in the sultan's victories. His actions in ridding Egypt of the Fāṭimids and Jerusalem of the Franks was accomplished by using the property of both groups for his own religious scholars so that he could command their loyalty and gratitude. His directorship in the pious endowment was made more prominent through a Sufi hospice (*ribāṭ*) that he established in 585/1189 for Sufis and the poor in Jerusalem; he named it after himself, 'al-Ṣaliḥiyya.' He further established a *madrasa*, his fourth in Cairo, with the same name – al-Ṣaliḥiyya – for the study of Shāfiʿī

43 A. L. Tibawi, 'Origin and Character of *al-madrasah*,' *BSOAS* 25 (1962), 232.

44 Hirschler, *Medieval Arabic Historiography*, 15–42.

45 J. E. Gilbert, 'Institutionalization of Muslim Scholarship and Professionalization of the 'Ulamā' in Medieval Damascus,' *SI* 52 (1980), 109.

46 M. Chamberlain, *Knowledge and Social Practice in Medieval Damascus, 1190–1350* (Cambridge: Cambridge University Press, 2002), 144.

jurisprudence.[47] Ṣalāḥ al-Dīn's commitment to ensure the establishment of religious provisions for the religious class enveloped the cities with an aura of Sunnī Islam and encouraged Sufi settlement in those lands. There was also an obvious practical dimension to these charitable endowments before the recapture of Jerusalem. By taking over religious institutions that had belonged to the Fāṭimids and the Christians, Ṣalāḥ al-Dīn was able to meet some of his fiscal shortages and reward his religious establishment.[48] Ṣalāḥ al-Dīn's accommodation of Sufis reveals not only the growth of the popular movement but also the extent to which a 'pious-warrior ethos,' one that was more palpable in the life of Nūr al-Dīn, was sustained under Ṣalāḥ al-Dīn. The latter's consideration of the religious prerequisites that would assure him of victories compels us to view Ṣalāḥ al-Dīn as someone motivated not only, or always, by secular motives but also by a genuine belief, consolidated by the likes of 'Imād al-Dīn and al-Qāḍī l-Fāḍil, that divine assistance was dependent on public and private displays of piety and the paying of homage to holy men by whose presence and supplication the *jihād* would succeed – ideas such as this also stemmed from books of *faḍā'il*. After Nūr al-Dīn's death in 569/1174, 'Imād al-Dīn al-Iṣfahānī, no stranger to the *madrasa* himself, having entered it in his teens, composed an elegy for his dead patron that depicted him as a victor for Islam, and praised him for his service to the religious classes: "He was a builder of mosques and *madrasas* / Voluntarily for God and sincerely from his heart."[49] Pious endowments were not the only means the Ayyūbids employed to recruit the civilian elite to rule cities and towns and also to become supporters and active participants in military initiatives; some *'ulamā'* were paid directly from the revenues of *dīwāns* and others entered the service of rulers and were financed from household revenues.

47 See al-Nu'aymī, *al-Dāris fī tārīkh al-madāris*, 1:331–333.

48 For a fuller discussion of Ṣalāḥ al-Dīn's use of *awqāf* see Y. Frenkel, 'Political and Social Aspects of Islamic Religious Endowments ("awqāf"): Saladin in Cairo (1169–73) and Jerusalem (1187–93),' *BSOAS* 62 (1999), 1–20; for more information on the *iqta'* (land grants) system in Egypt and Syria under the Ayyūbids, see T. Satō, *State and Rural Society in Medieval Islam: Sulṭāns, Muqta's, and Fallahun* (Leiden: Brill, 1997), 42–76; Nikita Elisséeff, *Nūr ad-Dīn un grand prince musulman de Syrie au temps des croisades (511–569H./1118–1174)* (Damascus Institut Francaise de Damas, 1967), 3:726–729; S. Heidemann, 'Economic Growth and Currency in Ayyubid Palestine,' in *Ayyubid Jerusalem: The Holy City in Context 1187–1250*, ed. R. Hillenbrand and S. Auld (London: al Tajir World of Islam Trust, 2009), 276–300.

49 Abū Shāma, *Kitāb al-Rawḍatayn fī akhbār al-dawlatayn al-nūriyya wa-l-ṣalāḥiyya*, ed. Ibrāhīm Shams al-Dīn (Beirut: Dār al-Kutub al-'Ilmiyya, 2002), 2:240.

Together with the *'ulamā'*, Sufis were a popular group that congregated in the courts of Nūr al-Dīn and Ṣalāḥ al-Dīn. The Ayyūbids endowed numerous Sufi hospices (*khānqāhs*) and Ṣalāḥ al-Dīn further demonstrated his commitment to Sufis by allotting them travel stipends.[50] Because the "power and appeal to the masses of everyday Muslim believers came from faith in the miraculous power of saints,"[51] the closeness of saints to temporal rulers served to legitimise the latter's authority and provide the religious conditions necessary for divine assistance. An outstanding example of the aforementioned can be observed in a scene in which Nūr al-Dīn's men advised him to cease the stipends distributed to the jurists, the poor, the Sufis, and Qur'ān reciters in favour of the army. Nūr al-Dīn retorted:

> By God, I do not hope for victory except by those men, for indeed you are provided and given support by your weak ones. How can I stop favours for a people who fight for me with arrows that do not miss while I am asleep in my bed and change them for those who do not fight for me except when they see me with arrows that miss and hit? Those people [the first group] will have a portion of the *bayt al-māl* [royal treasury] and I will spend from it for them, how can I give it to other than them?[52]

His critics were silenced. These displays of piety revealed that both personal and public *jihāds* were sought. They emphasised the spiritual dimension of the *jihād* and showed the depth and meaning of the relationship between religious and military leaderships.[53]

---

50 For *khānqāhs*, *ribāṭs* and *zāwiyas* built during this time, see al-Nu'aymī, *al-Dāris fī tārīkh al-madāris*, 2:139–222; some of the leading scholars from the Ḥanbalī Banū Qudāma, for example, travelled to Iraq to study with one of medieval Islam's leading Sufi jurists, 'Abd al-Qādir al-Jilānī (d. 561/1165). One such scholar was 'Abd al-Ghanī b. Surūr al-Maqdisī who travelled to Baghdad in 559/1164, to study under al-Jilānī. Upon his return, 'Abd al-Ghanī became a teacher of *ḥadīth* at the Umayyad Mosque in Damascus. H. Mahamid, '"Franks" Effect on Islamic Spirit, Religious and Cultural Characters in Medieval Syria,' *Nebula* 4.1 (2007), 167.

51 Ira M. Lapidus, *A History of Islamic Socities: Third Edition* (New York: Cambridge University Press), 254.

52 Ibn Wāṣil, *Mufarrij*, 1:136.

53 Al-Ghazālī addresses the idea of pretention at length in the *Naṣīḥat al-mulūk*. Concerning the 'holder of authority,' "his officials and servants will all work for the sake of their own interests in this life. They will cause injustice to appear good in the eyes of the ruler, and thus send him to hell, in order that they may attain their own ends." Al-Ghazali, *Naṣīḥat al-mulūk* (Ghazali's Book of Counsel for Kings), trans. F. R. C. Bagley, ed. Jalal Humā'ī and

The process of institution-building also had a more distinct function that placed the ruler at the centre of communal affairs. A new initiative, a medieval structure known as the *dār al-ʿadl* ('house of justice') was utilised for the *qaḍāʾ al-maẓālim* (public hearings held once or twice a week and presided over by the ruler himself or his deputies), who heard public grievances and sought to redress them. The earliest known *dār al-ʿadl* was built in Damascus, most probably in 558/1163, by Nūr al-Dīn.[54] Another such structure was established in Aleppo in the late sixth/twelfth century by Ṣalāḥ al-Dīn's son al-Malik al-Ẓāhir; it started to function in 585/1189 although al-Ẓāhir used it more for court ceremonials than for redressing public wrongs.[55] In any case the *dār al-ʿadl* provided a tenable opportunity for the ruling class to publicly demonstrate their concern for justice and correct Islamic procedure, and visually this must have gone some way in reinforcing their image as defenders of the Islamic faith and its people.

In line with Nūr al-Dīn's campaign to promote Sunnī Islam, he also sponsored the foundation of religious monuments such as minarets and inscriptions. These visually evocative constructs served to stress Islam's dominance in the cities in which they were built. They displayed elaborate arabesque decorations that alluded to paradise and the divine ordering of the universe. For the inscriptions, elaborate calligraphic forms of Arabic script were used, different than those of the Fāṭimids; this emphasised Nūr al-Dīn's loyalty to ʿAbbāsid caliphs.[56] These kinds of initiatives and Nūr al-Dīn's general pursuit of orthodoxy emerged in part through the influence of the ʿAbbāsid vizier and staunch Ḥanbalī theologian Ibn al-Hubayra (499–560/1105–65). The vizier was a strong religious presence in the courts of the ʿAbbāsid caliphs al-Muqtafī and al-Mustanjid. Through traditional preaching he emphasised the necessity of loyalty to the legitimate caliphs while emasculating the power of the Saljūq sultan. Ibn al-Hubayra's important place in the ʿAbbāsid political scene can also be gauged from his relationship to influential people of his time, including

H. D. Isaacs (London: Oxford University Press, 1964), 23. Al-Ghazālī's work belongs to the mirrors for princes genre; it was most likely composed between 498/1105 and 505/1111. For more information, see al-Ghazālī, *Naṣīḥat*, xi–lxxiv.

54 See Elisséeff, *Nūr ad-Dīn un grand prince*, 3:843–847.

55 See N. O. Rabbat, 'The Ideological Significance of the *dār al-ʿadl* in the Medieval Islamic Orient,' *IJMES* 27 (1995), 3–28.

56 Y. Tabbaa, 'Monuments with a Message: Propagation of *Jihād* under Nūr al-Dīn (1146–1174),' in *The Meeting of Two Worlds: Cultural Exchange between East and West during the Period of the Crusades*, ed. Vladimir P. Goss (Ann Arbor, MI: Medieval Institute Publications, 1986), 223–240.

nearly all of the major poets and scholars who, in turn, received his patronage and protection.[57]

The influence of the *ʿulamāʾ* during this time was paramount. In fact, Qurʾānic commentators placed them on a par with people of authority and influence; the role of the scholar in public life meant that the political decisions to prosecute military warfare could not be taken independent of the *ʿulamāʾ* who were, aside from the caliph, able to sanction war and justify it.[58] For Ṣalāḥ al-Dīn then, the defence of Jerusalem was dependent on the commitment and interest of his scholarly entourage and support base in Damascus. The scholarly status of shaykhs in Damascus was altogether distinctive; Damascenes associated great scholars, largely those from Damascus itself, with legendary heroes such as ʿAntar and Marwān b. al-Ḥakam. The *madrasa*s established in Damascus from the days of Nūr al-Dīn continued to function as social centres of learning, authorising *ijāza*s (certificates) and holding public readings. Ṣalāḥ al-Dīn also constructed at least two *madrasa*s in Damascus; in part, the schools established in Damascus enabled that city to retain its importance during the occupation of Jerusalem. The *madrasa*s functioned as a strong spiritual bulwark against the Franks.

In Egypt, among Ṣalāḥ al-Dīn's first actions was the establishment of two *madrasa*s in Fustat in 565/1170, one for the Shāfiʿīs and the other for Mālikīs. He also established a *madrasa* for the Ḥanafīs in Cairo in 571–572/1176–77. His concern to accommodate three of the major Sunnī schools of law was an attempt to expand the *madrasa*s in Egypt and to gain the patronage of the community; this contributed to his popularity and portrayed him as a defender of orthodoxy. Although the *madrasa*s were pivotal in strengthening Sunnī creed and jurisprudence as a counter to the Shīʿa, particularly under the Saljūqs and Ayyūbids, *madrasa*s in Egypt during the sixth/twelfth and seventh/thirteenth centuries further served to undermine the country's powerful Christian minority. In the latter part of the sixth/twelfth century the Shīʿa were no longer a strong presence in Egypt and since Sunnī Egyptians had not converted to Shīʿī thought in any sizeable numbers, the *madrasa*s could direct their focus on contributing to the ideological defence of Sunnī Islam against

57 See H. Mason, *Two Statesmen of Medieval Islam: vizir Ibn Hubayra (499–560 AH 1105–1165 AD) and Caliph an-Nāṣir li Din Allāh (553–622 AH/1158–1225 AD)* (Paris: Mouton, 1972).

58 They are *ahl al-Qurʾān wa-l-ʿilm* (people of Qurʾān and knowledge [of *ḥadīth*]) and *fuqahāʾ wa-l-ʿulamāʾ* (jurisprudents and scholars). See al-Qurṭubī, *Mukhtaṣar tafsīr al-Qurṭubī*, 1:523; they are *ʿumarāʾ* (rulers) and *ahl al-ʿilm wa-l-fiqh* (people of knowledge and jurisprudence). See al-Ṭabarī, *Tafsīr al-Ṭabarī*, ed. Hanī l-Ḥajj, ʿImād Zakī l-Bārūdī, and Khayrī Saʿīd (Cairo: Dār al-Tawfiqiyya li-Ṭibāʿa, 2004), 5:177–178.

the powerful Christian threat in Egypt.[59] Students of a *madrasa* trained in dialectics to counter different opinions and traditions (like those of the Shīʿī), could further use their skills to defend Islam against a dangerous rival faith; the bureaucrats trained in the *madrasa* system now competed with Christians for top government positions. The new-found anti-Christian emphasis in the *madrasas* might be shown in Ṣalāḥ al-Dīn's construction of a Shāfiʿī *madrasa* after the reconquest of Jerusalem in 583/1187 in the revered Church of St. Anne, which was believed to stand on the site of the birthplace of the Virgin Mary.[60]

According to Stephen Humphreys, there were 241 construction projects by 174 different patrons in Damascus from 589/1193 to 658/1260.[61] Naturally, the growth of *madrasas* in turn led to a demand for 'graduates' from these schools to take official positions as *khaṭībs* (preachers) and to administer other religious functions. It is for this reason that Makdisi referred to them as "colleges" in the medieval European sense.[62] The travel of scholars and students to fill teaching posts or to enrol as students added to the vibrancy of learning in this period, and attractive salaries and stipends for students provided by the endowment programmes of Nūr al-Dīn and Ṣalāḥ al-Dīn made *madrasas* formidable educational institutions; the manifold function of the *madrasa* meant it could promote Sunnī Islam to counter the Shīʿa and more importantly, advance the 'Islamic' cause in the face of Christian challenges, particularly in major cities such as Damascus, Aleppo, Cairo, and Alexandria.

59 See Gary Leiser, 'The *Madrasa* and the Islamization of the Middle East: The Case of Egypt,' *Journal of the American Research Center in Egypt* 22 (1985), 35–36.

60 Leiser, 'The *Madrasa*,' 29–47.

61 R. S. Humphreys, 'Politics and Architectural Patronage in Ayyūbid Syria,' in *The Islamic World from Classical to Modern Times: Esssays in Honor of Bernard Lewis*, ed. C. E. Bosworth, C. Issawi, R. Savory, and A. L. Udovitch (Princeton, NJ: Darwin Press, 1989), 169–171; D. Talmon-Heller, *Islamic Piety in Medieval Syria: Mosques, Cemeteries and Sermons under the Zangids and Ayyūbids (1146–1260)* (Boston: Brill, 2007), 12–13.

62 See G. Makdisi, 'The Significance of the Sunni Schools of Law in Islamic Religious History,' *IJMES* 10 (1979), 1–8. For further information see Devin J. Stewart, 'The Doctorate of Islamic Law in Mamluk Egypt and Syria,' in *Law and Education in Medieval Islam*, ed. Joseph Lowry, Devin Stewart, and Shawkat Toorawa (Cambridge: E. J. W. Gibb Memorial Trust, 2004), 45–90; Devin J. Stewart, 'The Students' Representative in the Law Colleges of Fourteenth-Century Damascus,' *Islamic Law and Society* 15.2 (2008), 185–218; Devin J. Stewart, 'Review of Jonathan Berkey, *The Transmission of Knowledge in Medieval Cairo: A Social History of Islamic Education*,' *Islamic Law and Society* 1 (1994): 363–372; Devin J. Stewart, 'Review of Michael Chamberlain, Knowledge and Social Practice in Medieval Damascus, 1190–1350,' *Comparative Education Review* 50.3 (August 2006), 531–533.

Nūr al-Dīn's establishment of *madrasas* did more than proclaim his public building programme, or counter the crusader threat. It was of course part of the ideology of the Sunnī revival of this period, propagated by the ʿAbbāsids and the Sunnī dynasties of the Ghaznavids, Saljūqs, Zangids, and Ayyūbids, that heterodoxy be challenged and supressed. The Qastal al-Shuʿaybiyya, a mosque originally renovated in the fourth/tenth century by a Shīʿa of Aleppo, Abū-l Ḥasan al-Ghadayrī, was converted by Nūr al-Dīn into a Shāfiʿī *madrasa* in 545/1150–51 for the jurist Shaykh Shuʿayb b. al-Ḥusayn b. Aḥmad al-Andalusī at a time of heightened tension between Sunnīs and Shīʿīs in Aleppo and as part of his policy of promoting Sunnī Islam. The conversion of what was previously a Shīʿī mosque into a Sunnī *madrasa* and the choice of Qurʾānic inscriptions used in the medieval building accent the anti-Shīʿī polemic in the renovation and use of the building, targeted toward Aleppo's predominantly Shīʿī population. The first *madrasa* Nūr al-Dīn renovated in the city of Aleppo (in 544–545/1149–50) was the Madrasa al-Ḥallāwiyya, previously the mosque of Sarrajin, another Shīʿī structure converted into a Ḥanafī *madrasa*. Nūr al-Dīn also put into place a series of restrictions against the Shīʿīs of Aleppo, forbidding public displays of Shīʿī Islam, such as the Shīʿī call to prayer and the practice of insulting the companions of the Prophet. These appropriations of Shīʿī sites of worship and restrictions on their public practices did much to antagonise relations between the two communities, and in 552/1157 some local Shīʿīs even destroyed some of the *madrasas* and *khānqāhs* that Nūr al-Dīn had built in Aleppo. However, Nūr al-Dīn's architectural patronage and competitive measures against the Shīʿīs were a calculated and essential part of an established policy of advancing Sunnī Islam and containing the threat of all heterodoxy.[63]

Although much historical attention has been paid to the *madrasa* as a successful and functional tool in the promotion of Sunnī Islam, and certain prominent examples, such as Ṣalāḥ al-Dīn's construction of a *madrasa* beside al-Shāfiʿī's tomb, seem to demonstrate this, and although the Ayyūbids were committed to Sunnism and the suppression of Shīʿī Islam, internal theological debates among Sunnīs must not be overlooked in the process of ascertaining the role and function of the *madrasa*. In this light, Ṣalāḥ al-Dīn's stipulation that those appointed in his *madrasas* be Ashʿarī in creed suggests that Ayyūbid

63 J. Raby, 'Nur al-Din, the Qastal shuʿaybiyya, and the "Classical Revival,"' *Muqarnas* 21, *Essays in Honor of J. M. Rogers* (2004), 289–310; Y. Tabbaa, *The Transformation of Islamic Art during the Sunni Revival* (Seattle and London: University of Washington Press, 2001), 21–24; Y. Tabbaa, *Constructions of Power and Piety in Medieval Aleppo* (University Park: Pennsylvania State University Press, 1997).

religious policy seems to have been directed at Sunnīs as much as Shīʿīs, and was certainly one of the hallmarks of the Sunnī revival in this period. It is the idea of seeing the *madrasa* as a strictly administered institution with a specified course of instruction that appears lacking; it appears more guided by "an elastic custom rather than by a rigid theory."[64]

The career of Ṣalāḥ al-Dīn (569–589/1174–93) has been much discussed and scrutinised in relation to the Muslim response to the crusader occupation of Jerusalem. Historians such as Stanley Lane-Poole and Sir Hamilton Gibb saw Ṣalāḥ al-Dīn as inspired throughout his reign by a resolve to wage a holy war against the Franks, and indeed as having wider aims, "to restore the rule of the Islamic law under the direction of the ʿAbbāsid Caliphate and not his own rule."[65] Ṣalāḥ al-Dīn thus came to be seen as a military leader interested in reviving Sunnī Islam and unifying Muslim political power such that he could bring about the subsequent reconquest. Such a romanticised image is contested, however, by historians such as Andrew Ehrenkreutz, who point to his record of unscrupulous schemes and campaigns aimed at personal and family aggrandisement.[66] Ṣalāḥ al-Dīn's rivalry with the Zangids took precedence over his concern to defeat the crusaders and Ehrenkreutz argues that "his alleged moral and religious attributes influenced neither the course of his public endeavours nor the conduct of his contemporaries."[67] Thus, his political and military experience, fused with his ambition to recapture former Zangid territory, should be considered when assessing Ṣalāḥ al-Dīn's successes. Malcolm Lyons and D. E. P. Jackson also focused their attention on ways in which expansionism, family aggrandisement, and religious convictions shaped his motives, and they suggest that his desire to maintain personal credibility following his failure to take Mosul in 581/1185 led him to focus military efforts on the Latin Kingdom of Jerusalem. In light of the aforementioned works, Ira Lapidus' assessment must be noted; he cautions against circumventing the plethora of interests at play in the socio-economic and religious milieu of Syria:

> To make any deep assessment of an historical personality we have to interpret his life in the context of the cultural values and expectations which informed his life. Behind Saladin's life lies the ethos of a whole culture – its ideas about the nature of the state and the role of soldier

64 Tibawi, 'Origin and Character,' 230. See also: Chamberlain, *Knowledge and Social Practice*, 69–90.

65 P. Holt, 'Saladin and His Admirers: A Biographical Reassessment,' *BSOAS* 46 (1983), 235.

66 Hillenbrand, *The Crusades*, 185.

67 A. S. Ehrenkreutz, *Saladin* (Albany: State University of New York Press, 1972), 238.

and ruler, its conceptions of worthwhile mundane and religious purposes. In particular there are the attitudes of diverse persons and strata of society toward war between Muslim princes, the norms defining legitimate objectives and tactics, Muslim attitudes toward the Crusaders – a plethora of mutually reinforcing and contradictory political, economic, and religious interests. How can we evaluate Saladin's career without this background of culture?[68]

Al-Ghazālī and the New Sunnism of the Saljūq Period

In the Saljūq period Abū Ḥāmid al-Ghazālī (d. 505/1111)[69] is prominently credited with reviving a new 'Sunnism' that centred on reviving the spirit of the inner *jihād*. Al-Ghazālī wrote his magisterial *Iḥyāʾ ʿulūm al-dīn* (Revival of the Religious Sciences) in an attempt to insire a religious awakening in a population that had succumbed to spiritual laxness.[70] A salient theme in the early poetry and *jihād* text of al-Sulamī is the idea that loss and defeat is a consequence of an internal religious weakness among Muslims. While early poets wrote of issues of apathy, indifference, division, misdirected zeal, and love of the world, each aspect fits into a broader consideration of religious neglect. The opprobrium levelled at such an internal state required a collective return to God (*rujūʿ ila-Allāh*), and this was the pivotal motivation for al-Ghazālī's *Iḥyāʾ ʿulūm al-dīn*. Al-Sulamī cited al-Ghazālī, a renowned Shāfiʿī theologian, to give credence and validity to his arguments in favour of *jihād*. Al-Ghazālī sought to show that it was one's spiritual relationship with God that needed to be addressed, and this was a far cry from the theological and *madhhab* wrangling of the fifth/eleventh century that often saw brawls spill over into the streets of Baghdad.

Another of al-Ghazālī's works, the *Naṣīḥat al-mulūk*, is quite significant, together with other texts of the same 'mirror for princes' genre. Though al-Ghazālī did not play a direct role in communicating the ideas of the anti-Frankish *jihād*, his viewpoints influenced some of the scholars who developed such ideas. These were formulated during the Sunnī revival of the Saljūq

68 I. M. Lapidus, 'Review of "Saladin" by Andrew S. Ehrenkreutz,' *JAOS* 94 (1974), 241.

69 For more information on al-Ghazālī see W. M. Watt, 'al-Ghazālī,' *EI*², 2:1038–1041; Ibn Khallikān, *Wafayāt al-aʿyān wa-anbāʾ abnaʾ al-zamān*, trans. M. de Slane, ed. S. Moinul Haq (New Delhi: Kitab Bhavan, 1996), 4:191–194.

70 Abū Ḥāmid al-Ghazālī, *Revival of Religious Learnings: Imam Ghazzali's Ihya Ulum-id-Din*, trans. Fazl-ul-Karim (Karachi: Darul-Ishaat, 1993).

period, and we see al-Ghazālī's emphasis in the *Naṣīḥat* on justice as a prerequisite of rightful political authority is accentuated in the poetry of this period. Al-Ghazālī wrote it for the Saljūq sultan Muḥammad b. Malikshāh who ruled from 498/1105 to 511/1118. In it, he underscores the dangers of failing to rule by precepts of justice and compassion:

> in government there is a great privilege and whoever carries out its responsibilities acquires a happiness beyond which there is no greater happiness, but if he falls short he falls into tribulation which is greater than all tribulation except unbelief; the greatest proof of the high nature of this privilege is that the Prophet of God said "the justice of one day of a just sultan is preferable to the worship of sixty years.[71]

The first part of al-Ghazālī's *Naṣīḥat* outlines the beliefs a Muslim ruler should abide by and the guiding religious principles that should inform his rule. The second part concerns the origin of many of his practical ethics. Magnanimity in kings and aphorisms of the sages make up some of the content in this section. In all, it is al-Ghazālī's Sufi outlook that is most noteworthy for the way it shapes the text. It should be noted that al-Ghazālī was not alone in his spiritual focus. The sixth/twelfth-century also brought with it the spiritual insights of the Baghdad-based Sufi master 'Abd-al-Qādir al-Jilānī (d. 561/1165) and the Persian philosopher Shihāb al-Dīn Yaḥyā b. Ḥabash Suhrawardī (548–587/1153–91), the latter was noted for his attention to asceticism, though such reformist methods, instead of injecting a new-found devoutness and spiritual vibrancy into the *umma*, led to a schism. In Aleppo Suhrawardī tutored the governor al-Malik al-Ẓāhir, the third son of Ṣalāḥ al-Dīn (d. 613/1216). However, his philosophical views earned him the disparagement of many orthodox jurists, and the famous judge al-Qāḍī l-Fāḍil advised Ṣalāḥ al-Dīn to have Suhrawardī put to death and by the sultan's order he was executed the same year that King Richard arrived at Acre. Nūr al-Dīn met the Baghdad-based founder of the Suhrawardiyya Sufi order, Abū l-Najīb al-Suhrawardī, in 557/1162 when al-Suhrawardī visited Damascus en route to Jerusalem. Though he was prevented from entering the Holy City, in Damascus Nūr al-Dīn received him with much esteem and honour, and arranged for al-Suhrawardī to preach at a number of assemblies. Another renowned ascetic, the Andalusian Muḥyī l-Dīn b. al-'Arabī (d. 638/1240), settled in Damascus toward the end of his life, and was criticised by some of his contemporaries, but defended by others.

71 Al-Ghazālī, *Naṣīḥat*, 8.

It is essential here to consider a further point. The new Islamic century, which began on the first of Muḥarram 500/2 September 1106, was awaited with anxiety and fear that was heightened by the fall of Jerusalem less than a decade before. Whereas al-Ghazālī, the Sufi mystic and theologian, was considered the *mujaddid* (lit. 'renewer') by not a few of his contemporaries, it could be argued that in the eyes of some, his lack of physical participation in the *jihād*, which might have been deemed a necessary prerequisite (particularly in the context following the events of 492/1099) made him less suitable to be considered the *mujaddid*. It is difficult to say. We do know, however, that the Egyptian Shāfiʿī jurist Jalāl al-Dīn al-Suyūṭī named him in his poem, *Tuḥfat al-muhtadīn bi-akhbār al-mujaddidīn*, as the *mujaddid* of the fifth Islamic century:

و الخامس الحجر هو الغزالي وعده ما فيه من جدال.[72]

It should be stated that al-Ghazālī was unrestrained in his legal verdicts concerning the obligation of *jihād*. The medieval "theologians became more ready to accept the mystics as respectable, while the mystics were more careful to remain within the bounds of orthodoxy"[73] – which meant of course, in part, the adoption of legal matters in relation to a respected *madhhab* (school of jurisprudence). Ideally the *mujaddid* combined qualities of the 'greater' inner *jihād* with those necessary for the more physical, albeit 'lesser' one. While there appears to be no explicit reference to indicate that Nūr al-Dīn or Ṣalāḥ al-Dīn considered themselves the *mujaddidīn* (sing. *mujaddid*) of their age, neither were they accorded the honorary title by their contemporaries. Perhaps this is not entirely surprising; those considered to have been 'renewers' of Islam were usually assigned the title decades or even centuries after their deaths. It is also plausible to suggest that Muslims might have generally expected a *mujaddid* to be an Arab. Furthermore, by this time a *mujaddid* would need to be from the *ʿulamāʾ*, and Nūr al-Dīn and Ṣalāḥ al-Dīn were not scholars to be considered 'renewers.'

The importance of political and religious patronage cannot be overstated. It provided the opportunity for many budding authors and poets to enter into courtly circles, to achieve recognition for their verse, and to contribute to the reputation of their patrons, most notably Nūr al-Dīn and Ṣalāḥ al-Dīn, as *jihād* warriors. Their verse often projected a religiosity and piety of their champions of the anti-Frankish *jihād*, and thereby helped to advance the new Sunnism of this period. However, it was not only poetry as a literary source that can be

72 Al-ʿAẓīm Ābādī, *ʿAwn al-maʿbūd: Sharḥ Sunan Abī Dāwūd* (Cairo, 2001), 7:359.

73 W. M. Watt, *The Faith and Practice of al-Ghazālī* (London: George Allen and Unwin, 1953), 15.

credited for this advancement. Other writings and initiatives also existed, including works on the *faḍāʾil al-Quds* ('merits of Jerusalem'), that deserve some mention at this point.

Faḍāʾil al-Quds (Merits of Jerusalem): Historiography and Relevance

The capture of Jerusalem in 492/1099 was eventually met by a popular Muslim response advocating the recovery of the Holy Land. This was manifested in part by an interest in *faḍāʾil al-Quds* ('merits of Jerusalem') literature which began to pick up after 555/1160, and there seems to have been a role for Nūr al-Dīn and later Ṣalāḥ al-Dīn in "stimulating" the proliferation of *faḍāʾil*. This literature served to reinforce the desire of Muslims to recapture the city. Such writings had existed before, but the importance of the crusades for the development of *faḍāʾil* ideas and literature is paramount to our understanding of sixth/twelfth-century Muslim attitudes.

For all its merits, one of the things lacking in Emmanuel Sivan's very influential *L'Islam et la Croisade* is the lack of attention it gives to Muslims' beliefs about the sanctity of Jerusalem before the crusades. In this section I first consider more recent historiography on *faḍāʾil al-Quds* studies and reveal not only a consistently held Muslim belief in the special status accorded to the city of Jerusalem, but one that also shows an evolution in the corpus of *faḍāʾil* texts by the sixth/twelfth century, and most importantly the way such texts came to be used to inspire a yearning for Jerusalem in the Muslims of Syria during the crusader occupation.

It was around the end of the first/seventh century that we can trace the beginning of the *faḍāʾil* literature, a genre of writing focused on the 'virtues' of places, the recitation of the Qurʾān – which appears to be the oldest strand – the Prophet's companions, the *ḥajj*, *jihād*, and other Islamic obligations. Much of the research concerned with the early *faḍāʾil al-Quds* literature pays particular attention to the information the texts provide about the sanctity of Jerusalem in the Islamic tradition; scholars and historians have utilised a range of treatises to determine how Muslim perception of the city evolved over time. Current political correctness arising from the Arab/Israeli conflict and its application in the study of the history of Jerusalem is certainly a hindrance to objectivity. In some scholarly circles, the *faḍāʾil al-Quds* genre seems to be examined for the purpose of questioning, or at best weakening, Islam's claim to the Holy City. While it is not the purpose of this book to delve into this area in any depth, an assessment of the historiography of the study of *faḍāʾil al-Quds* makes some clarification on the aforementioned question an unavoidable necessity.

One of the most noted authorities on the ideology and propaganda of the anti-Frankish Muslim struggle is Emmanuel Sivan, an author who devotes some of his study to the place of Jerusalem in Islam by assessing the dating and function of the *faḍāʾil al-Quds* literature.[74] Sivan concludes that most of the *faḍāʾil* literature originated as propaganda during and after the crusades, and thus it represents a late religious focus on the Holy City. His conclusions have been challenged by numerous studies that provide extensive documentation that the *faḍāʾil* of Jerusalem were very old and widely diffused. For instance, Amikam Elad demonstrated that Muslim worship, specifically pilgrimage rituals and visits to venerated places in and around the Dome of the Rock, can be traced to the Umayyad period, and the circulation of *faḍāʾil* literature went hand in hand with that.[75] Elad credits M. J. Kister for illuminating the role of the *faḍāʾil* phenomenon in the literary genre of *ḥadīth*, and its early origin and circulation.[76] According to G. H. A. Juynboll, the *faḍāʾil* may in fact be the oldest type of *ḥadīth* literature; it was circulated as early as the first/seventh century.[77]

In line with this, Ghada Hashem Talhami's important article "The Modern History of Jerusalem: Academic Myths and Propaganda" stresses that political views must not hinder accurate historical research.[78] Talhami contests Sivan's interpretation by pointing to an earlier work, entitled *Faḍāʾil bayt al-maqdis*, written by a Palestinian writer, al-Ramlī (d. 300/912) in the third/ninth century, about the companions of the Prophet who settled in Palestine. S. Mourad assessed al-Ramlī's text and understood the way it emphasised the early Muslims'

74 E. Sivan, 'The Beginning of the Faḍā'il al-Quds Literature,' *IOS* 1 (1971), 263–271.

75 A. Elad, 'The History and Topography of Jerusalem during the Early Islamic Period: The Historical Value of Faḍā'il al-Quds Literature: A Reconsideration,' *JSAI* 14 (1991), 41–70; Elad, *Medieval Jerusalem and Islamic Worship, Holy Ceremonies, Pilgrimage* (Leiden: E. J. Brill, 1995); Elad, 'Pilgrims and Pilgrimage to Hebron (al-Khalīl) During the Early Muslim Period,' in *Pilgrims and Travelers to the Holy Land*, ed. B. F. le Beau and Menachem Mor (Omaha, NE: Creighton University Press, 1996), 21–62; G. Le Strange, *Palestine under the Moslems* (London: Palestine Exploration Fund, 1890); O. Grabar, 'The Umayyad Dome of the Rock in Jerusalem,' *Ars Orientalis* 3 (1959), 33–62.

76 M. J. Kister, 'A Comment on the Antiquity of Traditions Praising Jerusalem,' in *The Jerusalem Cathedra* (1981), 1:185–186.

77 "Faḍā'il traditions may be considered as, if not the oldest, one of the oldest genres." G. H. Juynboll, *Muslim Tradition: Studies in Chronology, Provenance and Authorship of Early ḥadīth* (Cambridge: Cambridge University Press, 1983), 163 n4.

78 G. H. Talhami, 'The Modern History of Jerusalem: Academic Myths and Propaganda,' *Middle East Policy Council* 7 (Feb. 2000), 113–129.

perceptions of the sanctity of Jerusalem. The text allows for a reconsideration of the dating of books on the *faḍā'il* of Jerusalem, to at least two centuries before the crusades, and shows us a world in which the *faḍā'il* literature was circulating.[79] Other earlier works on the *faḍā'il* of Syria (Shām, i.e., Greater Syria) also exist.[80]

Moreover, Nasser Rabbat credits al-Wāsiṭī's tract for shedding crucial light on the function of Jerusalem in early Islam; the compilation of *faḍā'il* works during the *jihād* programmes of Nūr al-Dīn and Ṣalāḥ al-Dīn was an extension of an already existing tradition and must not serve as the sole means to interpret Jerusalem's early Islamic significance.[81] As Cobb explains, "the crusader-era collections of traditions about Jerusalem can be used as assemblages of earlier traditions from various early Islamic sources that no longer survive."[82] 'Abdul Aziz Duri expounds on other Jerusalem-related texts, such as the work by al-Ramlī, and geographical works that mention the Holy City. These predate the fifth-/eleventh-century tract by al-Wāsiṭī and illustrate an earlier Islamic interest in stipulating the merits associated with the Holy City.[83] The crusades did not, therefore, give birth to the *faḍā'il* literature. Instead, *jihād* leaders such as Nūr al-Dīn and Ṣalāḥ al-Dīn made use of existing material that had the emotional capacity to inspire a Muslim population to fight in the *jihād* and to liberate the cities (especially Jerusalem) that carry deep religious symbolism in Muslim religious imagination.

Meir Kister asserts the significance of the early *faḍā'il* treatises by acknowledging the early dating of *ḥadīths* found in them.[84] He relies upon the *tafsīr* (Qur'ān commentary) of Muqātil (d. 150/767), which contains traditions cited at particular junctions in which Jerusalem, al-Aqṣā Mosque or the prophets connected to the Holy Land are mentioned, or alluded to, in the Qur'ān. Similar to Livne-Kafri, Kister credits the *Isrā'īliyyāt* traditions as reinforcing

---

79 For a reconstruction of al-Ramlī's work by means of traditions contained from the *Faḍā'il bayt al-muqaddas* of al-Wāsiṭī and the *Faḍā'il bayt al-maqdis wa-l-Khalīl wa-faḍā'il al-Shām* of Abū l-Ma'ālī l-Musharraf b. al-Murajja al-Maqdisī, see Suleiman Ali Mourad, 'The Symbolism of Jerusalem in Early Islam,' in *Jerusalem: Idea and Reality*, ed. Tamar Mayer and Suleiman Ali Mourad (New York: Routledge, 2008), 86–102.

80 See Cobb, *White Banners*, 167 n33.

81 N. Rabbat, 'The Meaning of the Umayyad Dome of the Rock,' *Muqarnas* 6 (1989), 13.

82 P. M. Cobb, 'Virtual Sacrality: Making Muslim Syria Sacred Before the Crusades,' *Medieval Encounters: Jewish, Christian and Muslim Culture in Conference and Dialogue* 8 (Leiden: Brill, 2002), 40.

83 A. A. Duri, 'Jerusalem in the Early Islamic Period 7th–11th Centuries AD,' in *Jerusalem in History*, ed. K. J. Asali (Essex: Scorpion Publishing, 1989), 115.

84 Kister, 'A Comment,' 185–186.

the appeal of Jerusalem in the Muslim consciousness. Kister's approach is a more nuanced one, in that it at least acknowledges the indispensable science of *ḥadīth* in dating *faḍā'il* literature.

Here Samer Akkach provides some useful insights that the *faḍā'il* is quite simply "anchored in the Quran and the *ḥadīth*, which identifies and alludes to many sites of special significance."[85] It is Ibn 'Asākir's interpretation of *sūras* such as The Fig (95:1–3) in which allusions are made to the sanctities of Damascus, Jerusalem, Egypt, and Mecca that may be seen as formative for sixth/twelfth-century perceptions. As Akkach points out, Ibn 'Asākir "elaborates these references by reporting a set of traditions that describe the eschatological significance of these sites."[86]

The *faḍā'il* traditions are seen as a symbol of a broader recognition and commitment to *ḥadīth* studies that arose in the second half of the sixth/twelfth-century.[87] Nūr al-Dīn Zangī is credited for building the first Dār al-Ḥadīth *madrasa* in Damascus in 565/1170. It was in this setting that *faḍā'il al-Quds* gained popularity and was widely disseminated, bolstered by other literary devices including poetry and religious sermons aimed at rousing the Muslims to engage in *jihād* and recover the Holy Land. Keen interest in *ḥadīth* studies has always been a feature of Muslim religious communities, from which sprang many schools of *ḥadīth* throughout the Muslim world.[88]

This period also saw the writing of works on other Muslim cities threatened with occupation, such as Damascus, Alexandria, and Cairo; *faḍā'il* treatises served not only to reinvigorate the special place of cities and sites in the Islamic tradition but also the indispensable purpose of instructing the citizens and military forces. Some of these traditions expound on an earthly reward, such as an increase in wealth, while others promise a heavenly one for the residents of such centres. One can consider the particularly revealing case of the celebrated ninth-/fifteenth-century Muslim scholar Jalāl al-Dīn al-Suyūṭī (d. 911/1505) who composed an epistle on the virtues of Alexandria. The author intended to inspire pilgrimages and encourage Muslims to take up residence in Ascalon, Caesarea, and Alexandria to ensure a noteworthy position

85 S. Akkach, *Cosmology and Architecture in Premodern Islam: An Architectural Reading of Mystical Ideas* (Albany: State University of New York Press, 2005), 166.

86 Ibid.

87 'Abd al-Laṭīf Hamza, *Adab al-ḥurūb al-ṣalībiyya* (Cairo, 1949).

88 See J. P. Berkey, *Popular Preaching and Religious Authority in the Medieval Islamic Near East* (Seattle and London: University of Washington Press, 2001).

in paradise, and meanwhile ensure a build-up of Muslims in areas threatened with attacks by Christian pirates.[89]

The *faḍāʾil* works comprised panegyrics about particular cities, towns, or more specific locations such as mosques or shrines. We may note, however, that books of *faḍāʾil al-Quds* acted not merely as travel guides – a central purpose of many location-based *faḍāʾil* works[90] – but also promulgated the immediate purpose of taking up arms for the reconquest, and for the defence of homeland, particularly in cities like Damascus. The proliferation of *ḥadīth* that speak of victorious bands of warriors committed to Jerusalem and Syria until the end of time were the sort that conveyed the immediacy of the *jihād* and their proliferation is thus noted. Apocalyptic *ḥadīths* were useful in generating enthusiasm about future victory, and were easily applicable to the crusaders – as well as to the Shīʿīs. Medieval scholars were able to superimpose imprecise identities such as the 'Banū Aṣfar' (pale-faced ones) to distinct hostile groups, and the oft-repeated tradition championing the permanent struggle of a group of fighters in and around Jerusalem was advantageously employed for *jihād* participants in the inexact regions comprising the 'Bilād al-Shām' (or Greater Syria).

Within the corpus of this literature there is a focus on Jerusalem and Damascus as bastions of Islamic resistance against the 'unbelieving centres' of Constantinople and Rome in the latter days. In the sixth/twelfth century, the spiritual appeal of Damascus is often absent in historical considerations of the resilience of its people in the city's defence. During the occupation of Jerusalem, Damascus was substituted as a spiritual centre, and its sanctity

89 A. S. Atiya, *Crusade, Commerce and Culture* (London: Oxford University Press, 1962), 134; Alexandria was described by al-Muqaddasī, who wrote in the fourth/tenth century, as a fertile city rich in resources, that could provide protection from external threats: "Al-Iskandariyya (Alexandria) is a delightful town on the shore of the Romaean Sea. Commanded by an impregnable fortress it is a distinguished city with a goodly meed of upright and devout people. The drinking water of the people is derived from the Nile, which reaches them in the season of its food via an aqueduct, and fills their cisterns. It resembles Syria in climate and customs; rainfall is abundant; and every conceivable type of produce is brought together there. The countryside round about is splendid, producing excellent fruits, and fine grapes." Al-Muqaddasī, *Aḥsan al-taqāsīm fī maʿrifat al-aqālīm* (The Best Divisions for Knowledge of the Regions), trans. B. A. Collins (Reading: Garnet Publishing, 1994), 180–181.

90 We can discern from Ibn Jubayr's *Riḥla* that he relied on books of *faḍāʾil* (as travel guides); he mentions designations in Damascus that are important for travellers to the city, and was clearly dependent on a book extolling the virtues of Damascus and the *Tārīkh Dimashq* of Ibn ʿAsākir. Ibn Jubayr, *Travels*, 273, 274, 285, 290.

complemented and even strengthened the sanctity of Jerusalem. There is also a deliberate link between Jerusalem and Constantinople in Muslim literature, wherein the conquest of the latter was seen as conditional on the reconquest of the former. This seems to be a new development in *jihād* theory, in which the conquest of Constantinople was relegated to a position below that of the more immediate reconquest of Jerusalem.

Finally, whereas some historians have questioned Jerusalem's centrality to Islam by noting the late dating of *faḍā'il* tracts (as opposed to the earlier works on cities such as Mecca, Medina, Wasit, and Baghdad), from an Islamic eschatological perspective and one firmly embedded in the *faḍā'il* genre, it is Jerusalem and not the more prestigious cities of Mecca and Medina that loom large in the end of time scenario. Both cities are in fact seemingly subservient to the role of Jerusalem in Islamic tradition. Al-Muqaddasī in his *Aḥsan al-taqāsīm fī ma'rifat al-aqālīm* describes Jerusalem in a way that brought out its eschatological significance. The cities of Mecca and Medina have special places through Jerusalem and its functioning in the Last Day:

> As for the excellence of the city, is it not indeed to be the plain of the resurrection, and the marshalling place on the day of judgement for the risen dead? Now it is true that Mecca and Medina are in the ascendant with the Ka'ba and the Prophet – God's peace and blessings be upon him – but truly, on the Day of Resurrection, they will both hasten to Jerusalem, and the excellence of all of them will be encompassed there together.[91]

The Dome of the Rock in Jerusalem is eschatologically identified as the stage of the final drama of humanity, namely the resurrection and the last judgement. The caliph 'Abd al-Malik b. Marwān (26–86/646–705) was known to show a personal interest in this aspect of Jerusalem and the Dome of the Rock. A certain Nawf al-Bakkālī, in answer to 'Abd al-Malik's question concerning Jerusalem, enumerated the merits of Jerusalem in eschatological terms.[92]

To summarise, contemporary studies on the *faḍā'il al-Quds* are notable for the prominence they give to the *faḍā'il* tracts and what they tell us about the position of Jerusalem in Islam and how this may have changed over time owing to the scarcity of written works on the Holy City at some historical junctions and then the subsequent proliferation of works at other times. The connection of the *faḍā'il* phenomenon to the 'counter-crusade,' particularly during the

91 Al-Muqaddasī, *Aḥsan al-taqāsīm*, 152.

92 O. Livne-Kafri, 'Jerusalem in Early Islam: The Eschatological Aspect,' *Arabica* 53 (2006), 387.

sixth/twelfth century when that city was lost, thus deserves closer attention. Islam's position on Jerusalem is not an uncertain one; instead verses of the Qur'ān promulgate the importance of the city and early Qur'ān commentaries, as well as prophetic traditions, make clear the necessity of Muslim reverence for what is deemed a sacred space. In light of the delayed Muslim response to the crusader occupation of Jerusalem, Elisséeff's observation should be noted here. He argues that

> forgetting the obligation of the *Jihād* was not a new phenomenon in the Muslim world. It had been spreading ever since the end of the ninth (third H.) century when the caliphate abandoned its *ṣayfiyya*, summer raids along the northern borders (*'awāṣim*). The phenomenon seems to have been part of the gradual decline in the religious and moral conscience which occurred in the Muslim world at this time.[93]

The image and perception of Jerusalem in the minds of Ṣalāḥ al-Dīn's Arab, Kurdish, and Turkish troops was thus created and shaped, largely, by the *faḍā'il* literature. In light of this, preachers had an indispensable role.[94] Public readings, the selection of texts such as Ibn al-Mubārak's and al-Sulamī's *jihād* treatises, Ibn 'Asākir's *faḍā'il* selection, along with the assignment of *khaṭīb*s and the employment of poets, were instrumental initiatives that sought to enhance the public image of Nūr al-Dīn and Ṣalāḥ al-Dīn, to strengthen the *jihād* resolve, and to disseminate religious and political instructions pertaining to resistance, reconquest, political unity, and the merits accorded to Jerusalem, Damascus, and the Bilād al-Shām generally. While the massacre of the Muslim inhabitants in 492/1099 was highlighted in chronicles and poetry (as well as in the *faḍā'il* work of Ibn al-Jawzī), efforts to instil a yearning for the *jihād* were inspired by the belief that Jerusalem constituted a sacred space for Muslims. For those who had never witnessed Islamic dominion in the city, the site of Jerusalem triggered a web of associations enhanced by the merits associated with the place. Many of the traditions that shed light on these merits must have been memorised by the scholars and even laymen who flocked to the city from Egypt and Syria. The subsequent process of rebuilding was shaped

93 N. Elisséeff, 'The Reaction of the Syrian Muslims after the Foundation of the First Latin Kingdom of Jerusalem,' in *Crusaders and Muslims in Twelfth-Century* Syria, ed. Maya Shatzmiller (Leiden: Brill, 1993), 162.

94 See Hillenbrand, *The Crusades*, 223–224; Talmon-Heller, *Islamic Piety*, 87–144.

by Ṣalāḥ al-Dīn's desire to encase the city with a palpable Islamic character.[95] One may confidently argue that the proliferation of the *faḍā'il* genre enabled the Muslim population to fortify the city with their collective sense of religious duty, and to explain their recent success in terms that related to the city's role in Islamic eschatology.

The spiritual dimension of the anti-Frankish *jihād* was not only present, but was an intrinsic component of the theological attire and physical manifestation of the *jihād*; how much it speaks of general attitudes in the campaigns is only speculation, but the spiritual aura – and more overtly the *faḍā'il* – connected to places and personages was certainly unmistakeable. The *raison d'être* of the reconquest of Jerusalem was based on the city's spiritual appeal in Islam and the proliferation of *faḍā'il* books served to reinforce that.[96] The eschatological significance of the aforementioned areas in Islam – brought out in books of *faḍā'il* and also used in post-crusade books on *jihād* were clearly connected to the significance of Damascus, Jerusalem, and Syria generally as theatres of *jihād* in the anti-Frankish *jihād*. The *jihād* brought with it attention to the various and dynamic propaganda tools exploited by the Muslims – largely at the behest of *jihād* champions they were serving. Ephrat and Kabha cite the unequivocal devotion to the *jihād*, in which even those who opted for a spiritual life in Mecca during the crusader occupation were censured for their abandonment of the physical struggle.[97]

Aside from *faḍā'il* literature, public exhortation, whether orchestrated by *khaṭībs* or poets, was certainly a popular and traditional way to whip up public fervour, particularly for a people appreciative of the niceties of Arabic grammar and rhetoric; the poet's *jihād al-lisān* (*jihād* of the tongue) was, as Hitti notes, "as effective as his people's bravery. In peace he might prove a menace to public order by his fiery harangues."[98] The *minbar* also held a central place in Muslim public religious life and the *khaṭīb* an auspicious social standing.[99] The obligatory nature of the prayer the *khaṭīb* presided over was fused with his

95 Inscriptions are particularly telling in this regard; Sabri Jarrar notes the inscription above the entrance to the Ayyūbid Qubbat al-Miʿrāj (596–97/1200–01) which was believed to be the starting point of the Prophet Muḥammad's ascension to heaven, but which subsequently disappeared during the crusader occupation; another inscription, located above one of the entrances to al-Aqṣā Mosque, forbade entry to Christians. S. Jarrar, 'Suq al-Maʿrifa: An Ayyubid Hanbalite Shrine in al-Haram al-Sharif,' in *Muqarnas XV: An Annual on the Visual Culture of the Islamic World*, ed. Gülru Necipoglu (Leiden: E. J. Brill, 1998), 72.

96 See Hillenbrand, *The Crusades*, 162–165.

97 Ephrat and Kabha, 'Muslim Reactions,' 52.

98 P. K. Hitti, *History of the Arabs* (New York: Macmillan, 1958), 94.

99 For futher information, see Talmon-Heller, *Islamic Piety*, 87–114.

unrestricted scope and the virtuous status of Friday in general. The effect of the *khaṭīb*'s admonitions, moral instruction, and more pertinent *jihād* rhetoric was unquestionably potent for public propagation and *jihād* preaching; ʿImād al-Dīn al-Iṣfahānī in *al-Barq al-Shāmī* compared Nūr al-Dīn's *minbar* – temporarily stationed in Aleppo while awaiting its installation in al-Aqṣā Mosque by Ṣalāḥ al-Dīn at the reconquest – to "a sword in its protective scabbard."[100] It is also important to consider the potential effectiveness of public readings in light of the authoritative genre that they came to be recognized with. Unlike sermonizing and poetry, which has much to do with the eloquence and charisma of the preacher, texts selected for readings were approved based on the authenticity of traditions contained within them, and on the reputation of the author in the collective memory of the *umma*.[101] The effect of public readings was, while incalculable, certainly rousing. It is known that during the Second Crusade Ibn ʿAsākir chose to conduct public readings of ʿAbdallāh b. al-Mubārak's (d. 181/797) *Kitāb al-Jihād* in Damascus; this motivated Abū l-Ḥasan b. Munqidh, brother of the famous Usāma b. Munqidh, among others, to volunteer to help raise the siege of Ascalon.[102] Shortly before Ṣalāḥ al-Dīn's reconquest on 27 Rajab 583/2 October 1187, Abū Bakr Muḥammad al-Wāsiṭī's text on the virtues of Jerusalem, *Faḍāʾil al-bayt al-muqaddas*, was brought to the fore by a reading in the mosque of Acre in September 583/1187.[103]

This chapter provides some important background information about the religious, cultural, and political climate of Syria during the course of the sixth/twelfth century. It considers the place of patronage in this period; patronage that provided for religious communities through the building of *madrasas*, mosques, and other foundations in Syria, and thereby effected legitimacy for their patrons' political policies. A separate section was given to consider the

100 Hillenbrand, *The Crusades*, 156; Talmon-Heller, *Islamic Piety*, 37; Y. Tabbaa, 'Monuments with a Message,' 233–235.

101 A narration states, "Read the well-known (works) from the well-known (authors)." Some of his other provisions include the discouragement of acquiring sacred knowledge from those unqualified, immature in age, and or the blameworthy innovators (*ahl al-bidʿa*). Further stipulations include the meritorious act of walking to the *ḥadīth* reading, wearing fine clothing, and maintaining a deep sense of respect for the shaykh and the sacred gathering. Al-Khaṭīb al-Baghdādī, *al-Jāmiʿ li-akhlāq al-rāwī wa-adāb al-sāmiʿ* (Beirut: Dār al-Kutub al-ʿIlmīyya, 2003), 40 (no. 126), 48.

102 R. P. Mottahedeh and R. al-Sayyid, *The Idea of the Jihād in Islam before the Crusades*,' in *The Crusades from the Perspective of Byzantium and the Muslim World*, eds. Angeliki E. Laiou and R. P. Mottahedeh (Washington, DC: Dumbarton Oaks, 2001), 29; see Ibn al-Mubārak, *Kitāb al-Jihād* (Beirut: Dār al-Nūr, 1971).

103 Talmon-Heller, *Islamic Piety*, 73; Hillenbrand, *The Crusades*, 162–163.

influence of the theoloigian and mystic Abū Ḥāmid al-Ghazālī[104] who is credited with helping to revive a new 'Sunnism' in the Saljūq period, a religious outlook mirrored on that of Niẓām al-Mulk. The chapter elaborates, in sections about the sanctities of space and *faḍā'il* studies, on the importance given to the city of Jerusalem in Islam, as it emanated from the interpretation of Qur'ānic verses and from the corpus of *ḥadīth* literature, which gave sanctity to the Bilād al-Sham region, and to Jerusalem specifically. It was the sanctity afforded to such centres, promulgated and taught in *madrasa*s and through the writing of *faḍā'il* texts that bolstered the motivations of Muslims of Syria to fight for the protection, defence, conquest, liberation, and settlement in such areas. Further, I noted the contributions of the main authors and poets that figure prominently in this book.

---

104 For more information on al-Ghazālī see Watt, 'al-Ghazālī,' *EI*², 2:1038–1041 Ibn Khallikān, *Wafayāt*, 4:191–194.

CHAPTER 2

Poetry and Poetics in Medieval Arabic Discourse

In chapter 2 I present a bibliographical review of some modern historical works, in Arabic and English, concerned with the workings of poetry in the crusader era, namely, its relevance, function, and appeal in the course of the anti-Frankish *jihād*. I include poetry in a historiographical framework, draw on the 'historical' value of poetry in a significant historiographical context, and counter the often-held modern view that Arabic poetry in this period was a mere cultural artefact.

Historiographical Considerations

Poetry enjoyed the highest status in medieval Arabic culture. Men of *adab* were famed for having memorised large amounts of *jāhilī* (pre-Islamic) and early Islamic poetry; indeed it was a vital part of the traditional education of a litterateur (*adīb*).[1] The intellectual entourage of Ṣalāḥ al-Dīn, most prominently al-Qāḍī l-Fāḍil and ʿImād al-Dīn al-Iṣfahānī, were skilled poets of their time. Texts like al-Mutanabbī's *Dīwān* and Abū Tammām's *Ḥamāsa* were memorised in their entirety by rulers who sought to draw inspiration from ideals of courtly virtue, chivalry, and religious mores. Ṣalāḥ al-Dīn, for example was believed to have memorised the *Ḥamāsa* in full and carry with him Usāma b. Munqidh's *Dīwān*.

The composer of a powerful and meaningful *qaṣīda* (ode) was considered indispensable in the court, as someone who was able to convey the political will of the ruler. The *qaṣīda* can be seen symbolically as

> a formal testimony to the legitimacy of political authority. In its movement from chaos to order, from affliction to deliverance, from isolation to integration, the glory of the social order is proclaimed. Society and its values, present in the person of the ruler, are recreated triumphantly by

1 See M. Zwettler, *The Oral Tradition of Classical Arabic Poetry: Its Character and Implication* (Columbia: Ohio State University Press, 1978), 3–39; R. M. A. Allen, *An Introduction to Arabic Literature* (Cambridge: Cambridge University Press, 2000), 71.

 | DOI 10.1163/9789004345225_003

> the replay of symbolical events and the utterance of liturgical formulae of praise.[2]

The function of the poet was not limited to composing celebratory verses in the event of a victory; poetry was more eclectic, suitable for any kind of scenario including defeat – to encourage the faithful, to lampoon the enemy or exonerate the ruler. Poets saw themselves as "spokesmen of Islam" whose poetic "press campaigns" sought to echo Qur'ānic ideals and formulas.[3] Some scholars have focused on the 'origins' of poetic themes to highlight how individual poets may have been guided by an array of potential influences, be they religious (with reference to the large corpus of Islamic material) or political. It is entirely relevant, therefore, to apply some of the same standards of analysis to poetry as one would for other material. Contextualising poetry in the political, socio-religious, and economic conditions at the time of its composition enables us to see the works as more than cultural artefacts; both chronicles and poetry were products of their time, shaped by the events that they described. It is unreasonable to assume, in light of the growing entitlements of the civilian elite (*aʿyān*) and the relationships of scholarly companionship (*ṣuḥba/mulāzama*) that formed (and allowed for the transfer of ideas) between members of different backgrounds, that poets believed themselves to be entirely bound by the outlooks of their respected patrons. Not all poets were in fact dependent on patrons.

Poetry thus holds a valuable position in Arab culture and society. Considered to be the "quintessential Arabic literary achievement," Hitti notes that

> no people in the world, perhaps, manifest such enthusiastic admiration for literary expression and are so moved by the word, spoken or written, as the Arabs.... Modern audiences in Baghdād, Damascus and Cairo can be stirred to the highest degree by the recital of poems, only vaguely comprehended, and by the delivery of orations in the classical tongue, though it be only partially understood. The rhythm, the rhyme, the music, produce on them the effect of what they call "lawful magic."[4]

2 S. Sperl, *Mannerism in Arabic Poetry: A Structural Analysis of Selected Texts (3rd Century AH/9th Century AD–5th Century AH/11th Century AD)* (Cambridge: Cambridge University Press, 2004), 26.

3 Gabrieli, 'Religious Poetry in Early Islam,' 6–7.

4 Hitti, *History of the Arabs*, 90. Also see Hillenbrand, *The Crusades*, 297.

The huge corpus of poetry that has survived in *dīwāns* (poetry anthologies) and chronicles, though undoubtedly a remarkable testament to the vitality of this rich oral tradition, made the task of this book a difficult one from the outset; in time my approach became, of necessity, eclectic, whereby I pursued a few of the paths that seemed most fruitful, and neglected some others that may well be equally important and fascinating. Since Arabic poems are essentially open textured and incorporate multiple allusions, and because there are many *double entendres* in Arabic poetry, there is an inherent difficulty in translating Arabic into English. One is encumbered by a difficult style, imagery, and language, and unless the focus is a thoroughly literary one, we need not be particularly hindered by failing to replicate all of those aesthetically furnished literary features. Since the central concern in this study is the ideological content of the poetry rather than its literary artistry a more literal translation suffices. Though I have elucidated the meanings conveyed in the poetry and the word associations that may have been relevant for their original audiences, I have not embarked on the arduous task of concentrating on rhyme. As Irwin highlights,

> the closeness and profusion of rhyming and metrical patterns cannot be mimicked in English without serious strain. Of course, translating poetry from one language to another is always difficult, but translating Arabic poetry raises so many problems that [it] is impossible even to list them here. Just one particularly obvious and pervasive problem should be noted and that is the Arab poet's penchant for punning and word-play. Again and again, a translator will find he can translate one sense of a couplet, but only at the cost of sacrificing a second sense which the author also intended and which gave force and wit to his verse.[5]

This book's reliance on poetry to serve as an important source of information that sheds light on a previously understudied area of historical interest necessitates some discussion of the 'historical' value of poetry and how it fits into modern historiography and the study of Arabic texts.[6] Rhymed prose and poetry have long been used as historiographical tools; there are many examples

5 R. Irwin, *The Arabian Nights: A Companion* (London: Tauris Parke, 2005), 13.

6 Teresa Garulo adopts a nuanced approach in ascertaining the extent to which we may see, particularly Andalusian, Arabic poems as possessing 'documentary value.' Her assessment seeks to demonstrate that poetry must be included as a historical source for the history of the Arab woman. T. Garulo, 'Women in Medieval Classical Arabic Poetry,' in *Writing the Feminine: Women in Arab Sources*, ed. M. Marín and R. Deguilhem (I. B.Tauris: London, 2002), 25–40.

of the inclusion of poetry in historical narratives. Such poetry is often used to give the reader insight into individual opinion and emotion expressed publicly and without mediation. Saleh Said Agha outlines the use of Arabic poetry for reconstructing history and the ways in which the *akhbāriyyūn*, historians and authors of books on *adab*, used poetry as a source of historical knowledge.[7] Poetry shows how events were interpreted by contemporaries and though distinctions were made between contemporaneous verse and later verses used to historicise texts, poetry reflects on history though it is more concerned with general truths rather than specific events. Due to its association with rhetoric, hyperbole, and jesting (*hazl*), poetry can lack truth content; perhaps its essential value is in revealing how events were interpreted by contemporaries.

It is necessary to set out the rationale behind the use of sources that were previously deemed to possess little historical relevance. In Rosenthal's seminal work, *A History of Muslim Historiography*, which has been instrumental in shaping subsequent studies, poetry is set apart as an immaterial historical product, at least with regard to discerning historical truth.[8] Others, however, have investigated the topic with more sensitivity.

In the medieval Muslim period there existed an underlying religiosity in the study and recording of history. Usāma b. Munqidh, one of the most important contemporary Arab chroniclers during the crusades, stands out in this regard. The underlying theme in his work, *Kitāb al-Iʿtibār*, is the predetermination of life, death, victory, or loss. More important in relation to this study is the case of Abū Shāma, who adhered to the example set by his predecessors – he took a liking to history on the grounds of its religious benefits and utilised verses of the Qurʾān and the *ḥadīth* traditions. The historical works of Ibn Kathīr, al-Qurṭubī (d. 671/1273), and al-Ṭabarī (d. 310/923) – all of whom were also renowned commentators of the Qurʾān – reveal an exploration of human history twinned with precepts in the Qurʾān that outline a course of study for the purposes of contemplation (*tadbīr*), reflection (*tafkīr*), and moral instruction (*ʿibra*).[9]

While the incentive to study sciences intricately linked to the religion needed no justification, and had been popular since the time of the Prophet's

7 Saleh Said Agha, 'Of Verse, Poetry, Great Poetry, and History,' in *Poetry and History: The Value of Poetry in Reconstructing Arab History*, ed. R. Baalbaki, S. S. Agha, and T. Khalidi (Beirut: American University of Beirut Press, 2011), 7–8.

8 F. Rosenthal, *A History of Muslim Historiography* (Leiden: Brill, 1968), 67.

9 "Indeed in their stories, there is a lesson for men of understanding. It is not a forged statement but a confirmation (of existing Books) and a detailed explanation of everything, and a guide and a Mercy for the people who believe." Qurʾān, 12:111.

companions and was born out of explicit Qur'ānic verses and *ḥadīth*, the recording of history and knowledge of historical works was certainly a later development, but one that found its justification in the Qur'ānic paradigm of learning lessons from past events and civilisations.[10] It seems that Muslim legalists were concerned with the potential benefit (*maṣlaḥa*) to the religion and community when licensing a 'move' from the more familiar sciences.[11] Muslim scholars believed that the knowledge of history and historical works "brought with it the political wisdom and conventional skill which assured success in this world, and the humility and piety which assured blessedness in the other world."[12] For example, within both of these concepts of study, we often see issues related to Muslim apocalypticism, which came to feature during the crusades, as I discuss in subsequent chapters. This feature overtly manifested in *ḥadīth* literature and is crucial in providing a "history of the future."[13]

Historical writings were seen (and are still seen) as products of well-established religious, cultural, and political ideals. By applying Rosenthal's argument that the texts "written in the second half of the first century contained already all the formal elements of later Muslim historiography," one can see the

10 "These are some of the stories of communities which We relate unto thee: of them some are standing, and some have been mown down (by the sickle of time). It was not We that wronged them: They wronged Their own souls: the deities, other than God, whom they invoked, profited them no whit when there issued the decree of thy Lord: Nor did they add aught (to their lot) but perdition!" Qur'ān, 11:100–101. "So We made it an example to their own time and to their posterity and a lesson to those who fear God." Qur'ān, 2:66.

11 There exists in the literary realm of medieval Islamic scholarship a need to substantiate literature with a defined purpose, particularly when there is a divergence from the more conventional Islamic sciences such as *fiqh, ḥadīth, tafsīr, qirā'a*, etc. Ibn al-Jawzī's *Kitāb al-Quṣṣās wa-l-mudhakkirīn* is a vivid example of a scholarly attempt to solidify the practise of storytelling in an Islamic framework, and exonerate those who partake in it, while stressing the caution one must observe when narrating stories that have no firm historical authenticity or worse still, which may contradict beliefs and ethics delineated in the foundational Islamic texts such as the Qur'ān and *ḥadīth*. The author makes clear his purpose in his opening chapter: "Certain persons came to me with the following request: 'we observe that the views of the pious men of old (*salaf*) do not agree on the question of whether to commend or condemn the narrators of religious stories (*quṣṣās*). Some of them encouraged attendance at their meetings while others prohibited it. We, therefore, appeal to you to prepare a treatise which will clarify this matter for us.' I replied: 'There is no alternative but to lay bare the real nature of this matter in order to clarify that which ought to be commended and that which ought to be condemned.'" Ibn al-Jawzī, *Kitāb al-Quṣṣās wa-l-mudhakkirīn*, trans. M. S. Swartz (Beirut: Dār al-Mashriq, 1986), 95–96.

12 Rosenthal, *Historiography*, 60–61.

13 Ibid., 23.

historical works of sixth-/twelfth- and seventh-/thirteenth-century Syria and Egypt as compositions that were shaped in style and form by developments that took place in the four centuries preceding the arrival of the crusaders.[14] This approach implies that authors were simply following set standards and patterns and placing their texts in the framework of conventional historical writing. For Rosenthal, "history was not used as a means for the propagation of ideas, or, more exactly, historians as a rule did not consciously intend, in writing their works, to reinterpret historical data so as to conform to the ideas they might have wished to propagate."[15] By placing religion at the forefront of socio-political events, they served the cause of Islam through their writing. Many Muslim historians employed a didactic approach in their works;[16] *tafsīr* scholars further served as historians of general Islamic or world history, and it was the general acceptability of diverting focus from the more illustrious Islamic sciences in favour of historical writing (although oftentimes both were achieved by one person) as long as the truth of Islam was upheld, that not only provided the justification for such endeavours but also encouraged people to hearken back to what was more correct, and better established. This diadactic approach does much to limit the extent to which historians may have been affected by the age and society in which they were living. Yet we risk, in this case, a misreading of social history if we circumvent nuances, shades of meaning, choices of expression, titles, headings, and other literary features in their work, and we impute a set of ideas on their texts and allow no room to discern how events may have shaped their writing. In this respect, Hirschler considers some of these features from a fresh perspective. He focuses on the works of Abū Shāma and Ibn Wāṣil and sees them as "active interpreters of their societies," as men who "had considerable room for manoeuvre in both their social environment and the shaping of their texts."[17] We may see texts not merely as transmissions of events that were, indubitably, accurate historically because of the 'pietistic' consideration at play in their composition but also as a social phenomenon that was susceptible to contemporary socio-political influences.

The different historiographical approaches to Arabic writing can be categorised into four areas: a Formal-Cultural Approach, a Source-Critical/Factual Approach, a Contextual Approach, and a Textual Approach. Hirschler states

14 Ibid., 131.

15 Ibid., 61–62.

16 See M. H. M. Aḥmad, 'Some Notes on Arabic Historiography during the Zengid and Ayyūbid Periods (521/1127–648/1250),' in *Historians of the Middle East*, ed. Bernard Lewis and P. M. Holt (New York: Oxford University Press, 1962), 81.

17 Hirschler, *Medieval Arabic Historiography*.

that the latter two approaches emerged from limitations in the former two. Yet sometimes, by focusing on the search for historical veracity, we limit what we may learn from other telling features of a historical source; non-historical aspects are thus deemed relevant for our understanding of the text. If we fail to see a text in light of the social, religious, and economic factors in the author's society that shaped his composition we may emerge with an incorrect and simplistic understanding of the text as conventional historical writing with nothing original to present. The nuances and layers of additional meaning and styles of composition that we can discern are also telling in their own right. Hirschler argues for the importance of the often overlooked 'Textual Approach.' Proponents of this approach "have tended rather to see texts not as a direct reflection of societal developments, but as being an autonomous social reality by itself."[18] This view opposes the idea that medieval authors were simply transmitting events in line with cultural convention and pietistic ideals. It further credits medieval authors with a high degree of autonomy vis-à-vis societal forces that we assume may have significantly shaped their texts. In spite of ideas of patronage, medieval authors were influential enough not only to unilaterally shed light on the events in their societies, but also to decide how they depicted those happenings, even if that meant breaking from cultural conventions. El-Hibri also posits that a new reading of the sources would reposition our view of the intention behind the literary accounts "from one providing direct chronology to one offering historical commentary and seeking the active engagement of readers and narrators, listeners and dramatisers."[19]

In echoing el-Hibri's valid concerns that his interpretation of medieval Arabic historiography may be read or overly read as a literary critique of the chronicles he assesses, I place my analyses of poetry in the historical framework that I believe they require. My approach therefore does not profess to be entirely inclusive of finer elements of language, although some limited attempt at this has been both possible and necessary. Although chronicles, as seen through the Formal-Cultural Approach, are believed to have been inspired from older and more established texts, poetry is a far more fluid medium of expression. Poetry could communicate ideas in a discourse independent from prose, because it can delineate a formal speech, but can also be used to express the intensity of strong emotions like remorse, grief, or love. Ideas and themes that might also be culturally unacceptable could be explored in poetry,

18 K. Hirschler, 'Narrating the Past: Social Contexts and Literary Structures of Arabic,' PhD thesis (School of Oriental and African Studies, 2003) 32.

19 T. el-Hibri, *Reinterpreting Islamic Historiography: Harun al-Rashid and the Narrative of the 'Abbāsid Caliphate* (Cambridge: Cambridge University Press, 2002), 2.

as opposed to prose, because the competent poet could mask sentiments, reveal, and conceal, something the formalism of prose texts would preclude or make exceedingly difficult. Poetry does not follow the same rules or hope to achieve the same effects as a chronicle, nor was it composed for the same purpose. But by using formal 'texts' as a yardstick of what is important and worthy of 'historical' as opposed to 'literal' consideration, one runs the risk of bypassing a formidable medium that was perhaps the strongest and most rousing literary vehicle during this significant historical period. There is, however, something of value in all approaches. While we need to see beyond historical facts in a chronicle to search for layers of additional meaning, we also need to look within the literary makeup of a poem – and include nuances and shades of meaning, to discern historical 'meaning.'

While the Textual Approach affords chroniclers a greater autonomy than was previously accepted, we can also judge the extent to which poets described more than just the political outlooks of their patrons, particularly when they worked together in the same court circles. Alternatively, of course, such poets were sometimes not even bound by patronage, but instead were driven by simple and genuine pietistic considerations. Elisséeff highlights the case of the retinue that served Nūr al-Dīn, they were the

> men who were devoted to religion and who organised its propaganda. They were not dependent on him, and their activity was spontaneous and free. Financial recompense did not interest them, since they all considered themselves to be volunteers in the service of the *Jihād* and the defence of Dār al-Islām.[20]

Though one might question the extent of such spontaneity, some historians question the extent to which compositions in this time were entirely panegyrical and point to network alliances as an indicator that the flow of ideas in the Muslim Near East shaped the outlook of chroniclers.

Although I provide translations of poetry in this book, my methodology is not centred on an assessment of the texts' value for 'factual' considerations. In this respect chronicles remain the main source for historical information. In any case, we must not see poetry in the same light as chronicles, nor must we be dismayed by the disparity between the two genres in our search for historical 'truth.' The poetry sometimes reveals accurate historical 'information' albeit it is coated in rhythmical verse suited for rhetorical purposes. Yet it is the value attributed to poets in the sixth/twelfth and seventh/thirteenth centuries –

20 Elisséeff, 'The Reaction of the Syrian Muslims,' 171.

comprised either of loyal advocates of patrons or as displaced and exiled survivors of the Frankish crusade who had obvious axes to grind – that must be seen, together with an assessment of novel thematic features in their poetry, as instrumentally affecting the development of the anti-Frankish *jihād*.

The Place of Poetry and Modern Perspectives

In the twentieth century historians expressed an increased concern in delineating the backgrounds of and identifying the essential constructs that formed the crusades. It became, and is still, necessary and crucial to contextualise popular perceptions of the crusades, which have now come to be shaped by reactions to current political conflicts. We must credit Hans Eberhard Mayer, who, since publishing his *Geschichte der Kreuzzüge* in 1965, called for clarity with regard to the concept of the crusades, and the issue has been more widely debated since. There have emerged partisans whom G. Constable, in his article, 'The Historiography of the Crusades,'[21] places into four categories; each one represents an interpretation intended to express, to some degree, the fullness of the experience of the crusades. Some have attributed to the expedition exact legalistic formulae whereas others have advocated the need to observe the imprecision and fluidity of the crusades. As Rabbat points out, however,

> On the one hand, we have detailed analyses of every aspect of social, religious, political, military, economic, cultural, and artistic history of the Crusades and the dominant mindsets that generated and sustained them for several decades. On the other, we have mostly chronological surveys of the Muslim camp's reactions and glorifying or disparaging biographies of Muslim leaders such as Saladin and Baybars.[22]

The translations of vital Arabic sources that were previously either available in partial translation in Gabrieli's work or in the epic nineteenth-century French collection *Recueil des Historiens des Croisades* have led to developments and

21 G. Constable, 'The Historiography of the Crusades,' in *The Crusades from the Perspective of Byzantium and the Muslim World*, ed. A. E. Laiou and R. P. Mottahedeh (Washington, DC: Harvard University Press: 2001), 1–22.

22 N. Rabbat, 'The Visual Milieu of the Counter-Crusade in Syria and Egypt,' in *The Crusades: Other Experiences, Alternate Perspectives: Selected Proceedings from the 32nd Annual CEMERS Conference*, ed. K. I. Semaan (New York: Global Academic Publishing, 2003), 71.

focus on the Muslim reaction to the crusades.[23] In this regard the translations of Bahā' al-Dīn Ibn Shaddād's *al-Nawādir al-sulṭāniyya wa-l-maḥāsin al-Yūsufiyya* by D. S. Richards,[24] Ibn al-Qalānisī's *Dhayl Tārīkh Dimashq* by Gibb,[25] the early translation of Usāma b. Munqidh's *Kitāb al-I'tibār* by Hitti, and the most recent 2008 publication of the work,[26] and the indispensable translation of the crusading period from Ibn al-Athīr's voluminous *al-Kāmil fī l-Tārīkh* by D. S. Richards[27] reveal a continuing interest in providing western readers with an understanding of the conflict from the Muslim perspective. The latter translation by Richards is a refreshing change, particularly since there have been both a French[28] and English translation of Ibn al-Qalānisī's *Dhayl Tārīkh Dimashq* and two English translations of Usāma b. Munqidh's memoirs.[29] For the western reader the Muslim perspectives of the crusades are well represented in Carole Hillenbrand's *The Crusades: Islamic Perspectives* and more recently in Paul Cobb's *The Race for Paradise: An Islamic History of the Crusades.*[30] Hillenbrand's work is noted for its extensive translations and use of a wide array of primary source material, visual and written, that provide a clear and chronological basis for understanding the effects of the crusades on the Muslims and the anti-Frankish *jihād* strategy and implementation. Though Hamilton Gibb and Claude Cahen, the two towering figures that dominated the historiography of the medieval Near East, were averse to using poetry and belle-lettres as historical sources, in more recent times scholars have been more keen to investigate the topic with some sensitivity. Hillenbrand discusses the place of poetry in the anti-Frankish *jihād*. She translates and brings to light rousing literary examples from the verses of al-Abīwardī and Ibn al-Khayyāṭ (d. 1123), poets in the post-First Crusade era. She explores the theme of *jihād* through the verses of Ibn Sanā' al-Mulk, particularly in his celebratory poem after the victory at Ḥaṭṭīn in 583/1187; she also highlights the poet's use of Qur'ānic imagery, and uses the poem as evidence of how Ṣalāḥ al-Dīn was

23 *Recueil des historiens des croisades*, 16 vols. (Paris: Imprimerie royale, 1841–1906).

24 Ibn Shaddād, *The Rare and Excellent History of Saladin*, trans. Richards.

25 Ibn al-Qalānisī, *The Damascus Chronicle of the Crusades*, trans. H. A. R Gibb (New York: Dover Publications, 2002). See Niall Christie, 'Ibn al-Qalānisī,' in *Medieval Muslim Historians and the Franks in the Levant*, ed. Alex Mallett (Leiden: Brill, 2014), 7–28.

26 Usāma b. Munqidh, *Kitāb al-I'tibār*; Usāma b. Munqidh, *The Book of Contemplation.*

27 Ibn al-Athīr, *The Chronicle of Ibn al-Athīr.*

28 Ibn al-Qalānisī, trans. R. Le Tourneau, *Damas de 1075 à 1154* (Damascus: Institut Français de Damas, 1952).

29 Usāma b. Munqidh, *An Arab-Syrian Gentleman*, trans. Hitti.

30 Hillenbrand, *The Crusades*; P. M. Cobb, *The Race for Paradise: An Islamic History of the Crusades* (Oxford: Oxford University Press, 2014).

depicted by his contemporaries as an Islamic *jihād* leader authorised to fight the crusading infidels. The theme of *jihād* is further explored through the *dubayt*s composed by ʿImād al-Dīn al-Iṣfahānī for Nūr al-Dīn.[31]

The most recent and valuable overview of the place of *jihād* poetry in this period is further found in Carole Hillenbrand's article, 'Jihad Poetry in the Age of the Crusades,' which discusses many of the salient poetic themes of this period.[32] Among her particularly useful questions are those she poses about the authors of the poetry, the times and reasons for their compositions, the extent to which the poetry was understood and appreciated by the ruling class to whom it was addressed, and the extent to which it is useful as historical evidence of the military and religious environment of Syria in this period. Hadia Dajani-Shakeel also focuses attention on poetry and its uses during the crusades. Her article, 'Jihād in Twelfth-Century Arabic Poetry: A Moral and Religious Force to Counter the Crusades,' is a thorough study that draws on the earliest work of the two aforementioned post-First Crusade poets, and on complementary themes in the *jihād* work of al-Sulamī.[33] Her study generally underscores the idea that Muslims were far more aware of their enemy than was previously assumed.

Though authors like al-Sulamī regularly incorporated some poetry into their works, where passionate verses could strengthen their arguments or simply demonstrate the author's expansive belletristic knowledge and skills, some texts were composed entirely of poetry. Poetry is not simply aesthetically refined literature of rhythmic precision but is both a political and social act, a practical response to an event that was relevant to a community. Hillenbrand's most recent major work, *Turkish Myth and Muslim Symbol: The Battle of Manzikert* expounds on the important place of poetry in the legacy of the battle of Manzikert.[34] Her assessment of a panegyric poem by Amnet Yüzendag composed for the celebrations of the nine-hundredth-year anniversary (in 1971) of the battle illustrates how commemorative poetry could be used as battle narratives and stresses both the religious credentials of a pious Muslim ruler, pronounced in the poem as the archetypal *jihād* warrior

31 Hillenbrand, *The Crusades*, 69–71, 166–167, 179–180, 298.

32 Hillenbrand, 'Jihad Poetry,' 9–23. In this context, see also Osman Latiff, 'Qur'anic Imagery, Jesus and the Creation of a Pious-Warrior Ethos in the Muslim Poetry of the Anti-Frankish Jihad' in *Cultural Encounters during the Crusades*, eds. K. V. Jensen, K. Salomen and H. Vogt (Odense: University Press of Southern Denmark, 2013), 135–151.

33 Dajani-Shakeel, '*Jihād* in Twelfth-Century Arabic Poetry,' 96–113.

34 C. Hillenbrand, *Turkish Myth and Muslim Symbol: The Battle of Manzikert* (Edinburgh: Edinburgh University Press, 2007), 148–153, 182–184, 213–214.

preparing for conflict and for martyrdom, and as a propaganda tool to reinforce Turkish national identity through him.

Crediting Lyons and Jackson's *Saladin: The Politics of Holy War* for the way it utilises underused sources such as the letters of al-Qāḍī l-Fāḍil and the poetry of al-Wahrānī and Ibn ʿUnayn, in his assessment of crusader studies in the twentieth century Irwin stresses the need for scholars to pay more attention to the poetry of the Zangid, Ayyūbid, and Mamlūk eras for their value as a medium of heightened emotion, of *jihād* propaganda or even diplomacy.[35] In recent scholarship Christie incorporates the First Crusade poetry of al-Abīwardī, Ibn al-Khayyāṭ, an anonymous First Crusade poet, and two examples of Ibn al-Qaysarānī's poems on Frankish women; so too Phillips, in his second edition of *The Crusades: 1095–1204*, draws on the important place of Muslim poetry during the crusades.[36]

The timing of the introduction of *jihād* ideas following the events of 492/1099 has been a debated subject in modern historiography. For example, Helen J. Nicholson discusses it in 'Muslim Reactions to the Crusades,' though her study seldom mentions religious poetry.[37] Dajani-Shakeel notes the use of *faḍāʾil* works to inspire a Muslim yearning for Jerusalem, and their complementary role alongside poetry and *jihād* texts to create a religious awakening. She stops short, however, of providing examples of influence from *faḍāʾil* themes, i.e., the theme of Jerusalem. Elisséeff's article 'The Reaction of the Syrian Muslims after the Foundation of the First Latin Kingdom of Jerusalem' brings together the formative elements of the anti-Frankish *jihād* that materialised in the propaganda campaign of Nūr al-Dīn.[38] Further, he focuses on *jihād* theory according to the *Kitāb al-Jihād* of al-Sulamī. He elucidates the place of *faḍāʾil* books upon and in the religious institutions, the *madrasa* and *khānqāh* that housed male students of traditional learning in the former case and ascetic worship in the second. Elisséeff, however, makes only a cursory remark about poetry, which I believe requires a significant place in any discussion on the reaction of Syrian Muslims after the First Crusade.[39]

---

35 R. Irwin, 'The Arabists and Crusader Studies in the Twentieth Century,' in *Cultural Encounters during the Crusades*, ed. K. V. Jensen, K. Salomen, and H. Vogt (Odense: University Press of Southern Denmark, 2013), 283–298.

36 N. Christie, *Muslims and Crusaders: Christianity's Wars in the Middle East, 1095–1382, from the Islamic Sources* (Abingdon: Routledge, 2014), 129–131, 151; J. Phillips, *The Crusades 1095–1204* (second edition). (Abingdon: Routledge, 2014), 218–219, 237–239.

37 H. J. Nicholson, 'Muslim Reaction to the Crusades,' in *Palgrave Advances in the Crusades*, ed. Helen J. Nicholson (Basingstoke: Palgrave Macmillan, 2005), 269–289.

38 Elisséeff, 'The Reaction of the Syrian Muslims,' 162–172.

39 Ibid.

The work of ʿAbd al-Mahdī, *Bayt al-maqdis fī adab al-ḥurūb al-Ṣalībiyya* and Aḥmad Badawī's *al-Ḥayāt al-adabiyya fī ʿaṣr al-ḥurūb al-ṣalībiyya bi-Miṣr wa-l-Shām* are important in relation to my study, as they appear to be the most thorough studies on the poetry of the period.[40] Badawī's work includes a valuable dramatis personæ of the most important belletrists concerned with the *jihād* and the various forms of poetry composed to encourage *jihād*. The author highlights a multitude of themes in the poetry; these range from sorrow and grief (*asaf wa-ḥasrah*) to zeal/valour (*ḥamāsa*). The work is mostly focused on poetry and devotes little attention to other literature in this period, such as books of *faḍāʾil* and *jihād*. ʿAbd al-Mahdī's work is particularly beneficial in demonstrating the literary features that made up *jihād* poetry. The author highlights some insightful comparative literary expressions in compositions by poets from a variety of lands and times. The author's concentration on imagery, the influence of the Qurʾān, and connotations discerned from the usage of religious terminology in the poetry, helped to shape the methodological approach taken in this book. Both authors approached their studies with a literary sense and their work is thus afforded particular credit among those acquainted with Arabic.

There are obvious differences between poetry and history. Whereas poetry is emotive, history is discursive, and the subjectivity of poetry can be set against the objective nature of history.[41] In fact, both have their flaws, and often exhibit religious, social, or political bias on the part of their authors. In more recent times, Steven Caton's anthropological work, *Peaks of Yemen I Summon* stands out as an insightful example of the socio-cultural role played by poetry in this regard. He focuses on two forms of poetry used in the competitive poetic duels practiced by the Khawlānī tribe of Yemen, the *balāh* and *zāmil* forms of verse. Sung by men at a groom's celebration during Yemeni weddings, the poetic duels are also the preferred diplomatic form of poetic interactions between disputing tribes. The *balāh*, a poem created spontaneously and performed indoors at night, can act, therefore, as a symbolic ritual of violence as well as a mediator in cases of communal dispute. The *zāmil* is performed outdoors and is more politically oriented than the *balāh*; it stresses political, personal or tribal grievances.[42] In his assessment Caton shows that poetry, by

40 ʿA. J. Husain ʿAbd al-Mahdī, *Bayt al-maqdis fī adab al-ḥurūb al-ṣalībiyya* (Amman, 1989); Badawī, *al-Ḥayāt al-adabiyya*.

41 See also Roman Jacobson, 'Linguistics and Poetics,' in *Style and Language*, ed. Thomas Sebeok (Cambridge, MA: MIT Press, 1960), 374–375.

42 Steven C. Caton, *'Peaks of Yemen I Summon': Poetry as Cultural Practice in a North Yemeni Tribe* (London: University of California Press, 1990); See also Najwa Adra, 'Dance and

intensifying the ideology of tribalism, plays a central role in the tribe's socio-political system.

Similarly, in her study of Iraqi war poetry, Tramontini notes the significance of the annual Mirbad Poetry Festival held in Baghdad (organised by the Ministry of Culture and Information), in which renowned Arab poets tied lyrical verses to Iraqi politics and the war with Iran (1980–88). By politicising the collective memory of Iraqi society and history, the Baathists were able to successfully create a hegemonic and normative narrative outlook that disallowed alternative interpretations. This allowed them to create and control a collective memory of themselves and their enemies. Such a writing, or re-writing of history was done through the medium of art and literature, architecture and science. Cultural productions were particularly successful in advancing the hegemonic use of language in order to devise a communal identity. In this context, Yūsuf al-Ṣū'igh and Ḥamīd al-Saʿīd used their poetry to draw on traditional Iraqi themes and Arab nationalism, to deligitimise Iran as an enemy of Iraq. Al-Saʿīd's poetry carried a particularly admonishing tone that was aimed at Iraqi army deserters for their disloyalty to the state.[43] In a variety of ways the poets utilised Baathist ideas about national unity and Iraqi victimisation to encourage their countrymen to support Saddam Hussein and fight for Iraq. The 'truth' that their poetry depicts is entirely the 'truth' of the official government version of culture, history, and events. The use of poetry in political mobilisation is further seen in the poems of Mahmoud Darwish, written about the 2006 Lebanon War between Israel and Hezbollah. Darwish published a series of prose poems in *al-Karmel*, the literary journal that he edited; he introduced an innovative reworking of the narrative themes of the Arabic *rithāʾ* and *qaṣīda* metre and rhyme scheme. The transforming of the traditional genre allowed him to convey a strong protest and political message about Israeli aggression by memorialising Lebanese victims.[44]

This chapter examined some of the motivations of medieval authors and took a historiographical outlook to consider poetry a valuable source of information to complement accounts in chronicles and allow for the consideration

Glance: Visualizing Tribal Identity in Highland Yemen,' *Visual Anthropology* 11:1–2 (1998), 55–102.

43 Leslie Tramontini, 'Poetry Post-Sayyāb: Designing the Truth in Iraqi War Poetry of the 1980s,' in *Poetry and History: The Value of Poetry in Reconstructing Arab History*, ed. R. Baalbaki, S. S. Agha, and T. Khalidi (Beirut: American University of Beirut Press, 2011), 289–312.

44 Rebecca Dyer, 'Poetry of Politics and Mourning: Mahmoud Darwish's Genre-Transforming Tribute to Edward W. Said,' *Remapping Genre* 122, no. 5 (Oct. 2007), 1447–1462.

of more expressive sentiments that otherwise would have been conventionally unsuitable in prose texts. The chapter also showed the place of poetry in modern historiography, as historians have come to recognise the value of underused poetic sources. The majority of texts that identify poets and their works in the course of the anti-Frankish *jihād* are those of Arab scholars. Their studies are important for Arabic readers in this field, though the works in English by Hadia Dajani Shakeel and Carole Hillenbrand, which show the use of poetry as *jihād* propaganda and as the language of diplomacy and passion, are particularly valuable.

CHAPTER 3

Theories and Principles of *Jihād* and the Quest for Martyrdom

During both the crusades and the *jihād*s against them, religion was the initial and most powerful recruitment tool, and neither could exist without the approval of religious authority. Notwithstanding secular motives, Muslims and Christians both used their respected scriptures to sanction conflict against the other and the religious ties to Jerusalem were very important factors in the conflict. In this chapter I consider the theory and importance of the Muslim armed struggle as a physical response to the crusades and also draw on a major incentive for participants in the *jihād*, the pursuit of martyrdom as a way to attain heavenly favour.

I echo the view of Peter Partner, that "the only way to assess *jihād* is to look at it as part of a total religious situation."[1] As Partner points out, comparing the *jihād* with the crusade is akin to comparing a part with a whole.[2] Since the term 'counter-crusade' connotes an analogous activity and implies a response shaped by similar characteristics, it is instead essential to differentiate between the two religious experiences, their legalistic origins, their expressions, and formulae to allow for a better understanding and appreciation of the religious and political dynamics of the societies from which they emerged in this period. Any observations of the development of the *jihād* ideal in the crusader period must thus take into consideratation different strands of the expression of the *jihād*. The roots of the phenomenon lie in the Qur'ān and *ḥadīth* literature, which delineate both spiritual and physical efforts against one's self as well as an external enemy. A crusade was bound by its own legalistic formulae that subsequently entered into the popular imagination and allowed for the development of meaning and connotation. A 'counter-crusade' thus does not always best convey a meaning that fits the medieval phenomenon. Instead, I opt for "anti-Frankish *jihād*" to describe the Muslim response. Although martial activity is intrinsic to both the crusades and the *jihād*, there are difficulties in making a direct comparison between the two because each has dimensions that were markedly unique, and the failure to appreciate particular strands will

1 P. Partner, 'Holy War, Crusade and *Jihād*: An Attempt to Define Some Problems,' *Autour de la première croisade*, ed. M. Balard (Paris: Publications de la Sorbonne, 1996), 336.

2 Ibid., 333.

 | DOI 10.1163/9789004345225_004

inhibit our understanding of both. This being said, it must be stressed that different constituencies invoked the *jihād* for different purposes: some were driven by strong religious ideals, others were more pragmatic, and others were opportunists.

Sometimes referred to as the sixth pillar of Islam, *jihād* is mentioned many times in the Qur'ān. The Qur'ān grants the permission to physically engage the Meccans of Quraysh as a defensive step to safeguard the early Muslim community. It was regarded as a measure of true faith that a believer should 'struggle' with his life and wealth to draw closer to God, 'struggle' against temptations of life, establish the religion on earth, and fight the enemies of the faith.[3] The two broad considerations of what *jihād* entails and necessitates were stated as first engaging in military struggle against enemies of the faith, and second, as the lifelong endeavour to fight against the caprices of the soul. Later jurists and theorists taught that the need for the physical *jihād* is again divided into two realities: individual obligation (*farḍ al-ʿayn*) and collective duty (*farḍ al-kifāya*). It is held that the invasion of an army into a Muslim land renders those Muslim inhabitants responsible for bearing arms in defence; in that situation, the *jihād* becomes an obligation on all who are able; as the Qur'ān delineates, "Go forth [to war] lightly or heavily ..." (9:41). Concerning the rest of the *umma*, their obligation depends on the ability of the Muslim inhabitants to subdue their enemy; the obligation thus shifts from collective to individual and vice versa depending on needs and requirements. The general acceptance of this viewpoint by the Shāfiʿī school of thought in Syria – of which al-Sulamī was an adherent – is particularly noteworthy. Al-Shāfiʿī's (d. 204/820) legal

3 The Prophet is reported to have said: "The *mujāhid* is he who struggles against himself in obedience to God" المجاهد من جهد نفسه في طاعة الله. N. al-Albānī, *Silsilat al-aḥādīth al-ṣaḥīḥa* (Beirut, 1985), 2:81; according to Ibn al-Qayyim, *jihād* is of four types: *jihād* against the 'self,' against the *Shayṭān*, unbelief, and the hypocrites: "الجهاد أربعة مراتب: جهاد النفس، جهاد الشيطان، جهاد الكفر، جهاد المنافقين." Ibn al-Qayyim al-Jawziyya, *Zād al-maʿād fī hadī khayr al-ʿibād*, ed. Muṣṭafā ʿAbd al-Qādir ʿAṭā (Beirut: Dār al-Kutub al-ʿIlmiyya, 1998), 3:9. See also Qur'ān 91:7–10, 79:40–41; for more information see Ibn al-Jawzī, *Ṣayd al-khāṭir* (Cairo, 1999), 169–186. According to Ibn Taymiyya (661–728/1263–1328) however, "as for the hadith that some of them narrate that the Prophet (peace be upon him) said concerning the military expedition of Tabuk, 'We have returned from the lesser *Jihad* to the greatest *Jihad*,' then this has no bases and it had not been reported by anyone who has knowledge of the sayings and actions of the Prophet (peace be upon him). Undertaking the *Jihad* against the disbelievers is from the greatest of actions, indeed it is the best action that a person could opt to perform." Ibn Taymiyya, *The Decisive Criterion Between the Friends of Allāh and the Friends of Shayṭān*, trans. Abu Rumaysah (Birmingham: Daar Us-Sunnah Publishers, 2006), 144.

framework for the *jihād,* in which the eradication of unbelief was considered the principal justification for the holy struggle, should be borne in mind when considering al-Sulamī's *Kitāb al-Jihād.* We may infer, with regard to *jihād* rhetoric and the mentality of the Syrian population, that it was influenced by juristic considerations.

The Qur'ān stresses the necessity for believers to develop inner qualities, such as the fear of God (*taqwa*), steadfastness (*istiqāma*), and patience (*ṣabr*). Notwithstanding the requirement that believers obtain such qualities for admittance into paradise, they were also required for success in battle. The Qur'ān tells of how the early community, in spite of its fewer numbers and weaponry, overcame larger and better equipped enemies because of its devotion to the spirit of *jihād,* combined with the strength of their faith and piety.[4] Later Muslims demonstrated how the *umma* would continuously profit from divine assistance if it remained true to both the outer and inner struggle. In this light, the instructions of the second caliph ʿUmar b. al-Khaṭṭāb (r. 13–23/634–644) to his military general Saʿd b. Abī Waqqāṣ who led the Muslims against the Sasanian army in the battle of Qāḍisiyya (15/636) further advance this *jihād* ethos. The letter demonstrates how inner preparation constituted a form of 'spiritual armament': "I instruct you to be weary of the sins of your army, for the sins of your army are more deadly to them than their enemy."[5] (Inna maʿāṣiyat al-jaysh akhwafu ʿalayhim min ʿadduwihim). Such an exhortation attempts to appeal to strong religious sentiments, ones that required the *umma* to 'look within' with an attitude directed at attempting to provide a sense of continuous resistance and struggle for reform, both internal and external. The military and spiritual components of the anti-Frankish *jihād* of the sixth/twelfth century might be viewed in the context of a 'holistic' revival of Sunnī Islam in this period. Though the need of a 'holistic' revival was advocated by some scholars who stressed the trappings of sin as an impediment to military success, not everyone however heeded their warnings.

Niẓām al-Mulk's effort to establish a network of *madrasas* was intended, in part, to consolidate the Sunnī faith and undermine the Shīʿa. The physical *jihād* against the crusaders fit into this broad framework of resistance to everything that undermined the social order of Islam. It was, in the words of Irwin, "a moral rearmament movement"[6] that saw the active involvement of both rulers

4 Qur'ān 3:123.

5 Al-Nuwayrī, *Nihāyat al-arab fī funūn al-adab* (Cairo: Dār al-Kutub, 1925), 6:168–170.

6 R. Irwin, 'Islam and the Crusades,' in *The Oxford Illustrated History of the Crusades*, ed. J. S. C. Riley-Smith (Oxford: Oxford University Press, 1995), 226; A. R. Azzam, *Saladin* (London: Pearson, 2009), 45.

and members of the civilian elite (*aʿyān*), most notably scholars, to fight this upheaval (*fitna*) on all fronts, perhaps by finding support in the Qurʾānic paradigm that all forms of dissension must be fought, "hence, fight against them until there is no more oppression and all worship is devoted to God alone."[7] We also see that the pursuit of martyrdom (*ṭalab al-shahāda*) was not limited to the military class, but that such a religious propensity for martyrdom existed among some members of the civilian elite and lay population. For instance, Ibn Jubayr describes in his *Riḥla* that a local *shaykh* (elder) from Tyre informed him of a plan that was hatched in 518/1124 when the city was under siege. The *shaykh* recounts that some inhabitants thought women and children should go to the Grand Mosque and allow themselves to be put to death, in the belief that such an action was better than having the crusaders violate their honour and enslave them. The local jurists expressed their view that such an action was not permitted and so they chose to flee the city instead. Even though, by Ibn Jubayr's own admission, an extensive Muslim community remained in Tyre under crusader rule, the anecdote is still useful in that it outlines how some members of the lay population felt the need to engage in a 'jihād' of sort to ensure the protection of their honour. They contemplated the use of force against their own families to thwart what they considered to be a greater injustice. It reinforces the eclectic contributions that some felt they could make, the urgency of which must have been felt for a population well aware of the crusader onslaught and incursions into the Bilad al-Shām.[8]

In the course of military encounters, certain events could be mistaken for suicide, such as an individual venturing on his own to combat the enemy.[9] Muslim scholars discussed the permissability of such bravado. Since suicide is strictly forbidden in Islam, it was important to differentiate between a situation wherein the probability of death in battle was very high, and suicide.

We know of various examples of individuals who sought martyrdom during the period of the crusades. One pertained to Mūsā, a *muʿadhdhin* from Mosul who was prepared to risk his life by entering the besieged city of Edessa in 538/1144 as a spy. Dressed as an Armenian, he entered the Grand Mosque and climbed the minaret to make the call to prayer: "I shall go up and call to prayer, come what may." When he began to call out, rumour of a Muslim assault spread throughout the streets, causing the soldiers to abandon their posts, and thus

7 Qurʾān 2:193.

8 Ibn Jubayr, *Travels*, 321.

9 See David Cook, *Martyrdom in Islam* (Cambridge: Cambridge University Press, 2007), 31–44; D. Talmon-Heller, 'Muslim Martyrdom and Quest for Martyrdom in the Crusading Period,' *Al-Masāq* 14, no. 2 (Sept. 2002), 132.

allowing Zangī's men to enter. Although Mūsā was not afforded martyrdom for his brave feat, the anecdote serves as an example of how the ideal of bravery (*shajāʿa*) informed the actions of *jihād* participants, and how the pursuit of martyrdom carried an eclectic quality; martyrdom could be achieved anywhere as long as it served the Islamic cause and there were diverse actions that could be considered *jihād*.[10]

A somewhat similar display of courage and tenacity can be discerned in the case of the Sufi hermit, ʿAbdallāh al-Yūnīnī (d. 617/1220) from Baalbek. He set out to join al-Malik al-ʿĀdil in Frankish held territory. At a certain point, expecting an ambush by Franks, he was advised to be silent. The shaykh instead cried out "*Allāhu akbar*!" (God is great). Later in the day he imagined there were Hospitallers approaching him and he again called out, "God is great (*Allāhu akbar*). This is a blessed day. Today I shall go to my beloved friend." Sword unsheathed, he hurried toward the enemy only to discover that it was in fact a herd of donkeys approaching.[11] Though the tale might have been intended as a criticism of the other-worldliness of the Sufis, it also reflects a more relaxed attitude toward *jihād* at that time. One might also note a recurring pattern in the final cries of those seeking martyrdom. A Muslim's belief that through his martyrdom he would be assigned a place in paradise, was itself a form of heavenly witnessing.

Al-Sulamī dedicates two chapters in his *Kitab al-Jihād* to the topic of unexpected courage in the *jihād* fighter. He presents the Prophet as a paradigm of bravery by citing a report from Ibn Isḥāq who narrates that during the battle of Uḥud Umayya b. Khalaf exclaimed:

> "Where is Muḥammad, I will not be at peace if you [Muḥammad] are safe."
>
> Those with the Prophet said, "Let one of us go to him [to attack him]."
>
> The Prophet said, "Leave him" and then took the spear from al-Ḥārith b. al-Ṣamma.
>
> Some of the people then said, "When the Prophet took the spear he spread out from us just like flies spring off the back of a camel when it rises up."
>
> He then struck Umayya in the neck.[12]

10 Talmon-Heller, 'Muslim Martyrdom,' 133.

11 Ibid., 135.

12 Al-Sulamī, 'Kitāb al-Jihād,' 124.

Again, we must see the role and importance of the *jihād al-nafs* ethos in al-Sulamī's *jihād* outlook by considering the narration with which he concludes this section. It serves as a final remark about the true essence of courage and tenacity in battle. In the narration, a man approached the Prophet's cousin, son-in-law, and fourth caliph ʿAlī b. Abī Ṭālib and asked,

> "O Abū-l Ḥasan, who is the bravest of people?"
> He replied, "The one who has the anger of a tiger and leaps like a lion."
> ʿAlī then pointed to Zubayr [b. al-ʿAwwām], who was unaware of what ʿAlī had said.
> The man then approached Zubayr and asked him the same question.
> Zubayr replied: "[The bravest one] is he who was broken and was then repaired."[13]

It is plausible to suggest that this narration was included to counter the fear that these lofty ideals of physical courage were not attainable by all, or perhaps more to the point, that such ideals do not represent the essence of the Islamic spirit without also recognizing human limitations; the indeterminate 'broken' and 'repaired' could very well have a spiritual context that connotes the continual resistance to the path of rectification.

An outstanding example of a relatively early anti-Frankish stance can be seen in the formidable words and actions of the Shīʿī Aleppan *qāḍī* Abū l-Faḍl b. al-Khashshāb (d. 519/1125). Rather like the later al-Findalāwī, al-Khashshāb was known for temporarily setting aside the seat of traditional learning for the more engaging and volatile theatre of conflict. His active role in preaching and rousing the troops before the battle of Balat ('Battle of the Field of Blood') in 513/1119 is indicative of the indispensable role the religious class played in the conflict. The 'Islamicisation' or '*jihād*-ising' of military campaigns orchestrated by quite irreligious leaders – like Īl-Ghāzī – could only be done by members of the religious class. According to the Aleppan chronicler Ibn al-ʿAdīm, Ibn al-Khashshāb's versatility in tending to Aleppan affairs in the face of attack was supplemented by his robust desire to prosecute a *jihād* in God's cause against the unbelieving Franks:

> The *qāḍī* Abū l-Faḍl b. al-Khashshāb came, spurring the people to fight, riding on a mare and with spear in his hand. One of the troops saw him and belittled him saying: "So we have come from our lands only to follow this man in a turban!" He [Ibn al-Khashshāb] went up to the people and among the ranks preached an eloquent sermon in which he awakened

13 Ibid., 126.

their resolution and sharpened their resolve. He made the people weep, and there was agony in their eyes.[14]

Ibn al-Khashshāb's example is important to understanding how, in the sixth/twelfth century, the propaganda of *jihād* was first used politically. Sivan argues that Īl-Ghāzī's use of *jihād* propaganda after returning to Aleppo the second time, in the face of Roger of Antioch's attack, reveals an early attempt to use the strong language of *jihād* to inspire his troops with a religious mantle. We might question this, however, and consider the likelihood that Īl-Ghāzī, who had not been inspired by *jihād* rhetoric previously, may have done so between 512/1118 and the battle of Balat in 513/1119 for the sake of expediency. We further note his failure to follow up with the spirit of *jihād* after his victory against Roger of Antioch.

Yūsuf al-Findalāwī and the Pursuit of Martyrdom

The pursuit of martyrdom (*ṭalab al-shahāda*) gained a new momentum following the capture of Edessa in 538/1144; perhaps the most noted example of this that took place during the crusades is that of the Mālikī jurist Yūsuf al-Findalāwī (d. 543/1148). Al-Findalāwī was a *khaṭīb* at Bānyās, then a teacher of the Mālikī *madhhab* in Damascus and known for teaching the entire *al-Muwaṭṭa*.[15] He is mentioned in the chronicles as a worthy martyr because of his very old age and his scholarly standing; he was described as old and weak, a senior jurist from Damascus and a devout ascetic, and despite being encouraged to stay behind in the defence of Damascus in the failed crusader siege of the city in 543/1148, he preferred instead to participate in the *jihād*. In Usāma b. Munqidh's account he is the quintessence of virtuous *mujāhid*: "Among men there are those that go to battle just as the companions of the Prophet (may God be pleased with them) used to go to battle: to obtain entrance to Paradise, and not to pursue some selfish desire or to gain a reputation. Here is an example ..."[16] Abū l-Ḥakam al-Andalusī includes the martyrdom of al-Findalāwī in a poem described by Abū Shāma as a *sharḥ* (commentary) on the defence of Damascus during the Second Crusade of 543/1148, which was described

14 Ibn al-ʿAdīm, *Zubdat al-ḥalab fī tārīkh Ḥalab*, ed. Sāmī al-Daḥḥān (Damascus: al-Maʿhad al-Faransī bi-Dimashq lil-Dirāsāt al-ʿArabiyya, 1955), 188–189.

15 See al-Dhahabī, *Siyar aʿlām al-nubalāʾ* (Cairo: Maktaba al-Ṣafāʾ, 2003), 12:113–114.

16 Usāma b. Munqidh, *The Book of Contemplation*, 108; see also Ibn al-Qalānisī, *The Damascus Chronicle*, 284; Abū Shāma, *Kitāb al-Rawḍatayn*, 1:205–206.

in greater detail by Muslim chroniclers. In the poem al-Findalāwī is "Shaykh *al-faqīh* al-Findalāwī, a great supporter for the religion."[17] The significance of al-Findalāwī's pursuit of martyrdom is further developed by Ibn al-Qalānisī, who describes his resilience in the battle: "He was facing the enemy and refusing to withdraw, in obedience to the precepts of God Almighty in His noble Book. The devout ʿAbd al-Raḥmān al-Ḥalḥūlī met the same fate."[18] In the account of Ibn al-Athīr, al-Findalāwī is *ḥujjat al-dīn* ('proof of the religion'), a title he might have been accorded posthumously. Described as *shaykh kabīr*, he is an 'elderly man,' as well as being a learned jurist. When Muʿīn al-Dīn saw him marching on foot he approached him and said: "O *shaykh* you are excused [from fighting] because of your old age. We will undertake the defence of the Muslims." He asked him to return but he refused, and said: "I sold and he purchased from me, for by God I will not go back nor ask Him to cancel." He alluded to the words of God Almighty: "Indeed Allah has purchased from the believers their lives and properties because the Garden will be theirs" (9:111). It is interesting that Ibn al-Athīr does not credit the martyrdom of al-Findalāwī with a change in the fortune of the Muslims. He remarks instead how "the Franks grew strong and the Muslims became weak." It is the assistance of Sayf al-Dīn Ghāzī and his brother Nūr al-Dīn to Muʿīn al-Dīn in Damascus and the letters sent to the Franks warning them to withdraw from the city that serves as a syntactical medium between the martyrdom narrative and the re-emergence of Yūsuf al-Findalāwī at the end of the section wherein Ibn al-Athīr cites Ibn ʿAsākir:

> Al-Ḥāfiẓ Abū l-Qāsim b. ʿAsākir has mentioned in his *Tārīkh Dimashq* that one of the *ʿulamāʾ* related to him that he saw al-Findalāwī in a dream. He asked him, "How has God treated you? Where are you?" He replied, "He has forgiven me. We are in the Gardens of Eden, face to face on couches."[19]

Such dreams are common in the Muslim martyrdom tradition and are a way of confirming the status of martyrs after their death; the 'witnessing' of the martyr adds weight to his martyrdom. He also serves as a witness to the splendour of God's bounty and stands as a proof (*ḥujja*) for others; the dream of the martyr is important in influencing others to follow in his path.

The martyrdom of al-Findalāwī is venerated in a poem composed by Abū l-Ḥakam al-Andalusī, which reads rather like a list of descriptions that

17 Abū Shāma, *Kitāb al-Rawḍatayn*, 1:207.

18 Gabrieli, *Arab Historians of the Crusades*, 57.

19 Ibn al-Athīr, *al-Kāmil fī l-tārīkh*, 9:158–160.

Abū Shāma outlines as a commentary on the defence of Damascus in the Second Crusade of 543/1148:

1) On the banks of the river Darayya events occurred in a displeasing way.
2) Concerning a people who believed that the spilling of blood is like a religion.
3) 200,000 came to us, or maybe even more.
4) Some of them from Andalus, some from Palestine.
5) Some from Acre, Tyre, Sidon, and Tibnin.
6) If you saw them, it would be as if you were seeing a frenzied people.
7) For they immediately began by burning orchards.
8) They passed through Marj and our public squares.
9) If you could imagine them – riding hastily – like reptiles.
10) Among their tents they had pigs and sacrifices.
11) And flags and crosses on Masjid Khātun.
12) And we said when we saw them: "May God protect us from them!"
13) Muʿīn stood up to them, the one who helped his people and the religion.
14) And zealous youngsters, like ferocious devils.
15) They became lost while heading for Marj, in the east of Jisrin.
16) But they left Ilyās behind them, buried under the soil.
17) And the elder al-Findalāwī, a jurist and great supporter of the religion.
18) And some young men from Damascus who were great fighters, about seventy of them.
19) And from the Franks were two hundred *ʿilj* [pl. *ʿulūj*][20] and about ninety horses.
20) And the rest of them escaped death.[21] (1.1)

The poet castigates the crusaders for making a habit of 'spilling blood,' and seeks to contrast this with the humane method of battle in the Muslim ranks. The crusaders are frenzied (*majānīn*), not only because they kill incessantly but also because they destroy the natural environment, they 'immediately began by burning orchards.' They desecrate what is naturally pure – a senseless destruction; the similitude of 'reptiles' is a fitting one and aptly conjoined with the conventional mention of 'pigs' and 'crosses' which polluted the Khātun mosque. The collective religiosity of the Muslim camp is evidenced in line 12, by the supplication of the Muslims. Their response, cited in this line (And we said when we saw them: "May God protect us from them!") is very similar

20 The pejorative term *ʿilj* suggests a bestial, strong, obese individual.

21 Abū Shāma, *Kitāb al-Rawḍatayn*, 1:207.

to the Qur'ānic verse about the tenacity of the Prophet and his companions after the battle of Uḥud: "They said [when they heard this]: 'God is sufficient for us and He is the best disposer of affairs'" (3:173). The similarity between this and earlier Muslim struggles would have been picked up by some of the religiously minded among the poet's listeners; the later struggle was inspired by the former and religious justification was sought through it. Muʿīn al-Dīn's defence of his city is depicted as worthy and humane, the pun in line 13, *muʿīnun qad aʿāna* (Muʿīn [lit., 'the supporter'] supported us) shows how their defensive *jihād* is for the sake of the people and the religion (13), thus it is an honourable physical undertaking juxtaposed with the image of the crusaders' frenzied attacks. The martyrdom of al-Findalāwī is then featured. He is described as a supporter of the religion; the descriptive adjectives '*shaykh*' and '*faqīh*' both serve to illustrate the participation of the elderly and devout in the physical *jihād*. The struggle against the crusaders is validated through their contribution, whereby the desirability of participation in the physical struggle, even for the elderly and the religious scholars, is highlighted, as their memory and reputation is enhanced in the collective memory of the *umma* through the *jihād*.

The dream anecdote mentioned above, cited by Ibn ʿAsākir and Ibn al-Athīr, is also found in Sibṭ b. al-Jawzī's account, "some of his compansions saw him in their dream … in the Gardens of Eden, face to face on couches."[22] In the same poem partially cited by Sibṭ b. al-Jawzī the obscure 'Ilyās' in line 16 is the more meaningful priest (*qissīs*) in the author's concluding line (6): "The Franks ran away, leaving their priest behind, buried in the ground."[23] (1.2)

The poem carries an evident tone of valour (*ḥamāsa*). It seeks to extol the virtue of bravery and courage among the defenders of Damascus. The eyewitness Ibn al-Qalānisī says that 50,000 infantry and cavalry marched to Damascus, so the crusaders' numbers in the poem appear to be grossly exaggerated. The poet's numbers of Muslim and Christian dead cannot be verified, but the mention of two hundred *ʿilj* killed during the siege might be a more accurate way to reflect the crusader loss. The inclusion of al-Findalāwī further serves as a popular example of the dual roles some men of religion held during the crusades. The inclusion, in poetry, of such persons as the "shaykh" and "*faqīh*" al-Findalāwī, "a supporter of the religion" serves to underpin the idea that poets and propagandists were making, namely that the *jihād* was not only sometimes compulsory on all but that scholarly eminence rested on participation in such extramural feats.

22 Sibṭ b. al-Jawzī, *Mirʾāt al-zamān*, part 1, 8:201.
23 Ibid., part 1, 8:200–201.

This poem, cited by Sibṭ b. al-Jawzī, appears in his account of the Second Crusade. It seems similar in intent to a noted distinction he makes between the Qurʾān, the Bible, and a 'long-bearded' (Christian) priest[24] and reveals the way he considered cultural expectation in his chronicle. The contrast between 'their priest, buried in the ground' and the *shaykh* al-Findalāwī 'buried in the Great Mosque' is an obvious contrast that speaks of the intention of the poet (and here that of the author) to present the martyrdom of one and the abasement of the other. Al-Findalāwī is victorious because of the honour that is accorded to him; he is a *shahīd* (witness/martyr) for the believers as well as for God. His burial as a martyr ensures that he will be remembered as such and it serves as lesson for those committed to the *jihād* and for those still neglectful. In light of this it is also likely that the graves of al-Findalāwī, his friend ʿAbd al-Raḥmān al-Ḥalḥūlī, described as the *zāhid* of Damascus,[25] and other martyrs of the anti-Frankish *jihād* soon became sites for visits (*ziyāra*). Visiting the graves of martyrs was supposed to remind the faithful about the fragility of human affairs and the transitory nature of life. Muslims were instructed to visit the graves as a reminder of the hereafter and martyrs are specifically identified as sites for these visits because of their exalted status in the Islamic paradigm.[26]

This instance of an old man relinquishing his religiously sanctioned permit to abstain from fighting must be understood in light of the *jihād al-nafs* paradigm. *Jihād* was not only an activity centred on the defence of the Muslim community, but was also a chance for individuals to gain merit and increase in piety. In this respect, al-Findalāwī exercised a kind of *zuhd* in his insistence; he was, in the minds of the faithful, unconcerned about the comfort of this world (*dunyā*) and hoped through his martyrdom to 'purchase' a place in the hereafter. Predictably, such an ideal was also employed in al-Sulamī's preaching in favour of the anti-Frankish *jihād* in his *Kitāb al-Jihād*. He dedicated a short, albeit important section titled 'The joining of struggle against the self and struggle against the enemy – hoping for a good reward and recompense.' Al-Sulamī cited an incident in which some inhabitants of Damascus approached a certain Abū Muslim, "a fighter in the land of the Romans," who was fasting during his travel. The Damascenes questioned him:

24 Ibid., part 1, 8:198.

25 Al-Dhahabī, *Siyar aʿlām al-nubalāʾ*, 12:114.

26 See Christopher Taylor, *In the Vicinity of the Righteous: Ziyara and the Veneration of Muslim Saints in Late Medieval Egypt* (Leiden: Brill, 1999); Josef W. Meri, *The Cult of Saints among Muslims and Jews in Medieval Syria* (Oxford and New York: Oxford University Press, 2002).

> What makes you fast while you are travelling, and [you know that] eating has been permitted for you during fighting and travelling?

He said, "When the fighting is ready, I eat, and then I will be prepared for it and [be] strong; indeed horses do not run to far ends while they are stout but they run while they are lean."[27]

Al-Findalāwī's martyrdom was likely used to reinforce the obligatory nature of the defensive *jihād*, that physical struggle in such circumstances is an individual obligation (*farḍ al-ʿayn*), something well understood by the learned al-Findalāwī himself. In the syntactical inclusion of al-Findalāwī's martyrdom narrative it seems that the author was also hinting at the important relationship of dependency between the military and religious classes. This relationship is discussed in the earlier section, 'Ideological Pursuits – Nūr al-Dīn, Ṣalāḥ al-Dīn, and Political Patronage: An Overview.' Essentially, as cited by Ibn al-Jawzī the 'just ruler' is the one who shares in the reward of those who do good, "as if he is the servant of God in the service of everyone."[28]

In conclusion, partaking in *jihād* and even pursuing martyrdom was the most desired and striking response to the crusader occupation of Jerusalem. The religious class sought to impress on the community the obligation of *jihād* against their enemy, to draw inspiration from the first Islamic community guided by the Prophet, and to inspire the ruling class to also follow the more contemporary examples of Saljūq rulers who waged *jihād* against the Byzantines. In the course of the crusades one of the most celebrated religious participants in the *jihād* was Yūsuf al-Findalāwī. The poets of his time mentioned him prominently, as it helped them dramatize the events of the Muslim resistance in the Second Crusade. An elderly jurist, al-Findalāwī was distinguished on account of his age and his Islamic learning for his eagerness to participate; thus he served as a worthy example for the more reluctant and for others in the religious class. Might it also be surmised however that the overriding focus on al-Findalāwī suggests that the majority of the religious scholars (aside from occasional preaching) did not share the same enthusiasm of getting themselves directly involved in the *jihād*? In any case, an understanding of the dynamics of the *jihād* is crucial to our study of the crusades; it not only serves as a contrast to the crusade, but it also enables us to understand some of the reasons *jihād* was scripturally desirable for those who participated and how it was employed at the time.

27 Al-Sulamī, 'Kitāb al-Jihād,' 135.

28 Ibn al-Jawzī, *al-Shifāʾ fī mawāʿiẓ*, 45.

CHAPTER 4

Formative Muslim Responses: Franks (Faranj), Christians (Rūm), and the Making of a Christian Enemy

In chapter 4 I discuss three decisive events of the sixth/twelfth century in chronological order: the Frankish capture of Jerusalem (492/1099) and the Muslim poetic response; the fall of Edessa (538/1144) and the beginning of a clearer focus on the reconquest of Jerusalem with evidence of stronger *jihād* language in the poetry; and the Muslim reaction to Ṣalāḥ al-Dīn's reconquest of the Holy City in 583/1187. These sections complement existing research in similar areas, provide new translations of material, and offer alternative inferences and novel perspectives. Again, by seeking not to reproduce and/or comment on more 'superficial' elements of congratulatory poems, particularly after the fall of Edessa, I take a selective approach in these chapters in order to highlight areas that have hitherto not been analysed.

The First Crusade 488–93/1095–99: Syria and Internal Reform

On a Friday in August of 492/1099, almost a month after the capture of Jerusalem, a delegation left Damascus accompanied by the judge (*qāḍī*) of Damascus, Zayn al-Dīn Abū Saʿd al-Harawī. They reached Baghdad in Ramaḍān (August) of 492/1099 and requested support from the ʿAbbāsid caliph al-Mustaẓhir (487–512/1094–1118) and the sultan Barkiyāruq (487–498/1094–1105) against the Franks. The *qaḍī* stood up and conveyed the news to the others, offering a very moving account of the suffering. Ibn Taghrībirdī details a poem composed by Abū Muẓaffar al-Abīwardī that al-Harawī recited to a congregation in the mosque.[1] The recitation of poetry was of course an occasion for strong emotions, and listeners, whether genuinely moved by the words or maintaining a custom of projected expressions, wept freely. The poem fervently evoked the spirit of *jihād*, recalled elementary ideals of brotherhood, and drew on the kind of lay agitation that the crusades generated. Typical of motivational discourse, the underlying message of the poem points to an apathy in the Muslim world; the poet chided his listeners for succumbing to the world's comforts and

1 Ibn Taghrībirdī, *al-Nujūm*, 5:150–152.

 | DOI 10.1163/9789004345225_005

stated that their failure to act on his admonition only reinforced the laxness extant in the Muslim world.

(4) Dare you slumber in the blessed shade of safety, where life is as soft as an orchard flower?
(5) How can the eye sleep between the lids at a time of disasters that would waken any sleeper?[2] (1.3)

Although little of the early poetry has survived, what we have provides us with insight into the kind of political and religious insecurities that the poet saw as a product of his age. The lament is an internal one that seeks to impute blame on the Muslim *umma* generally, and more specifically, on the ruling elite and lay population of Syria. Here, the collective obligation (*farḍ al-kifāya*) on Muslims indicates that the people of Syria are principally responsible. Theirs is an immediate obligation. Together with this, since Syria and Palestine were still part of the Saljūq Empire, it was both the ʿAbbāsid caliph, al-Mustaẓhir bi-Llāh, and his sultan, Rukn al-Dīn Barkiyāruq that were the target of the poet's lament.[3]

The poets' lines were likely to have been especially evocative in rousing anger in their listeners since both al-Abīwardī and Ibn al-Khayyāṭ drew strong attention to the suffering of Muslim women and children. The euphemistic nature of these lines suggest sexual violations against womenfolk, the compromise of shame (*ḥayāʾ*) of 'sweet girls' is here connected to the notion of honour (*ʿirḍ*), the former staining the latter. Perhaps the greatest 'shame' that would dishonour the Muslim community was the violation of its womenfolk. Described as inviolable (*ḥarīm*), women are seen as sanctified, perchance echoing the instructive words of the Prophet in his Farewell Sermon (10/632) and thereby allowing the poet's listeners to empathise through a religious narrative framework already well familiar to them. In the Prophet's address the idea of sanctity of place is pointedly connected to the sanctity of Muslims:

2 Hillenbrand, *The Crusades*, 70–72.

3 Most historians who have appraised this period have commented on the initial Muslim reaction to the First Crusade and the early poetry that made up much of that response. Hadia Dajani-Shakeel's article on *jihād* poetry provides an overview of the topic. She highlights the key themes expressed in the poetry and its changing nature from the time of the First Crusade to Ṣalāḥ al-Dīn's recovery of Jerusalem. Dajani-Shakeel, '*Jihād* in Twelfth-Century Arabic Poetry,' 96–113.

> O People! Your blood and wealth is sacred until you meet your Lord, just like the sanctity of this day, and like the sanctity of this month and like the sanctity of this land …[4]
>
> أَيُّهَا النَاس إِنَّ دِمَاؤُكُم وَ أَموَالُكُم حَرَامٌ عليكُم إِلَى أَن تلقُوا رَبَّكُم كَحُرمَةِ يُومِكُم هَذَا
> فِي شَهرِكُم هَذَا فِي بَلَدِكُم هَذَا

The poets' dramatisation of the events emphasises the fear of the Muslims. Aside from killing, the theme of subjugation and humiliation is pramount in the early poetry; this was closely related to the migration of Muslims from Jerusalem to Ascalon.[5] We also have an early example of poetry that consolidates the sentiments that al-Abīwardī and Ibn al-Khayyāṭ appeal to in their lines. The poem is from the *jihād* treatise of al-Sulamī, in which he cites an incident from a chapter entitled 'Preventing women from fighting'; the wife of 'Abdallāh b. Zubayr, the companion of the Prophet Muḥammad, asked him, 'Shall we not go out to fight?' He recited:

> The worst sin for me is that a young, beautiful woman is killed
> Fighting is prescribed upon us, and for the chaste women [it] is to remain womanly [lit., draw the tails of their dresses].[6] (1.4)

In al-Abīwardī's line we find the following:

> (8) When blood has been spilt, when sweet girls must for shame hide their lovely faces in their hands! (1.5)

In Ibn al-Khayyāṭ's poem:

> (28) And how many young girls have begun to beat their throats and cheeks out of fear.

---

4 A. Z. Safwat, *Jamharat khuṭab al-ʿarab fī ʿuṣūr al-ʿarabiyya al-zāhira* (Beirut: al-Maktabat al-ʿIlmiyya, 1933), 1:156.

5 H. Dajani-Shakeel, 'Displacement of the Palestinians during the Crusades,' *Muslim World* 68, no. 3 (1978), 158–162.

6 S. Zakkār (ed.), *Arbaʿa kutub fī l-jihād min ʿaṣr al-ḥurūb al-Ṣalībiyya* (Damascus: Dār al-Takwīn, 2007), 97.

(29) And how many girls have not felt the heat [of the day] nor tasted the chill of the night.
(30) They are weakened and wasted away with grief and emotion
(31) So guard your religion and the inviolable ones; a legal profession for those who do not see loss in death.[7] (1.6)

Ibn al-Khayyāṭ's impassioned lines draw on the fear (*khawf*) and grief (*ḥuzn*) that the crusade cast on the population of Jerusalem and Syria. It distressed the entire social order and necessitated a pervasive response. Line 31 of Ibn al-Khayyāṭ's poem, a composition written for his patron ʿAbd al-Dawla (d. 502/1109), is significant in summing up what the poet sees as the responsibility of the Muslim nation.[8] It is "Islam and its people" that is under attack, the injustice meted out against "your Syrian brothers," "sweet girls," and "young children," ought to be enough to move his listeners to action. In both poems the poet stresses the importance of the collective jealousy/protection (*ghayra*) and honour (*ʿirḍ*) Muslims should have for their womenfolk.[9] The joining of women and children in his line is akin to a Qur'ān verse that calls on believers to partake in physical struggle for the purpose of defending the weak. They must consider the plight, specifically of women and children who suffer under tyranny, and the duty of *jihād* that such a situation warrants.

> And how could you refuse to fight in the cause of God and of the utterly helpless men and women and children who are crying, "O our Sustainer! Lead us forth [to freedom] out of this land whose people are oppressors, and raise for us, out of Your grace, a protector, and raise for us, out of Your grace, one who will bring us succour!".
>
> QUR'ĀN, 4:75

Fused with this lament at the crusader attack is a stern reproach directed inwards toward the Muslims for their apathy and misdirected zeal. The language of the poets is similar:

Al-Abīwardī states

(5) How can the eye sleep between the lids at a time of disasters that would waken any sleeper? (1.7)

7 Ibn al-Khayyāṭ, *Dīwān*, 182–187.
8 See Hillenbrand, *Turkish Myth and Muslim Symbol*, 148–153.
9 For a fuller discussion on 'honour' (*ʿirḍ*) see Frank Henderson Stewart, *Honor* (Chicago: University of Chicago Press, 1994).

And Ibn al-Khayyāṭ writes

(24) And how do you sleep and your eyes are only half open,
and you only open wide your eyes because of grudges you bear.
(25) The evil of grudges [continues] while grudges have become inflamed by unbelief. (1.8)

In these lines there is an expression of shock and bewilderment at how the community could remain indifferent in the face of such an outrage. The most infuriated tone complements the sentiments from the *Baḥr al-fawāʾid* in which a scholar complains that "in the early days of Islam two Muslims would stand fast against a hundred infidels, while today a hundred Muslims cannot stand against two Franks?"[10] The references to 'sleep' in the poets' lines denote docility but Ibn al-Khayyāṭ's lines turn the listener's the attention to the infighting between Muslims as a cause of their weakness. It is internal antipathy that prevents them from 'waking' from their 'slumber'; the poet chastises his listeners for responding only when personal, tribal or political loyalties are at stake, and the poet reminds them that their commitment to fighting would only avail them if it was now directed toward their crusader enemy. It is worth pointing out that in spite of the descriptions of suffering and his chastisement of Muslims for falling prey to the *fitna* of worldly trappings (*dunyā*), "refusing to believe that death will surely strike them," (al-Abīwardī) there is no despair in the poems; instead both poets intended to inspire their audiences through recollections of Islam's past heroes. In al-Abīwardī's poem they are "valiant Arabs," while Ibn al-Khayyāṭ, who beseeches his patron ʿAbd al-Dawla to fight in the *jihād*, concentrates on instructing his readers to overcome fear and apathy by taking up arms against the crusaders:

(33) So do not be bereaved by the spreading of the affair.
The weapons will give you strength against your enemies, and a firm and strong opinion. (1.9)

As a jurist al-Abīwardī's words are bound to have been oratorical. In this, his mention of the Prophet expresses an ability to draw attention to the idea of religious loyalty, defence and the responsibility of the ʿAbbāsid caliph, from the Hashimite 'sons of Hashim,' to serve as a defender of the Muslim nation:

10 Meisami (trans. and ed.), *The Sea of Precious Virtues*, 57.

(13) This is war, and he who lies in the tomb at Medina seems to raise his voice and cry: "O sons of Hāshim!" (1.10)

Although the emphatic contesting of religiosities had yet to pervade the anti-Frankish *jihād* poetry, the religious nature of the poets' lines – ideas pertaining to the preference of death in God's cause over the fleeting enjoyment of the world; the obligation to defend the weak and oppressed; the call to *jihād* and exemplary model of the Prophet – denoted an attack on the 'House of Islam' by the nation of *kufr* (unbelief). Al-Abīwardī calls on the 'sons of Islam' to remember the Muslim nation's illustrious victories; this exhortation is not limited by their contemporary knowledge of any military successes but instead is one that places them in the frame of Muslim victory from the time of Islam's earliest champions.

Al-Abīwardī states,

(3) O Sons of Islam, indeed behind you are battles in which heads rolled at your feet. (1.11)

Ibn al-Khayyāṭ, however, makes specific reference to the feats of Alp Arslān (d. 465/1072):

(41) His remembrance continues to remain like the guiding stars, and higher than the glorious sun.
(42) So that you return to the virtues and loftiness of what was before. (1.12)

The poem of al-Abīwardī refers to the "Rūm that feed on our ignominy." In Ibn al-Athīr's citation of the poem we discern a later and more accurate description of the crusaders as Faranj (Franks); the chronicler refers to the 'Faranj' six times in his section explaining the events of 492/1099.[11] Where 'Rūm' denoted Christians in general, Muslim contact with the crusaders taught them to differentiate between Byzantine Christians and western European Christians. Ibn al-Khayyāṭ's poem, written in Syria in the early decades of the sixth/twelfth century, calls to attention the war feats of Alp Arslān; the sultan was used as an exemplar for Muslims in the immediacy of the crusader capture of Jerusalem.[12]

11 Ibn al-Athīr, *al-Kāmil fī l-tārīkh*, 8:424–427.

12 Ibn al-Khayyāṭ, *Dīwān*, 182–187. For more information on the battle of Manzikert and the religious imagery that shaped the writing of the event, see Hillenbrand, *Turkish Myth and Muslim Symbol*.

The victory at Manzikert in 463/1071 was a heavy blow to the Byzantines – the Emperor Romanus was captured and the grip of Christian Byzantium on Anatolia ended. By deliberately referring to the Franks as Rūm, the poets placed their new enemy in the context of the defeat of the Byzantines only decades earlier; thus they shifted the focus politically from the Christian Byzantines to the new Christian crusaders and also geographically from Anatolia to Syria.

Although the massacre in the Holy City during the First Crusade was the most pressing concern in the early poetry, embedded in the collective social memory of the city's inhabitants was the place of Jerusalem as part of the abode (*dār*) of Islam; its sanctity as a precinct of Islamic governance was now compromised by an unbelieving foreign entity. The sacred boundary of 'Islamic Jerusalem' would have been a compelling incentive for the *jihād*, particularly for the religious classes, as Eddé notes, "la notion de pureté, dans l'islam ... est omniprésente."[13] *Jihād* was warranted not only to defend but also to repel since the *sharīʿa* 'cleanses' the impurity of unbelief. In light of this, we may consider the ways in which poets used terms congruous to well-established meanings that ordinary Muslims could easily relate to, as a way of saying and signalling more than what the lines literally stated. For example, in a poem presumably composed early after the First Crusade and collected by Ibn Taghrībirdī, an anonymous poet accentuates the dire state of the population and the crusader threat toward Islam.

(1) Unbelief has declared it lawful to inflict harm on Islam, causing prolonged lamentation for the religion.
(2) What is right is now lost [has perished] and what is protected [defended, guarded] is [now] made licit, the sword cuts and blood is spilt.
(3) And how many Muslim men have become booty, and how many Muslim women's inviolability has been plundered.[14] (1.13)

The lyrical mood in this part of the poem enables the poet to maximise yearning and sympathy for the victims of the First Crusade. In the poet's opening lines, "Unbelief has declared it lawful (*aḥalla*) ... what is protected is made licit (*mubāḥ*) ... Muslim women's inviolability has been plundered (*ḥarram*)," the poet uses derivatives of words congruous and indicative of the Islamic law code; *ḥalāl, mubāḥ*, and *ḥarām* are terms that are intrinsically connected to the *sharīʿa* and used to denote legal rulings pertaining to one's actions. It is

13 A. M. Eddé, *Saladin* (Paris: Flammarion, 2008), 214.

14 Ibn Taghrībirdī, *al-Nujūm*, 5:151–152.

plausible that the poet strung together his lines to appeal to the religious sensibilities of his listeners, or the sensibilities of the religious class. Even if this idea escaped the poet's intent, the words may have proven meaningful to the judges and administrators of law who held once valued positions in the framework of an Islamic political order. Whereas the lines were intended to evoke strong emotions pertaining to the honour of womenfolk, it is Islam, in all its elements, that is harmed; this includes the sanctity accorded to its governance. The crusaders quite simply upset the sacred balance of things. While the anonymous author of the mid sixth-/twelfth-century Persian 'mirrors for princes' text *Baḥr al-fawāʾid* began his work by noting that "all wise men agree that God is better than man,"[15] for the Muslims of Syria the conquest of Jerusalem signified a reversal of that divinely ordained social order. Such a concern was simply understood and did not need to be incorporated, for example, into the persuasive repertoire of those who travelled to Baghdad in 504/1111 in order to appeal for assistance from the son of Malik Shāh, Sultan Ghiyāth al-Dunyā wa-l-Dīn Muḥammad. While evoking the tangible reality of "the slaughter of men, and enslavement of women and children"[16] was decisive, even these lines stress the compromising of the sacred.

In this light the theme of Islam in which *sharīʿa* is its salient feature is further discerned from a later poem composed by the Damascene poet al-ʿArqala Ḥassān (d. 591/1195), who praised the last of the Būrid emirs, Mujīr al-Dīn Abaq (d. 565/1169),[17] after the failed crusader siege of Damascus in 543/1148:

(1) Who fought the Franks sincerely for the religion other than he, while the horses were like torrential floods in the battle?
(2) He pulled Islam in under his banner [authority], and was praised in the *sharīʿa* of Aḥmad.[18] (1.14)

The poem draws on the importance of legal 'sacredness,' similar to a panegyric composed by ʿImād al-Dīn al-Iṣfahānī in praise of Ṣalāḥ al-Dīn following the reconquest of Jerusalem. In al-Iṣfahānī's lines we see a more precise identification of Jerusalem as a land whose sanctity was compromised not only by the settlement of the crusaders, but by the absence of the 'laws of the

15 Meisami (trans. and ed.), *The Sea of Precious Virtues*, 3.
16 Ibn al-Qalānisī, *Tārīkh Dimashq* 360–555 H, ed. S. Zakkār (Damascus, 1983), 276; Ibn al-Qalānisī, *The Damascus Chronicle*, 111.
17 See J. W. Meri (ed.), *Medieval Islamic Civilization: An Encyclopedia* (Abingdon: Routledge, 2006), 1:123–124.
18 Abū Shāma, *Kitāb al-Rawḍatayn*, 1:208.

religion.' The conjoining of 'laws of the religion returned' (1.16 below) with the statement that patriarchs and priests were removed from the sanctity, implied that Islamic religious figures had retaken their places, and underscores how al-Iṣfahānī sought to show that al-Aqṣā had returned to its true Islamic state when its *sharʿī* (legal/sacred) authority was restored.

(21) You took off the garment of unbelief from the land of Jerusalem
And you clothed it with the religion which uncovers confusions (1.15)[19]

In this line an antithesis (*ṭibāq*) exists between the notion of clarity (*bayyināt*) and concealment (*tukhfī*); the poet alternates between removal (*nazaʿa*), and clothing or covering (*labasa*), uncovering or revealing (*kashafa*); this reflects a transformation from *rijs* (filth) which the poet focuses on in line 20, and culminates in garment of unbelief (*libās al-kufr*) in line 22 and the pure religion mentioned in the same line. He illustrates the polarities between crusaders and Muslims engaged in the *jihād* by isolating their contrasting qualities. The antithesis continues with Ṣalāḥ al-Dīn, who is nobler than those in the day (*aḍḥā*) and those in the night (*amsā*); he is quintessentially 'sanctified' (*muqaddasan*) by the reconquest of sanctified Jerusalem (*al-quds*). But, to remind his listeners that the sultan's eminence in not limited or entirely defined by the reconquest, he tells us that "before the reconquest of Jerusalem you were sanctified and your character is not lacking in purity (*ṭuhr*) and sanctity (*quds*)." (19)[20]

(22) And the laws of the religion returned to the house of God
So neither patriarch nor priest remained inside it. (1.16)[21]

Unlike the Muslim poets who wrote of the First Cruade and who did not refer to the occupation in unequivocal terms as a 'Christian' upturning of the city and a new religious landscape replacing a previous one, the poetry after the reconquest of 583/1187 was filled with Islamic symbols replacing those put in place by the Christians. The 'laws of the religion' here takes the place of 'patriarch' and 'priest.' These interpretations of the anonymous First Crusade poem speak of the way the capture of Jerusalem upturned the sacred order of things; it is akin to an approach taken by P. Smoor in his analysis of a poem commending Nūr al-Dīn. His inclusion of the juristic meaning of *ijmāʿ* (consensus) in the

19 Ibid., 3:233.
20 Ibid.
21 Ibid.

poet's diction opens up an array of possibilities. Smoor singles out the word as suggestive of "a new concept in that particular Egyptian climate," i.e., *ijmāʿ* in its juristic usage generally means a consensus of *ʿulamāʾ* in Sunnī Islam:

(14) He (Nūr al-Dīn) is the mainstay of the Banū Ayyūb in age and lordship; the reach of his arm is longest, gigantic is his majesty.
(15) When he causes his dewy rain to flow in abundance over an assembly, you observe both splashing rain and a jubilant multitude.
(16) A difference of opinion (*khulf*) occurred, but not with regard to the generosity of his hand; about that there was consensus (*ijmāʿ*) between both the opponent and the loyal friend.[22]

Whereas the poet's approach is estimable and should be considered, drawing obscure conclusions from a poet's apparent words may lead to less plausible conclusions. In this case we know that ʿUmāra al-Yamanī was initially a Sunnī Shāfiʿī, so he was likely accustomed to the juristic phrases of legal discourse. Extrapolating his meaning from the word *ijmāʿ* can, therefore, present difficulties, though searching for nuanced meanings is refreshing and can open up a host of previously unconsidered possibilities.

The anonymous post-First Crusade poet juxtaposes symbols of Christianity with those of Islam, presenting the crusade as an expedition that brought with it a change to the religious demographic of the city, violating sanctities of person, place, and scripture.

(1) How many a mosque has been made into a monastery, with a crucifix erected upon its *mihrāb*?
(2) The blood of pigs is suitable for it and Qurʾāns have been burned under the guise of incense. (1.17)

The mention of 'pigs' and the 'Qurʾān' in the same line is a deliberate poetic ploy to maximise the effect of the calamity on its listeners. The obvious distinction here is between the motifs of the foul and pure; the crusaders desecrated Jerusalem with their occupation, and the call for *jihād* is thus one that extends from the defence of people to the defence of the faith. The motif (*maʿānī*) is an idea one expresses through words; the subsequent line is, ingeniously,

22 P. Smoor, "ʿUmāra's Poetical Views of Shāwar, Ḍirghām, Shīrkūh and Saladin as Viziers of the Fāṭimid Caliphs,' in *Culture and Memory in Medieval Islam*, ed. F. Daftary and J. W. Meri (London: I. B. Tauris, 2003), 424.

a validation of the Qurʾān as much as it suggests a guided response. This is due to the Qurʾānic imagery in his line:

(6) Such events, were a child to reflect upon them, would turn white his hair. (1.18)

This metaphoric line resembles the Qurʾānic verse:

فَكَيفَ تَتَّقُونَ إِن كَفَرتُمْ يَومًا يَجعَلُ الوِلدَانَ شِيبًا

> Then how can you avoid the punishment, if you disbelieve, on a Day that will make the children grey-headed.
>
> QURʾĀN, 73:17

He thus creates an idea for his audience that equates the loss of Jerusalem with the cataclysmic day of judgement. Eschatological language and imagery was sometimes interwoven into narratives or poetry to amplify the extent of a particular upheaval. Sibṭ b. al-Jawzī, describing al-Muʿaẓẓam's dismantling of the fortifications of Jerusalem in 616/1219 explicates in his description the sense of panic among the city's inhabitants: "the *qiyāma* [lit., resurrection] was established in all the lands of Islam" and "a chaos occurred like that of *yawm al-qiyāma* [the day of resurrection]."[23]

(7) How can Muslim women be enslaved at every frontier, while other Muslims yet live in comfort?
(8) Do you not owe an obligation to God and to Islam, that you will defend the young and old men?
(9) Say to the men of understanding, wherever they may be, "Respond to God's call, woe to you, respond!" (1.19)

Continuing with his sequence of juxtaposing lines, the poet emphasises that the imprisonement and subjugation of Muslim women while the free and responsible enjoy comfortable lives is unacceptable. The intended response here was one of outrage, maybe his listeners could relate to the war feats of al-Muʿtaṣim in his siege of Amorium in 223/838 to respond to the cries of an imprisoned woman. Then 'owing an obligation to God' would have been relevant for the caliphal powers, notwithstanding the general duty on Muslims. The final line evocatively appeals to the religious susceptibilities of his audience;

23 Sibṭ b. al-Jawzī, *Mirʾāt al-zamān*, part 2, 8:601, 654.

he challenges them not only for enjoying their temporal pleasures at a time of calamitous events, but more pressingly, for the divine accountability that awaits them for their indifference. Thus, they must respond to 'God's call,' his appeal transcends political loyalties. The generality of his entreaty, 'wherever they may be' yet reveals the poet's anger, which shows through his imperative tone combined with the sorrowful expression encapsulated in the exclaim (woe to you). Ibn Taghrībirdī says, immediately after citing the poem, 'people said these kinds of words countless times.'

The early poetry offers us direct insight into the cultural and religious frameworks within which poets viewed and interpreted their history, and justified their responses. The poetry served to incite the rulers to come to the service of fellow Muslims. For al-Abīwardī, the *jihād* should equal the crusaders' attack in severity; it should furthermore be considered an individual obligation (*farḍ al-ʿayn*), which compels all Muslims (Arabs and non-Arabs) to participate. In political terms, however, *jihād* was not the primary response to the arrival of the crusaders. It took some decades before the Muslims of Syria were able to forego their political and religious disputes and unite under the banner of *jihād* and see their struggle as inherently religious, led by a committed political leadership to fight against the 'impure,' 'misguided,' and 'polytheist' crusaders. But these early poems certainly provide us with valuable insight into the crusader occupation of Syria. In addition, there are complementary ideas between al-Abīwardī and al-Sulamī's *Kitāb al-Jihād*. Both writers brought out the idea that the crusades were a concerted attack against Islam, although the kind of religious sensibility expressed in the early poetry is directed inward, toward the Muslims, rather than outward, against their Christian enemy. Such themes and others are discussed in the following section which considers the poems al-Sulamī incorporated into his *Kitāb al-Jihād*.

Verses in al-Sulamī's *Kitāb al-Jihād*

Aside from the early poetry cited by Ibn al-Khayyāṭ, al-Abīwardī, and the anonymous poet, and the arsenal of *ḥadīth* and juristic opinion that al-Sulamī includes in his *Kitāb al-Jihād*, it is important to consider al-Sulamī's text as a prosimetrum; it weaves poetry into theological discussions. Rhymed prose and poetry have long been used as historiographical tools, and al-Sulamī's incorporation of poetry not only supports his arguments and illuminates and embellishes the text, but also, by drawing on a wide spectrum of poets he was engaging in what many authors of his age were doing.

In the many sections that make up his book, his poetry serves to validate his points; the verses corroborate the themes espoused in Qur'ānic verses and in the *ḥadīth* he references. In a section about the superiority of remaining in the battle during violent combat he cites an Abū l-Qāsim al-Fārisī:

> I will continue to fight until I see no one standing to fight me.[24] (1.20)

The poem draws on the idea of the pursuit of martyrdom (*ṭalab al-shahāda*), that pursuing the enemy relentlessly not only represents an exemplary standard of bravery, but that conceding to the enemy conversely shows cowardice and weakness. The poem is a proclamation that typifies the self assurance common in *jihād* poetry but also connects with the idea of one's resolve (*'azm*), a theme memorialised in al-Mutanabbī's famous *qaṣīda* for Sayf al-Dawla (d. 356/967) after the battle of al-Ḥadath in 343/954–55, 'With the worth of men of resolve are resolutions in accordance.' Al-Mutanabbī was a professional poet who travelled through Syria seeking patronage; he found it most illustriously with the Hamdanid ruler of Aleppo, Sayf al-Dawla. The Arab prince fought dozens of battles against the Byzantines and became an inspiration for later *jihād* leaders. It was during the time al-Mutanabbī spent with his patron that he composed his most celebrated verses extolling the *jihād*, verses containing imagery that was utilised repeatedly by poets in the age of the crusades.[25] This poem cited by al-Sulamī is then followed by a couplet from an 'Umar b. 'Awf al-Kinānī:

> The people [enemy] are like you, they have hair on their heads
> And they will not come back to life after they are killed.[26] (1.21)

According to al-Sulamī, 'This means that they are people like you, if they are killed they will not live in the world again, so why are you afraid of death when they are unafraid, and you fear them and they do not fear [you].'[27] Such sentiments were likely to have been particularly meaningful in the event of enemy defeats; the poet emphasises how the *jihād* would limit the enemy's

24 Al-Sulamī, 'Kitāb al-Jihād,' 77.

25 For more information on al-Mutanabbī see M. Larkin, 'Al-Mutanabbī, Abū'l-Ṭayyib Aḥmad b. al-Ḥusayn al-Ju'fi,' in *Medieval Islamic Civilization*, ed. Josef W. Meri (Abingdon: Routledge, 2006), 542–544; W. Heinrichs, 'The Meaning of Mutanabbī,' in *Poetry and Prophecy: The Beginnings of a Literary Tradition*, ed. J. L. Kugel (New York: Cornell University Press, 1990), 120–139; C. Issawi, 'Al-Mutanabbī in Egypt (957–962),' in *Medieval and Middle Eastern Studies: In Honor of Aziz Suryal Atiya*, ed. S. A. Hanna (Leiden: E. J. Brill, 1972), 236–239.

26 Al-Sulamī, 'Kitāb al-Jihād,' 77.

27 Ibid.

incursions. Al-Sulamī's selection of these lines correlates to the widespread fear that for the crusaders, Jerusalem and the Islamic Near East were part of a wider Christian military scheme that began with conflicts in Sicily and Spain.

Another insightful poem cited earlier appears in his section about preventing women from engaging in the physical fighting. In it the wife of ʿAbdallāh b. Zubayr asked her husband, "Shall we not go out to fight?" He answered thus:

> The worst sin for me is that a young, beautiful woman is killed
> Fighting is prescribed upon us, and for the chaste women [it] is to remain womanly [lit., draw the tails of their dresses].[28] (1.22)

The womenfolk were not only exempt from fighting, they were also instructed to remain as housewives. In these verses Ibn Zubayr was certainly expressing cultural expectations; he contrasts male and female roles and even juxtaposes hard and soft sounds. For men there is *qatl* (killing) and *qitāl* (fighting), whereas the *muḥṣanāt* (chaste women) should 'draw the tails of their dresses' (*jarr al-dhuyūl*). These become signifiers for what is womanly and inherently unmanly. The poet iterates the obligation upon men to engage in the fighting and not to succumb to womanly pretences and refrain from the battle. Al-Sulamī's use and placement of the poetic verses lends emotive weight to his arguments, thereby showing how poetry was used in significant moments in narrative or prose texts. Al-Sulamī further cites poetic advice from a father, Quṭba b. al-Khaḍrāʾ al-Qaynī, to his son about the obligatory nature of physical struggle:

> My son one day your father will die, so protect his legacy even if you face only one battalion
> You be the one who initiates; the one who goes forth is not the one who loses
> You will face your death or maybe you will die from a wound [in battle]
> But remember that death will even come to the one who hid away and did not participate.[29] (1.23)

The verses draw on essential martyrdom tropes: fate and the nature of life as predestined; eagerness to engage the enemy; victory defined by participation even in the event of defeat; and death as an inescapable occurrence that must not dissuade participation. The encouragement to 'Protect the legacy of your father' that al-Qaynī evokes is one that emanates in a general sense from the

28 Ibid., 97.
29 Ibid., 132.

Islamic belief that the good deeds of one's children will benefit their deceased parents. Al-Qaynī makes this clear by reminding his son that 'your father is one day going to die'; it stands as an exhortation to continue a path of *jihād* hitherto trodden by the father; the son is now bound to continue. It is also strikingly similar to the papal bull *Quantum praedecessores* which called for the Second Crusade (540/1146), stating that crusaders should honour their fathers by pursuing the Muslims in battle to recapture the state of Edessa.[30] The final verses of al-Sulamī's poem seem to be inspired, at least thematically, by verses of the Qur'ān (4:74–78) which outline the incentives for fighting in the cause of God. These incentives include the hereafter and fighting to defend the oppressed; it notes that the reluctant harbour fears regarding fighting and states that death is an inevitability, as much as one tries to ward it off: 'Wherever you are, death will overtake you, though you are in lofty towers ...' (Qur'ān, 4:78) Similar ideas are evoked in another poem al-Sulamī cites; this one sees constancy in the *jihād* as key to the pursuit in spite of the strong likelihood of death. The second verse he cites in fact praises participation, even if one must flee from the battlefield, *jihād* is still a worthy pursuit, but seeking martyrdom by proceeding forward is more honourable.

> They refused to run away while the battle is raging
> And they did not leave the fighting out of fear of death
> And even if they ran away they would still have kept their dignity
> But they saw that patience in facing death is more honourable.[31] (1.24)

The extant poetry following the First Crusade includes responses from the Syrian region, responses that draw on the suffering of the inhabitants of the city and coastal regions. The poetry does not refer to distinct locations, however, the *faḍā'il* features that stem from the corpus of *ḥadīth* literature do have a central place in al-Sulamī's text but are absent in the early poetry. The salient themes in the poetry are predicated on the idea that Muslims succumbed to the trappings of worldly life, and that this was a cause for Muslim defeat and

30 'By the grace of God and the zeal of your fathers, who strove to defend them over the years and to spread the Christian name ... It will be seen as a great token of nobility and uprightness if those things acquired by the efforts of your fathers are vigorously defended by you, their good sons. But if, God forbid, it comes to pass differently, then the bravery of the fathers will have proved to be diminished in the sons.' *Quantum praedecessores*, 1 March 1146 in J. Phillips, *The Second Crusade: Extending the Frontiers of Christendom* (New Haven and London: Yale University Press, 2007), 280–282.

31 Al-Sulamī, 'Kitāb al-Jihād,' 134.

also a potential impediment to the 'rescue' ethos formulated around the idea of *jihād*. Sentiments of grief centre on the treatment and fear for young girls; the capture of Jerusalem was depicted as a violation of sacred Islamic boundaries and the humiliation of the Muslims was a result of internal weakness caused by the attraction of worldly comfort and misdirected zeal. A spirit of buoyancy also exists, however; the call for *jihād* is bolstered by calls to remember previous Muslim victors and illustrious triumphs. Importantly one comes to see how poetry was utilised by authors of *jihād* texts, often in al-Sulamī's case as poetic anecdotes, strategically placed in their works to corroborate and capture the highly charged atmosphere of the time.

The buoyancy of *jihād* spirit did not find the political strategy it required for another four decades. The next section shows that it made its strongest appeal following the capture of the crusader state of Edessa in 538/1144 by 'Imād al-Dīn Zangī. Most prominently, with Zangī's son, Nūr al-Dīn, Jerusalem became the focus of the inevitable and long anticipated *jihād*.

The Proximity of an Islamic Jerusalem: The Fall of Edessa, Banū Aṣfar, and the Revival of *Jihād*

Following 'Imād al-Dīn Zangī's (r. 521–541/1127–1146) capture of Edessa in 538/1144 and subsequent murder in 541/1146, his son Nūr al-Dīn Zangī led campaigns to unify the Muslims of Syria, and after taking possession of Aleppo and Edessa he directed his efforts to besieging Damascus. Tensions between Mujīr al-Dīn (r. 534–49/1140–54), the leader of Damascus, and Nūr al-Dīn were exacerbated while the former sought protection from the crusaders by renewing a treaty with them and agreeing to pay them an annual tribute. By 549/1154, however, Nūr al-Dīn managed to overthrow Mujīr al-Dīn and take control of Damascus. These events allow us to contrast the general formalism and artificiality of official court poetry with the exceptional cases of poets such as Ibn al-Qaysarānī and Ibn al-Munīr al-Ṭarābulsī (d. 548/1153); in the cases of these two poets there is a sense of truthful expression vividly employed particularly in the longing (*ḥanīnī*) type of poetry that reflected the reaction to the loss of the region.[32] Aside from the reality that both poets were what we would

32 Dajani-Shakeel, '*Jihād* in Twelfth-Century Arabic Poetry,' 102–103; the *Lament on Edessa* by Nerses Snorhali, written in 539/1145 or 540/1146 following 'Imād al-Dīn Zangī's capture of Edessa in 538/1144, is an example of a Christian equivalent to poetry of longing (*ḥanīnī*). It provides valuable insight into the Armenian Christian reaction to the crusades; this genre of poetry refers to poetry intended "to heal and to edify, to console and to strengthen each

term 'refugees,' there was a schismatic difference between them, the kind that prevented a unified response from the Muslim community, and was one of the reasons the First Crusade was so successful. Ibn al-Munīr was considered a Rāfiḍī by Ibn Khallikān; this term denoted one who held Shīʿī positions, whereas Ibn al-Qaysarānī was described in the sources as having been a devout Sunnī.[33] Aside from vehement poetic lampoons levelled against each other,[34] two of the most vibrant themes in their poetry are the importance of Jerusalem and the sanctity of al-Aqṣā Mosque – the notion of 'captivity' and the obligation to recapture the Holy City.

Ibn al-Qaysarānī used his poetry during Mujīr al-Dīn's reign over the city, and particularly in 544–545/1150 when there were signs of peace between the two leaders, to push for reconciliation and an alliance between Damascus and Aleppo that might threaten the Frankish occupation of Jerusalem.

> (1) [It is certain] that if you rule Damascus then those in Iliyā [Jerusalem] would certainly know that there would be slaughter [in Jerusalem].[35] (1.25)

The poet uses the hyperbolic *dhabḥ* (slaughter) to describe what is destined for the Franks if Damascus joined the struggle with Nūr al-Dīn, making it seem like an uncomplicated engagement in which victory is certain for the Muslims. In the same poem Nūr al-Dīn is *sayf fī kulli ḥālatin* (2) (a sword in every situation). The poet advances the idea that it is the sword that defends Islam from the crusaders and through it Islam has emerged victorious. The poet anticipates that his seizure of Damascus will facilitate the opening of Jerusalem; in the same poem he continues to remind his listeners that if Nūr al-Dīn took to fighting against the crusaders it would cause 'the heart of polytheism to grieve its wounds' (9).

Ibn al-Qaysarānī's competitor also advocated Muslim unity to advance the cause of *jihād* for the liberation of Jerusalem; Ibn al-Munīr al-Ṭarābulsī composed a poem directed at Nūr al-Dīn when the latter was threatening Damascus. The poet, using a lavish rhetorical style, presents Damascus as unable to prosper without Nūr al-Dīn, especially not while Jerusalem is under Frankish

---

Christian who reads or hears it." See T. M. van Lint, 'Seeking Meaning in Catastrophe: Nerses Snorhali's *Lament on Edessa*,' in *East and West in the Crusader States: Context – Contacts – Confrontations*, ed. K. Ciggaar and H. Teule (Leuven: Peeters, 1999), 29–105.

33 Ibn Khallikān, *Wafayāt*, 1:221.

34 Ibid., 1:221–223.

35 Abū Shāma, *Kitāb al-Rawḍatayn*, 1:241.

control. Following Nūr al-Dīn's request in 545/1150 for a thousand horsemen from the Damascenes to protect the people of Hawran from the Franks, the ruler of Damascus instead made a treaty with the Franks to fight off any invading force, though according to the Damascene chronicler Ibn al-Qalānisī, Nūr al-Dīn's "benevolent attitude" and "saintly status" afforded him the support of many Damascenes. The official Damascus response was unequivocal, "Between us and you there is nothing except the sword, and a party of Franks are now on their way to assist us and to repel you, if you advance towards us."[36] In light of this failure on the part of Mujīr al-Dīn and the Damascenes to assist Nūr al-Dīn against the crusaders, Ibn al-Munīr al-Ṭarābulsī describes their antagonism toward Nūr al-Dīn and their alliance with the Franks as a "building of hypocrisy (*nifāq*)," a kindling of a "fire that will burn them tomorrow at the resurrection."[37] In another poem composed around the same time and cited by Abū Shāma, Ibn al-Munīr equates the treachery shown by the inhabitants of Damascus toward Nūr al-Dīn with that of Nebuchadnezzar II's (d. 562 BC) repressive treatment of the Jews:

> (11) I swear that the Jews did not taste in Jerusalem and its surroundings from Nebuchadnezzar worse than some of what you have been forced to taste.[38] (1.26)

In the poem, after building up an image of betrayal and irreligiousness, Ibn al-Munīr then strikes his most serious tone. Because of Mujīr al-Dīn's alliances with the Franks, in the eyes of the poet he has become an unbeliever himself:

> (20) You have become a Christian from your mother's side, and indeed a Majūs [fire worshipper/Zoroastrian] from your father's side; so the vein of unbelief is repeated in you from many sides.[39] (1.27)

The similarity between Ibn al-Munīr and Ibn al-Khayyāṭ's line cited above in response to the First Crusade ('The evil of grudges [continues] while grudges have become inflamed by unbelief') is situated around the problem of Muslims turning their weapons on fellow Muslims over political squabbles and military alliances. The brunt of the poets' antagonism stems from the weakening of the

36 Ibn al-Qalānisī, *Tārīkh Dimashq*, 480; Ibn al-Qalānisī, *The Damascus Chronicle*, 299. [I have amended the English translation].

37 Abū Shāma, *Kitāb al-Rawḍatayn*, 1:254.

38 Ibid., 1:256.

39 Ibid., 1:256.

Muslim body politic. It is likely that this is what Ibn al-Munīr intended when he mentioned the different 'sides' from which Mujīr al-Dīn compromised his religious loyalties; clearly his becoming a 'Christian from his mother's side' was specifically due to his treaty with the Franks. His verses here reveal the incorporation of a legalistic discourse. He chooses words that convey a juristic matter about alliances and hostility intended for the people of Damascus; he speaks of the "summit of Islam – whoever seeks protection in it has believed, and whoever turns against it (*yatawallā*) has disbelieved."[40] Here Ibn al-Munīr uses the authority of a Qur'ānic edict that prohibits alliances with unbelievers against Muslims to threaten the Damascenes with damnation in the hereafter if they choose the crusaders over Nūr al-Dīn.[41] The poet's invective is further strengthened by the use of Qur'ānic vocabulary throughout his poetry. The poet's use of terms like *wa-anībū* (and turn to …) and *wa-firrū* (and flee to …) in the imperative probably have a Qur'ānic influence from *wa-anībū ilā rabbikum* (and turn to your Lord) (Qur'ān 39:54) and *fa-firrū ila-Allāh* (and flee to God) (Qur'ān 51:50) and his description of Jerusalem as *ṣarḥun 'alayhā mumarrad* (a smoothly paved palace) is almost certainly from *ṣarḥun mumarrad* (a palace paved smooth) (Qur'ān 27:44) in the Qur'ānic description of Prophet Sulaymān's (Solomon's) palace.

The poem is also interesting for candidly revealing the poet's incorporation of Frankish women as a desirable spoil-of-war – the fight against the Banū Aṣfar ('pale-faced ones') is for the prize of Banāt al-Aṣfar ('pale-faced women'):

(3) O light (*nūr*) of the religion (*dīn*) of God and the son of its support (*'imād*), and the Kawthar [lit. the fount (of abundance)],[42] son of Kawthar, son of the Kawthar

(4) Empty Damascus with the sword of those elderly people who prevented your horses from Banāt al-Aṣfar ['pale-faced women'].[43] (1.28)

Although we cannot measure the effect of Ibn al-Munīr's strong invective, it seems unlikely that ideas echoed in his poetry pertaining to unbelief (*kufr*) and hypocrisy (*nifāq*) were only put forward by him. On the contrary, it is likely that the religious community of Damascus harboured similar sentiments, and the poet's legerdemain – interspersing his poems with Qur'ānic imagery

40 Ibid., 1:255.

41 See Qur'ān, 5:43, 5:56, 9:23, 60:9.

42 See Qur'ān, 108:1.

43 Abū Shāma, *Kitāb al-Rawḍatayn*, 1:254.

while calling for the liberation of Jerusalem – went some way in bolstering the reputation of Nūr al-Dīn as a pious Muslim leader committed to the Islamic cause, as opposed to those who were governed by hypocrisy and unbelief, as the poet describes. Furthermore, due to the itinerant life led by someone like Ibn al-Munīr, a man who spent his time in different courts and cities of Syria, it is likely that the strong sentiments espoused in his poetry would have travelled across much of Syria.

After the capture of Edessa, a poem composed by Ibn al-Qaysarānī in praise of the vizier of Mosul Jamāl al-Dīn al-Iṣfahānī situates the conquest as the first in a string of victories leading to the reconquest of Jerusalem and the crusader-controlled coasts. Here the reconquest of Jerusalem is presented as an inevitable consequence of the Edessa victory. Jamāl al-Dīn earned the praise of many of his contemporaries, particularly the residents of Mosul. Jamāl al-Dīn was given the appellation *'jawād'* (generous) because it was said that he financed the construction of walls around Medina and the repair of the Prophet's Mosque. He was known to have been exceptionally charitable, and to have spent large sums on the poor and destitute in Mecca and Medina. He was, however, later imprisoned by Quṭb al-Dīn Mawdūd in mid 548/1153 because of what Ibn Khallikān describes as the latter's control over Jamāl al-Dīn after his influential rise to authority. Jamāl al-Dīn subsequently died in prison, in 559/1164, and his body was afforded the privilege of being interred in the Jannat al-Baqīʿ cemetery in Medina.[44]

(9) He struggled for God in a true *jihād*, hoping for reward from the Supreme One.
(11) If the conquest of Edessa is the deep sea then its shore is Jerusalem and the coast.[45] (1.29)

Perhaps the most influential voice, together with someone like al-Qāḍī l-Fāḍil, in directing Ṣalāḥ al-Dīn's focus toward the liberation of Jerusalem, was his secretary ʿImād al-Dīn al-Iṣfahānī. ʿImād al-Dīn's poetry of yearning (*ḥanīnī*) came to the fore in 570/1175 when Ṣalāḥ al-Dīn captured the town of Baalbek. Earlier, in a poem composed after Nūr al-Dīn's death, ʿImād al-Dīn lamented, in line 31 of his poem, "when will Jerusalem be cleansed from filth so that the Most Merciful can be sanctified in its purification?"[46] For ʿImād al-Dīn the opportunity was now ripe for an assault on Jerusalem. It was essential that Ṣalāḥ

44 Ibn Khallikān, *Wafayāt*, 3:295–299.
45 Abū Shāma, *Kitāb al-Rawḍatayn*, 1:197. ʿImād al-Dīn al-Iṣfahānī, *Kharīdat al-qaṣr*, 1:110.
46 Abū Shāma, *Kitāb al-Rawḍatayn*, 2:241.

al-Dīn's smaller successes be placed in the context of the most anticipated and more pressing matter of Jerusalem. The reconquest is described as the essential *itmām*: the completion of his *jihād*.

> (7) Satisfy yourself [with the conquest of Baalbek] and go forth for the conquest [of Jerusalem] which will surely be a completion of your conquests.[47] (1.30)

'Imād al-Dīn also describes the anticipated reconquest as the *fatḥ al-futūḥ*, the 'conquest of all conquests.' This phrase was also used in his hyperbolic prose, in his reporting of the day of the reconquest as recorded in Abū Shāma's *Kitāb al-Rawḍatayn*.[48] Gabrieli asserts, however, that in this style of writing many of "the concrete details are almost lost in an appalling mass of verbiage."[49] A less cynical approach, one that is more sensitive to the cultural expectations within which the text was composed, allows us to consider the literary qualities and imagery in 'Imād al-Dīn's descriptions and the extent to which it informs us about Muslim self-perceptions and the Muslim view of the Franks by 583/1187. For 'Imād al-Dīn his chronicles and poetry were part of the history he was describing. The words were not doggerel but had a semantic effect that was appreciated by many of his readers and listeners; for them the events described were memorable, vivid, and meaningful. In spite of the rhymed prose in his work, his words were not inexplicable; while it is true that attention to historical detail easily could have been circumvented for the sake of maintaining the finer literary elements, the rhetoric nevertheless may have been well appreciated and understood by his audience and readers; its effect in stirring up emotions was likely to have been considerable in spite of any 'historical' deficiency. More plainly, however, we have to see 'Imād al-Dīn for who he was:

> It is the pen that brings armies together, raises thrones, alarms the confident and gives confidence to the disheartened, raises up the one who stumbles, and causes the upright to stumble, sets the army against the enemy for the benefit of friends. So I gave good news to human lands with my pen and expressed the wonders of events … I grasped the importance of the reconquest of Jerusalem to the Muslim lands and adorned

47 Ibid., 2:245.

48 Ibid., 3:223.

49 Gabrieli, *Arab Historians of the Crusades*, 30.

> it, I explained its merit and clarified it, and I fulfilled the obligation of visiting it.[50]

It was with these words that ʿImād al-Dīn al-Iṣfahānī celebrated the Muslim conquest of Jerusalem on 27 Rajab 583/2 October 1187 – also the anniversary of Prophet Muḥammad's night journey and ascension (*al-isrāʾ wa-l-miʿrāj*). Accentuating the biographer's own importance, self-worth, and indispensable role in the victory, we are given a glimpse of the way in which men of *adab* in this period perceived their own contributions to the events that unfolded around them.

The description of the victory of victories (*fatḥ al-futūḥ*) in his rhymed prose was also used in his poetry, and was understood to represent the penultimate victory surpassing all others:

> (52) Rise for Jerusalem with the *fatḥ al-futūḥ* [victory of victories] in a way that will soothe rancour; and what is the difficulty in it?
> (53) Just ask God to ease the difficulties, because He has power over all things.[51] (1.31)

The great interest in the recovery of Jerusalem following the capture of Edessa can be discerned from subsequent victories against the Franks, events that were seen as promising precursors to the eventual liberation of Jerusalem. Following Nūr al-Dīn's victory at the battle of Inab in 544/1149, in which Prince Raymond of Antioch was killed, it was Jerusalem, and al-Aqṣā Mosque specifically, that was the primary focus of Ibn al-Qaysarānī. Poets frequently wrote their verses following a conquest. The poetry reveals that confidence in Syria was mounting following the victory at Edessa in 538/1144; the prospect of Muslim reprisals began to seem more likely with the recent spate of successes from the battlefields. It is clear from poetry such as this, in which the ideal of *jihād* and the outstanding qualities of its participants are closely intertwined, that the public's emotional attachment to the *jihād* was closely connected to the celebrated *mujāhid* who championed it; the model of *jihād* was thus shaped by its upholder.[52]

---

50 ʿImād al-Dīn al-Iṣfahānī, *al-Fatḥ al-qussī*, 131.

51 Abū Shāma, *Kitāb al-Rawḍatayn*, 2:244.

52 William of Tyre also highlighted the idea that Muslim fear of the Franks was replaced by a new *jihād* spirit after the capture of Edessa: "They ridiculed the shattered strength and broken glory of those who had represented the substantial foundations of the Christians." William of Tyre, *Guillaume de Tyr, Chronique, Édition critique, Corpus Christianorum*

Images of the Franks in Muslim Poetry

Some of the stereotypical imagery in the religious poetry of the crusading period was reminiscent of the style of Islam's fourth-/tenth-century poets, a style inherited from the wars with Byzantium. Whereas Byzantines were referred to as Banū Aṣfar ('pale-faced ones') so too the Franks were branded with this title. Thus it was easy for poets to make good use of al-Mutanabbī's earlier poetry that was anti-Byzantine in nature and infused with calls for *jihād*. The crusaders were still Banū Aṣfar, and the depiction of a struggle between monotheism and polytheism was well used by al-Mutanabbī against the Christian enemy Sayf al-Dawla was contending against. ʿImād al-Dīn al-Iṣfahānī cites some poems composed by ʿAbd al-Munʿim al-Jilyānī in the years preceding the reconquest in 583/1187. In the following line of a much longer poem composed a year before the reconquest, the poet compares the anticipated 'cleansing' of Jerusalem from the Franks to that of the conquest of Mecca by the Prophet in 8/630. In the Prophet's conquest, the pagan idols in and around the Kaʿba were destroyed; the line certainly alludes to the aspirations of the Muslims to remove the Christian symbols and objects of veneration in Jerusalem. Here there is a play on the words *ṣafirat* and Banū Aṣfar:

> When Jerusalem is emptied (*ṣafirat*) of the Banū Aṣfar [pale-faced ones], the scene will supersede that of the older conquest of the Mother of Cities [Mecca].[53] (1.32)

In another poem composed around the same time, al-Jilyānī first welcomes his listeners to consider the word play together with the oft-repeated 'Yūsuf from Egypt' pun. The line draws on the 'Otherness' of the Muslims' enemy; it suggests an entity whose struggle can become a frame of remembrance for the poet's listeners, suggesting a distant, foreign entity whose settlement in Jerusalem was both a sacrilege and an oddity.

> (1) God is the greatest; the land of Jerusalem is emptied (*ṣafirat*) of the Banū Aṣfar [pale-faced ones]
> (2) Those who replace them are children of Yūsuf from Egypt.[54] (1.33)

Continuatio Mediaevalis LXIII, ed. R. B. C. Huygens, H. E. Mayer, and G. Rösch (Turnhout: Brepols, 1986), 1:769.

53 Abū Shāma, *Kitāb al-Rawḍatayn*, 3:261.

54 Ibid., 3:262.

Ṣalāḥ al-Dīn also chose yellow, the Ayyūbids' favoured colour, for his banner. However, yellow, which remained the colour of the Mamlūk regime, is not one of the standard colours used for Islamic symbolism (these are black, green, white, red). The oft-repeated appellation Banū Aṣfar (pale-faced ones) must have seemed ironic with respect to the contrasting colour associations – according to ʿImād al-Dīn the sultan's martial entourage at the reconquest, "his knights, sons, brothers, Mamlūks, commanders, and friends in squadrons ranked according to their merit, in platoons drawn up in solemn cavalcades" were carrying "yellow flags that signalled disaster to the Banū Aṣfar."[55] The matter was picked up by the Damascene poet Fityān al-Shāghūrī (d. 615/1218)[56] following the reconquest of Jerusalem in 583/1187; the pun on yellow and colour imagery is apparent in the line:

(4) His yellow flag leaves for the battlefield and returns red, full of the blood of the Banū Aṣfar [pale-faced ones].
(5) Why didn't the proud kings compromise with him, [especially] since he has ruled over the coasts in [just] three months.[57] (1.34)

In the following poem composed to celebrate the feats of Ṣalāḥ al-Dīn, al-Jilyānī calls on the Banū Aṣfar to renounce their fighting and embrace Islam. He does not, in fact, order them to submit (*aslimū*), but to become monotheists (*waḥḥidū*); he uses his line to play on the superiority of the Islamic creed and to taunt the Franks for their excessive devotion to Jesus, which renders them polytheists. His message fuses the polemic with the conventional rhetoric in the poetry of this type. The poem states that cessation of conflict should herald victory for Islam. Here the poet denotes a twofold affront on the Franks: their defeat is inevitable and the best outcome for them would be to embrace Islam:

O pale-faced ones! Throw away your arms and become monotheists
Otherwise you will be met with fright from the one who took you captive.[58] (1.35)

An important area of discussion in light of pre-reconquest sentiments such as these is the attitudes of Muslims living under Frankish rule. Some of the strongest expressions of dismay about the Muslim subjugation came from

55 ʿImād al-Dīn al-Iṣfahānī, *al-Fatḥ al-qussī*, 120–121.
56 For more information on the poet, see Ibn Khallikān, *Wafayāt*, 4:4–7.
57 Abū Shāma, *Kitāb al-Rawḍatayn*, 3:266.
58 Al-Jilyānī, *Dīwān al-tadbīj*, 92.

the Andalusian pilgrim Ibn Jubayr. His invectives are strongly set against those Muslims who appear to have settled comfortably with the Christians. On his way from Tibnin to Acre in 580/1184 he remarked that Muslims existed with relative autonomy. Other than paying a tax of one dinar and five qirat, "they are not interfered with … their houses and all their effects are left in their full possession." He even notes that the justice afforded to Muslims under Frankish occupation was more than that provided by Muslim governors. He sees it nevertheless as a negative thing, a temptation (*fitna*); it is "one of the misfortunes affecting the Muslims."[59] Historians have relied on this positive description about the treatment of Muslim villagers, though it must also be seen in light of the Frankish strategy to keep the population content enough to prevent internal revolts. Ibn Jubayr was clearly disturbed by the process of assimilation, and was troubled by the indifference and apathy of the community in the face of Frankish subjugation. His most emotive lines concern the continuing plight of Muslim prisoners, "walking in shackles and put to painful labour like slaves. In like condition are the Muslim women prisoners, their legs in iron rings. Hearts are rent for them, but compassion avails nothing."[60] Ibn Jubayr, himself a jurist, speaks with the same kind of indignation as al-Sulamī did in the early years of the 492/1099 conquest of Jerusalem; he is troubled by the same kind of dispiritedness that was a marked feature of post-First Crusade Muslim poetry. Notwithstanding the taxes that were paid by the Muslim population to their rulers before the arrival of the crusaders, sometimes even higher ones, it was the mortification of unbelievers ruling over believers that lay at the heart of his discontent. At the Frankish fortress of Tibnin, "Customs duties are levied on the caravans. They go to the sow known as the Queen, who is the mother of the pig, who is the Lord of Acre – may God destroy it."[61] Here, both Baldwin IV and his mother, Agnes of Courtenay, are pigs (*khinzīr*). His inclusion of a woman is neither altogether surprising nor unwarranted for Ibn Jubayr. In a similar manner, in 587/1191 during the years of the Third Crusade, the renewed crusader interest in Jerusalem was met by the poetic indignation of al-Rashīd b. Nābulsī. His opening line also condemns both mothers and sons:

(1) Woe to the Franks, nay woe to their mothers, is there no one intelligent among them who can take heed?
(2) Consider how many of them you divided after they were gathered, and you then gathered them after their division by striking them.

---

59 Ibn Jubayr, *Travels*, 316–317; Ibn Jubayr, *Tadhkira*, 235–236.
60 Ibid., 241.
61 Ibid., 235.

(3) You made them drink a cup of humiliation many times, so it is not strange for them to commit lewdness since they are weak in intellect.
(4) If they wanted to come to you, then this is ignorance on their part, like the ignorant donkey that approaches the lion in the jungle.
(6) So protect the surroundings of Jerusalem without fear, and of course you are far from any fear and harm.
(7) Jerusalem is noble and it calls you 'al-Muʿtaṣim,' and there is no worrying about the majesty of Jerusalem after this.[62] (1.36)

Though news of the Third Crusade was met with apprehension among the lay population of Syria, it is difficult to discern a disquieting tone in sixth-/twelfth-century poetry related to the events of the crusades. The antithesis of 'gathered' and 'divided' in line 2 draws on the crusaders' subjection to the Muslims' strength, but since we do not know the exact date of the poem's composition it is difficult to surmise the poet's intent in relation to the many events of 587/1191 when the Third Crusade was in its stride. The Third Crusade was hitherto the greatest crusade undertaking. No other crusade saw the participation of the three most powerful rulers of Europe setting out to recover the Holy Land: Emperor Frederick Barbarossa of Germany (r. 1152–90), King Richard I of England (r. 1189–99), and King Philip II Augustus of France (r. 1180–1223). Though we do not know the full extent of the poet's familiarity with what was transpiring with the crusaders, such as their first major setback when Frederick drowned en route in mid 586/1190 and the outbreak of dysentery in Antioch that caused the death of thousands, Muslim sources did, however, comment on the trepidation elicited by the news of the King of England, "he was wise and experienced in warfare and his coming had a dread and frightening effect on the hearts of the Muslims."[63] Ibn al-Athīr considered him "the outstanding man of his time for bravery, cunning, steadfastness and endurance. In him the Muslims were tried by an unparalleled disaster."[64] Yet this fear was not a point of discussion in the poetry. Instead it was public resolve and solidarity that shaped the verses in the unsettling years of renewed crusader interest in Jerusalem. This is partly related to upholding and preserving the reputation of Islam's military leaders; poets were interested in evoking the memory of

62 Abū Shāma, *Kitāb al-Rawḍatayn*, 4:169. For more information on Abū Tammām's famous poem on Amorium, see M. M. Badawī, 'The Function of Rhetoric in Medieval Arabic Poetry: Abū Tammam's Ode on Amorium,' *Journal of Arabic Literature* 9 (1978), 43–56.

63 Ibn Shaddād, *The Rare and Excellent History of Saladin*, trans. Richards, 150.

64 Ibn al-Athīr, *The Chronicle of Ibn al-Athīr*, 2:387.

previous feats to empower the *jihād* spirit. Line 7 is interesting for its mention of the caliph al-Muʿtaṣim (d. 227/842). It seems that the personification of Jerusalem in the line may have been intended to suggest a connection between it and the personified city of Amorium in the ʿAbbāsid poet Abū Tammām's (d. 232/845) popular and celebrated poem, 'The sword is more truthful in tidings than books.' In the poem Amorium is depicted as a mother, a beautiful woman, a virgin, and as a miserly woman, and this image of the city, particularly in line 33 ('And nor are the cheeks, reddened with shyness …') is similar in imagery to line 28 of Ibn al-Khayyāṭ's First Crusade poem above ('And how many young girls have begun to beat their throats and cheeks out of fear').[65] Al-Muʿtaṣim's siege and sack of the city in 223/838 would have been well known to Ibn Nābulsī's audience and the connection between al-Muʿtaṣim and Ṣalāḥ al-Dīn is striking; the idea of the responsibility for the defence of Jerusalem in light of the captive Amorium is a key idea for the poet.

The Merging of Sacred Designations

One of the new developments of the sixth/twelfth century included the works composed by Muslim scholars to extol the virtues of Syria and specifically the city of Damascus. Religious sites in Syria, venerated in such works, acted as a substitute for Muslim devotion during the crusader occupation of Jerusalem, and in particular al-Aqṣā Mosque, and poets in the period around the time of the 583/1187 reconquest drew comparisons between the sanctity of Mecca and that of Jerusalem; they stressed the theme of lost sanctity and the hope that it would be realised through the 'merging' of such sanctities in Muslim consciousness.

Similar to al-Jilyānī's poem above, (1.32) which draws on the similarity between Jerusalem and Mecca, ʿImād al-Dīn al-Iṣfahānī composed one following the reconquest and directed it to the caliph al-Nāṣir li-Dīn Allāh (r. 575–622/1180–1225). What is interesting here is that the poet is careful not to present Ṣalāḥ al-Dīn as a '*nāṣir*' (victor). This is because the caliph had contended the sultan's use of the appellation due to his own namesake, 'al-Nāṣir li-Dīn Allāh' (lit. Victor for the Religion of God), though it was the Fāṭimid caliph in 564/1169 who bestowed the title al-Malik al-Nāṣir on Ṣalāḥ al-Dīn. Subsequently referred to as 'al-Nāṣir' (the Victor) he defended his title in light

65 See A. J. Arberry, *Arabic Poetry: A Primer for Students* (Cambridge: Cambridge University Press, 1965), 50–62.

of his 'uniting' Jerusalem with Mecca.[66] The poem begins by congratulating the caliph: "O leader of the believers, rejoice at the reconquest ..."

> (8) With the conquest of Jerusalem for Islam, the gates have been opened to curb the polytheist tyrant.
> (9) So now that Jerusalem is liberated we are proud that Jerusalem and the Sacred Mosque of Mecca are the same [both free].
> (10) And the Rock [in the Dome of the Rock] and the [Black] Stone that is kissed are now both a prayer niche for people.
> (11) The cross has now been expelled from Jerusalem as the statues and divinations were expelled from Mecca.[67] (1.37)

The religious motifs running through 'Imād al-Dīn al-Iṣfahānī's lines are many and carefully crafted to build on the appositions that the crusades represented for the Muslims. The oxymoronic references in lines 8 and 11 of 'Jerusalem ... polytheist tyrant,' and 'cross ... Mecca' make it appear as though the sacred designations of Jerusalem and Mecca are conjoined by a divine decree, as if the harm that befell the cities was only a preparation for the coming of a greater good; 'cleansing' and 'purifying' becomes necessary to stress that unbelief cannot settle in the two cities. The poet's lines make no attempt to withhold the polytheism (*shirk*) imputed upon the crusaders, rather it suggests that their right to status as 'people of the book' (*ahl al-kitāb*) was suspended during the conflict. The poet also says something about the collective social memory of the Muslims, in so far as his lines reflect their moods and feelings. Namely, the lost sanctity of Jerusalem manifested an incompleteness in the collective sacred domain of its precincts, the completeness of their sanctity requires an affirmation of the Islamic character of the cities as much as it demands a 'negating' (*nafī* – line 11) of 'other' symbols of worship. In his rhythmic prose 'Imād al-Dīn al-Iṣfahānī also connected the holy designations of Mecca and Jerusalem, the ideas from the poem and prose each correspond with one another:

> And Masjid al-Ḥarām was given glad tidings that al-Aqṣā has been liberated, and the Black Stone was congratulated because of the liberation of the White Rock, and the place of revelation [Mecca] was congratulated because of the liberation of the abode of ascent, and the abode of

66 H. Dajani-Shakeel, 'Some Medieval Accounts of Saladin's Recovery of Jerusalem (Al-Quds),' in *Studia Palaestina: Studies in honour of Constantine K. Zurayk*, ed. H. Nashabe (Beirut, 1988), 108.

67 Abū Shāma, *Kitāb al-Rawḍatayn*, 3:235.

> the leader of the messengers and the seal of the prophets was congratulated because of the liberation of the abode of messengers and prophets, and the station (*maqām*) of Ibrāhīm [Abraham] was congratulated because of the liberation of the footprint of the chosen one [the Prophet Muḥammad].[68]

However, his description lacks any references to 'crosses' or 'polytheist tyrants,' rather we can find this in poetry, which as a genre is better suited to emphasise these strong motifs. The description conjoins sites of virtue relevant to Mecca and Jerusalem, and demonstrates an analogous sequence of merits, which are celebrated individually in books of *faḍā'il* of those respective cities but are brought together in celebration of the reconquest. The merits of both cities are iterated and conjoined in the poem to delineate an all-encompassing victory for Islam; the poet reminds his listeners that 'guidance gave life and polytheism caused death' (line 7) – this is the most definitive line in the poem, as it immediately precedes the Mecca/Jerusalem descriptions. These motifs and rhetorical devices could in fact be more important than the whole poem. The antithesis of *hudā* (guidance) and *shirk* (polytheism) in the line is unmistakable and situates the conflict in the Qur'ānic paradigm of truth versus error, and monotheism versus polytheism. This comes through evocatively in post-reconquest poetry as discussed in subsequent sections.

As seen in 'Imād al-Dīn al-Iṣfahānī's aforementioned poem, the poetry draws attention to the meaninglessness of the Christian relic of the cross (line 11). Standing as the symbol of the trinity, Muslim sources emphasise the polytheism (*shirk*) it represents. The theological confrontation in these symbols epitomises the quintessence of the Muslim/crusader struggle; each side legitimised its encounter by underscoring the preponderence of its connection with the sacred, from land, sacred sites, symbols, and personages. This comes across vividly in the descriptions of Sibṭ b. al-Jawzī's account of the siege of Damascus during the Second Crusade in 543/1148. He recounts that "The whole population, men, women, and children, assembled in the Great Mosque and 'Uthmān's Qur'ān was displayed, and the people sprinkled their heads with ashes and wept and humbled themselves. And God heard their prayers."[69]

68 Ibid., 3:222.

69 Sibṭ b. al-Jawzī, *Mir'āt al-zamān*, part 1, 8:198; Ibn Jubayr brings out the spiritual aura associated with 'Uthmān's Qur'ān: "In the east corner of the New Maqsurah, inside the mihrab, is a large cupboard containing one of the Korans of (the Caliph) 'Uthman – may God hold him in His favour. It is the copy (of the definitive recension) which he sent to Syria. This cupboard is opened daily after the prayers, and people seek God's blessings by

It appears that the account of Sibṭ b. al-Jawzī may be an example of a Muslim chronicle working off cultural expectations; in one respect Sibṭ b. al-Jawzī's account of the siege portrays the Christians and Muslims in a similar light, with the priest carrying the holy scriptures before him while the Damascenes display 'Uthmān's Qur'ān.[70] The somewhat hyperbolic description of religious display in the priest's act of bringing together crosses to hang around his neck, the neck of his donkey, and holding others in his hand (all the while setting before him the scriptures) and the subsequent reliance on the Messiah may have been intended to demonstrate the Muslims' scriptural superiority as well as an implicit 'appropriation' of the Messiah. The sight of a "priest with a long beard" was not uncommon to Muslims, whether in their own ranks or among the native Syrians (Arabic-speaking Orthodox Christians), and Sibṭ b. al-Jawzī may have been focusing on such aspects to contest Christian religiosity vis-à-vis the way Christians were considered by Muslims in sixth-/twelfth-century Syria.[71]

Sibṭ b. al-Jawzī's description of Muslim penitence must also be noted; while overt displays of penitence on the Muslim side were certainly not lacking, the sprinkling of ashes does not appear to be customary religious practice.[72] It may, however, say something about the kind of humility that Ibn Rajab al-Ḥanbalī (d. 795/1393) draws upon in his *Faḍl al-ʿilm al-salaf ʿalā ʿilm al-khalaf* when he notes that some of the *salaf* (Muslim predecessors) said: "It is a requirement for the *ʿālim* [scholar] to put dust on his head as a sign of his humility towards his Lord," notwithstanding Sibṭ b. al-Jawzī's possible desire to replicate

touching and kissing the Book; and the press around it is very great." Ibn Jubayr, *Travels*, 279; Ibn Jubayr, *Tadhkira*, 209.

70 For more information on the symbolic value of the Qur'ān and the cross in the Second Crusade see Y. Frenkel, 'The Qur'ān Versus the Cross in the Wake of the Crusade: The Social Function of Dreams and Symbols in Encounters and Conflict (Damascus, July 1148),' *Quaderni di Studi Arabi*, 20–21 (2002–2003), 105–132.

71 "The most numerous group of indigenous Christians was Greek orthodox in confession, but among these a further distinction must be made between the ethnic Greeks of Antioch and the much larger number of Arabic-speaking Orthodox in the Kingdom of Jerusalem itself. Culturally, these Christians were Arab, and scarcely distinguishable in dress and manners from the Muslims; but ethnically they were native to what had once been the Roman provinces of Palestine and Syria. They were Greek Orthodox, but not Greek; Arab-speaking, but not Muslim; Christian inhabitants of a Christian state, yet subject to the rule of conquerors." A. Jotischky, 'Ethnographic Attitudes in the Crusader States: The Franks and the Indigenous Orthodox People,' in *East and West in the Crusader States: Context, Contacts, Confrontations III*, ed. K. Ciggaar and H. Teule (Leuven: Peeters, 2003), 3.

72 Some of the most elaborate displays of penitence can be discerned from the *Riḥla* of Ibn Jubayr. See Ibn Jubayr, *Travels*, 228–229.

descriptions of Christian penitential practice.[73] At this point, one can assert Chamberlain's observation that "where we may never know whether particular people in fact had the 'honour' or 'piety' that a particular source attributed to them, these anecdotes are likely to have been 'true' in the sense that these stories were believed by their contemporaries."[74] Such penitence can also be observed in Sibṭ b. al-Jawzī's participation in a raid on Frankish settlements after a sermon he delivered in Nablus in the summer of 606/1210. There, Sibṭ b. al-Jawzī dramatically awarded al-Muʿaẓẓam ʿĪsā (d. 624/1227) with the hair he had collected from penitents in Damascus; the raid followed.[75] With regard to Sibṭ b. al-Jawzī's description of events during the Second Crusade, it could also be argued that the author was attempting to depict the priest in a humiliating way to dissuade Muslims from cooperating or allying with the Franks, or even from converting to Christianity. It is essential to consider the possibility that chroniclers had such motives, since descriptions of the Franks served indispensable purposes for readers and listeners of Muslim works composed in this period. In light of Sibṭ b. al-Jawzī's depiction, we may consider Ibn al-Athīr's description of an envoy of Yūsuf (an Arab governor of the city of Gabes in Tunis, who was suspected of cooperating with the crusaders to strengthen their positions):[76] The envoy was captured in 541/1147 and brought before Yūsuf, who ordered that he be placed on a camel with a pointed cap and bells tied to his head and be paraded through the streets. The similarities in the descriptions of the two accounts are patent, and both were intended to rouse the Muslim population against the crusaders and against Christianity as a rival religion. The feelings they roused reached their climax at the reconquest of Jerusalem in 583/1187.

This chapter examined the array of early Muslim poetic responses that followed the capture of Jerusalem in 492/1099. Clearly the strength of emotions stems from the suffering, particularly of women and children, that the First Crusade brought with it. The blame, however, is less directed toward the Muslim foe and is instead turned inward toward the *umma*; it focused on the need for self-rectification, to bring to an end the disputes and political

73 Ibn Rajab al-Ḥanbalī, *Faḍl al-ʿilm al-salaf aʿlā ʿilm al-khalaf*, ed. Muḥammad Nāṣir al-ʿAjamī (Beirut: Dār al-Bashāʾir al-Islāmiyya, 2003), 82. There is, however, ample evidence that the clipping of one's *nāṣiya* (forelock) was a symbolic act of penitence. See D. Talmon-Heller, 'Islamic Preaching in Syria during the Counter-Crusade (Twelfth-Thirteenth Centuries),' in *In Laudem Hierosolymitani: Studies in Crusades and Medieval Culture in Honour of Benjamin Z. Kedar*, ed. I. Shagrir, R. Ellenblum, and J. S. C. Riley-Smith (Aldershot: Routledge, 2007), 70–71, and 71 n51.

74 Chamberlain, *Knowledge and Social Practice*, 19.

75 Talmon-Heller, *Islamic Piety*, 133.

76 Ibn al-Athīr, *al-Kāmil fī l-tārīkh*, 9:151–152.

rivalries that had weakened the Muslims of Syria. In line with the purpose of his work, the verses in al-Sulamī's *Kitāb al-Jihād* carry a more patent message of *jihād* and martyrdom. Short poems found a suitable place in his work, augmenting the tone of immediacy that urged Muslims to engage the crusaders in physical struggle.

The shift in the focus of *jihād* over the course of the sixth/twelfth century took shape after the conquest of Edessa in 538/1144, wherein ʿImād al-Dīn Zangī's victory inspired a new optimism in the poetry. Poets stressed the likelihood of recovering Jerusalem from the crusaders. The retinue of poets around Nūr al-Dīn and Ṣalāḥ al-Dīn called on their patrons to liberate the city of Jerusalem and al-Aqṣā Mosque, and began to fashion an image of the Franks (Faranj) as naturally weaker in might and resolve, as misguided Christ-worshippers, and as trinitarian polytheists; yet surprisingly, their women were noted as beautiful and elegant worshippers, at least for Ibn al-Qaysarānī, discussed in chapter 6.

CHAPTER 5

Poeticising the Reconquest and Future Expectations

(19) And this is the year; so honour it.
Unbelief is humiliated and victory has awoken.[1]

In this chapter I bring to light elaborate religious themes in some of the poetic verses composed after the reconquest of Jerusalem that concern the claim of the superiority of Islam. Among the themes are the victory of 'monotheism' over 'polytheism,' the place of al-Aqṣā Mosque in the sanctification of Jerusalem, and the way the reconquest of Jerusalem figured in future Muslim aspirations to conquer Constantinople. Furthermore, in a full translation and commentary of a poem (a declamation of the injustices a traveller witnessed in Alexandria) composed by the Andalusian traveller Ibn Jubayr, in this section I illustrate how the achievements of Ṣalāḥ al-Dīn against the crusaders were used in poetry to encourage the sultan's commitment to justice in other areas.

I describe and identify several poets' recurrent patterns of composition that relate to the sanctity of Jerusalem following the reconquest. Ideas pertaining to prophecies about Islam's triumph in the Holy City are shown, as are contesting religiosities between the Muslims and Franks. I also present depictions of the reconquest as an event comparable to Islam's earlier celebrated victories, and we come to learn that the image of the Holy City and its liberator found a special place in the collective imagination of the Muslims of the Near East.

The Reconquest of Jerusalem and Popular Piety

Ṣalāḥ al-Dīn's commitment to prosecute the *jihād* against the Franks with the definitive goal of recapturing Jerusalem must be attributed, in part, to the strong appeals from his circle of poets. The retinue sought to speak on behalf of a population that had witnessed an increase in focus on *jihād* to liberate Jerusalem and clear *jihād* vocabulary. This is also discernible from the type of *ḥadīth* that figure prominently in books of *faḍāʾil* during this period. It is

1 The Baghdadi poet Abū ʿAlī l-Ḥasan b. ʿAlī l-Juwaynī who congratulated Ṣalāḥ al-Dīn for the recovery of Jerusalem. Abū Shāma, *Kitāb al-Rawḍatayn*, 3:239.

 | DOI 10.1163/9789004345225_006

this focus that gained Ṣalāḥ al-Dīn the support of both religious and military classes and helped to shape his reputation as a champion of the Islamic cause. His avowed objective was the recovery of Jerusalem. Although he figures as an opportunist in his early years, the most determining influence in his later feats and campaigns against the crusaders appears to be his religious conviction. Aḥmad Aḥmad Badawī assembled a list of poets loyal to the cause of the reconquest, men who were supporters of Ṣalāḥ al-Dīn at one time or another who drew on the theme of his religious piety, celebrated his feats, and provided instructional directives through their verse. The collection of poets from Syria, Egypt, and the Arabian Peninsula (Jazira), who were from the secretarial class or embittered refugees, included Sunnīs and Shīʿīs who agreed on the necessity of the recapture of Jerusalem; they must have served as a pressure group and a strong stimulus for the campaigns of the Ayyūbid ruler.[2] The poets were oftentimes travellers from royal courts; they sought payments for their compositions and more importantly, patronage for their work. But they were not all professional poets. Some poets were wandering ascetics and many were scribes, advisers, and ministers of Turkish and Kurdish rulers.[3] Ṣalāḥ al-Dīn's scribe al-Qāḍī l-Fāḍil, his biographer ʿImād al-Dīn al-Iṣfahānī, and tax collector Ibn Mamātī all composed poetry.

Ṣalāḥ al-Dīn's image was very much bolstered by the reconquest. Though he received some criticism, notably from his advisers and from the Zangids, for directing his military efforts against rival Muslims, doubts about his service to the faith were put to rest with the liberation of Jerusalem. Ṣalāḥ al-Dīn was depicted as having been motivated by a desire to restore the *sharīʿa* under the authority of the ʿAbbāsid caliph, and the symbolic sanctifying of the city following the reconquest, the installation of Nūr al-Dīn's *minbar* from Aleppo

2 The list is made up of Usāma b. Munqidh, ʿImād al-Dīn al-Iṣfahānī, Ibn al-Harāwī, Ibn Qalāqis, al-Ḥakīm ʿAbd al-Munʿim al-Jilyānī, Ḥassān al-ʿArqala, al-Mahdhab b. Asʿad b. al-Dahhān al-Musulī, ʿAlam al-Dīn al-Shātanī, Maḥmūd b. al-Ḥasan b. Nabahān al-ʿIrāqī, al-Rashīd b. Badr al-Nābulsī, Ibn Zakī l-Dīn, Sibṭ b. al-Taʾāwīdhī, Ibn al-Saʿātī, Muwaffaq al-Dīn al-Irbilī, ʿUmāra al-Yamanī, Muḥammad b. Ismāʿīl al-Khayranī, Wahīsh al-Asadī, Ibn Saʿdān al-Ḥalabī, Saʿīd al-Ḥalabī, Saʿāda al-Aʿmā, al-Bahāʾ al-Sinjarī, al-Asʿad b. Mamātī, Ibn Jubayr, Nashwu al-Dawla Aḥmad al-Dimashqī, Ibn al-Athīr, Muḥammad b. Sulṭān b. al-Khaṭṭāb, Ibn Sanāʾ al-Mulk, Abū l-Faḍl b. Ḥamīd, Yūsuf al-Baraʾī, Saʿīd b. Muḥammad al-Harīrī, Abū Tayy al-Najjār, al-Qāḍī l-Fāḍil, Yūsuf b. al-Ḥusayn b. al-Mujāwir, al-Ḥasan b. ʿAlī l-Jawwīnī, Muḥammad b. Asʿad b. ʿAlī l-Jawānī, al-Ḥusayn b. ʿAbdallāh b. Rawāha, ʿAlī b. al-Mubārak b. al-Zāhida, Muḥammad b. Hibat Allāh al-Baramkī, ʿAlī b. Aḥmad b. al-Zubayr, Muḥammad b. Muḥammad b. al-Farrāsh, Abū Ṭālib b. al-Khashshāb, ʿUmar b. Muḥammad b. al-Shiḥna, Aḥmad b. ʿAlī b. Zanbūr, ʿAlī b. Mafraj, Abū l-Faḍl b. Ḥamīd al-Ḥalabī, ʿAlam al-Dīn al-Sakhāwī, Rashīd al-Dīn al-Fāriqī, Ibn Dhihn al-Musulī, Taqī l-Dīn ʿUmar b. Shāhnshāh. See Badawī, *al-Ḥayāt al-adabiyya*, 434–437.

3 Hillenbrand, '*Jihad* Poetry,' 18.

in al-Aqṣā Mosque, the selection of Ibn al-Zakī as the *khaṭīb* for the first Friday prayer, the sprinkling of rose water, and the purification of the mosque all played a major role in his public image as Islam's victor.

Following the reconquest Ṣalāḥ al-Dīn came to be depicted by his poets as the quintessence of Islam. This is suggested through the poet's use of contrasting light imagery (with darkness (*aẓlama*) and the sun (*shams*)) in the following poem, where the antithesis of light and dark stresses his religious commitment and elaborate purpose in fulfilling and serving the religion:

(12) So if the light of Islam is darkened then what comes from you
Will be like the sun to brighten it. (1.38)

Depicted by al-Jilyānī as a protector of the faith, instructed to 'fight the party of polytheism' (line 8), the crusaders' reversal of fortune comes to light through the poet's incisive play on words, in which the captive Prophet Yūsuf (Joseph), representing Ṣalāḥ al-Dīn, whose name was also Yūsuf, finds himself in a position to imprison the crusaders.

(29) And the Franks are either imprisoned or slain
And with this Yūsuf has disgraced them.[4] (1.39)

Ṣalāḥ al-Dīn's reconquest was described by the same poet as being a 'sudden' (*bāghitan*) attack,[5] the same word (*baghtatan*) appears at least six times in the Qur'ān in reference to the coming of the Last Day or divine punishment. His sudden and concerted attack with an army so large 'the tents could not be seen' (line 32) took place while the 'Franks in Jerusalem were venerating the cross (*ṣallabū*)' (line 32). The suddenness of divine reckoning is forcefully evoked in the Qur'ān: 'Nay, it may come to them all of a sudden and confound them: no power will they have to avert it, nor will they [then] get respite' (21:40). Elsewhere al-Jilyānī presents Ṣalāḥ al-Dīn in a similar light – as a victor aided by the divine to usher in Islam's ascendancy in Jerusalem. The repetitious use of similar motifs reveals precisely what the poet wanted his listeners to register about the sultan, the Ayyūbid House, Jerusalem, and the crusaders. We must not ignore, however, the underlying theological issues at play in his lines. Since theologians were normally present in the poet's audiences, the Qur'ānic imagery of 'early morning' and '*baghtatan*' would have made good sense to his listeners and moved them to consider the religious implications; the reconquest could be seen as a divinely ordained accomplishment bound by a time

4 Al-Jilyānī, *Dīwān al-tadbīj*, 94–95.

5 Ibid., 96.

frame that has religious associations; the Qur'ānic references to 'early morning' and 'sudden attack' usually appear in relation to a time of respite afforded to wrongdoers before God's punishment proceeds.

> In the early morning his sudden attack stunned the *mushrikīn* [polytheists]
> Travelling the entire night, his aim was to save Jerusalem. (14)[6] (1.40)

The line evokes Ṣalāḥ al-Dīn's unrelenting pursuit to expunge the crusaders from Jerusalem, here his commitment to the *jihād* is comparable to the sentiments espoused in 'Imād al-Dīn al-Iṣfahānī's *rubā'iyyāt* for Nūr al-Dīn, cited later. The crusaders are unequivocally cast as polytheists, twice in the space of a few lines, wherein in line 12 the sultan is defeating 'polytheism' (*shirk*) and in line 14 the 'polytheists' (*mushrikīn*) are outdone by his attack.

> And Ṣalāḥ al-Dīn rose up to annihilate the *shirk* [polytheism]
> With the collars at the necks of the kings becoming the blades of his swords. (12)[7] (1.41)

Al-Jilyānī's line here is remarkably direct. The presence of Christians, their displays and symbols were patently 'polytheism' and in the poem Ṣalāḥ al-Dīn's *jihād* is validated by descriptions that amalgamate the crusaders into a single polytheistic entity. In another of al-Jilyānī's post-reconquest poems, he celebrates the "Misfortune to the party of polytheism in Syria/A bird whose wing you cut at al-Aqṣā, a power that you shattered."[8] The validity of the *jihād* is suggested through the unequivocality of the enemy, characterised most strikingly by polytheism (*shirk*); the directness of his description could also be used to exonerate Ṣalāḥ al-Dīn from the causes that brought his previous actions into question – warring against his co-religionists instead of diverting his attention to the crusaders. In a poem he presented directly to Ṣalāḥ al-Dīn al-Jilyānī ingeniously used the word *yuwaḥḥid* (unite) to suggest a united crusader front; but the word also intimates the theological 'unity of God' and is juxtaposed with polytheism (*shirk*) in a double entendre that could be easily picked up by the listener:

> The people of polytheism united together
> And the priests of the trinity are frightened.[9] (7) (1.42)

6 Ibid., 91.

7 Ibid., 90.

8 Abū Shāma, *Kitāb al-Rawḍatayn*, 3:261.

9 Ibid., 3:262.

In this poem the word 'frightened' (*yarhabu*) in line 7 is juxtaposed with the word for 'affectionate' (*ḥusbān*) in the concluding line 9, where it describes an attribute of Ṣalāḥ al-Dīn's kingship and reflects the positive mood the poet believed encompassed the city of Jerusalem. The words 'frightened' (*yarhabu*) and 'priests' (*ruhbān*) is also a sharp play on words emphasizing the fear of the Christian clergy.

The victory at the battle of Ḥaṭṭīn provided poets with a great opportunity to extol Ṣalāḥ al-Dīn in light of the expected reconquest of Jerusalem. It was his climactic moment. Having amassed an army of around thirty thousand men from Syria, Egypt, and Iraq, an army so varied that communication between them was likely severely encumbered due to the multiple languages they spoke, Ṣalāḥ al-Dīn knew that such a loyal and diverse array of fighters would not be gathered again. In the events leading up to the battle it was the fatal decision of the King of Jerusalem, Guy de Lusignan, to direct his army to the village of Ḥaṭṭīn on 25 Rabīʿ II 583/4 July 1187 that blocked any progress the crusaders could have made. Engulfed by smoke from scrub fires that Salah al-Din instructed his men to light, cut off from water, and facing a larger and less fatigued force that saw the potential recovery of Jerusalem in their sights, the crusaders were forced to surrender.

ʿImād al-Dīn al-Iṣfahānī wrote many poems about the victory at Ḥaṭṭīn. Poets used the occasion to stress the superiority of Islam and degrade Christianity. ʿImād al-Dīn's tone is unequivocal, 'I saw on that day that the greatness of unbelief was humiliated' (2);[10] 'His sword is dripped in the blood of a people who are still dripping in unbelief' (7);[11] in the second hemistich of verse 8 we read that 'the filth from their house of unbelief has been swept away.'[12] Imputing unbelief to the crusaders is a familiar theme that runs through the poetry regularly; the most obvious differentiation between the two camps was the Otherness of the Faranj and the dichotomous motifs of guidance/misguidance, faith/unbelief, and monotheism/polytheism. In a poem composed by Fityān al-Shāghūrī, Ṣalāḥ al-Dīn's state of humbleness is set against the crusader arrogance and is implied as the cause for his victory. The poet declaims: 'Because you were humble before God the dominion of arrogance is now destroyed' (13);[13] he thus presents the sultan as outdoing the crusaders on both military and ethical terms. The Damascene litterateur Ibn al-Sāʿātī (d. 604/1209) wrote lines congratulating the sultan for the defeat of the crusaders at Tiberias, stating that 'your great determination glorified the clear conquest, and the

10 Ibid., 3:193.

11 Ibid., 3:194.

12 Ibid.

13 Ibid., 3:196.

believers' eyes were thus cooled' (1).[14] Line 4 appears then to provide the reason God's munificence descended on him; while al-Shāghūrī noted humbleness as the sultan's worthy attribute, Ibn al-Sāʿātī focuses on what differentiated him from other fighters, namely his genuine commitment to the religion: 'Every other king fights pretentiously but you fight your enemies for the sake of the religion' (4).[15] In the battle of Ḥaṭṭīn the capture of the True Cross[16] was a joyous success for the Muslim forces. It was Ṣalāḥ al-Dīn's nephew Ṭaqī l-Dīn who led the battle to capture the cross, protected in part by the bishops of Acre and Lydda. In spite of their unyielding commitment to protect the cross, the bishops were killed one after the other until Ṭaqī l-Dīn seized the prized relic. In line 3 Ibn al-Sāʿātī mentions the seizing of the cross: 'Capturing the cross was easy for you and you proceeded, it was of course difficult for the best of men to simplify such a task' (3).[17] Here, what the line leaves out is most telling. Aside from providing us with this nugget of factual information, for the poet the True Cross is simply *al-ṣalīb* (the cross) and is given no added reverential significance, similar to Ibn al-Qaysarānī's poem following the conquest of Edessa approaching Christmas Eve of 538/1144, in which he simply mentions 'ibn Maryam' (son of Mary) rather than satirising the Franks for their false belief, as detailed in chapter 4.[18] The poet wanted to remind his listeners that the 'True Cross' is simply a cross that was 'easily' seized, though the verb *hāna* could mean both 'to become easy' as well as 'to be despicable.' The *double entendre* thus encapsulates both meanings in the line. In the same poem the sense of collective happiness of the Muslims is expressed, 'So O God, how many hearts were pleased, and O God, how many eyes shed tears [of happiness] (6),[19] and in the first hemistich of line 29 we learn that it is of course 'the heart of Jerusalem that also finds joy' (29)[20] (1.43–1.51).

Another poetic interest in the reconquest of Jerusalem is one that relates to prophecy and Qurʾānic hermeneutics. In this regard Abū Shāma relates an incident in which he was informed by the Aleppan al-Rukn b. Jahbal al-ʿAdl that the respected jurist Majd al-Dīn b. Jahbal al-Shāfiʿī,[21] also from Aleppo,

14 Ibid.

15 Ibid.

16 Believed to have been the cross upon which Jesus Christ was believed by Christians to have been crucified. What was captured was actually a cross upon which a sliver of the original cross was attached.

17 Abū Shāma, *Kitāb al-Rawḍatayn*, 3:196.

18 The city was taken at dawn on 26 Jumāda II 539/23 December 1144.

19 Abū Shāma, *Kitāb al-Rawḍatayn*.

20 Ibid., 3:197.

21 For more information on Ibn Jahbal see ʿA. J. Ḥ. ʿAbd al-Mahdī, *al-Madāris fī bayt al-maqdis fī l-ʿaṣrayn al-Ayyūbī wa-l-Mamlūki* (Amman: Maktaba al-Aqṣā, 1981), 1:203–205;

came across a commentary (*tafsīr*) of the Qurʾān written by Abū l-Ḥakam al-Maghribī (better known as Ibn Barrajān). Ibn Barrajān commentary on the first verses of *Sūra Rūm* revealed that he believed that the Rūm would be defeated in the month of Rajab 583/October 1187. Majd al-Dīn b. Jahbal was reported to have read in the commentary on *Sūra Rūm* that "The Rūm will be defeated in Rajab 583 [1187], and then Jerusalem will be liberated and will remain in the abode of Islam (*dār al-Islām*) forever."[22] We should not be entirely sceptical about the information in this *tafsīr*; the *tafsīr*s of Abū ʿAlī l-Ṭabarsī (d. 548/1153) and Abū Ḥayyān al-Andalusī (d. 745/1344) have survived and also provide similar interpretations that relate the chapter to the crusader occupation. Again, the emphatic tone of Ibn Barrajān's commentary and his belief that Jerusalem would remain permanently under Islamic rule is not out of the ordinary.[23] In his eighth-/fourteenth-century *jihād* treatise *al-Ijtihād fī ṭalab al-jihād* [The book of assiduous pursuit of *jihād*] Ibn Kathīr, also a commentator of the Qurʾān, shares the same conviction.[24] According to Abū Shāma, when Ṣalāḥ al-Dīn captured Aleppo in 579/1183, Ibn Jahbal had written his prophecy on a note that he requested be given to the sultan. The jurist entrusted with delivering the letter instead chose not to because of its spurious nature; however, upon learning of the prophecy, and having faith in the scholarly standing of Ibn Barrajān, the *qāḍī* of Aleppo Muḥyī l-Dīn b. al-Zakī composed his own poem when Ṣalāḥ al-Dīn captured Aleppo in Ṣafar 579/June 1183:

> Your conquest of Aleppo with the sword in Ṣafar is a sign of your conquering Jerusalem in Rajab.[25] (1.52)

Sure enough, when Jerusalem was recaptured in Rajab 583/September 1187 Ibn Jahbal reminded Ṣalāḥ al-Dīn about the letter that he was supposed to have received, but Ibn al-Zakī's aforementioned poem was viewed by the sultan as an earlier prophecy, and Ibn Jahbal's was seen as a kind of *vaticinium ex eventu*. Yet Ibn Jahbal was not entirely deprived of the sultan's favours and

---

al-Nuʿaymī, *al-Dāris fī Tārīkh al-madāris*, 1:230–232.

22 Abū Shāma, *Kitāb al-Rawḍatayn*, 3:111.

23 See G. Bowering and Y. Casewit (eds.), *A Qur'an Commentary by Ibn Barrjan of Seville (d. 536/1141) Idah al-Hikma bi-Ahkam al-ʿIbra* (Wisdom Deciphered, the Unseen Discovered) (Texts and Studies on the Qur'an) (Leiden: Brill, 2015); for an insightful discussion on Ibn Barrajān and his understanding of *dawāʾir al-taqdīr* (cyclical spheres causing the determination of events), and his hermeneutical approach to the Qurʾān in relation to the future of Jerusalem, see Jose Bellver, 'Ibn Barrağān and Ibn ʿArabī on the Prediction of the Capture of Jerusalem in 583/1187 by Saladin,' *Arabica* 61 (2014), 252–286.

24 Ibn Kathīr, 'Kitāb al-ijtihād fī ṭalab al-jihād,' 413–436.

25 Abū Shāma, *Kitāb al-Rawḍatayn*, 3:111.

was afforded a high position as a teacher in the Dome of the Rock.[26] Ibn al-Zakī, on the other hand, went on to achieve more celebrated acclaim as the *khaṭīb* in al-Aqṣā Mosque on the first Friday prayer following the reconquest. Notwithstanding Ibn al-Zakī's scholarly status, it is plausible that his poem of 579/1183, in which he foretold the events, helped to secure his later role. We know that Ibn Barrajān's teaching in the Dome of the Rock was a result of his *tafsīr*-based prophecy and we may also interpret Ibn al-Zakī's position in al-Aqṣā Mosque in light of the same.

The Sanctification of Spaces

The mosque in the medieval Islamic world held a central place. The public *adhān* from the hundreds of mosques throughout Syria announced, firstly, the call to prayer; private devotion was thus regulated by the time of the day and the mosque was an important medium through which Muslims understood their relationship with the divine. Prayer times were also often used as indicators of other daily times, events occurred 'between the two prayers' or 'after' or 'before' a particular prayer. Further to this, the space of the mosque was also used to make important announcements, such as the arrival of a prestigious scholar or the appointment of a new judge. Aside from individual private devotion, the five fixed daily prayers in the mosque were communal, and the appointment of *imāms* and mosque administrators provided social roles for the faithful. Public readings (*samāʿāt*) were sometimes held in the mosque, as were *ḥadīth* classes and gatherings to recite the Qurʾān. While the epithet *bayt Allāh* (house of God) was used for all mosques, the Masjid al-Ḥarām (the sanctified mosque) or Kaʿba was accorded a prime designation of holiness, followed by the Masjid al-Nabī (the Prophet's mosque) and then Masjid al-Aqṣā (al-Aqṣā Mosque), and of course, the Masjid al-Umawī (the Umayyad Mosque) was afforded a noteworthy position, particularly since the city of Damascus became a kind of spiritual substitute for Jerusalem during the crusader occupation of the holy city. The number of mosques in Syria alone was sizeable. The effect of *faḍāʾil al-Quds* literature and its propagandistic role for the anti-Frankish *jihād* may be discerned from the sentiments expressed by the Muslim population when they learned of the impending victory. Although Ibn Shaddād began writing after the reconquest, he related that when Ṣalāḥ al-Dīn's intention to head for Jerusalem became known, "the ulema from Egypt and Syria made

26 Ibid.

their way to him, so much so that no-one of any note failed to be present."[27] It is likely that the desire to don the *iḥrām* (pilgrim's garb) and begin their pilgrimage from Jerusalem served as a strong motivation and the religious virtue that would accompany such a practice is cited in several books of *faḍā'il*. In the text of the mid fifth-/eleventh-century Abū l-Maʿālī l-Musharraf Ibn al-Murajja, who lived in Jerusalem, we find the following traditions:

> Whoever begins the *ḥajj* or *ʿumra* to the Sanctified Mosque from al-Aqṣā Mosque, his past sins are forgiven, or paradise is incumbent on him.[28]
> Whoever dons the *iḥrām* from Jerusalem, his journey is forgiveness for him.[29]

Here al-Aqṣā Mosque carries a specific worthiness, aside from the general sanctity accorded to the mosque, the practice of donning one's *iḥrām* from the mosque became contextually relevant in the heightened climate of the crusades. Abū l-Faraj b. al-Jawzī also accentuates the importance of the practice in the penultimate chapter of his *faḍā'il* work entitled, 'The reward for *ihlāl* [calling aloud with *talbiya* – proclamation for *ḥajj*] from Jerusalem.'[30] Clearly, Jerusalem and the city of Mecca were closely linked in the religious outlook of the Muslim population. Authors of *faḍā'il* works were sure to include traditions pertaining to the figurative sense of the 'subservience' of Mecca toward Jerusalem; al-Wāsiṭī, for example, cites a tradition explaining that "The Last Hour will not come until the holy sanctuary of Mecca visits Jerusalem."[31] The cosmological relationship shared by Mecca and Jerusalem is drawn upon vividly in *faḍā'il* literature. The two precincts share an earthly significance as well as a heavenly one; "the parallel systems of Mecca and Jerusalem reflect an attempt to elicit identical holy elements."[32]

This idea of linking Jerusalem to Mecca can also be discerned from the words of Ṣalāḥ al-Dīn when he defended his usage of the title 'al-Malik al-Nāṣir,'

27 Ibn Shaddād, *The Rare and Excellent History of Saladin*, 78.

28 Ibn al-Murajjā, *Faḍā'il bayt al-maqdis* (Beirut, 2002), 211.

29 Ibid., 212.

30 The manuscript that the editor of the work, Jibra'il S. Jabbūr, relied on contains only fifteen out of the seventeen chapters that Ibn al-Jawzī wrote. The author nevertheless listed his chapter headings in his introduction. Ibn al-Jawzī, *Faḍā'il al-Quds*, ed. Jibra'il S. Jabbūr (Beirut: Dār al-Afaq al-Jadīda, 1979), 63–65.

31 Al-Wāsiṭī, *Faḍā'il al-bayt al-muqaddas*, ed. Isaac Hasson (Jerusalem: Hebrew University of Jerusalem, 1979), 92–93.

32 O. Livne-Kafri, 'Jerusalem: The Navel of the Earth in Muslim Tradition,' *Der Islam* 84 (2007), 71.

which became the title of the caliph, al-Nāṣir li-Dīn Allāh (r. 575–622/1180–1225). The caliph reproached Ṣalāḥ al-Dīn for his use of the title, but the latter had of course earned it in 564/1169, long before al-Nāṣir became caliph and chose this title. ʿImād al-Dīn al-Iṣfahānī reported a conversation with Ṣalāḥ al-Dīn on this question and quotes him as having said, somewhat cynically: "Did I not recover Bayt al-Maqdis [Jerusalem] and unite it with al-Bayt al-Ḥarām [the noble sanctuary]. Indeed, I have returned to the native land a part that had been missing from it."[33]

In ʿImād al-Dīn's elegy (*rithāʾ*) for Ṣalāḥ al-Dīn, he shows the connections once again between the holy sites wherein Ṣalāḥ al-Dīn's persona is depicted as a marked feature of Jerusalem's sacredness.

> (28) And as usual the *bayt al-ḥaram* feels sorrow for the *bayt al-muqaddas*; indeed so does its ʿArafa.[34] (1.53)

The tone of euphoria in Muslim poetry following the recapture of the city in 583/1187 was thus connected to the retransformation of the mosques which saw the restoration of Muslim monuments which in turn symbolised the superiority of Islam over Christianity. Such elaborate themes are found in a poem composed by al-Rashīd b. Nābulsī following the reconquest. This poet from Nablus, like other poets, magnifies the victory, comparing the newly 'Islamised' Jerusalem to what was believed to have been defiled by the crusaders. Following years of fear and uncertainty, the poet relates the peace now present in the hearts and minds of the Muslims:

> (1) O the happiness of Jerusalem which woke with the unfurling of the flag of Islam, after it had been folded.
> (2) O the light of al-Aqṣā, how it now rises with verses and chapters [of the Qurʾān] after having the cross inside it.[35] (1.54)

Here we can understand the importance of the Qurʾān in relation to the sanctity of al-Aqṣā Mosque. Interestingly, in verse 6 the Qurʾān is not set against the Bible. Certainly the Muslims were not unaware of the importance of scripture in Christianity, since polemical treatises authored in the seventh/thirteenth and eighth/fourteenth centuries demonstrate a familiarity and perceptive-

33 ʿImād al-Dīn al-Iṣfahānī, *al-Fatḥ al-qussī*, 185.

34 Abū Shāma, *Kitāb al-Rawḍatayn*, 4:218.

35 Ibid., 3:264.

ness of the contrasting theologies and scriptural assertions.[36] Furthermore, in Islamic medieval legal thought the place of the Bible has been considered in some detail and it would not be unusual for the Muslim attitude toward Christian scripture to be shaped by juristic rulings during the period. In this regard the sixth-/twelfth-century Damascus-based Ḥanbalī jurist Ibn Qudāma al-Maqdisī (541–620/1146–1223), who wrote a Ḥanbalī legal textbook *al-Kāfī fī fiqh al-Imām Aḥmad b. Ḥanbal*, includes a discussion in his section on *jihād* concerning what should be done about the 'books of unbelief.' He says,

> whoever finds a book that contains unbelief (*kufr*) must destroy it because reading and examining it is disobedience. For example the Torah and the Gospel should be destroyed because they have been altered and abrogated [by the revelation of the Qur'ān] and it is forbidden to read them. If it is possible, then benefit from their covers or the pages when washed. Whoever finds alcohol must discard it because consuming it is a sin, and whoever finds a pig should kill it.[37]

Bringing together the topic of Christian scripture with alcohol and pigs is not entirely inadvertent, and perhaps an anti-Christian and anti-Frankish motive inspired his selection of impure items such that he included them in his chapter of *jihād*. In the poem above, the poet meant to show the superiority of the Qur'ān and the possibility that the Muslims would retake the mosque. The Muslim reading of the Qur'ān was the most oft-repeated ritual after the prayer and the poet argued for the replacement of the cross with the Qur'ān as a way to emphasise the necessity of the reconquest. This point is corroborated in a poem by Muḥammad al-Mujāwir composed after Frederick II took Jerusalem in 626/1229. Although the Muslims actually kept control of al-Aqṣā Mosque, the poet describes how the mosque lost one of its most definitive characteristics. The poet laments:

> (14) [Al-Aqṣā] is now empty of the prayer which is performed by one who is not saddened, but who recites verses and chapters with pleasure.[38] (1.55)

---

36 See, for example, Ibn Taymiyya, *al-Jawāb al-ṣaḥīḥ li-man baddala dīn al-Masīḥ*, ed. ʿAlī b. Ḥasan b. Nāṣir, ʿAbd al-ʿAzīz b. Ibrāhīm al-ʿAskar, and Ḥamdān b. Muḥammad al-Ḥamdān (Riyadh: Dār al-ʿĀṣima, 1993–94).

37 Ibn Qudāma al-Maqdisī, *al-Kāfī fī fiqh al-Imām Aḥmad b. Ḥanbal* (Beirut: Dār Ibn Ḥazm, 2003), 902.

38 Abū Shāma, *Kitāb al-Rawḍatayn*, 4:196.

Following the reconquest, ʿImād al-Dīn al-Iṣfahānī records Ṣalāḥ al-Dīn bewailing the dearth of worship in Jerusalem during the occupation; the Muslims were thus obliged to 'resanctify' the city through the institution of worship at its holy precincts: "For Jerusalem has been controlled by the enemy for ninety-one years, during which time God has received nothing from us here in the way of adoration."[39] Here we reintroduce a salient point in relation to the cosmological role of al-Aqṣā Mosque, the Dome of the Rock, and Jerusalem more generally; a point that stems from the Islamic notion of sanctity as elucidated in books of *faḍāʾil*. The idea that "chapters" and "verses" of the Qurʾān were an identifiable replacement for the Christian cross and worship fits into a broader conceptualisation of the 'purpose of space' as understood in the Islamic discourse. Both Christians and Muslims vied for divine preference insomuch as both believed that sacred space should not be occupied by the unholy, unclean, and undeserving. Therefore, Jerusalem, al-Quds, literally 'the holy,' must not be under the control of unbelievers who occupy "the awkwardly marginal position that is never in concordance with the order of things."[40] Akkach explains the point quite lucidly:

> the site, originally designated for Islam, could only tolerate an architecture that facilitates spatial practices that are in harmony with the Islamic creed of absolute unity … It is a determinedly Islamic version of geopolitics wherein God, along with the Muslims, acts as a central figure in the plotting, unfolding, and staging of events.[41]

According to Abū ʿAlī l-Ḥasan b. ʿAlī l-Juwaynī,

> (15) If this conquest was in the time of the Prophet then there would have been verses and Qurʾān revealed for it.[42] (1.56)

A poem composed by the Andalusian poet al-Jilyānī following the reconquest further complements this idea; the poem is unique for its profuse religious imagery. It complements the idea put forth by Ṣalāḥ al-Dīn's retinue of poets, who depicted him and the reconquest of Jerusalem as unprecedented events that were shaped by a divine design that secured Jerusalem's role in the narrative of the events of the end time. The religious class of preachers, *imāms*, scholars,

39 ʿImād al-Dīn al-Iṣfahānī, *al-Fatḥ al-qussī*, 122.

40 Akkach, *Cosmology and Architecture*, 168.

41 Ibid.

42 Abū Shāma, *Kitāb al-Rawḍatayn*, 3:239.

and *madrasa* teachers who comprised the poets' audiences would have approved of the religious imagery in the poetry but it is doubtful that the troops, who consisted of multiple ethnicities, would have understood or appreciated the nuances of the language. This notwithstanding, they would have had a familiarity with the well known vocabulary and Qur'ānic allusions, or simply with the fiery or melancholic tone which would have enabled them to relate to the poem's intent and the poetic tone. Al-Jilyānī marvels at "the way of goodness [which] took you from one end to the other; so we are in a time like that of the companions."[43] The poet draws on Islam's illustrious predecessors. Ṣalāḥ al-Dīn shares in the glory and feats of ʿUmar, Abu ʿUbayda, al-Ṣiddīq (Abū Bakr), ʿUthmān, ʿAlī, Yūsuf (the Prophet Joseph) and he concludes his poem by highlighting the "pride for this religion, as if you are in the time of prophethood."[44] The poet emphasises the sultan's religious qualities and also asserts his own status as the worthy recipient of a virtuous patron. Here we must stress the poem's partisan aspect: it incorporates the names of Islam's early caliphs, al-Ṣiddīq (Abū Bakr, d. 13/634), ʿUmar (d. 23/644), ʿUthmān (d. 35/656), and ʿAlī b. Abī Ṭālib (d. 40/661), who are celebrated in Sunnī Islam as the legitimate and honoured vicegerents of the Prophet Muḥammad. By contrast, the first three caliphs were criticised by the Shīʿīs; thus we must remember the theological positions inherent in referring to Ṣalāḥ al-Dīn in light of Sunnī Islam's earliest caliphs. By using the occasion of the reconquest to herald a victory for Sunnī Islam, the poet buttressed the grounds for the Sunnī revival which began well before the arrival of the crusaders, and part of which drew on the threat of Shīʿīs as a divisive and weakening element in the Muslim *umma*. This, together with the crusader threat, were the central components of the unified *jihād* theory espoused by Nūr al-Dīn and later the Ayyūbids, and Mamlūks.

This point is further illustrated by a poem composed by the Egyptian poet Ibn Sanāʾ al-Mulk (d. 608/1211), who held a high status in Egypt and Syria for his mastery of the Arabic language.[45] He was most renowned for his *muwashshaḥ* poetry, a five-stanza composition that had its roots in fifth-/eleventh-century al-Andalus. In the celebratory poem for Ṣalāḥ al-Dīn, Ibn Sanāʾ even incorporates in his lines the image of the angel Gabriel, to demonstrate the restoration of Islamic order to the Holy City. The line may be understood in light of Gabriel's role as the angel of divine revelation, and the great number of prophets that were related to the Holy Land:

---

43 Ibid., 3:235.

44 Ibid., 3:235–236.

45 See O. Zwartjes, *Love Songs from al-Andalus: History, Structure, and Meaning of the Kharja* (Leiden: Brill, 1997), 47–54.

(6) You gave life to it after it had died, and then you freed it after it was a captive.

(9) Gabriel yearned for his house [Bayt al-Maqdis], and his house yearned for him, so he came to it with a longing and a yearning.[46] (1.57)

The idea of the reconquest heralding a 'restoration' is emphasised with the mention of Gabriel, bringing to light a new epoch for the Holy City, a joining of earthly and heavenly celestial realms. Gabriel's yearning is the yearning of the collective body of Muslims; the verse suggests not only a divine validation of the victory but advances the repute of Ṣalāḥ al-Dīn for acting out the divine will of God, for acting as a medium entrusted to restore the natural order of things. In this, his legitimacy as a sultan, as a champion of *jihād* of the Ayyūbid house was not to be questioned. The shift of political power and religious hegemony in Jerusalem after the capture of Jerusalem in 492/1099 created a religious flux unparalleled in Islam's historical connection to the Holy City. The presence of Christian symbols in Jerusalem from 492/1099 to 587/1187 took on a new and ominous character because they had engulfed a sacred Muslim site. It was, of course, al-Aqṣā Mosque that aroused the strongest emotions, in a way comparable to the imagery denoting the captivity of the Holy Sepulchre that was used to bolster preaching for the crusades, and poets and chroniclers tried to accentuate these issues in the religious psychology of the Muslims in order to push them for a collective reaction.[47]

Lastly, in light of the positive expectations after the reconquest we should consider the kind of sentiments voiced in the first Friday sermon after the reconquest of Jerusalem. The sermon provides us with some powerful examples of the *jihād*-based emotions that Ibn al-Zakī (d. 598/1202) attempted to arouse among a congregation that had lived under the Frankish occupation of the city and participated in the *jihād* against them. The sermon was, of course, designed to highlight the heralding of a new stage in the history of the Holy Land, specifically the victory of the *umma* against her enemies. Without doubt Ṣalāḥ al-Dīn's entrance into Jerusalem was staged by Muslim scholars in a form intended to compare or compete with that of the caliph 'Umar's initial Muslim conquest of the city.

46 Ibn Sanā' al-Mulk, *Dīwān ibn Sanā' al-Mulk*, ed. Muḥammad Ibrāhīm Naṣr (Cairo: Wizārat al-Thaqāfa, 1969), 2:340.

47 See the reference to '*matrem aecclesiarum aecclesiam*' in Guibert de Nogent, *Dei Gesta Per Francos*, 113, and '*Mater ecclesia*' in C. W. David (ed. and trans.), *De Expugnatione Lyxbonensi: The Conquest of Lisbon* (New York: Columbia University Press, 2001), 79.

Similar to the ideas expressed in Ibn al-Zakī's sermon, Muslim poets of the period were also eager to depict the reconquest as one that could not have been won without divine approval and heavenly assistance. Abū ʿAlī l-Ḥasan b. ʿAlī l-Juwaynī (d. 586/1190), an Egyptian resident originally from Baghdad, composed a poem celebrating the conquest:

(1) The armies of heaven are support for this king.
Whoever doubts this, then this conquest is proof.
(3) This conquest is like the conquests of the prophets.
It cannot be appreciated by wealth, but only by gratitude [to God].
(8) For ninety years the lands of God cried out, but Muslim leaders were deaf and blind.
But now Ṣalāḥ al-Dīn responded to their request by order of Him who supports those who are in need.[48] (1.58)

Many of those who congregated for the sermon were from Ṣalāḥ al-Dīn's conquering army and while Ibn al-Zakī depended on eloquence and rhetoric in his sermon, this was combined with an enumeration of the merits of Jerusalem together with praise of the army and Ṣalāḥ al-Dīn.[49] Given that it was an immense privilege to speak and several other prospective *khaṭībs* certainly had been denied the chance, it is likely that Ibn al-Zakī used his valuable time at the pulpit to demonstrate once more and with heightened euphoria the propagandistic influence of the *khaṭīb* in the anti-Frankish *jihād*.[50] His message was designed as an official summation of the rationale behind the victory; he relished the new-found features of Jerusalem that had been popularised by the preaching of books of *faḍāʾil* that was accentuated during the reign of Ṣalāḥ al-Dīn. In light of the author's comparison of the reconquest to Islam's previous military feats and his proclamation of the victory as a sign of the last days, incorporated within such a description was an allusion to Ṣalāḥ al-Dīn's own position in the apocalyptic dimension of the event. Ibn al-Zakī linked Ṣalāḥ al-Dīn to Islam's early caliphs, Abū Bakr, ʿUmar, ʿUthmān, and ʿAlī, in what may have been intended as an affront to the ʿAbbāsid caliph for his lack of assistance in the

48 Abū Shāma, *Kitāb al-Rawḍatayn*, 3:238–239.

49 M. Ibrāhīm, 'Filasṭīn fī l-adab al-ʿarabī zamān al-ḥurūb al-Ṣalībiyya,' in *al-Ṣirā l-Islāmī l-Faranjī ʿalā Filasṭīn fī l-qurūn al-wusṭā*, ed. H. Dajani-Shakeel and B. Dajani (Beirut, 1994), 381.

50 For more information on the role of the *khaṭīb* in medieval Islam, see Talmon-Heller, *Islamic Piety*, 87–114.

reconquest.[51] It is certain that Ibn al-Zakī intended to stir the collective memory of his congregation in the hope that the achievements of past Muslim leaders might be compared to and matched by the reconquest. The speech contained, aside from the predictable anti-Christian rhetoric, a likening of the reconquest with the battle of Badr – the first battle *en masse* between Muslims and the Meccans of Quraysh (2/624). The Qurʾān draws attention to the miraculous nature of their victory, in which angels were believed to have supported the Muslims in their encounter; and Ibn al-Zakī praised God for ensuring a similar victory and procuring "the triumph of the miraculous powers displayed in the messenger's gift of prophecy … rejoice at the coming of the angels, sent down to thank you for the sweet odour of the profession of God's unity wherewith you have gifted this House …"[52] Eschatological features of Jerusalem were fused with other *faḍāʾil* characteristics that were so effectively highlighted during the propaganda campaigns of Nūr al-Dīn and Ṣalāḥ al-Dīn: "Jerusalem is the residence of your father Abraham, the place of ascension of your prophet, the burial ground of the messengers, and the place of the descent of revelations. It is in the land in which men will be resurrected …" A particularly telling aspect of the sermon, in light of Islamic eschatology and the popular perception of the *jihād* participants toward their own conflict, may be discerned from Ibn al-Zakī's exultant assertion, "How great a favour was that which rendered you the army by whose hand the Sacred City was recaptured in these latter times …"[53] As Cook discerns, "one of the most important purposes of both *jihād* literature and apocalyptic traditions is to establish the relative merits and rewards of those fighting in the battles."[54] He argues that sometimes apocalyptic traditions break a tendency that maintains that those chronologically closest to the Prophet are assigned more religious merit than those further away. In a general sense, the matter can be substantiated with reference to the Qurʾān and, in a specific sense, to *ḥadīth* that are non-apocalyptic in nature. In any case, Ibn al-Zakī's reference to the battle of Badr and the Prophet's companions must have gone some way to signal that Ṣalāḥ al-Dīn and his army were com-

51 "Blessings be on you for an army which hath procured the triumph of the miraculous powers displayed in the Apostle's gift of prophecy, which hath fought battles like those of Badr, which hath shown resolution like that of Abū Bakr, achieved conquests like those of ʿUmar's, behaved like the armies of ʿUthmān, and charged like those of ʿAlī! You have renewed for Islāmism the glorious days of Qādisiyah, the conflicts of Yarmūk, the sieges of Khaybar, and the impetuous attacks of Khālid Ibn al-Walīd." Ibn Khallikān, *Wafayāt*, 4:209.

52 Ibn Khallikān, *Wafayāt*, 4:209.

53 Abū Shāma, *Kitāb al-Rawḍatayn*, 3:248–253 (fa mādhā ʿalaykum min al-niʿma bi-an jaʿalakum al-jaysh alladhī yuftaḥu ʿalayhi al-bayt al-maqdis fī ākhir al-zamān).

54 D. Cook, 'Muslim Apocalyptic and Jihād,' *JSAI* 20 (1996), 81–82.

parable to their predecessors. As al-Juwaynī explained in the poem cited above (1.59), the conquest was "like the conquests of the prophets." Furthermore, in ʿImād al-Dīn's lengthy (232 line) elegy (*rithāʾ*), we find these lines:

> (25) If he had been [alive, i.e., done this] in the time of the Prophet
> Then verses would have been revealed in his remembrance.[55] (1.59)

It was with this sentiment that ʿImād al-Dīn concluded *al-Barq al-Shāmī*. Widely studied by scholars, the *rithāʾ* or *marthīya* (elegy) is considered a particular type of traditional *qaṣīda* and a subgenre of the *madīḥ* (panegyric).[56] In ʿImād al-Dīn al-Iṣfahānī's hyperbolic *rithāʾ*, Ṣalāḥ al-Dīn is depicted as an outstanding model of a Muslim sultan, enough to deserve mention in divine scripture. The death of a ruler provided opportune moments for a poet to eulogise his patron's favourable attributes and *jihād* achievements.

Constantinople and its Relation to Jerusalem

In the poetry of this period there was a further anticipated consequence of the capture of Jerusalem – the long awaited and much aspired conquest of Constantinople. Despite the established Muslim aspiration of conquering Constantinople, present from the early decades of the Islamic conquest, and the mention and prophecy of the conquest in books of *faḍāʾil* and *jihād* treatises during the crusades, in the poetry of this period there appears, from what is available, to have been little mention of Rūm or its sub-themes, except as the Banū Aṣfar. The interchangeable Rūm or Banū Aṣfar and *ʿilj* were simply designations for the Frankish 'Other,' and while authors of *faḍāʾil* or *jihād* works selected material and were keen to see the reconquest of Jerusalem in light of a progressive victory that would culminate in the capture of Constantinople, poets appeared less interested in the future victory. Their messages had a more immediate nature; they served the main concerns of their champions to praise and exonerate or lampoon their enemies. It seems that the reconquest of Jerusalem was, quite simply, yet ever-importantly, the victory of victories (*fatḥ al-futūḥ*) with nothing following it, at least in the domain of thought and expression. This circumvention of the future anticipated victory over Byzantium – if the idea was strong enough for that, of course served the obvious purpose

55 Abū Shāma, *Kitāb al-Rawḍatayn*, 4:218.

56 Allen, *An Introduction to Arabic Literature*, 93–98; M. M. Badawi, *A Critical Introduction to Modern Arabic Poetry* (Cambridge: Cambridge University Press, 1975), 3; V. I. Braginsky, *The Comparative Study of Traditional Asian Literatures* (Richmond: Curzon, 2001), 142–143.

of placing Jerusalem at the forefront of the military *jihād*. After the capture of Edessa in 538/1144, it became the central theme in the poetry; the distinctness of the goal rather than the prolonged road to Constantinople was the main aim.

However, Constantinople was not entirely absent from the poetry. Ibn al-Qaysarānī concluded his congratulatory poem in praise of ʿImād al-Dīn Zangī following the conquest of Edessa by alluding to the idea that the power of God worked through His army on earth – 'the army of God,' and was able to encompass Constantinople.

(27) And [God is] the owner of the heavens, so which land did the army of God not reach?
(28) And with God is the determination, beginning at the waters of Sayhān and taking its rest at the gardens of Constantinople.[57] (1.60)

The city of Constantinople features in more categorical terms in a poem composed by al-Jilyānī following the reconquest. Appearing toward the end of his poem (line 55), the poet brings together Jerusalem, al-Andalus, Syria, and Iraq as Muslim lands subservient to the sultan's power. In the distinct reference to Constantinople the poet says:

(55) Hagia Sophia pleads with you in remembrance of what you did in the Church of Resurrection.
Indeed this is the conquest that will shock the entire world.[58] (1.61)

The line is particularly insightful for what it reveals about the poet's identification of the role Ṣalāḥ al-Dīn plays as a champion of the Islamic cause. In this line the poet dispenses with the fuller description of the Church – *kanīsat al-qiyāma* – and instead uses *qiyāma* (resurrection). Whereas ʿImād al-Dīn al-Iṣfahānī's rhymed prose (*sajʿ*) and poetry plays on the words *qiyāma* (church of resurrection) and *qumāma* (waste), we could argue that al-Jilyānī's line "Hagia Sophia pleads with you in remembrance of what you did in the Church of Resurrection" is contracted to mean 'resurrection,' i.e., an end time association with the city of Constantinople, whose conquest was seen as one of the signs of the latter days.

In the Muslim literature during this period the loss and eventual gain of Jerusalem was contextualised in an eschatological milieu that, in some respects, was viable insofar as Jerusalem, Syria, and Constantinople were conveniently brought together; the position of each reinforcing the other. It may

57 Abū Shāma, *Kitāb al-Rawḍatayn*, 1:174.

58 Al-Jilyānī, *Dīwān al-tadbīj*, 93.

be noted, in light of Islamic eschatology, that any attitude toward the Franks was the culmination of centuries of mistrust between the Muslim world and Byzantium, and the position that Byzantium had been accorded as a resilient bastion of Christianity until the drawing close of the Last Day; the traditions about the Byzantines and the conquest of Constantinople came to unveil the greatest military ambition nurtured by the Muslims.[59]

It was thus the taking of Constantinople that loomed large in apocalyptic traditions and material to represent a definitive Muslim victory that would surpass all others and be the penultimate defeat of Christianity before the final apocalyptic battle/Armageddon (*malḥama*).[60] The victory is further accorded a miraculous status on account of its effortless opening: "The Muslims surround the city of infidelity on Friday night ... When the sun comes up, the Muslims give a [single] shout of *Allāhu akbar* [God is great], and the walls between the two towers fall."[61]

Since Constantinople was intrinsic to the mindset of Muslim apocalyptic thinkers, its future conquest could be exploited by way of signalling lesser conquests as prerequisite forerunners. In this light the reconquest of Jerusalem may be seen as an increase in the stakes when considered by those who attached religious meaning, as expected, to their participation in the anti-Frankish *jihād* and pursuit of martyrdom (*ṭalab al-shahāda*). The Prophet's companion and third caliph, ʿUthmān b. ʿAffān, reminded his subjects who looked forward to the conquest of al-Andalus that "Constantinople will be conquered from al-Andalus; if you conquer al-Andalus, you will be the partners of whosoever conquers Constantinople."[62] Al-Sulamī, the post-First Crusade jurist, was also eager to remind potential participants in the *jihād* against the Franks that the prize of Constantinople lay after the reconquest of Jerusalem; the capture of Jerusalem served to galvanize the pending conquest of Constantinople:

> If the *mujāhidīn* are from this party, among them are those who will succeed in driving them out of Jerusalem and other parts of these lands.

59 See A. Abel, 'Changements politiques et littérature eschatologique dans le monde musulman,' *SI* 2 (1954), 38. ("Certains évènements historiques revêtent d'ailleurs le caractère de grande tribulation, et, parmi eux, au premier plan, la prise de Constantinople, qui, dans les imaginations musulmanes, devait jouer un rôle significatif en annonçant l'établissment universel de l'Islâm, événement préalable au Jugement. Aussi les Apocalypses sur la prise de Constantinople se multiplièrent-elles.")

60 See T. Fahd, 'Malḥama,' *EI*^{2}, 4:247.

61 El Cheikh, *Byzantium Viewed by the Arabs* (London: Harvard Middle Eastern Monographs XXXVI, 2005), 68.

62 Ibid., 65; A. ʿU. al-Bakrī, *Jughrāfiyāt al-Andalus wa-Uruba*, ed. A. al-Ḥajj (Baghdad, 1968), 130.

> They are the ones who will conquer Constantinople ... So struggle hard, God have mercy on you, in this *jihād*, so that you may be the ones who will be victors with the merit of this great conquest, [having been] kept for this noble rank.[63]

Therefore, aside from al-Sulamī's attention to the 'victorious band in and around Jerusalem and Shām,' he too elucidated the reconquest of Jerusalem as a forerunner to the conquest of Constantinople; these victories were believed to be conditional upon one another. On the one hand, this could serve to agitate the Muslims because the loss of Jerusalem might be seen to impede any hope of achieving early Islam's long held aspiration to capture Constantinople. On the other hand, this situation could inspire a resolve to liberate Jerusalem vis-à-vis the conquest of Constantinople that would subsequently follow.

Jamāl al-Dīn b. Wāṣil recorded details of a letter from Nūr al-Dīn to the 'Abbāsid caliph in Baghdad, al-Ḥassān al-Mustaḍīʿ b. Yūsuf al-Mustanjid (536–575/1142–80), in which Nūr al-Dīn links Jerusalem to the prophesied tradition concerning the conquest of Constantinople:

> Constantinople and Jerusalem are both galloping to their time of conquest in the sphere of competition, and both are in the gloom of deep darkness, waiting for the crow of familiarity. God the exalted, by His generosity, will bring close the harvest of both conquests for the Muslims, and bless the servant [Nūr al-Dīn] to gain the pleasure of the *imām* [caliph].[64]

We might argue that the kind of apocalypticism that pervaded early Muslims' perception of their present was brought to the fore with the crusader conquests and occupation. Though interpreting communal attitudes on the basis of apocalyptic material is an over-simplification of the many working facets that shape the thoughts of a community, Constantinople is a unique example of the abundant and varied material associated with the city that reveal more than the expression of individual voices.[65] It seems that linking Jerusalem to Constantinople was a new development; importantly, it was always Constantinople rather than Jerusalem that figured prominently in *ḥadīth*

63 Al-Sulamī, 'Kitāb al-Jihād,' 54–55.

64 Ibn Wāṣil, *Mufarrij*, 1:235.

65 See El Cheikh, *Byzantium*, 66.

that prophesied major Muslim conquests.[66] Another eschatological dimension of the sixth/twelfth century that was stimulated by the crusades may be determined, therefore, from the relegation of the conquest of Constantinople to a position below that of the more immediate reconquest of Jerusalem.

We can ascertain a vivid example of the anticipated conquest of Constantinople that was generated by the 583/1187 reconquest of Jerusalem from the *Riḥla* of Ibn Jubayr. In his diary entry for his time in Sicily in the beginning of 580/1185 the pilgrim presents a confusing account. He begins by describing a usurpation of power by a cousin of the heir to the throne of Constantinople, an event that results in the usurper's (and his wife's) conversion to Islam, and a subsequent promise to provide assistance to the Muslims to conquer Constantinople, "slaying some 50,000 of its inhabitants" when entering. The result is that the Muslims seized Constantinople, and all of its wealth was transported to the *amīr*, Qilij Arslān b. Masʿūd. The conquest was heralded as one of the greatest portents of the Hour:

> There are others who see the levy as intended solely for Constantinople the Great, because of the momentous news which has come concerning it; news which inspires the soul with bodings of strange events, proving incontestably the truth of the traditions transmitted from the Chosen One [Muḥammad] – God's blessings upon him.
>
> ... its countless riches were taken to the Emir Masʿūd, who placed over forty thousand Muslim horsemen in the city, which now adjoined the Muslim lands. This conquest if it be true, is one of the greatest portents of the Day of Judgement. God best knows of hidden things.
>
> ... this news from Constantinople – God grant that it be true – is one of the greatest miracles and awaited manifestations of the world. God indeed is all-powerful in His decrees and in what He predetermines.[67]

Ibn Jubayr's euphoria is discernible from the author's repetition of the joyous, albeit inaccurate news. In fact he had confused some other events that took place in Byzantium during this time, namely that Andronicus, the cousin of Emperor Alexius II was killed during a rebellion in 1185 and succeeded by Emperor Isaac II. The killing of Andronicus was subsequent to the empire

66 See Ibn Kathīr, *Book of the End: Great Trials and Tribulations*, trans. Faisal Shafiq, ed. ʿAbd al-Aḥad (London: Darussalam Publishers, 2006), 72–73.

67 Ibn Jubayr, *Travels*, 354–356; Ibn Jubayr, *Tadhkira*, 265–267.

being plunged into an orgy of political violence.[68] Nevertheless, the anecdote demonstrates that the information brought from ships that arrived from Constantinople was fused with an apocalyptic narrative. Muslims and Christians heard that something of great consequence had taken place in Byzantium, and the eschatological expectations surrounding the city shaped his account. The account further corroborates the aforementioned idea that the eschatological figuring of Constantinople was well known, albeit the narrative is no more than a jurist's misunderstanding. Furthermore, the anonymous sixth-/twelfth-century Persian *Baḥr al-fawāʾid* also mentions the impending conquest of Constantinople. The author lists five significant events that the Muslim nation has and will pass through. While the "fourth was the conjunction of the fortunes of the ʿAbbāsids", "the fifth will be the conquest of Constantinople ... The Prophet said, 'The Hour will not arrive until God gives my community victory over Constantinople.'"[69] Although the text is very much contextualised by the sixth-/twelfth-century crusader occupations and what the author saw as the weakness of the Muslim nation and waning spirit of Islam at both the political and popular levels, the fact that the Frankish occupation is mentioned elsewhere – "Jerusalem is destroyed and is a place of dogs and swine, and the land of the Franks prospers"[70] – there is no mention of the reconquest in the author's aforementioned formulation; it is the conquest of Constantinople that is seen as the definitive victory. This lends weight to the argument that for some the reconquest of Jerusalem was seen in light of the greater expected victory at Constantinople. Its significance undisputed, it may have been consigned, nonetheless, to encourage an outlook informed by established eschatological belief, to inspire Nūr al-Dīn with the same, or perhaps even to invoke the idea that the reconquest of Jerusalem would be a forerunner of greater things to come – a prospect which therefore deserved greater mention.

We may also note the origins of the Frankish/Rūm connection in chapter 3 as one that stems from the early confusion about the true nature of the Franks, in part because of previous Muslim warfare with the Byzantines; this was bolstered by the fact that in 492/1099 the Franks marched south from Byzantium to Jerusalem. Further, consider the emotive focus of the rousing poetry contemporary with the First Crusade. Further still, Rūm was a term well understood. It

68 Ibn Jubayr, *Travels*, 387–389. See M. Angold, *The Byzantine Empire, 1025–1204: A Political History* (London: Longman, 1997), 295–303; J. Harris, *Byzantium and the Crusades* (London: Hambledon, 2003), 111–125.

69 Meisami (trans. and ed.), *The Sea of Precious Virtues*, 282.

70 Ibid., 56.

had a Qur'ānic reality – *Sūrat Rūm* – and the indecisiveness of the term meant that 'Franks' (Faranj), 'Romans', Greeks, Anatolians, and Byzantines could be used and were used interchangeably, one synonymous with the other. In spite of this, the use of Rūm could have been employed equally for the deliberate purpose of rendering the new enemy in light of the old one; 'Rūm' were, in reality, western Christians, and the early confusion could have been no more than a deliberate attempt to understand the enemy in light of what was already well-established in the religion.

Ibn Jubayr: Pilgrimage, Poetry, and Social Accountability

The context of the long poem assessed in this section by the traveller and jurist Ibn Jubayr relates to his travel in Alexandria during his second trip to Egypt 585/1189.[71] Ibn Jubayr witnessed the agents of Ṣalāḥ al-Dīn indiscriminately seizing pilgrims' money as *zakāt* payments without questioning the pilgrims about what they had possessed for the complete year (a stipulation of the *zakāt* calculation), and this served as the basis for his poetic complaint. The tone of Ibn Jubayr's poetry is congruent with other disquieting sentiments of social unease and division that he describes in his *Riḥla*, particularly in relation to what he witnessed in Damascus. A native of al-Andalus, it is likely that he was fully aware of the conflicts between al-Murābiṭūn (Almoravids) and al-Muwaḥḥidūn (Almohads), and although, as a Sunnī jurist, he would have understood the need to challenge what he believed was Shīʿī heresy and support the Sunnī revivalist aims outlined by his scholarly predecessors, the high tax payments on pilgrims were not only unethical but also contrary to his belief that Sunnī Islam was a morally superior religious code. Ibn Jubayr argued that the sultan had no idea that this was taking place, and the reputation he enjoyed because of his commitment to justice is described in Ibn Jubayr's poem, "So consider how many people in the East and West of the Muslim world praise

71 Ibn Jubayr's travels and sojourns in the Middle East described in his *Riḥla* occurred between 1 Dhū l-Ḥijja to 29 Dhū l-Ḥijja 578/28 March to 25 April 1183 before Ṣalāḥ al-Dīn recaptured Jerusalem and it is here that Wright's edition places the poem. The poem however makes clear references to the reconquest of Jerusalem so he could not have composed the poem at this timed. Secondly, the poem is not in Ibn Jubayr's *Rihla* but in the Introductory section that Wright wrote to his edition of the *Rihla*, and the poem is quoted from a much later source. It seems likely therefore that the experience he describes is from his second trip to Alexandria in 585/1189. See I. R. Netton, 'Ibn Jubayr: Penitent Pilgrim and Obervant,' in *Seek Knowledge: Thought and Travel in the House of Islam* (Richmond: Curzon Press, 1996), 95–102.

and thank you." (25)[72] In his travel account Ibn Jubayr juxtaposes what he observed of Ṣalāḥ al-Dīn's commitment to justice and the poor treatment of pilgrims overseen by the ruler of Mecca:

> For Saladin lifted from the pilgrim the customs duty, and in its stead provided money and victuals with orders that they should be sent to Mukhtir, Emir of Mecca. But when this consignment allotted to them was somewhat delayed, this Emir returned to intimidating the pilgrims and made show to imprison them for the dues.[73]

After appealing to the sultan's pietistic sentiments of establishing justice, Ibn Jubayr composed the following poem that reflects a fusing together of Ibn Jubayr's role as a cleric and a moral arbiter. Consideration is given to the unity of the poem as well as to individual verses and the variety of meanings they suggest.

1) May the happiness from this continuous universe blossom your successes.
2) So rejoice, for indeed the necks of your enemy will be given to your sharp sword.
3) After a short time, destruction [death] will descend on their treacherous plotting.
4) The most fertile day is the day the earth will be irrigated with their blood.
5) And how much have you caused them to suffer, like a lion in the thicket?
6) You forcibly broke their crosses, and may God bless you in being a fine breaker.
7) You changed what they left behind; nobody in this time will stand up for their monuments.
8) You spent your time fighting them, so let doom descend on their crippling majesty.
9) Their kingdom retreated and turned away from Syria just like what occurred on their previous dark days.
10) Your soldiers are victorious by instilling fear, so fight them [crusaders] whenever you please, or remain patient.
11) All of them are defeated in the torrent of your soldiers.
12) You have avenged the religion of guidance by fighting the enemies, so God has chosen you as a worthy avenger.

72 Ibn Jubayr, *Rihla*, ed. W. Wright (Leiden, 1907), 28–31.

73 Ibn Jubayr, *Travels*, 71–72. See also Phillips, 'The Travels of Ibn Jubayr,' 75–90.

13) You stood up for victory for God so you were named al-Malik al-Nāṣir [the victorious king]
14) You keep yourself awake for the sake of the One [God] who will please you for your alertness.
15) You have conquered the Holy Land so it [is] returned to its original pure description.
16) You came to the chosen Holy Land and purified it from the hand of the unbeliever.
17) And you raised up the minaret of guidance and gave life to the dead ruins [of Jerusalem].
18) For you is the honour of God in these conquests, like the [honour in the] first conquests [by ʿUmar b. al-Khaṭṭāb].
19) And [God] specified you for this task after you visited Him [through the reconquest] in Jerusalem, [and promised] to keep it for you [as a reward] in the hereafter.
20) Your love was thrown in the souls [of Muslims] and your commemoration flies among the people.
21) So they will say much about you as an example when they remember the kings.
22) You lifted all the difficulties of the Hijaz with your comprehensive and complete favour.
23) And you gave security to the Hijaz and its surroundings, and you eased the way for the travellers.
24) Your hands gave generously to the one who enters and the one who leaves.
25) So consider how many people in the East and West of the Muslim world praise and thank you.
26) And consider how many prayers there have been for you every year in Mecca, by the open fearless announcer.
27) And [now] consider how much the people persevere in fear of the injustice [in Alexandria], with the humiliation of pilgrims to the House of God, [those] who are dealt with unjustly.
28) Consider how humiliated they feel when their possessions are searched.
29) They are stopped as if they are prisoners of war.
30) He [the official] forced them to take false oaths that they had nothing left to give, the consequences of which fall on the official [in the next life].
31) And when they search the inviolable [women], they have no protection.
32) Does he not fear that tomorrow he will be exposed before God?
33) And is there no one jealous to protect the dignity of the Muslims?

34) And is there no one who can warn and advise him? What a humiliation he imposes on the one who tries.
35) Is there an adviser, a conveyer of this advice to the victorious al-Malik al-Nāṣir?
36) [The official is] an oppressor who controls the money of *zakāt* [obligatory alms giving], what a shame to such a loser.
37) He hides his treachery inside himself but in public he appears as a consultant.
38) Do something against him that would make him publicly ashamed.
39) No one can stop this evildoer except you and no one can give good orders except you.
40) God forbid, if you do not remove those injustices you will not have among the people one who will excuse you.
41) Removing these injustices will expand your honour without any need for publicising [it].
42) When you stop these wrongdoings you are in pursuit of honour, and those good actions will benefit the doer.
43) I vowed to advise you and it is a duty on the adviser to fulfil this promise.
44) And my love for you made me compose poetry, and I am not looking for what poets seek [financial reward].
45) And poetry is not my way of making a living, what a bad trade of a trader.
46) If the poetry became just an aim, then I am not looking to become famous.
47) And if my poetry is a vow then it was said that there is no judgement on the one who simply vows.
48) But all that I say is just the feelings of the heart which overtook me and came out as a poem.
49) And when my poetry has reached you then that is enough honour for me.
50) And if you accept what I wrote then that is the honour for the visitor.
51) And it is enough for me that you hear from the one who heard it from me, and enough for you to glance at the one who stands before you reading my poem before you.
52) And it is enough for the deliverer of my poem to stand before you, so much so that even the flowers in the garden will feel shy knowing that he stood before you.[74] (1.62)

Ibn Jubayr's poem has a clear structure divided into five sections of quite unequal length. Ascertaining the function of each group of verses is essential to

74 Ibn Jubayr, *Rihla*, ed. W. Wright (Leiden, 1907), 28–31.

understanding how meanings are interlaced in the lines. This not only adds to our appreciation of Arabic poetry composed in this period but it also allows us to notice the most striking recurring messages in those poems, for the way they elicit *jihād* against the crusaders. In Ibn Jubayr's poem the themes come to overlap and merge:

I. Lines 1–11: The defeat of the crusaders and Christian symbols in Jerusalem.
II. Lines 12–19: God's specification of Ṣalāḥ al-Dīn for the task of the reconquest and 'purifying' of Jerusalem.
III. Lines 20–26: The favour that Ṣalāḥ al-Dīn has found in the Muslim world.
IV. Lines 27–37: The injustice and corruption exhibited by tax officials in Alexandria.
V. Lines 38–42: Ṣalāḥ al-Dīn's responsibility to end the corruption.
VI. Lines 43–52: Ibn Jubayr's role as an advisory poet.

In the poem we notice an interesting palindrome-like ordering of lines in which the following set of lines share a similar purpose and theme: The opening and ending lines (1 and 49–52) are conventional examples of praise (*madīḥ*); lines 2–11 focus on the honour accredited to Ṣalāḥ al-Dīn for the defeat of the crusaders in Jerusalem, this is compared with lines 34–42 which carry sentiments expounding on the need for Ṣalāḥ al-Dīn to right the wrongs taking place. Although God honoured Ṣalāḥ al-Dīn with the reconquest, failing to check the injustice of the tax collector will sully his honour from the reconquest. In these lines the words *ḥurma* (inviolable), *ʿirḍ* (honour), *ghāʾir* (jealousy), and *dhull* (humiliation) are juxtaposed with *ʿizz* (glory) that Ibn Jubayr uses to appeal to Ṣalāḥ al-Dīn, "Removing these injustices will expand your honour without the need for publicising [it]."

Line 40 ('God forbid if you do not remove those injustices you will not have among the people one who will excuse you') is the most explicit line iterating that Ṣalāḥ al-Dīn could fall out of favour with those described in line 20 ('Your love was thrown in the souls [of Muslims] and your commemoration flies among the people') who admire him and hold him in high esteem. That is, 'The Muslims love you because of the reconquest. They will not excuse you if you fail in preventing this injustice.' The vehemence of the attack on the corrupt official in Alexandria with which the poem reaches its climax (lines 27–37) is counterbalanced by the poet's emphasis on Ṣalāḥ al-Dīn's responsibility, and the poet's obligation to 'advise' and 'compose.' In the poem Ibn Jubayr makes a point of twice repeating his description of what the agents had done.

Notwithstanding the poet's description of the corruption of Ṣalāḥ al-Dīn's agent, there is in Ibn Jubayr's poem an example of Ṣalāḥ al-Dīn's control over his affairs, he has an unbounded mastery; he did not simply 'destroy' the crusader plans, he has effectualised the crusaders' destruction. Perhaps by juxtaposing death and suffering with the fertility of the day (lines 3 and 4) the poet harkens to a Qur'ānic parable of "a garden on high, fertile ground: a rainstorm smites it, and thereupon it brings forth its fruit twofold" (2:265), though Ibn Jubayr's words are an inversion, the irrigation of blood will only worsen the crusader woes. In the poem there are many examples of antithesis. In line 2 the softness of *riqāb* (necks) is set against the *sayfak al-bāʾir* (your sharp sword); in line 37 the Alexandrian official hides his treachery 'inside himself' but in 'public' he appears as a consultant. Do something against him that would make him 'publicly' ashamed. By breaking crosses, akin to the role of the Islamic Jesus (ʿĪsā) who will 'break the cross' in his apocalyptic second coming, Ṣalāḥ al-Dīn is presented in his conquest not simply as an emulator but as someone whose role is that of a precursor, an agent of God's divine will to champion Islam's triumph. The motif of 'breaking crosses' is emblematic of defeating the crusaders and their religion; Ibn Jubayr presents Ṣalāḥ al-Dīn's unrelenting 'breaking' of crosses and capturing of the sacred space of Jerusalem as representative of a decisive victory, enough to thwart any subsequent crusader attempts to wrestle control of the city. When referencing 'their monuments' the poet does not present the sultan as a 'destroyer' of those monuments, but only as a restorer of the landscape of Jerusalem to the sacred Islamic order of things, 'so that it [is] returned to its original pure description,' giving 'life to the dead ruins.' The poet uses the typical pun commonly associated with victors, 'al-Malik al-Nāṣir.' In his feat, Ṣalāḥ al-Dīn is again comparable to the illustrious caliph ʿUmar; he thus shares not only in the triumphs of his predecessor, but can sentimentally, through the 'love' and 'remembrance' of his supporters, associate himself to the regal privilege as a worthy defender of Islam. The poet's point becomes clear – 'So how much they will have to say about you as an example when they remember the kings.'

The laudatory lines for the sultan as a victor and protector of the faith earned him the supplications of pilgrims in Mecca, something immediately relevant and symbolic for the pilgrim poet, but so too in the same regard is Ibn Jubayr's outrage at the mishandling of affairs that results in hindering and obstructing pilgrims to the Holy City. The esteem of the benediction apparent in the congratulatory note is juxtaposed with a lament about corrupt tax officials operating in the Hijaz. The way in which the poet sets the reverence afforded to the sultan in Mecca against the humiliation and fear that has befallen the pilgrims to the sanctified city is aptly fit. Not only does the lament offset the congratulatory tone, Ibn Jubayr weaves into his description the contrast between Ṣalāḥ al-Dīn's 'lifting of difficulties,' the provision of security for travellers with the injustice and corruption exhibited by the officials. Ṣalāḥ al-Dīn thus remains in the frame as a vanguard; his piety is the impetus for correcting the wrongs of the official. Since the official is the embodiment of oppression (*ẓalūm*), a description twice repeated in the poet's lines (one to stress the state of affairs in Alexandria and the other a personal descriptive), both in the active participle form, he emphasises the extent of the injustice. Since Ibn Jubayr praises Ṣalāḥ al-Dīn for restoring justice by expelling the crusaders from Jerusalem, it would make good sense to the poet's listeners to entrust him to maintain the integrity of Islam's social order by taking action against the corrupt. This of course is his first point in the description as his pilgrim group arrived in Alexandria. Ibn Jubayr makes a point of twice repeating that the agents of the sultan seized their money as *zakāt* payments without questioning them about what they had possessed for the complete year, which is a stipulation of the payment. Clearly, the author/poet sees in the disturbance of standard Islamic practice a violation that warrants swift restitution. Ibn Jubayr concludes the opening section in the *Riḥla* by also detailing the misconduct of customs officials and drawing on the sultan's predisposition to establish justice if he comes to hear of such a transgression – of course it is Ibn Jubayr, through the medium of his poem, who becomes the adviser (*nāṣiḥ*) that he entreats in his poem. His focus on wrongs committed against women, his description of them as inviolable (*ḥurma*) is akin to the sentiments expressed by Ibn al-Khayyāṭ in his First Crusade poem,

> So guard your religion and the inviolable ones ...[75]
> (*Fa-ḥāmū 'ala dīnikum wa-l-ḥarīm*)

And similar to the anonymous First Crusade poem cited by Ibn Taghrībirdī:

> And how many Muslim women's inviolability has been plundered.[76]
> (*Wa muslimatun lahā ḥaramun ṣalīb*)

What makes Ibn Jubayr's poem compelling is that it was not composed for the purpose of obtaining a monetary reward, nor was it written so that the pilgrim could gain Ṣalāḥ al-Dīn's patronage. He uses the *madīḥ* section of his poem, which focuses on Ṣalāḥ al-Dīn's defeat of the crusaders, to appeal to the sultan's sense of shame and pity, in other words to make a generous sacrifice

75 Ibn al-Khayyāṭ, *Dīwān*, 185.
76 Ibn Taghrībirdī, *al-Nujūm*, 5:151–152.

to undo the wrongs committed in Alexandria. Ibn Jubayr used the medium of his correspondence with the sultan to both vindicate himself from the pretention often seen in poetry and for its effectiveness as a literary device. Though this was a standard practice for poets, Ibn Jubayr separates himself from other poets of a 'retinue'; unlike the dozens of court poets that typified this kind or celebratory verse in their poetry, Ibn Jubayr was not a refugee poet. Instead, his verses seem to suggest a sincere instructive tone of voice, in part moved by his role as a religious pilgrim, and in part emanating from his social position as a jurist. The poet set himself apart from Ṣalāḥ al-Dīn's courtly circles; in fact his verses can be read as a criticism of those who compose adulatory verse for their patrons. Despite the flattering verses with which he begins and concludes his poem, Ibn Jubayr juxtaposes the financial benefit that poets seek with "the feelings of the heart which took over" him in line 48 of his poem, 1.63. His style is oratorical, persuasive, and emotive. Ibn Jubayr combines his *madīḥ* with tones of address in his poem which include advice, warning, and instruction. While poets would often boast of their poetic skill, and since poems were often arranged and rearranged, Ibn Jubayr here uses the latter part of his poem to instead emphasise his earnestness. Sumi writes,

> The Arabic panegyric genre potentially contains both a literary portrait of the patron and a poet's self-portrait in one and the same ode: a double portrait. Portraiture is a representation or depiction of a human subject, and it can be visual, verbal, or musical ... Although the professed purpose of the Arabic panegyric is to praise a patron – an Arab poet portrays the praised individual in the *madīḥ* section (and portrays himself in the *nasīb*, the *raḥīl*, and the *madīḥ* sections) – the *qaṣīdah* thus comes to be investigated as a verbal portrait or as a self-portrait.[77]

By using the medium of ornate verse to convey his message to Ṣalāḥ al-Dīn, Ibn Jubayr subtly merged his sentiment of sincerity while vaunting his dexterity in verse. The poetic structure and examples of antithesis in the poem further show that it was not a random stringing together of words but a sequence of rhetorical images contained in a coherently organised structure.

77 Akiko Motoyoshi Sumi, *Description in Classical Arabic Poetry: Waṣf, Ekphrasis, and Interparts Theory* (Leiden: Brill, 2004), 155.

CHAPTER 6

Literary Underpinnings of the Anti-Frankish *Jihād*

> Poetry is the mine of knowledge of the Arabs and the book of their wisdom, the archives of their history, the reservoir of their epic days, the wall that defends their exploits, the impassable trench that preserves their glories, the impartial witness for the day of judgement.[1]

In chapter 6 I consider key themes in the Muslim poetry of this period, themes that enable us to appreciate how poets used religious motifs to strengthen pro-*jihād* efforts, to offset crusader interest in the city of Jerusalem, and to challenge Christian religious ascriptions. The first theme underpins the theological influences that steered both sides of the conflicts, and the way Muslims perceived that Christians were 'appropriating' the personality of Jesus Christ and thus accentuating a misguided claim to him and to the land made holy through him. The second theme is the creation of what may be termed a 'pious warrior ethos,' developed through the person of Nūr al-Dīn Zangī. By examining the spiritual resonances in poetry composed for Nūr al-Dīn, we see the growth of Sufism in the period and the role of Damascus as a city of immense spiritual worth. The vast retinue of poets operating in Syria frequently enjoined Nūr al-Dīn to take on the role of his illustrious Muslim predecessors, and in this light his pietistic tendencies were praised in poetry, which served an important purpose and basis for his anti-Frankish *jihād* programme. I also examine the influence of popularised *ḥadīth* that filtered into compositions intended for Nūr al-Dīn. Notwithstanding the strong themes of religious superiority evidenced in the poetry of this period that I cite in this chapter, of the influence of Sufism on the poetic discourse, or the frequent use of Qur'ānic imagery to drive home the poet's political and ideological messages, and the eschatological motifs running through the Andalusian poet 'Abd al-Mun'im al-Jilyānī's verses, in the final parts of this chapter I reveal some divergent and surprising attitudes toward the Frankish Christians.

1 Ibn Qutayba, *'Uyūn al-akhbār* (Cairo, 1973), 2:185; Garulo, 'Women in Medieval Classical Arabic Poetry,' 25.

 | DOI 10.1163/9789004345225_007

Steering an Image: The Figure of the Christian 'Other' in Muslim Poetry

In this section I examine the way Muslim poets utilised Christian references related to Jesus, the Bible, and Christian clergy in their poetry. We find that Muslim poets sought to express the supremacy of Islam by deriding their Frankish enemy for their misdirected worship and for having false religious hopes; the poets depict both of these factors as reasons for the failures of the Franks. The *jihād* consequently allowed the poets to exploit the disparity between the two faiths and the Franks were distanced from their status as 'people of the book' (*ahl al-kitāb*). It was, for the most part, Christian belief in the trinity, which the Muslims consider at odds with and anathema to the belief in oneness (*tawḥīd*) espoused in the Qur'ān that provided the strongest theological weapon in the arsenal of the Muslim polemic against Christianity. The anti-Frankish *jihād*, in line with Nūr al-Dīn's educational ambitions, incorporated traditional polemics to sow seeds of dissent and further demonstrate to the Muslim population that Christians had no right to the Holy Land or to the personage for whose sake they defended it.

In this period *jihād* poetry was composed and performed for three or four main purposes. A complex layered composition, the *qaṣīda* (panegyric ode) could serve the purpose of praise (*madḥ*); it was also used to lampoon (*hijā'*) the Christians for their military failures, misdirected worship, theological errors, and weaknesses – often to draw a contrast with the qualities of the poet's patron; it was also employed to celebrate the feats of the dead in elegies (*rithā'*). In light of the elements of *hijā'* and *munāqaḍāt* (polemics) in the poetry, Muslims relished what may be considered the aspired theological implications of the crusader defeat. This was vividly expressed in a poem composed by Ibn Maṭrūḥ (d. 649/1251)[2] after King Louis IX (d. 1270) lost his army at the battle of Fariskur in Muḥarram 648/April 1250 and was captured by the Egyptians. During certain periods Ibn Maṭrūḥ was the chief of the army (*nāẓir al-jaysh*), treasurer (*nāẓir al-khizāna*), and senior adviser to al-Malik al-Ṣāliḥ Ayyūb.[3] The poet calls on the French to consider the defeat in light of God's decree; predestination and divine decree in the event of defeat and humiliation must serve a purpose, and the poet emphasises that this must be considered. His message

2 See Ibn Khallikān, *Wafayāt*, 7:31–39.

3 Hirschler, *Medieval Arabic Historiography*, 23.

is akin to the voices of thirteeth-century western critics who were dissatisfied with the crusade.[4]

(1) Speak to the Frenchman, if you visit him, a true word from a good counsellor:
(2) 'God requite you for what has happened, the slaughter of the Messiah's adorers!'
(7) God help you in other similar adventures: who knows that in the end Jesus will not breathe freely!
(8) If your Pope is content with this, how often is a statement guilty of deceit!'[5] (1.63)

The poet rebukes the crusaders for their false trust in Jesus; in verses 2 and 3 he uses sarcasm to highlight how their adoration for Jesus does not avail them. We may trace this particular focus toward the religious status of the crusaders to the relationship between Ibn Maṭrūḥ and Ibn Wāṣil. Ibn Wāṣil spent much of his time in Hama before he was summoned to Cairo by the Mamlūk sultan Baybars (r. 658–76/1260–77) who sent him as an envoy to King Manfred of Sicily (r. 1258–66) where he spent two years.[6] While in Egypt, Ibn Wāṣil formed a close friendship with Ibn Maṭrūḥ. Although they had known one another before Ibn Maṭrūḥ's time in Sicily (in Hama Ibn Wāṣil had tutored Ibn Maṭrūḥ), once there, the pair were known to have met regularly. It is possible that while in Sicily Ibn Wāṣil became familiar with disputes in the church and learned that many Christians were indifferent toward the crusade. Knowing of Manfred's troubles with Pope Innocent IV and Louis IX must have allowed Ibn Wāṣil to develop insights into Christian and Church affairs; these ideas likely filtered down to the likes of Ibn Maṭrūḥ. Tibawi notes that "the rapidity with which ideas and scholars moved in those days of slow communication is often under-estimated."[7]

---

4 Humbert of Romans (d. 1277), Master General of the Dominican Order, authored his *Opusculum tripartitum* between 1272 and 1273. The text reveals the kind of objections, however popular they were, to taking up the cross and sheds light on the diversity of criticisms that Humbert sought to refute. See J. A. Brundage, 'Humbert of Romans and the Legitimacy of Crusader Conquests,' in *The Horns of Ḥaṭṭīn*, ed. B. Z. Kedar (London: Variorum, 1992), 302–313.

5 Gabrieli, *Arab Historians of the Crusades*, 294–295; al-Kutubī, *Fawāt al-wafayāt wa-l-dhayl 'alayhā*, ed. Iḥsān 'Abbās (Beirut: Dār Ṣādir, 1973), 1:232; Ibn Taghrībirdī, *al-Nujūm*, 6:371.

6 See G. Wiet, 'Baybars I,' *EI*², 1:1124–1126.

7 Tibawi, 'Origin and Character,' 234.

Another poet, this one anonymous, struck a similar message. The fact that the Muslims felt free to provoke the Franks to warfare indicates the buoyancy of the Muslims following the capture of King Louis.

(1) Say to the Frenchman: all the Muslims are grateful to him.
(2) Because he is good to us for sending us his armies.
(3) And the nation of Jesus (*ummatu ʿĪsā*) brought to Egypt much of what they possessed of munitions.[8]

Muslim poets were aware of the pope's significance to Christians and understood that he had the authority to sanction a crusade. Again, following Ibn Wāṣil's stay in Sicily, he noted that "The Pope in Rome is the caliph of the Messiah for them, standing in his place. He can declare what is forbidden and what is licit, [he can] cut and separate [excommunicate]."[9] The poet places the pope at the centre of the catastrophe; the decision to capture Damietta transpired through him:

(6) The Pope aspired to many things but destiny did not desire what he wanted.
(7) The ferocity of war infuriated them; it made them alert but with nothing to see.
(8) Their eyes did not become blind, but in fact their hearts were blinded.

While the poet's aforementioned line (8) (lam taʿma abṣāruhum wa-lakin qad ʿamiyat minhum al-baṣāʾir) disparages the crusaders for their superciliousness in the battle, the Qurʾānic imagery in the line represents a scornful view of the crusaders for their lack of religious intuition. The reference to the blindness of eyes and hearts is found in several Qurʾānic chapters; a few striking similarities can be noted in the following verses:

> (Lā taʿma al-abṣār wa-lakin taʿma al-qulūb allatī fī l-ṣudūr)
> Verily, it is not the eyes that grow blind, but it is the hearts which are in the breasts that grow blind.
>
> QURʾĀN, 22:46

8 Al-Kutubī, *Fawāt al-wafayāt*, 1:233.

9 Ibn Wāṣil, *Mufarrij*, 4:249.

And

> (Qāla rabbī lima ḥashartanī aʿmā wa-qad kuntu baṣīrā)
> He will say: "O my Lord! Why have you raised me up blind, while I had sight before?"
>
> QUR'ĀN, 20:125

The poet continues:

(13) And the Messiah takes his rest from them – from every *ʿilj* and from every unbeliever (*kāfir*).[10] (1.64)

The negative appelations *ʿilj* and *kāfir* serve as a contrast to the positive Messiah (*masīḥ*), an affirmation of the Islamic position and, again, a challenge of religious ascriptions. The crusaders were commonly described as *ʿilj*. A poem composed by Ibn al-Qaysarānī in celebration of the victory at Edessa in 538/1144 praised ʿImād al-Dīn Zangī (d. 541/1146), atabeg of Mosul, for his exceptional military qualities and religious piety. The poet also emphasises the Christian faith of the crusaders; he stresses that along with the military defeat of the crusaders, Christianity itself was also defeated. It is the misguided aspirations of the crusaders and their misplaced trust in their religion that is the focus. The *ʿulūj* (pl. of *ʿilj*), the 'unbelieving,' 'bestial foreigners' failed in their strategy. The term is also used contemptuously to refer to those religiously lacking;[11] and could also be seen as a reference of the debasement of the Christian clergy:

Ibn al-Qaysarānī wrote:

(8) There was a special significance in the conquest of Edessa, one that differed from what the *ʿulūj* believed.
(9) They hoped that the birthday of the son of Mary would give them victory, but what they believed about his birth was of no benefit.[12]
(19) And there is no *minbar* except that it is now proud
And there is no *muṣḥaf* [Qur'ān] except that its ink is now illuminated
(22) To where O prisoners of misguidance after this?
Your deviation has become humiliation and his right guidance has become honoured.

10 Al-Kutubī, *Fawāt al-wafayāt*, 1:233.
11 E. W. Lane, *An Arabic-English Lexicon* (Beirut: Librairie du Liban, 1968), 2128.
12 Abū Shāma, *Kitāb al-Rawḍatayn*, 1:173.

(25) Tell the kings of unbelief to surrender their kingdoms after this. Indeed the countries are his countries.
(27) God is the owner of the kingdoms of the heavens, so which land did the army of God not reach?
(28) With God is the determination, beginning at the waters of Sayḥān and taking its rest at the gardens of Constantinople.[13] (1.65)

The poem juxtaposes the pride of the Muslims with the defeat of the crusaders. To ossify the Muslims' belief that the crusaders were wicked and misled, the poets present God as having the same belief about them. The Franks are *"ulūj'* who were defeated in a theological victory that was symbolised through the conquest of Edessa; references to the *minbar* (pulpit) and *muṣḥaf* (Qur'ān) rejoicing are the kind of personification found in the poetry of the post-reconquest period; it validates the conquest and Zangī's feat on religious terms and reflects a new spiritual epoch. The antithesis of *ḍalāla* (misguidance) and *rashād* (guidance) in line 22 is metonymical, and relates to the mistake about the birthday of Jesus Christ, of Christian faith generally, and of crusader aspirations. The siege of the city of Edessa lasted for a month, from November to December 1144 (538), and the city fell to the Muslims on 26 Jumāda II 538/23 December 1144. Ibn al-Qaysarānī refers to the city as "a city of sin for the last fifty years" (10).[14] The poetry reveals Muslim awareness of the special occasion of Christmas and imputes to the Franks the expectation of victory because of the sanctity of that day. Their added incentive to defend Edessa failed to prevent the Muslim victory. Muslims of course do not believe that Christmas has any special value; instead of satirising the Franks for their false belief, the poet pointedly refers to Jesus as 'ibn Maryam' (son of Mary) in contrast to what the Franks would have believed sanctified the day, i.e., the birth of the son of God. The crusaders are presented as arrogant, "the Pope wanted many things," as a people who placed their trust in their own strength and in the worship of a false God. These reasons are presented as the cause of their defeat.

Abū Shāma introduces Ibn al-Qaysarānī's poem by citing three anecdotes from Ibn al-Athīr's *al-Kāmil*. They detail miraculous incidents, the first involving a Shāfiʿī jurist, Shaykh Abī ʿAbdallāh b. ʿAlī b. Mihrān, noted for his miraculous acts who, after retreating to his private lodge (*zāwiya*) emerged elated and informed his company that Zangī had captured Edessa. He also repeatedly claimed that Zangī would not be harmed because of his achievement. The anecdote concludes with a group of soldiers who participated in the conquest

13 Ibid., 1:174.
14 Ibid., 1:173.

swearing that they had seen the shaykh present at the battle. The second anecdote is a popular one. Some Muslims of the Near East considered the Norman rulers of Sicily hostile enemies, as exemplified by the cunning military tenacity of Roger II of Sicily. The fall of Edessa in 538/1144, however, did much to instill a newfound confidence in Muslim victory, and furthered by means of a popular story which circulated in Syria. In the story, the ruler of Sicily was elated at the successful incursions into the North African coast that he administered. When the news of success was brought to him, he announced, in the presence of his Muslim adviser, "O Jurist! Our forces have defeated the Muslim forces! Where was Muḥammad at the time of the Muslims' defeat? Why couldn't he support them!" The Muslim adviser looked at the ruler and replied, "At that particular time, Muḥammad was supervising the recovery of Edessa."[15] Lastly, Ibn al-Athīr relates that he heard one of the pious say: "I saw in my sleep a martyr in the best of states after he had been killed. I said to him: 'What did God do for you?' He said: 'He has forgiven me.' I asked, 'On account of what?' He said: 'On account of the conquest of Edessa.'"[16]

Another example of the Muslim awareness of the religious rationale behind the crusade and the importance of Jerusalem as a land that constituted a sacred space for Christians (because of the Christian belief about Jesus' death and his burial in the Holy City) can be discerned from a poem composed by ʿAbd al-Munʿim al-Jilyānī (d. 602/1207). The poet sought to promote the Ayyūbids through the feats of Ṣalāḥ al-Dīn, and rather than encouraging caution in the wake of the Third Crusade, the poetry instead advocates inner tenacity and fearlessness. The poet scorns the crusaders for their false worship and marvels at the Christian conviction and loyalty to Jesus. It is not altogether surprising that the poem lacks the *faḍāʾil al-Quds* sentiments evoked in the poetry preceding Ṣalāḥ al-Dīn's reconquest, since such sentiments now sufficiently permeated the outlook of the Muslims of Syria. He states that, in spite of the great numbers and extensive preparations, it was the divine decree (*qadr*) that denied the crusaders victory:

(1) O rescuer of Jerusalem from the hands of tyrants, the Franks swore that with their Lord's support they would enter it [a second time].

15 Ibn al-Athīr, *al-Tārīkh al-bāhir*, 32; H. Dajani-Shakeel, 'A Reassessment of Some Medieval and Modern Perceptions of the Counter-Crusade,' in *The Jihād and its Times*, ed. Hadia Dajani-Shakeel and Ronald A Messier (Ann Arbor, MI: University of Michigan Press, 1991), 47–48.

16 Abū Shāma, *Kitāb al-Rawḍatayn*, 1:172.

(2) So they spoke their lies in their description of their Lord, and the promise of God has instead been delivered in favour of the Muslims.

In these opening verses the religious motivation for the crusade is underscored. Mention of *rabb* (Lord) appears twice in this poem, initially to show how the sincerity of the crusaders' faith and certainty in victory was undermined by Ṣalāḥ al-Dīn and the Muslims. Secondly, the following verse refers to the polemic in 'their description of their Lord' in which the pronoun 'their' is distinct and differentiates from the Muslims' belief in God. Al-Jilyānī contends that the defeat of the crusaders was due to their transgression against God Himself; 'their lies' and 'their' manifestation of 'their Lord' are not juxtaposed, however, as one might expect, with motifs of 'monotheism' and 'true faith' that we saw featured in other poems. Verses 3 and 4 juxtapose Ṣalāḥ al-Dīn's fearlessness and tenacity in respect to other Muslim leaders of the time – the salient point being that Ṣalāḥ al-Dīn was able to recapture Jerusalem when others could not. The fact that, in this verse, Ṣalāḥ al-Dīn is referred to as the 'son of Ayyūb' is revealing for what it asserts about the Ayyūbid ruler's ascendency over members of the Zangids, because of his liberation of Jerusalem.

(3) Have you not seen the son of Ayyūb who, by himself, did what the era and its people could not do?
(4) The Franks became infuriated and cowardice afflicted them, and they became frightened and terrified.
(5) When Ṣalāḥ al-Dīn took Jerusalem, they said: "How can we leave it while our Lord is buried there?"
(6) Consider how many kings sailed there by sea to give support to the grave, but destiny was not on the side of those kings.
(7) Consider how many huge armies travelled to reach there, yet their destiny was to meet hyenas on the way.
(8) They cried out for help, spreading infections that divided them, and they gathered, for the war, much money which became booty [for us].

In verses 6–8 the poet outlines ways in which the crusaders' efforts were frustrated. Verse 6 uses the description '*shaqq al-biḥār*' which means 'sailed the sea,' but also connotes a more intense image of splitting and slashing the sea, an image that symbolises the drowning of Pharaoh and his army in the Red Sea and is described in the Qur'ān (25:63–67). The image suggests an overturning, an upturning; it is used in the Qur'ān in several places in relation to rocks (2:74), in relation to those contending against God and His Messenger (8:13); and in reference to the splitting of the earth (19:90, 50:44, 80:26).

(10) [He is like] a sword in front of Palestine. The one who produced the sword produced it sharp and strong for cutting.
(11) Their preparations were many, yet they divided and became factions without fighting.
(12) And indeed it is the name 'Ṣalāḥ al-Dīn' that frightens them when he is remembered in the army of the enemy.[17] (1.66)

The sword motif and metaphor in verse 9 reinforces the image of Ṣalāḥ al-Dīn as a protector of Palestine; the climax of the poem is reached by bolstering his repute as one who engenders fear in the crusader camp, the frightening (*marhūb*) description in verse 4 refers to the dread and terror he inspires in his enemies. The poem thus draws together motifs of war and religious imagery, and frames these around the achievements of Ṣalāḥ al-Dīn. Efforts of the crusader kings defending the land and the Muslim sultans recovering it are challenged by fate, which allowed Ṣalāḥ al-Dīn to emerge as the sole protector of the Holy Land.

The Muslims were aware of Jerusalem's importance to Christians and of the special place of the Holy Sepulchre, the liberation of which sacred site provided the central rationale for the crusade. ʿImād al-Dīn was eager to show his understanding of Christian belief through his rhymed prose (*sajʿ*) about the reconquest of Jerusalem in 583/1187. The Christians say that "this is our *qumāma* (waste), in it is our *maqām* (sanctuary) and from it our *qiyāma* (day of resurrection) will be established."[18] The play on the word *qiyāma*/*qumāma* was a popular one at the time, but here there is also a consideration of *qiyāma*, from the Kanīsat al-Qiyāma (Church of the Resurrection), and with respect to its eschatological meaning, the reference to *yawm al-qiyāma*, the day of resurrection. In relation to this, ʿImād al-Dīn also imputes these sentiments to the Christians: "Every one of us is worth twenty and every ten worth two hundred, and to defend the *qumāma* we will establish the *qiyāma*, and for our love for its safety, we will end all peace."[19]

---

17 Ibid., 4:68–69.

18 Ibid., 3:215; al-Harawī, who visited Jerusalem in 569/1173, said Christians call the Sepulchre the '"Resurrection' because they believe the Messiah's resurrection took place at that site." The play on the *qiyāma*/*qumāma* confused him; he noted, "the truth is that the spot was called 'The Refuse heap' because it served as a garbage heap for the city." Al-Harawī, *A Lonely Wayfarer's Guide to Pilgrimage*, trans. Josef W. Meri (Princeton, NJ: Darwin Press, 2004), 76.

19 ʿImād al-Dīn al-Iṣfahānī, *al-Fatḥ al-qussī*, 125.

According to ʿImād al-Dīn, Christians say that,

> in it [Jerusalem] Jesus was crucified … God took a body and the body became God, and the mixture was established and the cross was erected and light descended, and darkness went away; the nature of God was fused, and in it the existing and the non-existing were mixed; the church of God was built up, and the virgin gave birth; they add misguidance to what they worship and are misled by doubts – and they abandoned the clear proofs.[20]

As the aforementioned poem reveals, Muslims were therefore aware that the Christians accorded this sanctity to the tomb and that in the sixth/twelfth century this provided unfailing vigour for the repeated crusades which sought to secure, repossess the Holy City, and defend 'the grave,' meaning the Holy Sepulchre. ʿImād al-Dīn continued his rhymed prose with this description: "Before they get to the grave, we will die defending it, how can we not fervently dispute [their claim to it] and how can we not fight [for it]."[21]

It has been generally acknowledged that the fall of Edessa in 538/1144 sparked Muslim interest in the anti-Frankish *jihād*, and that with this a clearer and more distinct *jihād* vocabulary emerged. Hillenbrand, however, highlights earlier examples of *jihād* titulature in tomb inscriptions dedicated to Ṭughtikin, the ruler of Damascus, the Artuqid prince Balak, and Zangī.[22] The defeat of the Franks at the battle of Balat ('Field of Blood') in 513/1119 between the crusader principality of Antioch and Īl-Ghāzī (500–516/1107–22) near Sarmada in Syria was also a key event. After the victory, Īl-Ghāzī, in spite of his religious transgressions (he was known to drink excessively), was depicted as a *mujāhid*.[23] In light of Hillenbrand's notes, the following couplet, composed as a celebration of the victory, reveals an early demonstration of the kind of

20 Abū Shāma, *Kitāb al-Rawḍatayn*, 3:215.

21 Ibid., 3:215.

22 C. Hillenbrand, 'Jihad Propaganda in Syria from the Time of the First Crusade until the Death of Zengi: The Evidence of Monumental Inscriptions,' in *The Frankish Wars and Their Influence on Palestine*, ed. K. Athamina and R. Heacock (Birzeit: Birzeit University Publications, 1994), 60–69.

23 "Forty days later, Baldwin stood in battle array against Īl-Ghāzī. The latter was so constituted that whenever he drank wine he would feel drunk for twenty days. Now it happened that after he had routed the Franks and put them to the sword, he drank wine and entered his period of intoxication, from which he did not recover until King Baldwin, the prince, had arrived in Antioch with his army." Usāma ibn Munqidh, *An Arab-Syrian Gentleman*, 149.

religious contention that was more frequent in the poetry composed after the taking of Edessa in 538/1144. The fact that the Qur'ān was set against the Bible is telling of the existence, however unrepresentative, of a psychological climate in Syria, some decades preceding the later unified *jihād* efforts, that was focused on the liberation of Jerusalem.

After the victory in 513/1119 an anonymous poet wrote:

(1) Say whatever you want, your saying is accepted; and after the Creator, we depend on you.
(2) And the Qur'ān rejoiced when you gave it victory and the Injīl [Bible] cried when it lost its men.[24] (1.67)

In verses composed by the Egyptian poet As'ad b. Mamātī in praise of Ṣalāḥ al-Dīn, we find an interesting reference to '*umm al-ṣalīb*' (lit., 'mother of the cross'). The poet contrasts the high spirits of the Muslim camp with the sorrows of the crusaders, here epitomised by the word 'mother,' although it would seem that *umm* was intended to mean *umma* (nation).[25] But, it could also be 'mother,' the effect of which would be a gendered imagery of women mourners.

(23) When he went out to the battle the sheath of his sword rejoiced
(24) While the nation of the cross wept
(25) And conquering the land of Syria appeared easy for him after it was initially difficult.[26] (1.68)

One can therefore see in 'Imād al-Dīn al-Iṣfahānī's verse an example of contraction. His perception as a poet, showing his listeners that he perceives a twofold reality in the exploits of the crusaders, allows him to maintain his rank as a worthy lyricist. Arabic poetry in its Islamic mode was limited by conventionality – originality was not central to the poet's intent. The imaginative stylistic features, however, allow us to appreciate the poetic dexterity of the writer. In medieval Islamic courts, poetry lay at the centre of political and public discourse. Great fortunes of wealth and political status could be gained by mastering poetic conventions which could be used and subverted to demonstrate one's innovation and mastery.

24 Abū l-Fidā, *al-Mukhtaṣar fī akhbār al-bashr: tārīkh Abī l-Fidā* (Cairo, 19–), 1:231.

25 In (أم) '*umm*' the (ة) is disconnected to assure the fixed meters of the rhythmical poem. The intended meaning then with the addition of the (ة) would render the meaning أمة (nation).

26 'Imād al-Dīn al-Iṣfahānī, *Kharīdat al-qaṣr*, 1:108.

This incorporation of religious symbolism was even more evident decades later, in the words of ʿImād al-Dīn al-Iṣfahānī, who clearly sought to advance the cause of the *jihād* by inciting Ṣalāḥ al-Dīn to exact revenge on the Franks and to purify the occupied lands from their unbelief. The religiosity advocated by the poets around Nūr al-Dīn and Ṣalāḥ al-Dīn is similar; descriptions of the afterlife and the day of judgement were evoked to stimulate pietistic considerations – these were part of the religious milieu of the *jihād*s of this age and were important in creating political motivation. There was no exemption for Christian clergy as far as ʿImād al-Dīn was concerned; the role of the clergy in advocating the crusade was of course well known to the Muslims, and men of religion were also targets of *jihād* poetry of the period. It is essential to remember that many poets wrote to put forward their perspective of their religious superiority, this appears not only in poetry, but also intermittently in Muslim chronicles.[27]

ʿImād al-Dīn al-Iṣfahānī wrote,

(4) So rise and conquer Jerusalem, and cause bloodshed in it. When the blood flows, it will cleanse the city.
(5) And bestow death upon the Asbatār [Hospitallers] and push the ceiling down on the bishop.
(6) And rescue those countries from unbelief, so that God will save you [when you] stand [before Him] on the day of judgement.[28] (1.69)

In spite of the stereotypical nature of the poet's sentiment, these verses carried quite an emotional charge. The sequence of imperatives in the lines, *fa-sir* (so rise), *iftaḥ* (conquer), *isfak* (shed), *ihdi* (bestow), *wa-hudd* (push), *khalliṣ* (rescue), generates a tone of immediacy in the poem's concluding lines. The poet charges Ṣalāḥ al-Dīn with the obligation of recapturing Jerualem, punishing the Christian clergy, and purifying the Muslim lands as a form of salvation for him in the hereafter. The imagery in the final line is comparable to the poetic exhortation levelled at Nūr al-Dīn in relation to his taking high taxes: 'What would you say if you stood on the station [day of judgement] by yourself, humiliated and with a heavy accountability? (6).[29] The *mawqif* (standing) mentioned in this poem and in line 6 of al-Iṣfahānī's poem above refers to man's accountability to God on the day of judgement, used here as a religious

27 A case may be made, for example, of Sibṭ b. al-Jawzī's account of the siege of Damascus (543/1148) in the Second Crusade: Sibṭ b. al-Jawzī, *Mirʾāt al-zamān*, part 1, 8:198.

28 Abū Shāma, *Kitāb al-Rawḍatayn*, 2:296.

29 Ibn Kathīr, *al-Bidāya wa-l-nihāya*, 12:299.

warning and incentive. The reference to the Asbatār in verse 5, a name used to designate the Hospitallers, originated during the crusades and reveals the Muslims' understanding of the importance of military orders. Muslim appreciation for the religiosity of the Hospitallers may be discerned from the inclusion of the bishop in the same line. For 'Imād al-Dīn, the Christian clergy and Hospitallers represented the *kufr* (unbelief) that Ṣalāḥ al-Dīn was entrusted to repel.

An important feature of a study such as this hinges on what we are able to understand about the audiences of this poetry. The references analysed in this book pertaining to the personage of Jesus – as Muslims see him – allow us to consider three things. First, whether his inclusion in the poetry was intended simply to demonstrate Muslim loyalty and attachment to him; secondly, that Christians were misled into fighting Muslims in their sacred precincts, this was based on their false belief in Jesus – the very person for whose sake they set out to fight; and thirdly, the poetry was also directed to Christians who lived among Muslims in Syria and Egypt. The indigenous population were seen as either 'Franks' or 'non-Franks.' The native Christian population did not use the term they would have used for themselves, 'Naṣāra' (Nazarenes) and so did not confuse their indigenous co-religionists with the European Franks, and so too did the Muslims distinguish between the Faranj (European Franks) and the local Christians.[30]

There is convincing evidence that Muslims of Syria showed some partiality toward Oriental Christians in Syria, Palestine, and Egypt before the First Crusade, on account of their status as 'people of the book' (*ahl al-kitāb*). In spite of the evolution of juristic formulae concerning the treatment of the *ahl al-kitāb*, some called for a cautious approach toward them, thereby strictly enforcing the view of the superiority of Islam and Muslims and the subordination of Jews and Christians, nevertheless, justice and protection were recognisable rights granted to the indigenous communities of the Muslim Near East. Their inclusion in the military, their roles in society – as physicians, scholars, and merchants – and the relative autonomy granted to them to practice their faiths and build places of worship, stemmed from Qur'ānic injunctions and prophetic instruction pertaining to the treatment of the *dhimmīs*. The observation of Runciman, who credits the crusaders' bloodthirsty zeal for what became "the

30 P. K. Hitti, 'The Impact of the Crusades on the Near East,' in *A History of the Crusades*, ed. K. M. Setton, N. P. Zacour, H. W. Hazard (Madison, WI and London: University of Wisconsin Press, 1985), 5:120.

fanaticism of Islam," seems patently incorrect and simplistic.[31] Hillenbrand cautions against oversimplified statements such as this because they may lead to slanted interpretations and inform modern political or religious agendas.[32] Nonetheless, it is worth emphasising that Muslims seemed to have an emotional detachment from Christians during the crusader period, at least as seen in the poetry, in spite of the latter's *dhimmī* status. Poets seemed keen to scorn the Franks for their belief, loyalty, and adherence to Christianity. This may be read as an emphasis on the religious differences between the two camps, but may well also have intensified the antagonism toward indigenous Christians. Or the poetry may, of course, be seen as a by-product of the growing antipathy toward indigenous Christians because of the crusaders (although Ibn al-Qaysarānī's gender-based poetry cited later in this chapter appears to suggest otherwise). In light of this, to what extent did the anti-Frankish *jihād*, through the themes and focus of *jihād* poetry, also increase tensions with the indigenous Christian population? It seems likely that the poetry was an a posteriori product of sixth-/twelfth- and seventh-/thirteenth-century religio-political considerations that spoke of a reshaping of Christians – be they Frankish or Oriental – in the popular Muslim outlook. This position may be understood inversely by examining the way in which the reconquest of 583/1187 resulted in a change in the relationship between the Franks and indigenous Orthodox Christians. We may also see a change in the Muslim treatment of *dhimmīs* as a consequence of the capture of Jerusalem in 492/1099 and the establishment of a crusader settlement, wherein, in spite of Latin mistrust for their native co-religionists, Muslim suspicion of them fostered an antagonism that was, partly, created through their image.

Because of the mixed evidence from chroniclers and poets about the treatment of Oriental Christians during the crusades, it is difficult to clearly assess the influence of the crusades on Muslim behaviour toward the *dhimmīs*. What seems clear is that there was greater toleration of Christians in the Ayyūbid period than in the Mamlūk period. Though conflict with the crusaders was a direct cause of hostility with Christians, the Mongol onslaught in the seventh/thirteenth century and consequent suspicion toward the Copts in Egypt further created a fervent desire among many Muslims to behave with intense hostility toward any potential anti-Islamic forces. While the crusades facilitated

31 S. Runciman, *A History of the Crusades*, vol. 1: *The First Crusade and the Foundation of the Kingdom of Jerusalem* (Cambridge: Cambridge University Press, 1951), 1:287.

32 Hillenbrand, *The Crusades*, 407–420, 411, E. Sivan, *L'Islam et la croisade: idéologie et propagande dans les réactions musulmanes aux croisades* (Paris: Adrien Maisonneuve, 1968), 180–183.

the contact between Egyptian and Frankish Christians, the interaction did not always produce positive outcomes. Crusader victories in Egypt sometimes led to Muslim attacks against indigenous Christians. Wilfong suggests that Muslim rulers of Egypt did not distinguish between the two groups, though we must also acknowledge a more general anti-Christian feeling in the Mamlūk period.[33] We know that Coptic administrative effectiveness in the Mamlūk bureaucracy was viewed with some concern; some Copts were considered to have become too powerful, corrupt, and pretentious. We may further attribute Muslim reprisals in light of accusations of Coptic collaboration with Frankish crusaders and cases of Christian glee following, for example, the arrival of the Mongols in 658/1260.[34] Hillenbrand notes that the nature of Islamic society was unique in the sense that it renewed and purified itself from within, and the *jihād* focus of the sixth/twelfth century and onwards may have sprung from this phenomenon alone. Notwithstanding the division and disagreements that existed at the time, on religious or political matters, it is likely, she argues, that "the coming of the crusaders with their 'new brand' of fanatical Christianity acted as a catalyst, or even a direct agent, in the process of hardening Sunnī Muslim hearts against people of other faiths, and indeed against any kind of religious deviancy within the ranks of the Muslims themselves."[35] We must be cautious however of over-simplifying the place and role of non-Muslim communities and the extent of their *dhimmī* status, and instead appreciate the complexity in the social, political, and religious milieu of the *dhimmīs*. MacEvitt and Werthmuller do not accord with Wilfong's view that the Muslims did not distinguish between the local Christians and the Franks, and that many were in fact aware of the distinction and did not seek retaliation. The authors further stress the flexibility of non-Muslim communities in their religious and social identities, that medieval Islamic state and society retained a vibrant non-Muslim community, "Non Muslims often found themselves pressured and yet privileged, marginalised and yet integrated, partly shaped by external forces and yet often clearly acting – rather than merely *reacting* – through internal agency and conscience."[36]

---

33 T. G. Wilfong, 'The Non-Muslim Communities: Christian Communities,' in *The Cambridge History of Egypt*, ed. M. W. Daly and C. F. Petry (Cambridge: Cambridge University Press, 1998), 195.

34 See Hillenbrand, *The Crusades*, 416–417.

35 Ibid., 419.

36 K. J. Werthmuller, *Coptic Identity and Ayyubid Politics in Egypt 1218–1250* (Cairo: American University of Cairo Press, 2010), p. 5. See also C. MacEvitt, *The Crusades and the Christian World of the East: Rough Tolerance* (Philadelphia: University of Pennsylvania Press, 2008).

Thus far, consideration has not been given to the place of Jesus in the popular imagination of Fāṭimid Shīʿīs during the crusades, nor have we asked whether a similar idea of 'appropriation' as discerned in Zangid and Ayyūbid Sunnī circles existed among the Shīʿīs. The idea of the Messiah and future redemption is entrenched in Shīʿī Islam. Pieter Smoor, for example, has examined eschatological ideas pertaining to the Mahdī, Dajjāl (Antichrist), and Jesus in third-/ninth- and fourth-/tenth-century Fāṭimid poetry by, or for, Shīʿī *imāms*.[37] There does exist, however, an oft-quoted verse by the contemporary Shīʿī Ibn al-Munīr al-Ṭarābulsī that draws on the image of Jesus as shaped by the conflict, and whose poetic satires are similar to those found in material composed by Sunnī Muslims. The line was originally brought to the fore by Sivan in his acclaimed 1968 publication *L'Islam et la croisade: idéologie et propagande dans les réactions musulmanes aux croisades*.[38] The last lines of the poem are translated below.

(15) It is as if his battlefield is paradise, and for fighting he is rewarded [with] the aroma of the heavenly fountain.
(17) *Jihād* is by night and day and when you are patient and grateful therein, you succeed.
(18) The best someone can hear about you is shown through the shaking of the *minbar* [pulpit] at your description.
(19) God has kept for you the world and the religion, and has brightened your face.
(20) Until you see Jesus fleeing from Jerusalem to seek protection under your sword.[39] (1.70)

Surprisingly, it seems that Sivan's translation of line 20 from Ibn al-Munīr's poem of 544/1149 was incomplete and is thus misleading, as it suggests a disdainful tone not in keeping with the Muslim reverence for Jesus. The translated line from Sivan, "until you see Jesus flee from Jerusalem"[40] (20) speaks of a popular new Christian view that is shaped by theological provenances that, in general, were not traditionally ascribed to the Christian belief in Jesus. Irrespective

37 P. Smoor, 'Al-Mahdi's Tears: Impressions of Fāṭimid Court Poetry,' in *Egypt and Syria in the Fāṭimid, Ayyūbid, and Mamlūk Eras: Proceedings of the 4th and 5th International Colloquium Organized at the Katholieke Universiteit Leuven in May 1995 and 1996* (Leuven, 1998), 131–170, 142.

38 Sivan, *L'Islam et la croisade*.

39 Abū Shāma, *Kitāb al-Rawḍatayn*, 1:214.

40 D. Pinault, 'Images of Christ in Arabic Literature,' *Die Welt des Islams* 27 (1987), 111.

of the mistranslation, the image of Jesus was certainly influenced by the crusades; the crusader-induced rivalry between the personages of Jesus and the Prophet Muḥammad entered the domain of Muslim thought whereas previously the kind of sentiments expressed by poets may have been considered an affront to religious orthodoxy. One thus sees that the polemic against the crusaders was given a new edge with the victory at the battle of Fariskur (648/1250). Both poets quoted use ascriptions for the crusaders specific to the person of ʿĪsā (Jesus), whereas earlier poetry uses 'ibn Maryam' to refer to Jesus and Banū Aṣfar (pale-faced ones) was used for the crusaders. Unfortunately, Sivan's mistranslation entirely distorts what was suggested by the poet and is an error that has been adopted by others.[41] A careful reading of the verse presents a different picture entirely. Far from being disdainful, it is instead more in line with the kind of Muslim sentiments expressed vis-à-vis Christian and Muslim claims to 'appropriate' Jesus for themselves.

To stress the sword's achievement verses 15 and 17 both draw on success, one worldly and the other anticipated in 'paradise' and the 'heavenly fountain' – for which 'God has kept for you the world and the religion' (19). Though Ibn al-Munīr was Shīʿī, he credits Ṣalāḥ al-Dīn with the good news of divine favour. His poem is imbued with religious terminology: 'paradise, *minbar*, God, religion, Jesus, Jerusalem,' are all sentiments that likely gained him acceptance from his listeners and show that he maintained religious conventions. Contrasting motifs of 'day' and 'night' are popular in poetry and were used for the sultan by others, like al-Jilyānī; so too the poet used motifs of light imagery.[42] Since great fortunes of wealth and political status could be gained through the mastery of poetic conventions which could be used and subverted to demonstrate innovation and mastery, Ibn al-Munīr's concluding verse sets forth an original perspective with regard to the 'appropriation' of Jesus for the purpose of the anti-Frankish *jihād*. He presents Jesus as so disaffected with the Christian crusaders fighting in his name, that he wants to 'flee from Jerusalem' and seek Ṣalāḥ al-Dīn's protection. His verse does not draw on the same tropes of 'purifying' Jerusalem that ʿImād al-Dīn al-Iṣfahānī draws on – 'When Jerusalem is emptied (*ṣafirat*) of the pale-faced ones (Banū Aṣfar)' – but suggests a more positive reading focused on 'rescuing' the sacred personage Muslims believed they had more right to; here Jesus is not abased under Ṣalāḥ al-Dīn's sword, but protected.

41 See Sivan, *L'Islam et la croisade*, 62; E. Sivan, 'Le caractère sacre dé Jérusalem dans l'Islam,' *SI* 27 (1967), 155; Pinault, 'Images of Christ,' 111; C. Tyerman, *God's War: A New History of the Crusades* (London: Penguin, 2006), 344.

42 Al-Jilyānī, *Dīwān al-tadbīj*, 94.

The *jihād* consequently allowed the poets to exploit the disparity between the two faiths; Christian crusaders were far removed from their *ahl al-kitāb* status and Muslim poets were ever eager to reveal the differences. The poet Ibn al-Mujāwir (d. 600/1204) presented his poem to the sultan in the Holy City, congratulating him for the reconquest and depicting it as a victory for monotheism. Ṣalāḥ al-Dīn emerges in the poem as someone who acted based on his unyielding commitment to *jihād* – his struggle was predicated on religious principles and he sought to reflect the disparity between the two religious communities. The poet declaims: "He [Ṣalāḥ al-Dīn] put *tawḥīd* [oneness of God] into effect after their trinity, and the laws of the Qur'ān were established over the Gospel" (10)[43] (1.71).

The poet first welcomes his listeners (lines 1–5) to consider the enormity of the Islamic obligation to participate in the *jihād* in the face of crusader threats. The poet adeptly begins his poem by stressing the gratuitous use of lyrical verse at a time when serious effort (*jidd*) is paramount (line 2): 'The time is more serious than listening to a poem (*aḍyaqu min samāʿi qaṣīdatin*) (line 1). Ṣalāḥ al-Dīn is described as the one who guided the way to the *jihād* (line 3), trusts in God (line 4), and who 'strengthened in power the pillars of the prophetic faith (*millat Aḥmad*)' (line 5). Line 10 cited above is intended to celebrate the Muslims' theological victory over the Christians with the juxtaposition of oneness (*tawḥīd*) and trinity (*tathlīth*), and the Gospel (Injīl) and scripture of the Qur'ān (*muṣḥaf*). The poets of this time reminded their listeners of the ongoing struggle between Islam and Christianity. In the purification of Jerusalem there is a sensory connection to the heavenly/natural order of things, the *adhān* takes the place of church bells as the recitation of the Qur'ān replaces the Bible. Ṣalāḥ al-Dīn is also described as having 'given life to and established the religion of Muḥammad' (line 24). Contemporary poets fused conventional Islamic rhetoric with Muslim disparagement of the underlying salient motive of the crusaders, including, *imitatio Christi*, aware that the crusaders were motivated by their love for Christ and their desire to protect the Holy Sepulchre.[44] Muslim attachment to Christ and their perception of Christian transgressions in his name nevertheless created opportunities for Muslims to scorn their enemy while claiming the moral high ground by using the person of Christ in their favour. This line of thinking was employed to good effect by the Fāṭimid vizier Malik al-Ṣāliḥ Ṭalāʾiʿ b. Ruzzīk (d. 556/1161).

43 Abū Shāma, *Kitāb al-Rawḍatayn*, 3:237.

44 See W. Purkis, 'Elite and Popular Perceptions of *imitatio Christi* in Twelfth-Century Crusade Spirituality,' in *Elite and Popular Religion*, ed. K. Cooper and J. Gregory (Woodbridge: Ecclesiastical History Society, 2006), 54–64.

Ṭalā'iʿ b. Ruzzīk composed a poem lamenting the presence of the Franks in Jerusalem, particularly their violation of the sanctity of al-Aqṣā Mosque. The poem was composed for the bereaved Usāma b. Munqidh, ruler of Shayzar, following the loss of his family in a series of earthquakes which began in 551/1156.[45] Jerusalem is seen to have been polluted by pigs and alcohol, both of which are referred to in the Qur'ān as repugnant.

(5) There are pigs and alcohol in the middle of it, and the Franks compete to ring the bell, and inside it is the cross.
(6) If the Messiah saw it he would not be pleased by such actions; they falsely allege that such actions are preceded by him.
(7) The furthest people from the worship of the Lord of mankind are a people whose deity is crucified.[46] (1.72)

Usāma b. Munqidh describes the following incident:

> I saw one of the Franks come up to the amir Mu'in al-Din (may God have mercy upon him) while he was in the Dome of the Rock, and say, 'Would you like to see God when He was young?' 'Why yes,' Mu'in al-Din replied. So this Frank walked in front of us until he brought us to an icon of Mary and the Messiah (Peace be upon him) when he was a child, sitting in her lap. 'This is God when He was young,' he said. May God be exalted far beyond what the infidels say![47]

This is certainly typical of the attitude of the Muslims. The Frankish occupation of the mosques was deemed a grave violation of the religious sanctity of these places. The transformation of the mosques with explicit Christian symbols of faith could be deeply humiliating for some Muslims of the city and those outside it who heard of the desecrations. Muslims thus held that the expulsion of the crusaders from Jerusalem was a divinely sanctioned purification.

Finally, in terms of the new-found focus on *jihād* in Muslim poetry and the greater interest in polemics (*munāqaḍāt*) during this time, we may consider the interesting and popular anecdote cited earlier and examine it in light of the various inclusions of the mention of the Prophet in anti-Frankish *jihād* literature. The story, mentioned earlier, concerns the ruler of Sicily, who was elated by the successful incursions into the North African coast that he administered;

45 Usāma b. Munqidh, *The Book of Contemplation*, xxviii–xxix.
46 Ibn Ruzzīk, *Dīwān Ṭalā'iʿ Ibn Ruzzīk* (Najaf: al-Maktabat al-Ahliyya, 1964), 63.
47 Usāma b. Munqidh, *The Book of Contemplation*, 147–148.

when he challenged one of his Muslim advisers about the reason the Prophet Muḥammad did not defend the city, he was informed that the Prophet was supervising the conquest of Edessa. One need not be hindered by what may be an unreliable narrative here – what is important is the purpose behind the story and how it fitted into the social logic shared by the source and its subject. The story had a distinct social use that must be interpreted in light of the changing state of Muslim affairs and the new focus on *jihād*; "these anecdotes are likely to have been 'true' in the sense that these stories were believed by their contemporaries."[48] Since Jesus is revered as a prophet and messenger in Islam, in the poetry he is sometimes conveniently set against the crusaders and their actions. Though the crusaders were necessarily evil, their actions were considered as based on their religious principles, and not by their failure to follow their religion correctly. The idea of Jesus' not finding favour with the crusaders' actions underscores the superiority of Muslim conduct in the crusades – they adhered to Islamic guidelines, and this justified the Muslim response. This is in contrast to Walter the Chancellor's presentation of Īl-Ghāzī as "star of the law," and his description of Īl-Ghāzī as someone who viciously tortured Christians, while acting in accordance with the guidelines of his religion.[49] Mallett's article on Walter the Chancellor's account of the battles between the forces of Antioch and those of their Muslim neighbours in northern Syria in the 1110s and 1120s highlights the presentation of the Muslim 'Other' in Latin writings of the early period of the crusades. Murray notes that the writings of William of Tyre, Walter the Chancellor, and Fucher of Chartres describe the Franks in a way that emphasises their distinction from other peoples of the Middle East, and that their use of terms such as *Franci* and *Latini* directly contrasts terms such as *Turci, Saraceni,* and *Suriani*.[50] The disparaging epithets that reflect the crusaders' perceptions as misguided pagans is akin to the presentation of Īl-Ghāzī in Walter the Chancellor's *Bella Antiochena* as the "minister of death" and a savage torturer of prisoners.[51]

48 Chamberlain, *Knowledge and Social Practice*, 19.

49 Alex Mallett, 'The "Other" in the Crusading Period: Walter the Chancellor's Presentation of Najm al-Dīn Il-Ghāzī,' *Al-Masāq*, 22 (2010), 121.

50 A. Murray, 'Ethnic Identity in the Crusader States,' in *Concepts of National Identity in the Middle Ages*, ed. Simon Forde, Alan V. Murray, and Lesley Johnson (Leeds: Leeds Texts and Monographs 14, 1995), 61–64.

51 "[T]his wicked man was delighted by their torments and he laughed at them as if he were refreshed by some food to fuel his cruelty … at his order a thousand or more soldiers were ready, carrying naked swords in their hands so that by striking out they could at the same time tear the prisoners to pieces and delight the unholy one." Alex Mallett,

Even though Muslim preachers did not invoke the Prophet Muḥammad for assistance, the crusaders were eager to understand Muslim loss through their own Christian outlook in which invoking Jesus is an accepted practice. Although the aforementioned anecdote about the Prophet Muḥammad supervising the recovery of Edessa in no way speaks of a case of a Muslim vision akin to those in crusader accounts of heavenly assistance, it is nevertheless worth noting what Muslims may have believed about physical heavenly support and the ways in which the poetry of the period, as discussed below, reveals this. During the crusades, Jesus was believed to be ever-present, instructing and encouraging the holy warriors. Although there is no comparable volume of 'visions' in the course of the Muslim *jihād*s, the few that we know of reveal a novel feature of the way *jihād* events were recorded. Visions of saints were, and still are, a feature of Sufism that gained a particular prominence in the medieval period. The sixth/twelfth century was an extremely important time for the spiritual shaping of Sufism. The fusion of intellectual scholarship with the inwardly-oriented piety of the Sufis in the sixth/twelfth century and beyond produced a situation not entirely bound by rigidities of one mode of religious acuity and practice or another. Thus, one sees an interlacing between Sufism and traditional intellectual discourse.

While Christian chronicles therefore make much mention of signs, prophecies, and visions, Muslim contemporary sources, though less frequently, also contain cases of visions of divine assistance. The Christian defeat at the battle of Balat in 513/1119 by the Artuqid Īl-Ghāzī was, according to Ibn al-Qalānisī "one of the finest of victories, and such plenitude of divine aid was never granted to Islam in all its past ages." Those present, he comments, were privileged "to witness the splendid miracle sent by God."[52] While vivid details of the victory are not ignored by the contemporary Ibn al-ʿAdīm, he takes care to further describe a man "renowned for his strength who had been captured by a weak, short and ill-armed Muslim."[53] Bemused by such a capture, Muslim soldiers came to learn from the prisoner that the latter was in fact captured by a larger-than-life warrior, "a great man, greater than me and stronger, and he handed me over to this individual. He wore a green robe and rode a green horse!"[54] The chronicler's reference to green may allude to the Prophet's intervention,

'The "Other" in the Crusading Period: Walter the Chancellor's Presentation of Najm al-Dīn Il-Ghāzī,' *Al-Masāq*, 22 (2010), 113–128.

52 Ibn al-Qalānisī, *Tārīkh Dimashq*, 320; Ibn al-Qalānisī, *The Damascus Chronicle*, 161.

53 Ibn al-ʿAdīm, *Zubdat al-ḥalab*, 190.

54 Ibid.

but there are other explanations.[55] These examples stem, in part, from a new approach toward Sufism in some quarters of the medieval Muslim world, as the impact of the conflict with the crusaders and Mongols together with the growing influence of Sufism created a "new and *political* sphere of operation for glimpses of the Unseen, portents of triumph or doom, spiritual energies channelled in the cause of war against infidels."[56] The role of the religious class in this period was unique as men of religion had also become integral to the military conflict with respect to bearing arms – a matter that will now be explored further with particular reference to Nūr al-Dīn Zangī.

Nūr al-Dīn and the Creation of a Pious Warrior Ethos

> Even though the renown of the might of a son of Adam reach east and west, and men from east to west acknowledge his rule and pay taxes to his diwan, he yet must die alone, be laid in the grave alone, and pay his accounts alone.[57]

---

55 The Qur'ānic figure of Khiḍr (lit., green one) seems, particularly in Turkey, to be a vague personality conceived of mainly as a helper to those in need. It is worth noting that Ibn ʿAsākir mentions Khiḍr as a phantasmic night visitor to the Umayyad Mosque in Damascus. Ibn ʿAsākir, *Tārīkh Dimashq*, 16:402. Furthermore, it should be noted that in Islamic tradition it is angels who are usually entrusted with delivering divine assistance. See Qur'ān, 3:123–125. As noted, this could also be a reference to the elusive *abdāl*. For more information on the veneration of al-Khiḍr in the medieval period, see J. W. Meri, 'Re-Appropriating Sacred Space: Medieval Jews and Muslims Seeking Elijah and al-Khaḍir,' in *Medieval Encounters: Jewish, Christian and Muslim Culture in Confluence and Dialogue* (Leiden; Brill, 1999), 5:237–264. Ibn ʿAsākir's *Tārīkh* contains an interesting narration: "Elias and Khaḍir both fast in Jerusalem during Ramaḍān, and both perform the *ḥajj* every year ..." Ibn ʿAsākir, *Tārīkh Dimashq*, 16:428.

56 T. Khalidi, *Arabic Historical Thought in the Classical Period* (Cambridge: Cambridge University Press, 1994), 212. We may extend our analysis to other literary genres circulating in the Muslim world at this time. The *Baḥr al-fawā'id* contains an opening chapter on 'The Book of Conduct of Holy War'. The author begins and concludes his chapter by bringing the indispensable component of inner, spiritual motivations for the "lesser" physical *jihād* to the fore. The chapter concludes with a narration that blends ideas pertaining to divine help, ideas about *ṭalab al-shahāda* (pursuit of martyrdom), and the possibility of miraculous occurrences. Anecdotes like these may have gone some way in motivating participation in the anti-Frankish *jihād*, since it is likely that the readership spread beyond the author's patron, Arslān Aba b. Āq Sunqur. See Meisami (trans. and ed.), *The Sea of Precious Virtues*, 34–35.

57 Meisami (trans. and ed.), *The Sea of Precious Virtues*, 50.

The aforementioned instruction from the *Baḥr al-fawāʾid* evokes the kind of pietistic sentiments found in chronicles that established Nūr al-Dīn's reputation as a devout warrior for the Islamic cause. While chronicles provide examples of his magnanimity and piety, the poetry allows us to consider his representation in light of Islam's illustrious predecessors. This section examines some of those similarities and shows that the growth of Sufism in this period augmented his noted reputation for piety.

The Zangids and Ayyūbids strongly encouraged poets and scholars of religion and science to take a position within their courts. Often chroniclers and poets who impressed the rulers with their works were appointed as *qāḍīs*, *wazīrs* (viziers), court poets, royal biographers or other court functionaries who served to bolster the political positions of their patrons and contribute to the cultural and religious life of the major cities. When ʿImād al-Dīn al-Iṣfahānī was introduced to Nūr al-Dīn, for example, his presentation of a *qaṣīda* impressed Nūr al-Dīn enough to grant him a post in his chancery.

Aside from literary skills that could provide opportunities for wealth and status, friendships with the civilian elite (*aʿyān*) often provided lucrative prospects as well. The friendship of ʿImād al-Dīn's uncle al-ʿAzīz with the brothers Ayyūb and Shīrkūh, the father and uncle of Ṣalāḥ al-Dīn, facilitated ʿImād al-Dīn's own *entrée* into prominent social and religious circles when he came to Syria. By incorporating skilled litterateurs the court sought to enhance the supremacy of the caliph and the civilian elite while reinforcing its cosmopolitan Islamic identity. In the context of an established divide between the cosmopolitan and urban milieu in which, in relation to the latter, Islam concerned itself with individual piety, humility, and asceticism and taking refuge from the trappings of the worldy life, Nūr al-Dīn came to be seen as a ruler who fused both of these worlds and emphasised that holy men and martyrs could be equated. The flourishing of Sufism thus allowed Nūr al-Dīn and his entourage of Sufis to bring about a pious-warrior ethos that was, clearly, relevant because of the crusader threat. The particular focus on spirituality may also be explained by the diffusion of Sufi ideas from Baghdad to Damascus and Jerusalem. It was the Ḥanbalī adherents, the Banū Qudāma, who often travelled to Baghdad to study with the renowned spiritual jurist ʿAbd al-Qādir al-Jilānī.[58]

58 Ibn Kathīr and Ibn Ṭūlūn biograph for example, the case of ʿAbd al-Ghanī l-Maqdisī (541–600/1146–1203) who travelled to Baghdad alone and returned to teach *ḥadīth* at the Umayyad Mosque of Damascus. Ibn Kathīr, *al-Bidāya wa-l-nihāya*, 13:76; Ibn Ṭūlūn, *al-Qalāʾid al-jawhariyya fī tārīkh al-Ṣāliḥiyya*, part 2, ed. Muḥammad Aḥmad Dahmān (Damascus, 1980), 439–441.

In a poem that brings to light the ways in which such an ethos of piety was created, Abū Shāma notes that Nūr al-Dīn asked ʿImād al-Dīn to compose short *dubayt* poems on the subject of *jihād. Dubayt*s or *rubāʿī* (quatrains), were short four-line compositions that conveyed very precise messages.[59] They comprised two verses – four hemistichs with a rhyme scheme of a-a-b-a. They were easy to learn and memorise and in this context were used to present a clear image of Nūr al-Dīn as a warrior whose only concern was *jihād* against the Franks. ʿImād al-Dīn composed three *dubayt*s, and the propagandistic effect of the compositions was likely to have been great. They were read aloud in public centres and presumably oft-quoted. In one *dubayt* that ʿImād al-Dīn composed for Nūr al-Dīn, he states that the mainstay of Nūr al-Dīn's earthly purpose is simply *jihād*:

(1) My activity and passion is in raiding (*ghazwa*).
It is my only aim in life.
(2) With effort and with *jihād* the sought after is gained.
And rest is dependent on effort [in *jihād*].[60] (1.73)

Though Nūr al-Dīn's role in the anti-Frankish *jihād* may be questioned because of the many other activities he engaged in during his rule, many of them social, which likely kept him preoccupied and in turn perhaps undeserving of titles such as *mujāhid*, we must consider two points. First, the broad extent of *jihād*-based activity in this period, at least that which could be proven to be so, meant that his social roles and focused spirituality did not encumber his suitability for the title of *mujāhid* and instead complemented it in light of the spirituality of the period. Second, Nūr al-Dīn's own personal piety must be considered in light of the extent to which he wanted to be seen as a *mujāhid*.

In another *dubayt* ʿImād al-Dīn presented the same set of virtues by contrasting rest (*rāḥa*) with effort (*jidd*) and *jihād*. The messages sought to present Nūr al-Dīn as one uninterested and unaffected by the worldly trappings that might affect others. The *dubayt* form enabled the poet to emphasise the message in few words. Since ʿImād al-Dīn reiterated the same kind of sentiments in his *dubayt* compositions, which were recited from memory and unadorned by any subtle literary features, the strongly inspiring element behind the poems was clearly the main intention. The poems not only extol the bravery and military focus of Nūr al-Dīn but also place him in the historical context of Islam's

59 W. Stoetzer, 'Rubāʿi,' *EI*², 8:578–585; also see H. Dajani-Shakeel, '*Jihād* in Twelfth-Century Arabic Poetry,' 97; Hillenbrand, *The Crusades*, 166.

60 Abū Shāma, *Kitāb al-Rawḍatayn*, 2:157.

illustrious champions. In fact, ʿImād al-Dīn's poems may allude to verses recited by the Prophet Muḥammad, who is reported to have used a similar short poetic feature during the 'Battle of the Trench' ('*khandaq*') in 5/627. During the preparation for the battle he saw the Anṣār (lit., 'Helpers') digging on a very cold morning. Noticing their fatigue and hunger, he said in a rhyming couplet:

> O Allāh! The real life is that of the Hereafter, so forgive the Anṣār [supporters] and the Muhājirīn [emigrants].

In their reply the Muhājirīn and the Anṣār said,

> We are those who have given the *bayʿa* [pledge] to Muḥammad, promising that we will carry on with *jihād* for as long as we live.[61] (1.74)

There are similarities between ʿImād al-Dīn's verses and those of the Prophet. Both were composed for the purpose of *jihād*; the *ḥadīth* that includes the poetic exchange comes from a chapter in *Ṣaḥīḥ al-Bukhārī* entitled 'Rousing and exhorting people to fight.' There are similarities in meaning as well: both poems render the life (*ʿaysh*) of the world unimportant and propagate the idea that the most meaningful and purposeful existence is striving for God's pleasure, and more specifically, engaging the enemy in battle.

(1) There is no rest in life except in raiding.
My sword strikes with passion.
(2) In humiliating the unbelievers there is honour.
And capability in other than the *jihād* is in fact disability.[62] (1.75)

Another of ʿImād al-Dīn's *dubayt*s for Nūr al-Dīn contains a similar meaning:

(1) I swore that I have no aim except *jihād*.
And rest in other than it wearies me.
(2) Aims cannot be achieved except with serious effort.
And life without serious effort (*jidd*) is a playful (*laʿib*) *jihād*.[63] (1.76)

---

61 Al-Bukhārī, *Summarized Ṣaḥīh al-Bukhāhrī*, trans. Muḥsin Khan (Riyadh: Maktaba Dar-us-Salam, 1994), 589–590.

62 Abū Shāma, *Kitāb al-Rawḍatayn*, 2:157.

63 Ibid., 2:158.

Perhaps the comparison in this *dubayt* for Nūr al-Dīn and the opening of the famous *qaṣīda* of Abū Tammām in praise of the caliph al-Muʿtaṣim in his conquest of Amorium in 223/838, wherein both poets juxtaposed *jidd* and *laʿib*, was purposely arranged to evoke a comparison between al-Muʿtaṣim's victory at Amorium and Nūr al-Dīn's victories against the crusaders. Although there is no way of knowing that this was the poet's intent, or that he was in any way influenced by Abū Tammām, because of the popularity of Abū Tammām and his *qaṣīda*, such a comparison would have magnified Nūr al-Dīn's achievements. The role of the ʿAbbāsid poet is essential in appreciating many of the *jihād*-based motifs used by later poets. There are recurring *jihād*-based motifs in his praise of the third/ninth-century *ṣayfiyya* (summer campaigns) against the Byzantines led by al-Muʿtaṣim, and in particular about the Muslim victory at the battle of Amorium.

Abū Tammām wrote:

> The sword is more truthful than the written word
> On its edge is the boundary between serious effort (*jidd*) and play (*laʿib*).[64]
> (1.77)

The antithesis of *jidd* and *laʿib* also finds a similar place in verse 68 of Abū Tammām's poem, which draws on the contrast of rest (*rāḥa*) and weariness (*taʿab*), in precisely the same way as in the aforementioned *dubayt*. Abū Tammām states – "You have beheld the greater repose and you have perceived that it is not attained except over a bridge of toil" and in Nūr al-Dīn's verse – "I swore that I have no aim except *jihād* / And repose in other than it is toil for me." 'Repose' suggests something different in each verse. In Abū Tammām's poem it comes to mean a state of peace (*ṭumaʾnīna*) reached as a result of the piety of the caliph al-Muʿtaṣim, and for Nūr al-Dīn it denotes the trappings of the world, anything that would dissuade one from devotion to the *jihād* to which Nūr al-Dīn was committed.

The sentiments behind the play on the word *jihād* in the above *dubayt* may also stem from the content of a popular poem by the second-/eighth-century ʿAbdallāh b. al-Mubārak (d. 181/797), composed as a directive to al-Fuḍayl b. ʿIyāḍ (d. 187/803). The poem criticises al-Fuḍayl who, although originally from Samarqand and educated in Kufa, later chose a life of spiritual seclusion in Mecca that caused Ibn al-Mubārak to expose the religious deficiency of one who would opt for a life of ease in worship in the face of other more strenuous and demanding religious obligations like *jihād*. Some scholars argue that the

64 Abū Tammām, *Dīwān Abī Tammām*, ed. M. A. Azzam (Cairo: Dār al-Maʿārif, 1951), 45–79.

priority of engaging in the *jihād* against unbelievers was so pervasive that those who left Syria for pilgrimage/visitation (*ziyāra*) to Mecca – where Muslims led ascetic lifestyles – were criticised for neglect and failing to give precedence to the overriding obligation.[65] Ibn al-Mubārak wrote:

(1) O you who worship in the vicinity of the Two Holy Mosques!
If you but see us, you will realise that you are only jesting in worship.[66]
(2) He who wets his cheek with his tears should know that our necks are wet with blood.
(3) He who tires his horses without purpose, know that our horses are tired in battle.
(4) Yours is the scent of perfume, while ours is the glimmer of spears and the stench of dust [in battle].[67] (1.78)

It is possible that Ibn al-Mubārak did not intend to diminish the importance of these acts of worship, but meant to associate *jihād* with them. This would be meaningful in light of Ibn al-Mubārak's work on the importance of asceticism, in his *Kitāb al-Zuhd* and his work on *jihād, Kitāb al-Jihād*.[68] Although the nature of a *dubayt* is to avoid elaborate description, clearly the imagery and memories evoked through its simple, short lines presented Nūr al-Dīn in terms comparable to his illustrious predecessor.

---

65 Ephrat and Kabha, 'Muslim Reactions,' 52.

66 The lines are strikingly similar to sentiments expressed by al-Mutanabbī (d. 354/965) more than a century later in a poem entitled, 'Death in war is (like the taste of) honey in the mouth':

(1) Till when will you continue to be *muḥrim* [wear the *iḥrām*] and until when will you be in hardship, and until when?
(2) If you do not die honourably under swords, you will die without dignity in humiliation.
(3) So rise, while trusting in God, as one who is honourable who sees death in battle like honey in the mouth.

Al-Mutanabbī, *Dīwān al-Mutanabbī* (Beirut: Dār Bayrūt lil-Ṭibāʿa wa-l-Nashr, 1975), 16; Dajani-Shakeel has noted the similarities in the *Rūmiyyāt* of al-Mutanabbī composed in praise of Sayf al-Dawla in his battles with the Byzantines and poetry composed against the crusaders. The former were believed to have inspired the anti-crusade compositions of the sixth/twelfth century. See H. Dajani-Shakeel, '*Jihād* in Twelfth-Century Arabic Poetry,' 96.

67 Ibn Kathīr, *Tafsīr*, 2:363–364.

68 Ibn al-Mubārak, *Kitāb al-Zuhd wa-yalīhi kitāb al-raqāʾiq* (Beirut: Dār al-Kutub al-ʿIlmiyya, 2004); Ibn al-Mubārak, *Kitab al-Jihād*.

(1) He possessed two *jihāds*, one against the enemy and the other against his *nafs* [lit., 'self'], so he is therefore always in battle.[69] (1.79)

Here the spiritual dimension of his *jihād* is equated with his physical *jihād*. The humility of Nūr al-Dīn served the purpose of making authentic the examples of Islam's past champions upon which he based his *jihād*. Nūr al-Dīn was known to beseech God for assistance, particularly at dire moments in military campaigns, when he was depicted as being humble, in a weak and desperate state. This reveals that he incorporated a strong spiritual focus in his military *jihād*, and shows the earnest devotion behind the ideologies that spurred these conflicts.[70] Nūr al-Dīn's position as a 'warrior-ascetic' was justified by Ibn al-Athīr who referred to personages greater in rank than him, like the Prophet Sulaymān (Solomon) who, according to some Muslim belief, remained an ascetic in spite of his vast kingdom. Similarly, the Prophet Muḥammad's far-reaching governance, and by extension that of his successors, points to the fact that "*zuhd* is the heart's seclusion from love of the world and not from the hand toward it."[71] Some of the most relevant elements of Nūr al-Dīn's piety relate to his humility and trust in God. When acclaimed for his indispensable position in the military *jihād* and the loss that would befall Islam if he were killed in battle, Nūr al-Dīn reminded his discerning scholarly audience that "who is Maḥmūd that such a thing is said to him?[72] Who protected the lands of Islam

69 Abū Shāma, *Kitāb al-Rawḍatayn*, 1:128.

70 Strikingly, and much to our benefit *à propos* appreciating the oftentimes little considered graceful religiosity on each side of the conflict, we note the intimate reflection of the Anglo-French priest Raoul following the capture of Lisbon in 541/1147: "For our God has delivered the enemies of the cross into our hands. And divine vengeance has pressed upon them with such severity that, as we see the city in ruins and the castle overthrown, the fields depopulated, the land reduced to solitude, with no inhabitant in the fields, and as we behold their mourning and lamentations, we are inclined to feel pity for them in their vicissitudes and evil fortunes and to suffer with them on account of their infirmities and to feel sorry that the lashings of divine justice are not yet at an end; and particularly are we moved to sorrow because not even among us Christians have sins been corrected amid the scourging of this action. There is a necessity for both sorrow and rejoicing … Not in our own righteousness have we overthrown the enemy, but through the great compassion of God. Accordingly, let not the Abundance of his gifts arouse our pride …" C. W. David, (ed. and trans.), *De Expugnatione Lyxbonensi: The Conquest of Lisbon* (New York: Columbia University Press, 2001), 183–185.

71 Abū Shāma, *Kitāb al-Rawḍatayn*, 1:100.

72 Although Ibn Jubayr lamented the pretention in the grand setting of Ṣalāḥ al-Dīn's Damascus court with the leading men of the city 'with imposing appellations of distinction, which they confer on all alike, and all referring to *dīn* (religion) …

before me? It was God of course, of whom there is no other."[73] Nūr al-Dīn might have been inspired by an anecdote collected in al-Ghazālī's *Naṣīḥat al-mulūk*, in which Islam's second caliph ʿUmar b. al-Khaṭṭāb instructed his audience: "'O people,' he asked, 'am I your prince?' They answered 'Yes.' 'Then call me the Prince of the Believers,' he said; 'but I am still the same son of al-Khaṭṭāb.'"[74] One of the most interesting lines of poetry to mark Nūr al-Dīn's feats in light of his struggle, both military and spiritual, against the crusaders, can be found in an undated celebratory poem composed by Ibn al-Munīr al-Ṭarābulsī:[75]

> (12) You have an advance [in battle] and for that, you rose as an expert. You have pleased your God, the Messiah [Jesus] and Aḥmad [the Prophet Muḥammad].[76] (1.80)

In this very telling verse Nūr al-Dīn emerges as a champion of the faith. Ibn al-Munīr brings together God, Jesus, and Aḥmad (another name for the Prophet Muḥammad), and effectively lays forth Islam's claim on the person of Jesus and satirises the crusaders for their sole and misguided claim to him. His struggle is then 'sanctioned' with the inclusion of the three. By fighting against the crusaders he has the support of Jesus, an idea seen elsewhere in poetry extolling the feats of Ṣalāḥ al-Dīn, in which Jesus is 'rescued' by Muslims from the crusaders; the name Aḥmad as opposed to Muḥammad also reveals the reaction the poet sought to elicit from his audience. The Qurʾānic verse that appears to be the inspiration for the poet's line is found in *Sūra Ṣaff*:

> And remember, Jesus, the son of Mary, said: "O children of Israel! I am the messenger of God (sent) to you, confirming the Law (which came) before me, and giving glad tidings of a Messenger to come after me, whose name shall be Aḥmad." But when he came to them with clear signs, they said, "this is evident sorcery!" (61:6)

فتسمع ما شئت من صدر الدين أو شمسه أو بدره أو نجمه أو زينه أو بهائه أو جماله أو مجده
أو فخره أو شرفه أو معينه أو محييه أو زكيه أو نجيبه

... without a limit to similar false titles,' Nūr al-Dīn appeared to sometimes relinquish his own 'al-Dīn' title for the more unadorned 'Maḥmūd.' See Ibn Jubayr, *Travels*, 308–309; Ibn Jubayr, *Tadhkira*, 230.

73 Ibn al-Athīr, *al-Kāmil fī l-tārīkh*, 9:395.

74 Al-Ghazālī, *Naṣīḥat*, 67.

75 See Ibn Khallikān, *Wafayāt*, 1:221–227.

76 Abū Shāma, *Kitāb al-Rawḍatayn*, 1:134.

Following Nūr al-Dīn's recovery from a severe illness that afflicted him in 552/1157, one of a few such illnesses that instilled in him an acute consciousness of God and a spiritual re-awakening, Ibn al-Munīr composed a poem to congratulate him on his recovery. The poet hopes that God will preserve his patron; his poem echoes the themes of dependence and reliance; Nūr al-Dīn's commitment to the *jihād* against the Franks was depicted as his most identifiable achievement, for he is "always active in striking."

(1) O sun without eclipse and without concealment, lights request that your light remains.
(2) The full moon is incomplete while you are complete. You have full light while it has a glow.
(3) Your cure is with Islam, and your healing causes stagnation for your enemies.
(4) You are always a sword that does not become rusty, and you are always active in striking.

Here conventional *madḥ* motifs are used, wherein Nūr al-Dīn is compared to the sun and the moon. The play on the words *adwāʾ* (diseases) and *aʿdāʾ* (enemies) in verse 3 reveals how the crusaders symbolised not only a disordering of the Islamic world, but an affliction on Islam itself; the words for 'disease' and 'enemy' are intended to be synonymous in the poet's line. It was of course Nūr al-Dīn's illness that was central to the poet's motive; as part of his consolation he is reminded that Islam too has suffered because of its enemies. Defeating the crusaders then would be a healing for both Nūr al-Dīn and Islam. His commitment to the *jihād* is unwavering, as symbolised through the hard consonance in *ṣadda ṣaddan*, which allows the poet to move his audience to consider the rigorous striking of his sword.

(4) If a loss comes to you, the eyes of your people take it away from you.
(5) If the earth was paid as a ransom so that the sky does not fall, then the kings were paid as a ransom, so that you will not be harmed.
(6) You provide for them if rain is withheld, and fulfil their needs. And when we recount the worthy, you are indeed the best of them.
(7) And in the bed of the kingdom is a kingdom for God. And its happiness and bounty are hidden for [the sake of] God.
(10) He spread the religion in this kingdom, so that those who remain secretly awake in the night do not steal from it.
(11) Its buildings have risen, and they are in his hands. And they are fenced like a protective bracelet.

(13) O Nūr al-Dīn [lit., 'light of the religion'], the horizons will darken if you do not illuminate them.

(15) May you be saved for Islam, to protect the lands of Islam if they give in to laziness or if they become oppressive.

(16) You became sad and distressed, and when you do then the world becomes troubled.

(19) Your hopes will forever remain with you, and you take what you want from them.

(20) Time does not permit you to stay forever with us, and every wound of yours is enormous for us.[77] (1.81)

In these verses 'kingdom' and 'religion' are associated, with Nūr al-Dīn embodying the quintessential model for both. His spreading of the religion throughout his empire (verse 10) originates from his personal devotion to his faith, with the 'bed of the kingdom' perhaps indicating Nūr al-Dīn's private devotional chamber, 'a kingdom for God.' Ibn al-Munīr thus used the occasion of Nūr al-Dīn's illness to draw not on explicit religious sentiments, but on the relationship between ruler, kingdom, and religion, and to show how each was dependent on the other. The salient detail of the poem is mentioned in line 13, wherein the poet notes that without Nūr al-Dīn the religion of Islam would suffer. This is shown through the antithesis of *nūr al-dīn* (the light of the religion) and *aẓlamat* (darken) in line 13, and without enaging in *jihād* against the crusaders Nūr al-Dīn would not be 'healed.' It is Nūr al-Dīn whose religious practice is also scrutinised by the poets of his time, however, they sought to inspire in him a religiosity that must have complemented the new spiritual focus of the fifth/eleventh century, yet he was censured for misappropriating taxes and for religious laxity in the army; "how can you be supported when you have wine and drums in your army?"[78] Ibn Kathīr cites a poem that severely scorns Nūr al-Dīn and calls on him to consider the consequences of his actions in light of the hereafter.

(3) And though you have finished drinking wine, you have recklessly drunk from the cup of oppression.

77 Abū Shāma, *Kitāb al-Rawḍatayn*, 1:317.

78 In Ibn Kathīr, *al-Bidāya wa-l-nihāya*, 12:299, we find an idea similar to one found in the *dīwān* of al-Mutanabbī:

(6) And do not think that glory is found in alcohol and female singers; there is no glory except in a sword and in fighting.

Al-Mutanabbī, *Dīwān al-Mutanabbī*, 189.

(4) You prevented cups, and now upon you is the sin of the distribution of forbidden cups.
(5) What would you say on a day when you are carried to the grave by yourself?
And Munkar and Nakīr [angels of the grave] come to you.
(6) What would you say if you stood on the station of the Day of Judgement by yourself, humiliated, and with a heavy account?
(7) And clinging to you are the rights of others [whom you have wronged], and on the day of judgement you become a chained criminal.
(8) And your soldiers desert you, and you lie in the narrowness of the grave.
(9) You would wish that you were not a guardian and that people would not have called you an *amīr* [leader].[79]
(10) And know that after having been honoured, you will be subject to a pit in the world of the dead, and you will be despicable.
(11) And you will be gathered without clothes, sad, crying, and worried, and you will not find anyone from creation there to help you.
(14) [So] Prepare for yourself a witness that can deliver you on the day of appointment, and on the day when there is no concealment.[80] (1.82)

This poem also bears the traits of a *zuhdiyya* (poem of asceticism), as it contains several motifs present in the opening of traditional *qaṣīdas*, namely the interrogation of the occupants of the grave, the fleeting nature of life, the drawing close of death, and divine accountability. Mention of the '*ḥisāb*' (account), '*yawm al-ḥisāb*' (day of reckoning), and *qabr* (grave) are prominent forms of religious imagery in this poem, brought together to appeal directly to Nūr al-Dīn to not be hampered in the hereafter by any of his current political policies. The sentiments are similar to those found in the *zuhdiyya* of Abū l-ʿAtāhiyya

79 This line strikes an interesting chord with what al-Ghazālī considered one of ten indispensable rules of justice in his 'mirrors for princes' text, 'Kīmiyā-yi saʿādat': (1) The ruler should rule in such a way that he is the subject and the other person is the ruler. C. Hillenbrand, 'A Little-Known Mirror for Princes of al-Ghazali,' in *Words, Texts and Concepts Cruising the Mediterranean Sea*, ed. R. Arnzen and J. Thielmann, (Leuven: Peeters, 2004), 595. Given our frequent mention of the *Baḥr al-fawāʾid* in this book, it is important to note the influence of al-Ghazālī's *Kīmiyā* on the aforementioned text. See Meisami (trans. and ed.), *The Sea of Precious Virtues*, xiv–xv.

80 Ibn Kathīr, *al-Bidāya wa-l-nihāya*, 12:299.

(d. 211/826): 'All brought to nought by Him who brings great kings to nought' (line 9) and '… I have forgotten my lasting abode; I have inhabited a house that will not stay' (line 10).[81] In this light, the simple message was intended to strike a chord with Nūr al-Dīn's sensibility, and it was essential for Nūr al-Dīn's scholarly entourage that the *jihād* fighter did not transgress religious boundaries and succumb to *maẓālim* (oppression/injustice) (line 3).[82] Moreover, Sufi focus on the hereafter and on self-accountability – invigorated by the fifth-/eleventh-century ascetic al-Ghazālī – was an imperative for everyone, especially an *amīr*. An anecdote in al-Ghazālī's *Naṣīḥat al-mulūk* clarifies the matter: "Adorn yourself with righteousness, for at the tribunal of the resurrection no man will lend you his adornment."[83] Furthermore, in the *Baḥr al-fawā'id* the author narrates exhortations for those who might be tempted to prefer temporal power to the hereafter. In a tone that delineates the mood of the aforementioned poem, the author chastises:

> O ye who boast of reason, and have built a house on a bridge and cast it over the waves of the sea: when you see the forelock of the Angel of Death you will come to your senses and cry out, "*Alas! for that I have been negligent in my duty to God*" (39:57).[84]

Nūr al-Dīn likely found solace in his spirituality and much of the poetry written for him addresses this notion. For Ibn al-Qaysarānī, he is "as a worshipper, succour for the *abdāl*, and in fighting, the king of lions."[85] The *abdāl* are believed to be an enigmatic group who come to the aid of Muslims in times of difficulty. Ibn Kathīr corroborates Nūr al-Dīn's attention to such reproaches by narrating an episode in which a group of Sufis recount what they heard from some Franks in the kingdom of Jerusalem. The jurist Abū l-Fatḥ Banjīr

81 Geert Jan Van Gelder, *Classical Arabic Literature: A Library of Arabic Literature Anthology* (New York University Press: New York, 2013), 49–50.

82 Nadia Maria El Cheikh emphasises that, "the most laudable feature of the ruler is his justice, *'adl*, and his primary function is the administration of justice, guided by the Qur'ān and Sunna." Nadia Maria El Cheikh, 'Byzantine Leaders in Arabic-Muslim Texts,' in *Elites Old and New in the Byzantine and Early Islamic Near East*, ed. J. Haldon and L. I. Conrad (Princeton, NJ: Darwin Press, 2004), 120. See also M. Khadduri, *The Islamic Concept of Justice* (Baltimore: Johns Hopkins University Press, 1984); F. Rosenthal, 'Political Justice and the Just Ruler,' *IOS* 10 (1980), 92–101.

83 Al-Ghazālī, *Naṣīḥat*, 73.

84 Meisami (trans. and ed.), *The Sea of Precious Virtues*, 49.

85 Abū Shāma, *Kitāb al-Rawḍatayn*, 1:264; al-Harawī describes Nūr al-Dīn as 'one of the saints,' al-Harawī, *A Lonely Wayfarer's Guide*, 34–35. نور الدين محمود زنكي من الأولياء

al-Ashtarī (d. 579/1183), who was said to have composed an abridged life history of Nūr al-Dīn, said:

> We heard that he turned to a group of Sufis regarding what they said when they entered Jerusalem for *ziyāra* in the days when the Franks had taken Jerusalem, and he heard them say that al-Qusaym b. al-Qusaym thinks that Nūr al-Dīn is being helped by God in secret, for [otherwise] he will not triumph and will not be victorious over us with the size of his army and soldiers, but he will indeed triumph over us and be victorious with supplication and night prayers for indeed he prays in the night and raises his hands to God and beseeches Him, and indeed He answers him [Nūr al-Dīn] and gives him what he asks for and so he triumphs over us. He said: This is the true speech of the unbelievers.[86]

The anecdote of the obscure Qusaym b. al-Qusaym bears striking resemblance to the conversation between Kerbogha, *atabeg* of Mosul during the First Crusade, and his mother in the *Gesta Francorum* that also appears in the chronicles of Robert the Monk, Guibert of Nogent, Peter Tudebode, and Baldric of Dol. As Hodgson notes, the case of Kerbogha's mother is very telling of attitudes toward women in the crusades, but it also reveals the camp-gossip and inter-religious perceptions.[87] The acknowledgement of piety and godly support of unbelievers is what makes Kerbogha's and the aforementioned anecdotes so compelling for their readers. The jurist reinforces his claim by allowing no doubt about the veracity of his spurious tale; "this is the true speech of the unbelievers." The anecdote recorded by Ibn Kathīr and others like it is valuable, not for its historical accuracy, but for the religious sentiments that the author intended to arouse among the Muslim population of Syria. In light of the presentation of Nūr al-Dīn, the idea of personal and public reform (*iṣlāḥ*) becomes a vital feature for success.

Perhaps the simplicity of some of the poetry assessed here speaks of what Nabih Amin Faris calls the "depressing effect of Arabic poetry" in this period. Due to the influx of foreigners into the Arab world and the transfer of political authority from Arab to Persian Buwayhids (Būyids), Turkish Saljūqs, or Kurdish Ayyūbids, it is plausible to think that poets were writing in a culture

86 Abū Shāma, *Kitāb al-Rawḍatayn*, 1:118; Ibn Kathīr, *al-Bidāya wa-l-nihāya*, 12:300; Ibn Abī l-Wafā l-Maqdisī, *Īqāẓ al-ghāfil bi-sīrat al-Malik al-ʿĀdil Nūr al-Dīn al-Shahīd* (Beirut: al-Maktabat al-ʿAṣriyya, 2006), 59.

87 N. Hodgson, 'The Role of Kerbogha's Mother in the *Gesta Francorum* and Selected Chronicles of the First Crusade,' in *Gendering the Crusades*, ed. S. B. Edgington and S. Lambert (Cardiff: University of Wales Press, 2001), 163.

in which literary benchmarks were in the process of being redefined.[88] While each poet was judged on his own merits, and any further discussion of what those 'merits' are lies well beyond the remit of this book, it is plausible too that the dissemination of ideas during the crusades was done in a language simple enough for those in the poet's audience whose mother-tongue was not Arabic. Though the poetry was composed for and recited in the presence of Turkish and Kurdish rulers of Syria, Egypt, and Palestine, it is not certain that they would have understood, much less appreciated, all of the poet's rhetorical devices, double entendres, and ornate imagery. They were of course accustomed to verses in their own languages. The public recitation of poetry was, however, an important part of court ceremonies and it is possible that a translator was used to interpret the subtleties.

Finally, can we assume that Nūr al-Dīn's concern to be depicted as a pious fighter, or 'Imād al-Dīn al-Iṣfahānī's concern to depict his patron as such, arose from the same kind of historicism that influenced him to wear coarse clothing or to order that his troops hang their swords from their shoulders because the Prophet Muḥammad had done the same thing?[89] It seems that his appreciation for style, appearance, and subtle associations was a patent and effective feature that shaped the image of Nūr al-Dīn as a 'holy warrior' and allowed for the creation of an image in which his religious humility and *jihād* against crusaders found an ideal equipoise.

The same kind of 'image-making' we find in regard to Nūr al-Dīn's character and feats in the *jihād* also appears in the *Maqāmāt* of Aḥmad b. Abī Bakr al-Rāzī l-Ḥanafī, a sixth-/twelfth-century work dedicated to the *qāḍī* of Aleppo, Abū Ḥāmid Muḥammad al-Shahrazūrī (d. 586/1190). D. Stewart makes a convincing case to show that the text has an important place in the anti-crusader religious propaganda which flourished during the Zangid and Ayyūbid dynasties; he presents it as the direct ideological message of a *jihād* programme promoted by Nūr al-Dīn and Ṣalāḥ al-Dīn. The initiative was centred on fighting the crusaders together with a focus on resisting the enemies in the internal body of the *umma*, namely Twelver and Ismāʿīlī Shīʿīs.[90] The pair of episodes (XXVII–XXVIII) specific to the anti-Frankish *jihād* are most revealing. The events described in the poem of *Maqāma* XXVIII by Ibn Bassam are those he

---

88 N. A. Faris, 'Arab Culture in the Twelfth-Century,' in *A History of the Crusades*, vol. 5: *The Impact of the Crusades on the Near East*, ed. K. M. Setton, N. P. Zacour, and H. W. Hazard (Madison: University of Wisconsin Press, 1969–89), 31.

89 Abū Shāma, *Kitāb al-Rawḍatayn*, 2:111.

90 Devin J. Stewart, 'The Maqāmāt of Aḥmad b. Abī Bakr b. Aḥmad al-Rāzī al-Ḥanafī and the Ideology of the Counter-Crusade in Twelfth-Century Syria,' *Middle Eastern Literatures* 11, no. 2 (2008), 211–232.

claimed occurred the year he witnessed what strikingly resembles the battle of Bānyās in 559/1164. Ibn Bassam recites a poem to commemorate this victory.

> The Victory of God came, without holding back,
> to give us glad tidings while we were in Bānyās.
> Giving glad tidings of victory and conquest,
> the remembrance of which will stay with me.
> Over a group whom we made to drink from the cup of death,
> Each of them sipped from it.
> There gave them to drink the cup of death, all of a sudden,
> one endowed with great power, generous and mighty:
> A lion, Master, King, Noble,
> a generous and virtuous man like Abu Firās.
> How can one compare, tell me, O companion,
> the stone pellet of a slingshot with towering mountain peaks?
> O champion of Islam, fight for God, without holding back.
> Tell the doubtful unbeliever to go away, as the Samaritan did, cut off completely.
> Do not despair, for one may hope for victory from the Beneficent after despair.[91]

The appellations Ibn Bassam uses to describe the unnamed 'champion of Islam' – 'lion, Master, King, Noble,' and the revealing comparison to Abū Firās al-Ḥamdānī (d. 357/968), the famed poet of the third/ninth and fourth/tenth century, who inspired poets of the sixth/twelfth century in their *jihād* rhetoric, and who was a cousin of Sayf al-Dawla al-Ḥamdānī (r. 333–56/945–67), celebrated for his military expeditions against the Byzantines in the fourth/tenth century, must be Nūr al-Dīn. The capture of the fort of Bānyās from the crusaders in 559/1164 was an illustrious victory, celebrated by other poets, including Ibn al-Munīr.[92] The poem that focuses on the capture of Bānyās and the descriptions of its victor that resemble Nūr al-Dīn suggest that the *maqāmāt* of al-Ḥanafī must have been written after 559/1164.

The poetry underpins the presentation of Nūr al-Dīn as a just ruler, devout, and determined in the cause of the *jihād*. The repeated celebration of his 'victory' is expressed in a poem by Ibn al-Munīr, who writes that it was a 'conquest that would [cause] all other conquests to be forgotten' (verse 11) (*tunsīy al-futūḥ bihā-l futūḥ*). The appellations in Ibn Bassam's poem, 'great power,

91 Stewart, 'The Maqāmāt,' 217–218.

92 Abū Shāma, *Kitāb al-Rawḍatayn*, 1:376.

generous and mighty, lion, Master, King, Noble' are enhanced in the verses of Ibn al-Munīr al-Ṭarābulsī, in which he presents Nūr al-Dīn as undertaking an important eschatological role:

> If doubts are harboured about you, then know that you are the Mahdī who blows out the fire of the Dajjāl [imposter/Antichrist].[93] (1) (1.83)

Sunnī Muslims believe that Jesus Christ himself would defeat the Antichrist, but the poet could not equate Nūr al-Dīn with the Prophet Jesus because of the theological implications that such an idea entails. Poets sometimes stressed what they believed were Christians' false theological claims about Jesus, and emphasised the name 'ibn Maryam' (son of Mary); other times they presented the *jihād* as one that would rescue Jesus from Jerusalem. Here, however, the 'Mahdī' is used in the poem to afford Nūr al-Dīn an eschatological place and to embellish the crusader presence and threat.

Another of Ibn al-Munīr's poems composed to celebrate the victory of Bānyās reveals the way poets incorporated Qur'ānic allusions in their poems to display their knowledge of the sacred text and demonstrate a poetic competence that would appeal particularly to the religious class. Though this is further noted in the next section, one specific case is highlighted here, since it is relevant to the victory of Bānyās. The poet begins with the recurring motif of the full moon (*badr*), popular in laudatory (*madīḥ*) poems:

> A full moon in the fourteenth night that takes its light from the fifteenth [verse] of *Sūrat al-Anfāl*.[94] (16) (1.84)

The fifteenth verse of *Sūrat al-Anfāl* (i.e., 8:15), to which Ibn al-Munīr directs his listeners, is an exhortation to remain steadfast in battle when Muslim and unbelieving forces meet; the verse proscribes retreat as ignominious. The verse was used to exemplify Nūr al-Dīn and his army. Even without specific knowledge of what the verse denotes, the name of the chapter, *Sūrat al-Anfāl* (The Spoils of War) makes plain the thematic intent of the chapter.

> O you who believe! When you meet the unbelievers in hostile array, never turn your backs to them.
>
> QUR'ĀN 8:15

93 Ibid.

94 Ibid., 1:377.

In Ibn al-Athīr's account of the battle of Bānyās, he reports that the poetry complements the underlying message that Nūr al-Dīn was a just ruler blessed by heavenly favour. He relates a dialogue at the end of his account about Nūr al-Dīn and the son of Muʿīn al-Dīn Unur who had handed Bānyās to the crusaders in 534/1140. In the dialogue Nūr al-Dīn remarked to Muʿīn al-Dīn: "The people rejoice once for this conquest, but you can rejoice twice." He asked, "How is that?" Nūr al-Dīn replied by acclaiming his father, "Because God – may He be exalted – cooled today your father's skin from hellfire."[95] The scene is one that establishes Nūr al-Dīn's authority and reveals a recurring motif in which the protagonist seeks safety from punishment in the hereafter, which becomes his reward and incentive. The sentiment is similar to ʿImād al-Dīn al-Iṣfahānī's poetic plea to Ṣalāḥ al-Dīn, in which the poet sees the recapture of Jerusalem as a form of salvation in the hereafter, 'so God will save you,' and the exhortation levelled at Nūr al-Dīn for his high taxes cited earlier – 'prepare an excuse that will save you [when you stand] before God.' Nūr al-Dīn's extensive *madrasa* building programme and promotion of Sunnī Islam in this period meant that his *jihād* carried a dual purpose; he vanquished the external crusader threat and strengthened Sunnī Islam to ward off internal heresies.

The Inspiration of the Qur'ān in *Jihād* Poetry

The aforementioned example of Ibn al-Munīr's description of the battle of Bānyās shows the significance of the Qur'ān in Muslim literature, and the poet's desire to provide moral justification for the events he depicts by using perceptible imagery from the sacred scripture. In this part of the chapter I provide further examples of insightful Qur'ānic imagery in sixth-/twelfth- and seventh-/thirteenth-century poetry. Oral transmission of the Qur'ān was an important undertaking, it was in fact the most oft-repeated ritual after the prayer. The prayer is made up of reciting verses and chapters of the sacred text, connecting listeners to the revelation directly. Qur'ānic recitals, the most favoured place for reading, formed part of the socio-religious public reading experience, and for the ordinary Muslim, who memorised some parts of the Qur'ān, a Qur'ānic verse evoked and likely produced strong emotional responses. Aside from the mosque, the Qur'ān was recited in other locations and occasions. It could be recited at a grave, during a funeral, and at festivals. It could be performed both spontaneously and as part of an organised routine session. Ibn Jubayr carefully highlights the ongoing recitations of the Qur'ān in the Umayyad Mosque

95 Ibn al-Athīr, *al-Kāmil fī l-tārīkh*, 9:311–312; Abū Shāma, *Kitāb al-Rawḍatayn*, 1:377.

in Damascus and states that some participants received stipends for their recitation.[96] Jurists also recommended how much of the Qurʾān ought to be recited on a daily basis.[97]

Putting aside assumptions, it is impossible to realistically assess the effect of poetry on an audience – not least an audience 800 years ago – and we have no evidence of the size of the poet's audience, but we can discern, with some clarity, that the language and ideas were chosen with intelligent intent. A verse from the Qurʾān was evocative of the divine, and the majority of Muslims knew parts of the Qurʾān, even long parts, by heart.

A simple Qurʾānic allusion can be found in a celebratory poem composed by the Egyptian poet al-Jawwānī (d. 587/1192) and written for Ṣalāḥ al-Dīn following the reconquest of Jerusalem in 583/1187:

(4) The victory of God and the conquest have come – which the Messenger promised, so glorify God and seek His forgiveness.
(5) Syria has been conquered and Jerusalem, which is the gathering place for creation at the resurrection, is purified.[98]

The poet's line 'the victory of God and the conquest have come' (qad jāʿa naṣr Allāhi wa-l-fatḥ) is strikingly similar to the Qurʾānic verse, 'when the victory of God comes and the conquest' (idhā jāʿa naṣr Allāhi wa-l-fatḥ),[99] and the line 'so glorify God and seek His forgiveness' (fa-sabbiḥ wa-stagfirū) is similarly akin to the Qurʾānic verse 110:3, 'so glorify the praises of your Lord and seek His forgiveness' (fa-sabbiḥ bi-ḥamdi rabbika wa-stagfirhu). The poet's diction reveals the influence of the Qurʾān on his celebratory poem, which was meant to remind listeners of God's divine 'design' for His servants. The verses also reflect the motif of finality of the prophetic mission, 'so glorify the praises of your Lord' suggests a requirement to engage in spiritual self-focus, and may be interpreted as a need to thank God for the victory, and focus one's attention on the inner *jihād*. The short Qurʾānic chapter is the sort that would have been memorised by a majority of Muslims and even young children; the allusions are strikingly noticeable and connect the feat with Islam's earlier illustrious victories. The Damascene poet Fityān al-Shāghūrī,[100] following the reconquest of Jerusalem in 583/1187, wrote,

96 Ibn Jubayr, *Travels*, 282–284.
97 Talmon-Heller, *Islamic Piety*, 66–69.
98 Abū Shāma, *Kitāb al-Rawḍatayn*, 3:240.
99 The reference, from Qurʾān 110:1, concerns the conquest of Mecca (8/630).
100 For more information on the poet, see Ibn Khallikān, *Wafayāt*, 4:4–7.

(6) And he rescued the purified house by force with every pure person (*muṭahhar*) from every impure one (*najis*).
(7) And you showed them when both armies met (*lammā taqa-l-jam'ān*)[101] in Jerusalem the dread of the Day of Gathering.
(8) You have returned the religion of God to al-Aqṣā Mosque, which now appears with a beaming face (*bi-wajhin musfir*)[102] after its sadness.[103] (1.85)

In verse 6 the antithesis of 'pure' Muslim and 'impure' Christian crusader has deeper resonations directed at the rescuing of the 'purified house' of Jerusalem; the theme of the 'restoration' of the natural order with Islam's triumph is implicit in this line. There are two examples of Qur'ānic allusions in verses 7 and 8. The phrase in line 7, *lammā taqa-l-jam'ān* ('when the two armies met') emanates from a Qur'ānic reference to the battle of Uḥud (4/625), "and all that befell you on the day when the two armies met in battle happened by God's leave, so that He might mark out the [true] believers" (3:122). Aside from the simple incorporation of a Qur'ānic phrase, the verse in question has a *jihād*-based context, one which calls on the believers to reflect on God's divine purpose behind victory and loss in battle, and thus would have aroused sentiments associating Ṣalāḥ al-Dīn's reconquest with the Qur'ānic narrative of battle. Imagery of light and darkness occurs frequently in the Qur'ān, often with *īmān* (belief) likened to light and *kufr* (unbelief) to darkness. In line 8 *bi-wajhin musfir* relates to the ending of the previous line, *yawm al-maḥshar* (day of gathering). The poet's reference to a 'beaming face' likely stems from a verse about the events of the day of judgement/gathering – 'Some faces that day will be beaming' (80:38), suggesting both an earthly acceptance and divine approval of his feats.

We may consider another example. Following al-Malik al-Kāmil's request for assistance from his two brothers after the Fifth Crusade captured Damietta in 616/1219, Ibn al-Nabīh (d. 619/1222), who worked in the chancery of al-Malik al-Ashraf (d. 693/1293) composed a poem likely intended to quell fears in the Muslim camp. Damietta was a focal point of crusader interest, as it facilitated the journeys of western Christians to the new land.[104] The symbolic

101 See Qur'ān, 3:155, 3:166, 8:41.

102 See Qur'ān, 80:38.

103 Abū Shāma, *Kitāb al-Rawḍatayn*, 3:266.

104 The strategic advantages of Damietta were numerous. According to al-Muqaddasī, "you may travel in this lake for a day and a night, sometimes meeting with fresh water, and narrow straits, until reaching another town, which is better [than Tinnis], more spacious, wider, more open, more frequented; with more fruits, better construction, more water,

significance of al-Malik al-Muʿaẓẓam's destruction of the walls of Jerusalem and the practical threat the Muslims faced from the Mongols added to the growing consternation in the Muslim world. Al-Malik al-Ashraf's decision to set out to Damietta and meet with al-Malik al-Kāmil was a cause of great public jubilation. The following lines of a longer poem draw on several strands of pietistic evocation; namely Qur'ānic imagery and *faḍā'il* sentiments.

> Damietta is Mount Sinai, the fire of war is kindled, you are Moses and this is the day of appointment.
> Throw the rod and it will swallow what they have made, and do not fear; the ropes of the people are not living.[105] (1.86)

Al-Malik al-Ashraf is equated, from the perspective of the mission and – essentially 'ordained' – commission, with the prophet Moses. His name of course was also 'Mūsā' (Moses), thus allowing the poet to draw an obvious connection. The underlying theme of the poem is one of resolve, hope, and security in the face of fear; the poet calls for action, equating military endeavour with the rod of Moses, and the decisive engagement with the Franks at Damietta with the 'day of appointment' mentioned in the Qur'ān (the day that saw Moses defeat the magicians of the Pharaoh). The language of the poet incorporates the vocabulary of the Qur'ān to connect his listeners to the great display of God's power working through the rod of Moses, and to draw on an event and theme that the poet's audience would have been familiar with. In the Qur'ān the following words are used to describe God's command to Moses: 'And throw that which is in your right hand! It will swallow up that which they have made' (wa alqā mā fī yamīnika talqaf mā ṣanaʿū) (20:69). The poet's language is noticeably similar: 'And throw the rod! It will swallow that which they have made' (alqī-l-ʿaṣā tatallaqaf mā ṣanaʿū). Furthermore, the poet's exhortation, 'and do not fear,' is one that recurs in the Qur'ānic narrative concerning Moses.[106] The poet's attention to the Islamic prophet was also intended to bring out the *faḍā'il* (merits) of Egypt; this can be discerned in the association of Damietta with the al-Ṭūr, a reference to Mount Sinai, which holds a particularly elevated position in the Qur'ān because of its relation to the prophethood of Moses.[107]

artisans more skilful, cloths finer, more furnished workmanship, better baths, stronger walls, and fewer vexations." Al-Muqaddasī, *Aḥsan al-taqāsīm*, 185.

105 Ibn Taghrībirdī, *al-Nujūm*, 6:243.

106 See for example, verses 20:21, 20:68, 27:10, 28:31.

107 Qur'ān, 95:2.

References to prophets, the Prophet Muḥammad and his companions, by way of word play and associations were common for the poets of this era.[108]

The influence of the Qur'ān also permeated the landscape of the medieval Islamic world in Qur'ānic inscriptions which featured in mosques, *madrasas*, Sufi lodges, minarets, and other buildings. The oldest monumental inscription is preserved in the Dome of the Rock, an impressive edifice erected around 72/691 by the Umayyad caliph ʿAbd al-Malik b. Marwān (r. 65–86/685–705); we consider the long inscription in gold mosaic on the drum of the dome in the Dome of the Rock dated to the reign of Ṣalāḥ al-Dīn. The inscription is significant in light of the ideology surrounding the re-establishment of Muslim authority over the Dome of the Rock and over the newly sanctified Jerusalem.[109] The inscriptions in the Dome of the Rock reveal associations that connect the Qur'ānic prophet Moses (Mūsā), the companion and second caliph ʿUmar b. al-Khaṭṭāb, and Ṣalāḥ al-Dīn. The association of prophets and the Prophet's Muḥammad's companions with Nūr al-Dīn and Ṣalāḥ al-Dīn was a prominent feature in the Muslim poetry of this period, and the inscriptions considered here reveal similar associations and point to a historicism in the outlook of Ṣalāḥ al-Dīn's religious acquaintances.

The inscription contains the first twenty-one verses of *Sūra Ṭā-hā* (Qur'ān 20:1–21). The verses relate the dialogue between God and Moses, the latter's ordainment as a prophet, and his witnessing of the miracle that God placed in his rod. It is difficult to deduce the exact purpose behind this choice of verses, but there are a few indicators. The key subject matter in these first twenty-one verses is that of Moses. The Moses/Pharaoh dichotomy, the most oft-repeated narrative in the Qur'ān, demonstrates the victory of good over evil and belief over unbelief. The comparison that Ṣalāḥ al-Dīn's contemporaries made between him and the caliph ʿUmar b. al-Khaṭṭāb as the first conquerer of Jerusalem and Ṣalāḥ al-Dīn as the one who reconquered it might have been further augmented in the Muslim historical imagination through the symbolic

108 A wonderful display of this is found in the chronicle of the Egyptian chronicler Aḥmad b. ʿAlī l-Maqrīzī (766–845/1364–1442) in his account of al-Malik al-Kāmil's victory at Damietta in 618/1221 during the Fifth Crusade. Al-Maqrīzī, *A History of the Ayyūbid Sulṭāns of Egypt*, trans. R. J. C Broadhurst (Boston: Twayne Publishers, 1980), 187; Abū Shāma, *al-Dhayl*, 196.

109 O. Grabar, *The Dome of the Rock* (London: Thames and Hudson, 1996), 174; See also Jaroslav Folda, *Crusader Art in the Holy Land: From the Third Crusade to the Fall of Acre, 1187–1291* (Cambridge: Cambridge University Press, 2005), 25–26; R. Hillenbrand, 'Qur'ānic Epigraphy in Medieval Islamic Architecture,' in *Studies in Medieval Islamic Architecture* (London: Pindar Press, 2001), 1:308–327; R. Hillenbrand, 'The Legacy of the Dome of the Rock,' in *Studies in Medieval Islamic Architecture* (London: Pindar Press, 2001), 1:1–19.

intent of the inscription. The Qur'ānic Moses was the closest comparison that they could make between a Qur'ānic prophet and 'Umar. This argument may be substantiated by a *ḥadīth* in which the Prophet is reported to have once told 'Umar: "You are similar O 'Umar to the Prophet Moses."[110] Furthermore, the biographies of the Prophet Muḥammad reveal that 'Umar's conversion to Islam took place when he heard the verses of *Sūra Ṭā-ha*.[111] We can assume that Ṣalāḥ al-Dīn's religious entourage knew this.

Secondly, verse 21 of *Sūra Ṭā-ha* (20:21) speaks of the "return" of Moses' rod to its "former state" after it became a "serpent"; perhaps it was deliberately chosen to celebrate Ṣalāḥ al-Dīn's and the *umma*'s return to Jerusalem. Furthermore, there is a tone of consolation to the *sūra*, and in particular in the narrative concerning Moses, who is told to "grasp it and fear not; We shall return it to its former state." While the first verses speak of Moses, the last verses of the *sūra* call for reflection, for the "many generations We have destroyed before them, in whose dwellings they walk." Muslims are told to "bear patiently what they say" and are commanded to "strain not your eyes in longing for the things We have given for enjoyment to various groups of them, the splendour of the life of this world, that We may test them thereby" (20:131). Such verses allowed listeners to draw parallels with the crusaders and benefit from the lessons of God's power and grace – something much needed after Muslims had endured almost ninety years of a Christian occupation of the city. In light of what might have been their intended use, the verses further suggest the closing of a historical chapter, that is, the end of the crusader rule of the city and the removal of 'impurities.' The idea of 'conversion' was certainly significant in the context of the post-reconquest sanctification of the Holy City and this was a central message in the poetry. The Egyptian poet Ibn Sanā' al-Mulk composed these words: (6) "You gave life to it [Jerusalem] after it had died, then you freed it after it was a captive."[112]

We can surmise that the lasting significance of the themes of the *sūra* in the imagination of the Muslim inhabitants of Syria was inspired by the impact of the crusades on the Muslim world. This is seen in a poem composed by the Egyptian administrator As'ad b. Mamātī (d. 605/1209) in praise of al-Malik al-Ẓāhir al-Ghāzī (d. 613/1216), one of Ṣalāḥ al-Dīn's sons who ruled Aleppo, and who was an important architectural patron in the city.

---

110 Ibn Kathīr, *Tafsīr*, 702.

111 Ibn Kathīr, *al-Sīrat al-nabawiyya*, ed. Muṣṭafā 'Abd al-Wāḥid (Beirut: Dār al-Iḥyā' al-Turāth al-'Arabiyya), 2:34.

112 Ibn Sanā', *Dīwān*, 2:340.

> Ask Jerusalem, and it will inform you of the *sūra* [chapter] of its conquest (*bi-sūrati fatḥihi*) when it is related.
> The bells and crucifix have disappeared from it and affirmed in it now are "*Hal Atā*" and "*Ṭā-hā*."[113] (1.87)

The poem refers to three Qur'ānic chapters in its verses, *Sūrat al-Fatḥ, Sūrat al-Insān*, and *Sūra Ṭā-hā*. Looking beyond the poet's straightforward rhyme is a layer of meaning that may have been discerned by his audience. Whereas *al-fatḥ al-mubīn* (decisive victory) in the first verse of *Sūrat al-Fatḥ* is oft-repeated in the poetry of this period, the first verse of *Sūrat al-Insān* is one that emphasises the notion of humility, by calling on man to consider his lowly origins – "Has there not been over man a long period of time, when he was nothing – (not even) mentioned?" (Qur'ān 76:1). Although *'Hal atā* (*Sūrat al-Insān*) could have been used with *'Ṭa-hā'* simply for the purpose of rhyme, other *sūras* could have achieved a similar effect, most predictably the *sūra* that follows, *al-Anbiyā'* (The Prophets). The poet's choice of *Hal atā* thus appears to have been thoughtfully chosen rather than randomly selected, and may have been intended to commemorate the reconquest in light of Ṣalāḥ al-Dīn's displays of piety.

The transformation of the religious sanctities of Jerusalem, namely that of al-Aqṣā Mosque and the Dome of the Rock, redefined the character of the buildings after the reconquest. The original inscriptions which attest to a strong religious association with the building were intended to demonstrate the theological errors of the Jews and the Christians and the affirmation of the One True God. The inscriptions of verses from *Sūras* 112, 17:111, 4:171–172, 19:33–36, and 3:18–19 all relate specifically to the deviations of the Christians, or the 'people of the book' generally, and thus contain verses asserting belief in One God.

Heightened Fears and Eschatological Undercurrents in Muslim Poetry

As noted in the previous section with Ibn al-Munīr's juxtaposition of the designations of the Mahdī and Dajjāl in his celebratory poem following the capture of Bānyās in 559/1164, or Ibn al-Zakī's reference to the 'end of days' in his Friday sermon at al-Aqṣā Mosque, the eschatology was essential to Islam's outlook on

113 See 'A. J. Ḥusain 'Abd al-Mahdī, *Bayt al-maqdis fī adab al-ḥurūb al-ṣalībiyya* (Amman: Dār al-Bashīr, 1989), 282.

the *jihād* to take back Jerusalem. Here I consider some of the eschatological motifs in the Muslim poetry of the sixth/twelfth century, and focus in particular on the poet ʿAbd al-Munʿim al-Jilyānī. By taking into consideration the fears and hopes of the Muslims of the Near East, as heightened by eschatological beliefs and happenings, we can see the picture already constructed of a society defined by religion, sectarian discord, dynastic rivalries, and military and political events even more clearly.

Abū Shāma, in his description of al-Malik al-Muʿaẓẓam's pre-emptive razing of the walls of Jerusalem in 616/1219, wrote that "a clamor occurred like that of the day of resurrection."[114] Sibṭ b. al-Jawzī explicated the sense of panic: "the *qiyāma* was established in all the lands of Islam"[115] and "a chaos occurred like that of the *yawm al-qiyāma* (day of judgement)."[116] References to the day of judgement were common in poetry of this period, wherein poets sought to arouse religious emotion to elicit political and military responses. ʿImād al-Dīn al-Iṣfahānī appealed to Ṣalāḥ al-Dīn to exert physical effort in order to find comfort in the next life; when Nūr al-Dīn was reproached for his heavy taxation, a poet spoke of references to the grave and the day of judgement as a means of awakening a waning religiosity.[117]

Poets also used vocabulary pertaining to scenic descriptions of the day of judgement as found in the Qurʾān, including terms such as *nushūr* (resurrection) or *qāriʿa* (the sudden calamity) to establish connections between their audiences and familiar eschatological imagery.[118] Apocalyptic notions are fused with the expectation of chaos and disorder. The end of the world will be a catastrophic occurrence and signs heralding the Last Day commonly represent the replacement of order with disorder, tranquillity with panic, and, above all, religiosity with sin and transgression. The state of chaos and disorder will come to an end with the second coming of Jesus, which will conclude the final victory of Islam. Prior to the First Crusade, Muslims were particularly focused on the proximity of the Islamic year 500 and, as Irwin explains, "for Muslims, Christians, and Jews the late eleventh-century Near East was a time of acute insecurity."[119] This sense of anxiety can be discerned from revealing information provided in the *faḍāʾil* work of ʿAbd al-Raḥīm b. Shīth, *Miftāḥ al-maqāṣid wa-miṣbāḥ al-marāṣid fī ziyārat bayt al-maqdis*:

---

114 Abū Shāma, *al-Dhayl*, 175.

115 Sibṭ b. al-Jawzī, *Mirʾāt al-zamān*, part 2, 8:601.

116 Ibid., 8:654.

117 Abū Shāma, *Kitāb al-Rawḍatayn*, 2:296; Ibn Kathīr, *al-Bidāya wa-l-nihāya*, 12:299.

118 Abū Shāma, *Kitāb al-Rawḍatayn*, 2:242; Abū Shāma, *Kitāb al-Rawḍatayn*, 1:308.

119 Irwin, 'Islam and the Crusades,' 217.

Bayt al-maqdis, known for its distinctive beauty and its unique candelabra, remained [with the Muslims] until its destruction by the Franks [492/1099]. According to some reports, a silver chandelier in its mosque, holding 500 lamps, crashed in the year 452/1060, thus creating some fears that a great calamity would befall Islam. It was not long after this incident [in 492/1099], that the Franks attacked the region of Syria and captured Jerusalem from the representatives of the Fāṭimids who failed to fortify it. The Franks had planned [for years] to assassinate the Muslims [in Jerusalem] and succeeded finally on Friday, the 22nd of Shaʿbān, the month corresponding to July 492 [15 July 1099]. When the Franks captured [the city], the Muslims were performing the Friday prayer while the Jews were preparing for their Sabbath. Like assassins, the Franks attacked the undefended city, killing and enslaving the free citizens as well as the slaves.[120]

120 ʿAbd al-Raḥīm b. Shīth, 'Miftāḥ al-maqāṣid wa-miṣbāḥ al-marāṣid fī ziyārat bayt al-maqdis,' in *Faḍā'il bayt al-maqdis fī makhṭūṭāt ʿarabiyya qadīma*, ed. M. Ibrāhīm (Kuwait: Maʿhad al-Makhṭūṭāt al-ʿArabiyya, al-Munaẓẓama al-ʿArabiyya lil-Tarbiyya wa-l-Thaqāfa wa-l-ʿUlūm, 1985), 266–267; H. Dajani-Shakeel, 'Jerusalem and the First Crusade,' in *Jerusalem's Heritage: Essays in Memory of Kāmil Jamil Asali*, ed. Ṣāliḥ Hamarneh (al-Jāmiʿa al-Urdunīya: Amman, 1996), 39; here we can make a comparison with the sentiments of the crusaders after their defence of Jerusalem in 583/1187 failed and the great cross that had been installed to celebrate the capture of the city in 492/1099 fell. "The breach in the wall was in the same spot from which the first Crusaders had entered the city in 1099. When the wall fell, the great cross that had been installed there to celebrate the capture of Jerusalem by the Latins in that year also fell." M. C. Lyons and D. E. P. Jackson, *Saladin: The Politics of the Holy War* (Cambridge: Cambridge University Press, 1982), 274. A clearer example of the agitation of fears caused by the falling of prominent icons can be seen from Ibn Jubayr's *Travels*, in which he recounts the support that the Almohads received, based on their justice and correctness in religion; Ibn Jubayr was himself a fervent supporter. The Andalusian jurist explained how the belief of Muslims in the Hijaz is strengthened by "certain omens which fell to the notice of some of them and gave warning of coming events which they saw in the result to be true. Amongst the omens leading to this is the following. Between the mosques of Ibn Tulun and Cairo are two old and closely-built towers. On one is a statue facing the west, while on the other there had been a statue looking to the east. They used to relate that if one of them should fall, it would give warning of conquest by the people in whose direction it faced over the lands of Egypt, and others besides." The power of the omen's effect is further discernible from what also seems to be Ibn Jubayr's belief about the impending Almohad victory: "There remains nothing but the happy prospect of an Almohade conquest of these lands, and attentively they watch for it one auspicious morning, being certain of it, and expecting it as they expect the (last) hour, the fulfilment of the promise of which no one feels doubt." Ibn Jubayr, *Travels*, 73–74; *Tadhkira*, 57–58. There actually exists something of a mystery surrounding the

From the description in the text it seems that the foreshadowing event complemented the fears extant in Syria; it is the author's – and even the population's – hindsight that brings into play the significance of the occurrence, which stems

manuscript of ʿAbd al-Raḥīm b. Isḥāq b. Shīth al-Qurashī. Another manuscript with the same name, *Miftāḥ al-maqāṣid wa-miṣbāḥ al-marāṣid fī ziyārat bayt al-maqdis* by an ʿAbd al-Raḥmān b. Isḥāq b. Shīth 'al-Qunawī' also exists. The latter can be found in Dār al-Kutub al-Miṣriyya, Cairo. It is unlikely that two authors with similar names and exactly the same titles of works dealing with the same topic are two different people. The Cairo manuscript is only a section of a longer work and the text analysed by Maḥmūd Ibrāhīm is also a section of another manuscript located in Aleppo. It is possible that both sections belong to one manuscript – pending investigation of the complete manuscript in Aleppo – and that 'Raḥmān' and 'Raḥīm' represents a forgivable oversight on the part of a copyist, and that القونوي and القرشي are both the author's titles or that a copyist was relying on a script that was unclear and the similarities in the two titles may have led to the misspelling. Whatever the case however, the unpublished 'al-Qunawī' Cairo manuscript does provide us with some edifying information. There are allusions in the work that point to a post-reconquest awareness of the exceptional place of Ṣalāḥ al-Dīn's victory in light of God's protection of the city during the prophetic era of Sulaymān (Solomon) and the Jewish nation, Banī Isrāʾīl generally. I have translated what is relevant in this context and adopted a positive reading of the text to suggest that the author may have noted the absence of wonders (*ʿajāʾib*) that were decreed by God to the Children of Isrāʾīl to reflect the favouring of the Prophet's nation by not trying them in the same way. The author writes: "After the death of ʿAbd al-Malik (b. Marwān) it was left as it was built, then the unbelievers took it after that, so Ṣalāḥ al-Dīn then conquered it on Friday 583/1187. After the reconquest many unusual events did not occur to the Muslims (as they had before). From them was a sign in that in some of the nights there was a great fire that descended from the sky. So whoever committed a sin against God on that night, the fire burned him if he looked at it. And they [believed] that if an arrow was fired inside Jerusalem that arrow would come back to the one who fired [it]. Another sign was that there was a dog made of wood at one of the gates of Jerusalem. If the doer of magic passed by it the dog would bark at him. He would then forget what he knew of magic before he entered Jerusalem. Another sign was the particular gate, which, if any of the wrongdoers entered it, the gate would squeeze him. Another sign was that, in the time of Solomon, there was a chain dangling from the sky to the earth. If two people had a dispute they would come to the chain, so whoever was truthful would have access to the chain and would touch it with his hand while the liar was unable to touch it." ʿAbd al-Raḥmān b. Isḥāq b. Shīth al-Qunawī, *Miftāḥ al-maqāṣid wa-miṣbāḥ al-marāṣid fī ziyārat bayt al-maqdis* (M/S copying department, 1963, no. 46304/514), 53–54; the information pertaining to strange happenings in Jerusalem in ancient times is not important here. Such events made up sections of other *faḍāʾil* texts, including the *Faḍāʾil al-Quds* of Ibn al-Jawzī, who also incorporates the Qurʾānic figure Dhū l-Qarnayn; but Ibn Shīth's inclusion of the information in the context of Ṣalāḥ al-Dīn's reconquest makes it significant here. See Ibn al-Jawzī, *Faḍāʾil al-Quds*, 81–83.

from a search for signs and special reasons to explain the Muslim loss of sacred locations. A similar example may emphasise the point. A poem composed by Ṭalāʾiʿ b. Ruzzīk (d. 556/1161), the Fāṭimid vizier, for the caliph al-ʿĀḍid (r. 555–67/1160–71), for the bereaved Usāma b. Munqidh, ruler of Shayzar, following the latter's loss of his family in a series of earthquakes which began in 551/1156, attributes the misfortune and calamity to the crusader presence in Jerusalem; the poem highlights the connection between natural phenomena and social trepidation. In further calls for an alliance with Damascus, Ibn Ruzzīk advocated cooperation between the Egyptian and Syrian armies to liberate Jerusalem and delivered messages with advice to Nūr al-Dīn Zangī through Usāma, his acquaintance in Syria: "In my opinion, and opinions are like arrows that could miss or hit. Indeed this earthquake occurred because of Islam's absence from Jerusalem"[121] (1.88).

Abū Shāma's *Rawḍatayn* contains an elaborate section entitled "Qaṣāʾid qudsiyyāt li-l-ḥakīm al-Jilyānī wa-ghayrihi" [Jerusalem poems by the sage al-Jilyānī and others]; this section immediately follows the details of the expulsion of the Franks from Jerusalem. Abū Shāma cites selected pieces from five different poems of ʿAbd al-Munʿim al-Jilyānī. His poetry is distinctive for its use of non-Arabic words such as al-Isbatār (Hospitallers), al-Dāwiyya (Templars), and al-Brins (The prince), which highlight an attempt to make a conclusive pronouncement about the fate of Islam's enemies; for showing how the Muslim camp was well informed about crusader plans; for demonstrating a Muslim awareness of the crusaders' most skilled and resilient fighters; and for celebrating Ṣalāḥ al-Dīn's feats around earlier acclaimed personalities (Iskandar ahl al-zamān, Ghaḍanfar, ʿUmar, Dhū l-Qarnayn). We must bear in mind that poets, patrons, and audiences did not entirely believe, literally, what was said about the patron, rather the hyperbolic praise reflected a particular atmosphere and mood.

What is especially revealing about al-Jilyānī's verses is his repetition of the idea that the crusaders brought with them what would culminate in a new Islamic era of victory. His poetry contains more eschatological motifs than that of other poets and is enmeshed in a web of allusions that place Ṣalāḥ al-Dīn in a narrative frame.

(3) The Hospitallers and the Knights Templars came together
As if they are from the barrier of Gog [Yaʾjūj] when they flow forth.[122]
(1.89)

121 Ibn Ruzzīk, *Dīwān*, 63.

122 Abū Shāma, *Kitāb al-Rawḍatayn*, 3:262.

Al-Jilyānī's association of the military orders with the Ya'jūj (Gog) has clear Qur'ānic and eschatological undertones. This reference likely served to embellish the crusader threat and emphasise Ṣalāḥ al-Dīn's victory, but it also tied in with an undercurrent whereby scholars sought to link the occupation of Jerusalem, the crusader presence in Syria, and the reconquest to the *ḥadīth* literature. Al-Jilyānī's interest and expertise in esoteric studies might explain his attention to eschatological imagery in several poems which congratulate Ṣalāḥ al-Dīn for the reconquest of Jerualem. He draws on eschatological motifs, referencing the 'end of time' in relation to the divinely intended epoch he believed he was witnessing. In this, Ṣalāḥ al-Dīn is in the position of a forerunner of unfolding end of time events. Al-Jilyānī describes the "Hospitallers [who] merged in the wilderness ... as if they are coming from the barrier of the Ya'jūj" (Gog) (3). The reference to the crusaders as Ya'jūj magnified Ṣalāḥ al-Dīn's victory and inflated the magnitude of the crusader threat by staging the enemy as comparable to end of time actors, a reference that is part of a semantic field in the poem wherein motifs pertaining to end time occurences draw on the special era the poet believed his listeners were witnessing. In addition, a reference to the Qur'ānic prophet Shu'ayb and his disbelieving townspeople (7) further stages the conflict as one related to the scale of prophecy, as one of faith set against unbelief. In line 15 the poet notes that "the end time generation is proceeding ..." (15),[123] and led in glory by "The king which the Prophet gave glad tidings about ... In the trial of rebellion he would be the support of Islam" (18) and "Because of him the *malāḥim* [epic battles] of Dhū l-Qarnayn are forgotten ..." (19).[124] In another poem al-Jilyānī heralds Ṣalāḥ al-Dīn as "The Alexander of this time [who] has made us victorious."[125]

Eschatology is a pervasive element of Islamic religious literature, and since conflict stimulates powerful feelings of fear and hope, some elements of 'end time' apprehension are noticeable in chronicles, *jihād* and *faḍā'il* treatises, and also in poetry. It is important to remind ourselves that the *ḥadīth madrasa* was the institutional centre for Nūr al-Dīn's struggle against the enemies of Sunnī Islam, and the renowned scholar and historian Ibn 'Asākir sought to contribute to Nūr al-Dīn's focus on the *jihād* by authoring a treatise to this end, *Arba'ūn fī l-ijtihād fī iqāmat al-jihād* [Forty in the cause of *jihād*] and *Faḍl 'Asqalān* [The virtues of Ascalon], in an attempt to inspire Muslims to retake the town of Ascalon which the Franks had captured in 547–8/1153.[126] Ibn 'Asākir's eldest son, al-Qāsim (d. 600/1203), also wrote a work dealing specifically with the

123 Ibid., 3:262.
124 Ibid., 3:263.
125 Ibid.
126 See Mourad and Lindsay, *The Intensification and Reorientation*.

merits of Jerusalem and al-Aqṣā Mosque; it was entitled *al-Jāmiʿ al-mustaqṣā fī faḍāʾil al-masjid al-Aqṣā* [The verified compendium of the merits of al-Aqṣā].[127] Unfortunately the work is lost, but parts of it are preserved in Burhān al-Dīn Ibn al-Firkāḥ's (d. 729/1329) *Kitāb Bāʿith al-nufūs*, which is a summary of al-Qāsim's text and Abū l-Maʿālī's *Faḍāʾil al-Quds wa-l-Shām*. In his treatise, Ibn al-Firkāḥ mentions Jerusalem's specific role in end time scenarios, some of which do not appear in other previous *faḍāʾil* works. Here Ibn al-Firkāḥ brings together several end time events in Jerusalem, beginning with the release of Gog and Magog:

> Gog and Magog shall conquer the entire world except Jerusalem. And God shall destroy them in the land of Jerusalem … And the Migration in the Last Day shall be to Jerusalem … God prevents the enemy of God from entering Jerusalem … There will remain no believer, man or woman, who shall not go to Jerusalem. All the lands shall be destroyed, but Jerusalem shall prosper … Hell-fire is heated in Jerusalem. A door of Heaven will open onto Jerusalem.[128]

Reynald of Châtillon's raid into the Red Sea in 1182–83 and his threats against Mecca and Medina represent a specific episode that reveals how fears of upheaval following the loss, or expected loss of a sacred location generated eschatological concerns.[129] A few years earlier, in 577/1181, Reynald, lord of Kerak and Transjordan, set out toward Taymāʾ (an area en route to the city of Medina) in spite of a truce between the King of Jerusalem and Ṣalāḥ al-Dīn. To thwart Reynald's attempt to reach the holy city, Ṣalāḥ al-Dīn's nephew and the governor of Damascus, Farrūkshāh pillaged the areas around Kerak to make Reynald rethink his decision. The lord of Kerak, however, was undeterred, and in 578/1183 he organised another incursion to the Red Sea; his aim was to disrupt relations between Syria and Egypt and to profit by plundering the caravans of merchants who frequented the area.

127 See Mourad, 'Ibn 'Asakir,' 1:351–352.

128 Charles Matthews, *Palestine-Mohammedan Holy Land* (London, 1949), 30, 32, 33.

129 Aside from the extent to which these ideas may or may not have been true in Reynald of Châtillon, Marcus Milwright provides some interesting speculations about how Reynald would have perceived Muslim ritual practices concerning the treatment of the dead and ideas about pilgrimage and the veneration of saints and shrines during his sixteen-year imprisonment in Aleppo from 1160 to 1176, and how these ideas may have influenced his notorious undertaking. See M. Milwright, 'Reynald of Chatillon and the Red Sea Expedition,' in *Noble Ideas and Bloody Realities: Warfare in the Middle Ages*, ed. Niall Christie and Maya Yazigi (Leiden: Brill, 2006), 235–257.

Aside from Islam's holiest precincts being at risk, Ibn Jubayr's contemporary account is based on a rumour that the crusaders intended to "enter the City of the Prophet – may God bless and preserve him – and remove him from the sacred tomb. This intent they spread abroad, and let report of it run on their tongues."[130] If the raid had been successful, it would have obstructed the pilgrimage routes to the holy cities and trade routes to India, causing substantial economic loss to Egypt, Ṣalāḥ al-Dīn's major source of power. But it was the belief that the holy cities might be attacked and the Prophet's body might be disinterred that greatly aggravated the fears.[131]

Information pertaining to the raid is also found in Abū Shāma's *Rawḍatayn* which preserves the accounts of ʿImād al-Dīn al-Iṣfahānī and al-Qāḍī l-Fāḍil; both Sibṭ b. al-Jawzī and Ibn Wāṣil, however, also copied part of the letter al-Qāḍī l-Fāḍil sent to Baghdad describing the raid.[132] My commentary is limited to a small section of what is broadly similar in the accounts of Abū Shāma, Ibn Wāṣil, and Sibṭ b. al-Jawzī, though in fact the accounts of both ʿImād al-Dīn and al-Qāḍī l-Fāḍil can be found in a surviving fragment of ʿImād al-Dīn's *al-Barq al-Shāmī* and Abū Shāma did not copy the full account of both authors.[133]

Al-Qāḍī l-Fāḍil reports

> The fear of the people of those areas grew, especially that of the *ahl al-qibla* [Muslims] when the consequences flashed before them. The Muslims were sure that it was the day of judgement and that its portents were clear, and that the world would be laid out and spread [for the judgement]. They waited for the anger of God to end [the danger to] His sanctified house, and the station of His noble friend [Abraham], the legacy of the past prophets and the tomb of His greatest prophet – may

130 Ibn Jubayr, *Travels*, 52; *Tadhkira*, 40.

131 In light of this, there is a story of particular interest that developed out of the pietistic persona of Nūr al-Dīn. It pertains to the sultan being visited by the Prophet on three occasions in one night. The Prophet calls on him thus: "O Maḥmūd save me from these two blond-haired individuals" while pointing to his assailants. After counting all the inhabitants of Medina, two individuals were unaccounted for. The two were Andalusians who matched the description of the assailants in Nūr al-Dīn's dream; they were discovered attempting to disinter the body of the Prophet. The story is not found in any contemporary chronicle featuring Nūr al-Dīn but complements the aura of piety that developed out of his persona; he is the unadorned 'Maḥmūd,' defender of Islam and *mujāhid* against the *umma*'s enemies. Ibn Qāḍī Shuhbah, *al-Kawākib al-durriya fī l-sīrat al-nūriyya* (Beirut: Dār al-Kitāb al-Jadīd, 1971), 72–73.

132 Sibṭ b. al-Jawzī, *Mirʾāt al-zamān*, part 1, 8:370; Ibn Wāṣil, *Mufarrij*, 2:129–131.

133 See Gibb, 'Al-Barq al-Shāmī,' 93–115.

> the peace and blessings of God be upon him – they hoped that a miracle of this house would sharpen their eyes, like [it did] when the companions of the elephant intended to take it. They entrusted the affair to God who was sufficient for them and the best disposer of affairs … and no one survived except the one who lost hope of returning and knew that the command of the Last Hour remained.[134]

The words of al-Qāḍī l-Fāḍil clearly reveal that the feared destruction of the sacred precincts induced eschatological fears coupled with hopes for a divine miracle. Although the incomparable significance of the holy cities and the Prophet himself was certain to evoke such strong sentiments, the fact that the Franks were the source of such trepidation indicates that their role in shaping Muslim perceptions complemented existing attitudes that arose from the occupation of Jerusalem. Even though it was not stated, one can assume that the eschatological fears of the Muslims were exacerbated because Jerusalem, Islam's third holiest precinct, was already in crusader hands; it must have felt as though the end of the world was imminent, "for no Rūmī [western Christian] had ever before come to that place."[135]

Ṣalāḥ al-Dīn's naval reforms in Egypt allowed for a quick response to the crusader incursions. A fleet was dispatched by the sultan's brother al-ʿĀdil, the port of ʿAqaba was retaken, and the crusaders aboard the fleet were taken prisoner. While Ṣalāḥ al-Dīn's reputation as a defender of Islam may have been marred because of the crusaders' nearness to the holy cities, Ṣalāḥ al-Dīn's

134 Abū Shāma, *Kitāb al-Rawḍatayn*, 3:91–92; Ibn Wāṣil, *Mufarrij*, 2:129–131.

135 Ibn Jubayr, *Travels*, 52; *Tadhkira*, 40; Alex Mallett attempts to offer a more nuanced analysis of the motives for Reynald's raid into the Red Sea and pillaging in the Hijaz. It allows for the consideration of other alternatives that differ from the matching accounts found in Muslim sources – namely, that it was Reynald's intent to attack the cities of Mecca and Medina and unearth the body of the Prophet – this caused a particular Muslim hatred for Reynald. Although I believe the Muslim account should not be rejected – in light of Reynald's acute anti-Muslim bitterness that likely shaped his actions after he was released from incarceration in Aleppo, where he was imprisoned from 1160 to 1176 – Mallett's focus on the political benefit of Reynald's raid and his attempt to thwart the joining of Aleppo to Ṣalāḥ al-Dīn's territory is in turn convincing. See Alex Mallett, 'A Trip Down the Red Sea with Reynald of Châtillon,' *Journal of the Royal Asiatic Society* 18 (2008), 141–153. See also Carole Hillenbrand, 'The Imprisonment of Reynald of Chattilon,' in *Texts, Documents and Artefacts: Islamic Studies in Honour of D. S. Richards*, ed. C. F. Robinson (Leiden: Brill, 2003), 79–102; Bernard Hamilton, 'The Elephant of Christ: Reynald of Chatillon,' *Studies in Church History 15: Religious Motivation*, ed. D. Baker (Oxford: Basil Blackwell, 1978), 97–108.

chancery was nevertheless able to exploit the event to reveal his unyielding commitment to the *jihād*; the crusader threat was given a new edge, as al-Qāḍī l-Fāḍil's letter reveals. Aside from the praise accorded to Ṣalāḥ al-Dīn, the admiral Ḥusām al-Dīn Lu'lu', an Armenian freedman instructed by al-ʿĀdil to pursue the Franks from Egypt, was included in a panegyric composed after the event by the Egyptian poet Ibn al-Dharawī.[136] It appears that Ḥusām al-Dīn was a Mamlūk, since the name 'Lu'lu'' (lit., pearl) was often given to slaves. His description 'al-Hājib' (chamberlain) does not reveal much; he may have held the position under the Fāṭimids in Egypt, in which case he was an important court official but not a military figure.[137] His piety is noted by the chroniclers who describe him as someone who was committed to the service of the religion.[138]

(1) There passed a day that was strange, wherein happiness was almost frozen.
(2) When the respectable chamberlain came with prisoners of war who were tied with a chain.
(3) They were tied to camels that looked like mountains and the *ʿulūj* looked as if they *were* mountains.
(4) I said: after the *takbīr* [exclamation – *Allāhu akbar*] when everything was clear: 'It's like this, like this, that the *jihād* should be' (*hakadhā hakadhā yakūn al-jihād*).[139] (1.90)

Aside from congratulating Ḥusām al-Dīn, verse 3 of the poem presents a seemingly inaccurate historical image that amplifies the scale of what was an isolated case of plunder rather than a sweeping incursion to acquire new territories, instigated by a man seeking revenge after spending sixteen years in an Aleppan jail. Verse 4 appears to denote a euphoric expression that goes some way in explaining the great significance of thwarting the incursion. The description represents what Ibn al-Dharawī perceived to be an outstanding example of *jihād*. His diction is akin to what Ibn Waṣil uses for both Nūr al-Dīn and Ṣalāḥ al-Dīn, 'like this, rulers should be!' *wa-hakadhā fa-l-takun al-mulūk* and 'like this, the

---

136 See ʿImād al-Dīn al-Iṣfahānī, *Kharīdat al-qaṣr*, 1:187–188.

137 See C. L. Klausner, *The Seljuk Vezirate, a Study of Civil Administration, 1055–1194* (Cambridge, MA: Harvard University Press, 1973).

138 See G. L. V. Leiser, 'The Crusader Raid in the Red Sea in 578/1182–83,' *Journal of the American Research Center in Egypt* 14 (1977), 93.

139 Abū Shāma, *Kitāb al-Rawḍatayn*, 3:89.

sultan should be' *fa-mithli hadhā li-yakun al-sulṭān*.[140] The same way that both of these descriptions centre on the rulers' legitimacy, Ibn al-Dharawī's sentiment serves to legitimise the *jihād* initiative.

Here the poet's voice is similar to that which Ṭalā'i' b. Ruzzīk adopts in a poem he composed following Ṣalāḥ al-Dīn's reconquest of Jerusalem.

> Indeed this is how, for God, determinations proceed
> And it is the strong determinate swords that proceed in this war.[141] (1.91)

These two poets may have been inspired by the memorable verses of the fourth-/tenth-century poet al-Mutanabbī in his famous *qaṣīda* for Sayf al-Dawla after the battle of al-Ḥadath in 343/954–55:

> With the worth of men of resolve are resolutions in accordance
> And in accordance with the worth of the generous are generous deeds
> Great in the eye of the small are small deeds
> And small in the eye of the great are great deeds,

and Abū Tammām's gnomic musing in his equally famous *qaṣīda* in praise of al-Mu'taṣim's conquest of Amorium in 223/838, which opens with the reflection: "The sword is an intelligencer more truthful than the written word."[142]

The poet subsequently congratulates Ḥusām al-Dīn by drawing attention to the clear religious rationale behind the counterattack, "You were sufficient [protection] for the people of the Ḥaramayn [two sanctuaries] from their enemies, and you protected Aḥmad [Prophet Muḥammad] and the Ka'ba."[143] His defence of the 'sacred' was the most illustrious feature of the attack, and the safekeeping of the Ḥaramayn may have reminded the Syrians of their responsibility to recapture the third *ḥaram*, Jerusalem. In light of this, the connection between the Ka'ba and the Dome of the Rock in later poetry may have stemmed in part from this kind of sentiment – one that was evoked by 'Imād al-Dīn al-Iṣfahānī following the reconquest:

140 Ibn Wāṣil, *Mufarrij*, 1:135; Ibn Wāṣil, *Mufarrij*, 2:277.

141 Ibn Ruzzīk, *Dīwān*, 135.

142 See M. M. Badawi, 'The Function of Rhetoric in Medieval Arabic Poetry: Abu Tammam's Ode on Amorium,' *Journal of Arabic Literature* 9 (1978), 43–56.

143 Abū Shāma, *Kitāb al-Rawḍatayn*, 3:89.

(9) So now that Jerusalem is free, we are extremely proud that Jerusalem and al-Bayt al-Ḥarām are the same [i.e., both free].[144] (1.92)

To summarise, in this section I examined the ways in which poetry was used to ascertain some of the theological provenances that shaped the socio-political landscape of Syria in the sixth/twelfth century. The image of Jesus was perhaps intended to tie in with *faḍāʾil* themes that strengthened Muslim attachment to Jerusalem, and derided the Christian enemy. Furthermore, Nūr al-Dīn was a keen benefactor of religious centres and placed great emphasis on private and public acts of devotion; he thus gained a reputation as a religiously committed military leader, as shown by the compositions analysed in this chapter, which enhanced that image. Nūr al-Dīn wanted to be seen in light of the religiosity of his predecessors, and as a contributor to the Sunnī revival of the period. In this chapter I further considered examples of the pervasiveness of Qurʾānic scripture in the poetry of the period. Allusions to scriptural passages were mostly understood by the religious classes in the poet's audience, though it is likely that such references were also grasped by others and might have been pointed out by scholars or interpreters in the audiences. Such references were often used to cast events between crusader and Muslim camps and the heroic feats of *jihād* warriors with an identifiable Islamic character, and this was a sure way to ward off the objections of critics. The poetry of this period, however, did not always ossify binaries between the two camps. As shown in the following section, the melodrama that typifies dichotomous conflicts is seemingly abated in light of a cultural encounter between Ibn al-Qaysarānī and Frankish women.

Gendering the Anti-Frankish *Jihād*

Notwithstanding the strong themes of religious superiority evidenced in the poetry of this period, of the influence of Sufism and the ways it shaped the poetic discourse, as shown in earlier sections, or in the frequent use of Qurʾānic imagery to drive home the poet's political and ideological messages, in this part of the chapter I reveal some divergent and surprising attitudes toward Frankish Christians. These complement and complicate the *jihād* message our poet Ibn al-Qaysarānī espouses elsewhere. The same intensity of anti-Frankish feeling found in his other poems does not permeate the following verses of his poems.

In 541/1146 Ibn al-Qaysarānī visited some areas under Frankish occupation and during these travels, particularly to Antioch, he disclosed to his readers a

144 Ibid., 3:235.

particular liking he had developed for Frankish women. He marvelled at their beauty and their bashful nature. The gender perspective in what appear to be *ghazal* poems present in his *dīwān* is very revealing for what it highlights about the boundaries of social acceptability, spoken or otherwise, that may have influenced the poet's choice of subject. Clearly differentiating them from native Christians, it is the Faranja that he so brazenly admires.

> I moved away but I left in their lands a heart that longed for a sight to observe them.
> And I will always envy the one who lived among them because of his closeness to them, until I even envied the captive.[145] (1.93)

During his visit to Antioch in 541/1146 Ibn al-Qaysarānī either visited a church, superimposed an image he had formulated about Christian women onto his poetry, or wrote from what he had heard about female worship in churches. Some of his verses seem to acknowledge a sincerity in their devotion and their propriety served as the basis for his infatuation. The reverential tone of his poetry might be understood in light of his fixation with the physical beauty of the opposite gender; the same tone does not extend, for example, to male worshippers. Perhaps we can understand the poet's lines in light of a merging of physical beauty and religious devotion, one that could not be explored with his own female co-religionists, because of its social unacceptability.

> (1) How many women [wet with tears] are in churches, like a deer whose beauty is her shyness?
> (2) For every female worshipper [lit., one who prostrates] there is a picture of her on the wall [an icon of the Holy Virgin Mary]. If she were placed on the wall [as a picture], then the [other] pictures would prostrate to her.
> (4) Modesty is planted on her cheeks like a rose. The branches of the rose are watered by [my] looking [at her].
> (5) The eyelashes have spoken. So if you talk to her, the *ḥūr* [celestial maidens] will reply.[146] (1.94)

145 Ibn al-Qaysarānī, *Dīwān Muḥammad b. Naṣr*, 64; ʿImād al-Dīn al-Iṣfahānī, *Kharīdat al-qaṣr*, 1:100; for a valuable work on Ibn al-Qaysarānī's *Dīwān*, see Maḥmūd Ibrāhīm, *Ṣida al-ghazwu*. See also Nizar F. Hermes, *The [European] Other in Medieval Arabic Literature and Culture: Ninth-Twelfth Century AD* (New York: Palgrave Macmillan, 2012), 135–169.

146 Ibn al-Qaysarānī, *Dīwān*, 62; ʿImād al-Dīn al-Iṣfahānī, *Kharīdat al-qaṣr*, 1:120.

Ghazal poetry, poems with themes of love and longing, first began to appear during the Umayyad period. Bauer points out that it is difficult to find an exact definition of the *ghazal* because of its different manifestations, and the interplay between elements of form and content.[147] Aside from the form and structure of the poem as a criterion, Meisami's definition that emphasises content sees the *ghazal* as "poetry about love, whether incorporated into the *qaṣīda* or in an independent brief poem."[148] A *ghazal* therefore must have the theme of love as its centrepiece. The *maʿānī* (syntactic meanings) present in this poem, *mahāt* (deer), *ḥafr* (shyness), *ḥayāʾ* (shyness), *ward* (roses), *jufūn* (eyelashes), *ḥūr* (celestial maiden), and *qamar* (moon) (line 6) are symbols of the physical attributes of Frankish women, according to the poet's observations. The figurative language Ibn al-Qaysarānī uses to describe the beauty of the Faranja involves metaphors typical of *ghazal* poetry. Bauer's analysis of *ghazals* of the third/ninth and fourth/tenth centuries found that all themes and motifs were incorporated into five thematic categories: 'praise' of the beloved's beauty; 'complaint' of the lover's separation from his beloved; 'declaration' of the love of the lover; 'reproach' toward the beloved for the unfulfilled duties of love toward the lover; and the 'portrayal' of individual traits of the beloved.[149] The poem contains, almost entirely, the *ghazal*-based themes of 'praise' and 'portrayal' of his beloved. Using the words 'moon' and 'celestial maiden' the verses emphasise the ephemeral elements of light and heavenly associations. In a way akin to a lover enjoying the beloved's presence, Ibn al-Qaysarānī's Faranja could be imagined in the the sense that the occasion could be a genuine 'close encounter.' It was typical of *al-ghazal al-ʿudhrī* poetry that the poet might invent his beloved, and although the poem meets the criterion of a *ghazal* – containing themes of 'portrayal' of Ibn al-Qaysarānī's infatuation and 'praise' of his beloved's beauty, the element of 'reproach' here is not directed toward the beloved for the unfulfilled duties of love toward the lover. Rather, the poet deems the Frankish women a *fitna*, a temptation that might stem not only from her beauty, but also from the sense of distance and othering of her person, an unrequited and inadmissable love, it was thus an infatuation that bordered on religious as well as cultural sensitivities, particularly since the

147 Thomas Bauer, 'The Arabic Ghazal: Formal and Thematic Aspects of a Problematic Genre' in *Ghazal as World Literature II: From a Literary Genre to a Great Tradition. The Ottoman Ghazel in Context*, ed. Angelika Neuwirth, Michael Hess, Judith Pfeiffer, and Börte Sagaster (Beirut and Würzburg: Ergon, 2006), 3.

148 Julie Scott Meisami, 'Ghazal,' in *Encyclopedia of Arabic Literature*, ed. J. S. Meisami and P. Starkey (London: Routledge, 1998), 1:249.

149 Bauer, "The Arabic Ghazal."

infatuation might suggest that local beauty was less desirable. Although the motifs are conventional they are not entirely intimate but are mitigated by the Otherness that his beloved represents. Since Ibn al-Qaysarānī seems to be depicting what he would have seen inside a church, it may have been that he was permitted to attend a Frankish church service, which is interesting for what it tells us about cultural encounters and modes of cultural acceptability between Franks and Muslims; in times of antagonism there were also glimpses of apparent conciliation.

In another poem, the poet is clearly entranced by a 'white Christian.' Far removed from the Banāt al-Aṣfar ascription that Ibn al-Qaysarānī's contemporary Ibn al-Munīr used, the poet does not view the Frankish women as a promising consequence of the *jihād*, i.e., as a spoil of war. Indisposed to use the Banāt al-Aṣfar description, we have the impression that perhaps he sought to humanise the Franks, or felt comfortable in the belief that it was not the enemy 'crusaders' that he was so impressed with, but Frankish settlers. Still, however, the image was his own fashioning of the Faranj as the Muslim 'Other.'

(1) I have so many desires in Antioch, and I will not conceal them out of shyness
(3) [My desires are] for every fair Christian woman. You cannot even compare the full moon to her.
(5) You cannot look at her eyes out of fear of [their] evil eye, but the heart is not absent from looking upon them.[150] (1.95)

Poets did not stress the whiteness of the crusaders. In Islamic tradition white suggests virtue and honour, purity, and the angelic. It plays an important role in Ibn al-Qaysarānī's poems however. The poem contains themes of 'portrayal' with a specific emphasis on 'whiteness' and also 'complaint,' for being unable to attain his beloved. The diffident remark is similar to what is found in another of his poems – By comparing her to a full moon the Frankish woman is described as transcending everything else. His sentiment is comparable to that found in Imru' l-Qays' *Mu'allaqa* in which Jamīl depicts Buthayna as the 'full moon' surpassing the 'minor stars' in brightness:

She is the full moon,
whereas the other women are [merely minor] stars
And what a great distance between them

150 Ibn al-Qaysarānī, *Dīwān*, 62; Ibrāhīm, *Ṣida al-ghazwu*, 94.

> She is superior in beauty to other people,
> just as the Night of Qadr is preferred
> over one thousand months.[151]

In line with the tropes and motifs found in *al-ghazal al-ʿudhrī* poems, in which comparative phrases are used to show the matchless beauty of the beloved, al-Harthi highlights the ethereal nature of this beauty. Ibn al-Qaysarānī's comparison of the Faranja to the paradisical *al-ḥūr al-ʿīn*, unsurpassed in beauty, suggests that the women he sees are beyond 'worldly' beauty. His is a desire that remains unfulfilled, or fulfilled only in a transient way. The feelings of the beauty expressed in *al-ʿudhrī* is not always purely erotic or sensual but focuses on describing a beauty that transcends human or natural qualities, the moon and the sun or any other woman is incomparable to her. Furthermore, Ibn al-Qaysarānī also reveals the semantic exchange between religion and love, which is another indicator of the *al-ʿudhrī* influences on the poetry. This comes through when describing, 'For every female worshipper there is a picture of her on the wall. If she is placed on the wall (as a picture) then the (other) pictures would prostrate to her.' The act of prostration is sanctified in the religious texts as owing to God alone, and not permitted to anyone else, including the Prophet. In what is most likely a reference to icons of the holy Virgin Mary, the image of the beloved being prostrated to might have been viewed as anathema for some Muslims and the imagery he creates may reveal a critical outlook toward Christian devotion. Hamori describes how 'The poaching of religious language is meant in the *ʿudhrī* lyric to express the extent of this dangerous devotion.'[152] This could be true in Ibn al-Qaysarānī's poetry if we juxtapose Ibn al-Qaysaranī's fascination with Frankish women with the general contempt he had for the Franks because of their presence in his homeland and the other occupied Muslim states. Some of his most evocative lines seek to persuade 'Imād al-Dīn Zangī and his son Nūr al-Dīn to advance the *jihād* against the crusaders and liberate Jerusalem. For example, in his praise of Nūr al-Dīn, Ibn al-Qaysarānī was concerned about following another kind of 'whiteness' (*bayḍāʾ*):

---

151 Jamīl b. Muʿmar, *Dīwān Jamīl Buthaynah: Jamīl b. Muʿmar*, ed. Fawzī ʿAṭawī (Beirut: Dār Saʿb, 1980), 37; J. M. al-Harthi, 'I Have Never Touched Her: The Body in al-Ghazal al-ʿUdhrī,' PhD thesis (University of Edinburgh, 2010), 146.

152 A. Hamori, 'Love Poetry (*Ghazal*),' in *Abbasid Belles Lettres*, ed. J. Ashtiany, T. M. Johnstone, J. D. Latham, and R. B. Serjeant (Cambridge: Cambridge University Press, 1990), 206.

> O the king who brought people to the clear white path (*al-maḥajjat al-bayḍāʾ*)
> You showed up the other kings by way of your justice when you followed the conduct of the caliphs.[153] (1.96)

His gender-based poetry may even be a demonstration of his love for his homeland and the occupied states. Was the seductive power of Frankish women a warning sign that Muslim men would be unable to live among the Franks and that the danger of acclimatisation carried with it not only an acquiescence of Frankish authority and domination but also an inclination toward matters prohibited in the religion?[154] In this light, Ibn Jubayr, in his description of Tyre in the month of Jumāda II 580/September 1184, lamented the state of affairs between the Muslims and the Franks. His prescription that "there can be no excuse in the eyes of God for a Muslim to remain in an infidel country, except when passing through it, while the way lies clear in Muslim lands …"[155] followed the description of a wedding procession that he and other Muslims witnessed. The Christian bride he saw

> was most elegantly garbed in a beautiful dress from which trailed, according to their traditional style, a long train of golden silk. On her head she wore a golden diadem covered by a net of woven gold, and on her breast was a like arrangement. Proud she was in her ornaments and dress, walking with little steps of half a span, like a dove, or in the manner of a wisp of a cloud. God protect us from the seduction of the sight.[156]

Notwithstanding the "alluring sight" that even Muslims chose to observe, it was still a *fitna*, a temptation that Ibn Jubayr recognised. Moreover, there appears to be a syntactical structuring in this section of the *Riḥla*, whereby the author sought to build up a sense of the catastrophe that afflicted the city of Tyre. The devastating events he describes begin with the *fitna* of a wedding procession; he then describes an account of the severe hunger that befell the Muslims in Rabīʿ II 518/June 1124, such that the Muslim inhabitants were forced to flee the city; Ibn Jubayr then castigated the natives against returning to crusader occupied lands; he detailed the dire state of Muslim prisoners, male and female;

153 Abū Shāma, *Kitāb al-Rawḍatayn*, 1:128.

154 See Qur'ān, 24:30–31.

155 Ibn Jubayr, *Travels*, 321–322; Ibn Jubayr, *Tadhkira*, 240.

156 Ibn Jubayr, *Travels*, 320; Ibn Jubayr, *Tadhkira*, 239.

and told the story of the apostasy of a Maghribi (North African) whose mixing with Christians led him to renounce Islam and become Christian. As Ibn al-Qaysarānī candidly acknowledges in his poem, if passing through the occupied states has had a harmful effect on his religious conscience, then those who lived with the 'white Christian women' risk being predisposed to greater harm. Here Ibn al-Qaysarānī invokes the colour blue:

> The Frankish woman has become a *fitna* for me, the strong scent of perfume emanates from her.
> In her dress she is like a soft thin branch and her crown is like a lightning moon.
> And if there is some blueness in her eye, then the sharp-pointed lance is bluer.[157] (1.97)

By the ʿAbbāsid era, poetry comprised lighter genres, including love and licentious poetry. In another of Ibn al-Qaysarānī's poems we see more specific references to *ʿudhrī* motifs, including the mention of 'satin,' 'silk,' 'morning sun,' and 'necklace'; these were interlaced with religious motifs that are most compelling reflections of a crossing of religious/cultural boundaries as a consequence of Frankish presence. The poem is brazen with respect to the cultural/religious syncretism it seems to present. Though the point of *ʿudhrī* poetry is to exaggerate the impossibility of the love affair and the hardships and risks that the poet-lover is willing to undertake, the poem still allows the possibility, however, that Ibn al-Qaysarānī was, at least in part, motivated by a fear of the dangers represented by the Frankish presence. The drawing together of love-based words and motifs of physical appearance produce a *ghazal* imagery that speaks of the poet's infatuation: 'in every colour of satin'; 'girdles encircling their waists'; 'vestments of silk burdening them'; 'every charming woman'; 'face bare of a veil in the morning sun'; 'beauty of the sight'; 'necklace silent'; 'kisses.'

Joseph Sadan has assessed the *maʿānī* (syntactic meanings) in descriptions of women's hair, skin, and clothing, and, although the religious element in Ibn al-Qaysarani's poetry may preclude it being read in light of strong love or erotic symbolism, a case can be made for the existence of other *maʿānī* prevalent in *al-ghazal al-ʿudhrī* poetry.[158] Invention was a marked feature in medieval Arabic poetry intended for maximum audience impact. Strings of embellished

---

157 Ibn al-Qaysarānī, *Dīwān*, 66–67.

158 For more information on the place of women in Muslim and Christian literature during the crusades, see N. Christie, 'Crusade Literature: 9th to 15th Century,' in *Encyclopedia of*

verses and rhetorical devices were skilfully composed to challenge overt meanings; the more mendacious a poem the more it allowed for invented meanings and the more it appealed to the intellectual wit of the listeners. This, of course, was only meaningful if they were skilled enough to understand the subtleties. Multifaceted meanings then underscored the poet's perceptive genius, the scrutinising of meaning allowed the poet to display an acumen not bound by religion and pious truth. The importance of such independence of thought and meaning is expressed by the fifth-/eleventh-century Ibn Rashīq (d. 471/1078):

> A poet is called this because he perceives (*shaʿara*) what others do not. For if the poet did not form a concept or invent one, or did not embellish an expression or give it an original twist, or did not expand the concepts others treated clumsily, or shorten the expressions others made excessively long, or use a concept in a different way than it had been used before, then the name of poet would be given to him in a figurative sense and not in a real one, and he would not possess any merit other than that of metre, which in my opinion is no merit at all.[159]

Although Ibn al-Qaysarānī's poems might be read as standard *ghazal* (love poems) popular in the medieval courts from the Umayyad period onward, and reveal common conventions depicting women and their bodies, in fact, the depiction of Frankish women as part of an occupying presence in Antioch is not characteristic of his poetry, which generally focused on the *jihād*. The poetry also shows that sometimes we cannot find simple dichotomous categories, in which Franks are depicted in an entirely negative way. Though the Byzantine women were known as Rumiyya, the feminine of Rumi, distinguished for her physical beauty and her sexual immorality and described as an enticing *fitna*, was different than Ibn al-Qaysarānī's Faranja. So too, the poet's fascination with Frankish women is very distinct from ʿImād al-Dīn al-Iṣfahānī's elaborately prurient description of women who undertook (as a noble deed) to provide sexual relief to soldiers.[160]

Though Muslims may have been fascinated with the *othered* exotic, she was not the stereotypical Rumiyya. A literal reading of Ibn al-Qaysarānī's lines indicates an accommodation of the Frankish 'other'; they might in fact challenge religious and social boundaries that deemed the Franks as distant and

---

Women and Islamic Cultures, Vol 1: *Methodologies, Paradigms and Sources*, ed. S. Joseph et al. (Brill: Leiden, 2003), 1:16–21.

159 Vincente Cantarino, *Arabic Poets in the Golden Age* (Leiden: Brill, 1975), 38.

160 Gabrieli, *Arab Historians of the Crusades*, 204–206.

dehumanised. On the other hand, they might fit well into the *ghazal* type, or they could be an example of the multi-faceted nature of inventive meanings, they could be reflective and refractive. Of course it was the poet's adeptness at being inventive that marked him as a proficient poet; it was his ability to transcend 'the obviousness of objective truth' while keeping to the standard of aesthetics, to use his mastery of language to expose, challenge, and confront, and the Franks could well be a typified enemy and a grave *fitna* that the Muslim world should not accept.[161]

161 See S. A. Ali, *Arabic Literary Salons in the Islamic Middle Ages: Poetry, Public Performance, and the Presentation of the Past* (Notre Dame, IN: University of Notre Dame Press 2010), 69–71.

CHAPTER 7

The Place of Egypt in Poetic Discourse

One of the important uses of poetry in this period is the way it served as a medium of diplomacy and cross-cultural exchange between rulers and states. As Caton has shown in his anthropological work on Yemeni poets discussed in chapter 2, poetry could be used as a source of mediation between rival families or tribes. Poets could antagonise relations, or appear as peace brokers. In this regard the role of the contemporary Fāṭimids and their use of poetry is particularly relevant. Therefore, in this chapter I draw on the conflict between Shāwar (d. 564/1169) and Shīrkūh (d. 564/1169), and the changing role of al-Qāḍī l-Fāḍil as an instrumental figure in the Fāṭimid chancery and then as a highly skilled administrator under the Ayyūbids.[1] In this part I also highlight examples of realpolitik at play in the poetry.

In the second section of the chapter I address the relationship between Usāma b. Munqidh and Ṭalāʾiʿ b. Ruzzīk, who worked under the Ayyūbids and Fāṭimids respectively.[2] I emphasise the way in which poetry was used as a medium of diplomacy between representatives of the Fāṭimids and Ayyūbids and I analyse key themes in the series of correspondences between the two, themes such as the need for unity between Syria and Egypt in order to liberate Jerusalem from the crusaders. Unlike official dispatches produced by the secretarial classes, which essentially only echoed the views of their patrons, poetic correspondence between the civilian elite, particularly in cases in which companionship (*ṣuḥba*) between them was evident, allows us to observe expressions pertaining to ideas of political unity and the outlooks on the crusaders different from the more "official" aspect of the other literature.

1 C. Cahen, 'Ayyūbids,' *EI*², 1:796–807.

2 Usāma's religious leaning has been a matter of some question. According to Robert Irwin, the Banū Munqidh were Twelver Shīʿīs and Usāma's dislike for *jihād* may serve as a further indicator of his Shīʿī faith. Hitti suspects that he might have harboured some sympathy for the Shīʿa. According to Cobb, however, no conclusive evidence of his precise theological leaning appears to exist; he was most probably a Sunnī with some "acceptable Shi'ite tendencies." See Irwin, 'Islam and the Crusades,' 233; Irwin, 'Usamah ibn Munqidh,' 78; Hitti, *An Arab-Syrian Gentleman*, 14; Usāma ibn Munqidh, *The Book of Contemplation*, 77.

 | DOI 10.1163/9789004345225_008

Egypt and the Language of Realpolitik

In this section I show that poets sometimes compromised on theological conventions in favour of politically-oriented views. I draw on the relationship between the Fāṭimid vizier Ṭalā'iʿ b. Ruzzīk, the Yemeni historian and poet ʿUmāra al-Yamanī (d. 571/1175), and Usāma b. Munqidh. Although Ibn Ruzzīk was a Shīʿī and ʿUmāra and Usāma were Sunnī, their political loyalties sometimes took precedence over their religious differences and attitudes toward internal schismatic disputes.

It is the *qaṣīda* (panegyric ode) that was central to medieval Arabic poetry. Aside from praise of a ruler, the *qaṣīda* also praised the tribal society in which the poet lived. Pre-Islamic attributes such as courage, noble lineage, patience, forbearance, and hospitality were coated with Islamic ideals of fear of God, guidance, worship, support of the faith, and ideas pertaining to legitimate authority.[3] As Sperl notes, "The ancient themes have preserved their power but acquired a new meaning: the formal recitation of the *qaṣīda* is still a ritual act, celebrating no longer the heroic model but the model of political authority in Islam."[4] Praise in a *qaṣīda* was also not limited to rulers. The civilian elite generally – viziers, secretaries, and religious scholars – were sometimes the subject of praise, particularly during political conflicts. In the 540s/1150s, the viziers Usāma b. Munqidh and Ṭalā'iʿ b. Ruzzīk were lauded, sometimes by each other, for their efforts in pursuing the *jihād* against the Franks.

During this period the rivalry that ensued between the Fāṭimid caliphate and the vizierate was a major political conflict. When the Fāṭimid vizier Abū ʿAlī b. al-Afḍal (d. 515/1121) took over from his father Badr al-Jamālī (d. 487/1094) – during what has been termed the 'Jamālī' dynasty, an age when nearly all power, political and military, was in the hands of the vizierate while the caliph held only a nominal position of head of state – the Sunnī poets of Syria showed a keen interest in supporting this change of Fāṭimid political power. Al-Qāḍī l-Fāḍil, who went on to become Ṣalāḥ al-Dīn's scribe and leading administrator, praised the Fāṭimid coup in his *dīwān*.

(2) You only became like lions toward your enemies, when they had become like dogs.[5] (1.98)

---

3 See J. S. Meisami, 'Madiḥ, Madḥ,' in *Encyclopedia of Arabic Literature*, ed. J. S. Meisami and P. Starkey (London: Routledge, 1999), 2:482.

4 Sperl, *Mannerism in Arabic Poetry*, 27.

5 Qāḍī l-Fāḍil, *Dīwān al-Qāḍī l-Fāḍil* (Cairo: Dār al-Maʿrifa, 1961), 46.

The vision of Ṣalāḥ al-Dīn was best articulated by his scribe and adviser ʿAbd al-Raḥīm b. ʿAlī l-Baysānī, known as al-Qāḍī l-Fāḍil. The instrumental role of al-Qāḍī l-Fāḍil in overhauling the administrative system of Ṣalāḥ al-Dīn's power base in Egypt developed from 558/1163, from the unwavering attitude he displayed in the years before Ṣalāḥ al-Dīn's emergence in Egypt, during the rivalry between Shāwar and Shīrkūh. Born in Ascalon, al-Qāḍī l-Fāḍil settled in Egypt where he started his career in the Fāṭimid chancery of the state (*dīwān al-inshāʾ*). He rose through the ranks and in 565/1170 became the director of the *dīwān*; he supported the Fāṭimid struggle against Shīrkūh and Nūr al-Dīn's desired takeover of Egypt. Although al-Qāḍī l-Fāḍil was not a Shīʿī and later expressed contempt for this creed, possibly out of political expediency, it was what he described as his love for Egypt, the Nile, the pyramids, and the fertile land that prompted him not only to support Egyptian autonomy but to use his administrative aptitude to strengthen the footing of Shāwar (and later his son al-Kāmil) even at the expense of his co-religionists in Syria; he even – initially – enlisted Frankish support to fight off the Syrian threat.[6] Al-Qāḍī l-Fāḍil used his political position to strike a chord with his audiences and readers by employing language particularly pertinent to the Fāṭimid Shīʿīs as he congratulated Shāwar for "supporting the Prophet and his household." Instead of depicting the Franks in light of their enemy status, they are presented, paradoxically, as supporters of Islam for protecting the Fāṭimid state from the Syrians:[7]

(6) You stood up in support of the Prophet and his family, so God the Most Merciful owes you a reward for that.
(7) The king of the Franks, those whose unbelief had been feared, marched by night in order to support their cause [of the Prophet's family].[8] (1.99)

This may be an example of the language of realpolitik in al-Qāḍī l-Fāḍil's poem. It reads as if composed by a Shīʿī but al-Qāḍī l-Fāḍil instead played to his audience's religious and political sensibilities to evoke their support for Shāwar and Egyptian independence. It is his inclusion of the *ahl al-bayt* (lit., 'people of the house,' i.e., the household of the Prophet Muḥammad) that is distinct

6 According to Ibn Khallikān he was even called 'al-Miṣrī.' See Ibn Khallikān, *Wafayāt*, 3:142–148.

7 For further information, see H. Dajani Shakeel, 'Egypt and the Egyptians: A Focal Point in the Policies and Literature of al-Qāḍī al-Fāḍil,' *Journal of Near Eastern Studies* 36 (1977), 25–38; A. S. Ehrenkreutz, *Saladin*, 58; Lyons and Jackson, *Saladin*, 25–26; Y. Lev, *Saladin in Egypt* (Leiden: Brill, 1999), 14–25.

8 Qāḍī l-Fāḍil, *Dīwān*, 1:200–201. See also Dajani Shakeel, 'Egypt and the Egyptians,' 26.

here. Notwithstanding the special place of the Prophet's family for both Sunnīs and Shīʿīs, it is clear that the reference would have struck a distinct chord with the Shīʿīs.

The power of the literary word in medieval Muslim society can thus be gauged from the brilliance of al-Qāḍī l-Fāḍil who, by 567/1171, had come to occupy the highest civil office of vizier during the reign of Ṣalāḥ al-Dīn. Al-Qāḍī l-Fāḍil is credited for his instrumental role in establishing the Ayyūbid regime in Egypt, and for his political involvement at all levels of government.[9] He managed to turn the chancery into an effective propaganda instrument for Ṣalāḥ al-Dīn, by dispatching letters across the Muslim world, letters in which he depicted the sultan as a holy warrior intent on waging *jihād* against the Franks. His literary skill was acutely appreciated by Ṣalāḥ al-Dīn who remarked, "I have not conquered the countries with the sword, I conquered them with the pen of al-Qāḍī l-Fāḍil."[10] Prior to the rule of Ṣalāḥ al-Dīn, al-Qāḍī l-Fāḍil's political acumen allowed him to call for the consolidation of Muslim resources in Egypt so as to protect it from crusader attack; however, this followed his initial calls for Frankish intervention against Syrian contingents during a military confrontation between Shāwar, the Egyptian vizier, and Asad al-Dīn Shīrkūh, who headed the Syrian contingents. Al-Qāḍī l-Fāḍil effectively used poetry to rouse popular support in favour of the vizier and his entourage when they sought to cooperate with the crusaders in 561/1166 and then, in 563–4/1168, during the reign of Shāwar's son al-Kāmil, he did the same to resist a Frankish invasion of Egypt.

Al-Qāḍī l-Fāḍil's support for al-Kāmil in the following lines is juxtaposed with the idea that the crusaders, because of their campaigns against Nūr al-Dīn's forces, would be useful in ensuring Egyptian independence. In one of his poems he explains that "The crosses served the guidance [Islam] in his [Kāmil's] support (47)."[11] After Shāwar was deposed by his rival Dirgham in 558/1163 he escaped to Damascus, where he beseeched Nūr al-Dīn for assistance to be reinstated as vizier in return for a third of Egypt's revenues. Nūr al-Dīn responded by dispatching an army led by Shīrkūh, accompanied by his nephew Ṣalāḥ al-Dīn; they succeeded in killing Dirgham and reinstating Shāwar. Eager to have Shīrkūh's army leave Egypt, Shāwar enlisted the support of King Amalric of Jerusalem; he attacked Shīrkūh in 559/1164 and 562/1167 until Shāwar switched alliances and enlisted the support of Shīrkūh against

9 Dajani-Shakeel, 'Egypt and the Egyptians,' 25.

10 See Ibn al-ʿImād al-Ḥanbalī (ʿAbd al-Ḥayy b. Aḥmad), *Shadharāt al-dhahab fī akhbār man dhahab* (Cairo, 1931–32), 4:324; Dajani-Shakeel, 'Egypt and the Egyptians,' 25.

11 Qāḍī l-Fāḍil, *Dīwān*, 1:150.

King Amalric when the latter attacked Egypt again in 563–4/1168. Shīrkūh, with Ṣalāḥ al-Dīn, forced Amalric to withdraw, and conquered Egypt in 564/1169. Shāwar was subsequently killed by Ṣalāḥ al-Dīn in December of the same year.

We may see al-Qāḍī l-Fāḍil in a light similar to al-Afḍal, Badr al-Jamālī's son. Hamblin makes a case that explains, in part, the lack of early Shīʿī response to the crusader occupation of Jerusalem. The undermining of the caliphate by the Jamālī viziers meant that any *jihād* against the crusaders could not be endorsed or sanctioned officially because of the indispensable role of the caliph in managing such affairs. The vizierate's use of *jihād* propaganda was further complicated by the large numbers of Armenian Christians in the military; any call for a *jihād* would not be conducive to the vizierate's need for military support to undermine the power of the caliphate. Al-Afḍal's attempts to subvert the power of the Fāṭimid caliph by ensuring that a young child was placed as his successor – a child that would be al-Afḍal's puppet – despite the fact that his antics hampered the growth of Fāṭimid religious expansion indicates that political priorities sometimes overrode religious loyalties. According to Ibn al-Qalānisī however, al-Afḍal "was a firm believer in the doctrines of the Sunna";[12] a tribute that may have been true or may again be a case of a sectarian pretext.[13]

Following the taking of Egypt, Usāma b. Munqidh described Ṣalāḥ al-Dīn in terms that were intended to contrast with the character of Shāwar: "You have straightened the pillars of Islam." This straightening of "the pillars of Islam" suggests the political compromises made by the Fāṭimid Shīʿīs. We might also surmise that the 'pillars of Islam' – a religious phrase denoting matters of creed and practice – were previously crooked due to the theological unorthodoxies of the Shīʿīs. While questions over Usāma's own theological leaning may make this less plausible, his patronage by Ṣalāḥ al-Dīn and contempt for Shāwar may have superseded any indecision on his part regarding his assertion of Ṣalāḥ al-Dīn's superiority over Shāwar and the former's opposition to the Shīʿa.

(1) You have straightened the pillars of Islam when the transgressing Shāwar tried to bend them toward the Franks.

(2) You have defeated the party of unbelief till you sent them back in humiliation; so upon them is only loss and further humiliation.[14] (2.0)

12 Ibn al-Qalānisī, *Tārīkh Dimashq*, 325; Ibn al-Qalānisī, *The Damascus Chronicle*, 164.

13 See Hamblin, 'To Wage *Jihād* or Not,' 31–39.

14 Abū Shāma, *Kitāb al-Rawḍatayn*, 2:37.

In light of our focus on Egypt it is interesting to note that fear of the enemy was not a theme that was expressed in the poetry of this period; the caveats centred instead on self-rectification, political unity, and military preparation. Poets were not eager to highlight the strengths of the Franks. We can discern an allusion to Muslim belief in Islam's superlative strength, in part, in the oblique criticisms directed at Islam's political establishment, particularly the caliph. It seems that poets sought instead to encourage activity by imploring God for assistance and thus appealing to religious sensibilities. Another tactic involved recounting previous feats and describing various personages as an incentive or praising military leaders to inspire confidence. By the time of the Fifth Crusade (614–18/1217–21) the Muslim world was troubled by the threat of the Mongol invasion and the newfound crusader interest in Egypt.[15] The strategic significance of the port of Damietta was unquestionable; launching a new attack on Jerusalem would first require control of Egypt. Al-Kāmil recognised this and, in 616/1219 offered the crusaders Jerusalem if they would bring their siege of Damietta to an end. He also requested that his brother al-Muʿaẓẓam dismantle the walls and major buildings of the Holy City to obviate the enemy's use of them.[16] Early Frankish interest in Egypt and the Frankish recognition of its vital geographical and economic position aroused the fears of earlier poets such as the loyal Fāṭimid supporter ʿUmāra al-Yamanī[17] who, upon hearing of

15 "From the West came the Franks, who took a city like Damietta in Egypt because of its lack of fortifications to protect it from enemies." Ibn al-Athīr, *al-Kāmil fī l-tārīkh*, 10:307–308.

16 Ibn al-Athīr, *al-Kāmil fī l-tārīkh*, 10:308.

17 Following the death of the last Fāṭimid caliph al-ʿĀḍid in 567/1171 we know that there was a plot a few years later to restore the Fāṭimid dynasty to power. Upon discovering the plot, Ṣalāḥ al-Dīn had the eight leaders of the conspiracy, including ʿUmāra al-Yamanī hanged on 26 Shaʿbān 569/6 April 1174. See Jamāl al-Dīn ʿAbd al-Raḥīm al-Isnawī, *Ṭabaqāt al-Shāfiʿiyya* (Beirut, 1987), 2:321; for more information on the poet see Ibn Khallikān, *Wafayāt*, 3:437–442. According to the historian al-Ṣafadī, however, it was ʿUmāra's laissez-faire poetic style, wherein he failed to shift from praise of Fāṭimid viziers such as Shāwar and regularise his poetry within the constraints of Sunnī orthodoxy that may have played a part in his execution. Smoor highlights the intrinsic heresy in ʿUmāra's lines that equate Ṣalāḥ al-Dīn with God (425). ʿUmāra may therefore have been declared an unbeliever by Sunnī scholars – thus legitimising his execution. In another controversial poem, ʿUmāra writes about Ṣalāḥ al-Dīn, "I flirted like a coquettish lover and said: 'He did not approach me in an unrefined manner, nor did he apply affectation.'" (426). According to al-Ṣafadī it is likely "that this *qaṣīda* was one among several reasons to have him [ʿUmāra] strangled. But Allāh is most informed! For kings ought not to be addressed in such a manner, nor to be confronted by these wordings and this coquettish flirtation (*idlal*). This then, will lead to humiliation (*idhal*). I imagine this *qaṣīda* has remained without any profit." (426) Smoor, "Umāra's Poetical Views,' 410–432. Another example of the dangers

crusader interest in Egypt particularly during Shāwar's[18] alliance with Amalric in the early 550s/1160s, composed a prayer-like poem on behalf of the *umma*, in which he beseeches God for the protection of Islam.

> O Lord, I see that Egypt is beginning to notice the enemy, after it was previously asleep.
> So let the path of Islam remain in Egypt, and protect its decades of guidance so that it does not go astray.
> And grant us from yourself support that will protect us from this trial that only intensifies its flame.[19] (2.1)

There is a tone of desperation (*iḍṭirār*) running through the verses of the poem. While the threat was a real one, the poet does not divulge the fears extant in the Muslim population, nor does he highlight the strengths of the formidable approaching Frankish army. It is Islam itself that is threatened by enemy occupation, therefore such an appeal most befits the context of the poem; God is most concerned with His religion and worship. This type of appeal resembles that made by the Prophet himself at the battle of Badr (2/624), when worship of God and the survival of the Muslims were inter-related; the Prophet implored God with these words, "O God, they are barefooted, so carry them; naked, so clothe them; O God if this contingent from the nation of Islam is destroyed, then you will not be worshipped on earth."[20] The Frankish threat is described as a *fitna*, a trial. *Fitna* often denotes a religious trial and temptation – a real danger to the Muslim body analogous to *shirk* (polytheism), punishment, and social tumult.[21]

One of the most telling features of sixth-/twelfth-century poetry is the extent to which it suggests lay agitations in the Muslim population; these included consternation at the growing threat of the Franks, particularly before the capture of Edessa, and the inner awareness of the *umma*'s political weakness in the face of the disunity that had already led to the occupation of Jerusalem. Muslim chroniclers such as ʿImād al-Dīn al-Iṣfahānī, Ibn al-Athīr, and perhaps

---

of non-conformist poetic tendencies is the case of the famous fourth-/tenth-century poet al-Mutanabbī (303–54/915–65). He was imprisoned for two years for a poem in which he equated himself with the Qur'ānic Prophet Ṣāliḥ. Larkin, 'Al-Mutanabbī,' 542; Heinrichs, 'The Meaning of Mutanabbī,' 126.

18 For more information on Shāwar, see Ibn Khallikān, *Wafayāt*, 2:418–422.

19 Badawī, *al-Ḥayāt al-adabiyya*, 478.

20 Al-Wāqidī, *Kitāb al-Maghāzī*, ed. M. Jones (Beirut: ʿAlam al-Kutub, 2006), 54.

21 Qur'ān 2:193, 8:73, 5:71.

most influentially al-Qāḍī l-Fāḍil noted the dire consequences of political disunity in Syria, Egypt, and the Jazira (Arabian Peninsula); their concerns about crusader interest in Egypt and Syria translated into the popular sentiments espoused by several poets. The fact that ʿUmāra first composed poetry for Ibn Ruzzīk, and then, during Shāwar's vizierate, supported the alliance with Amalric, and subsequently praised Shāwar as a *mujāhid* following the 563–4/1168 attack on Egypt, and thereafter even praised the soldiers of Nūr al-Dīn and Ṣalāḥ al-Dīn, highlights how financial and political incentives could easily mask true sentiments.

Poetry in Diplomacy and Calls for Unity

In this section I consider the way poetry was used to initiate diplomacy between the vizierates of Egypt and Syria. I highlight the significance of calls for an alliance between Egypt and Damascus in the 540s/1150s, and Fāṭimid concerns about Syrian disunity. Poetry provided an important measure of the hopes and fears of the Muslims of the Near East. The sentiments voiced in *jihād* poetry of the period were certainly intended to be and likely were representative of the concerns of the Muslim population. A poet's care to convey a message that would resonate with his listeners may be compared to the *khaṭīb* who aims to rouse his audience with a pertinent message fused with Arabic niceties that would strike subtle chords. On the whole, it was the relevance of what was being communicated that ensured its dissemination. The poet's fears may therefore be seen as an illustration of his community's fears. Similarly, strategic initiatives espoused by the poet were the sort that allowed his audience to accept the poet and his message. An example of this may be discerned from Ṭalāʾiʿ b. Ruzzīk,[22] the Fāṭimid vizier of Egypt who, in 550/1156, sent a message (in the form of a poem) via Usāma b. Munqidh to Nūr al-Dīn urging him to form an alliance with the Fāṭimids in order to collectively assail the Franks.

In the context of his concern we can see, in addition to a shared religious Shīʿī standpoint, the companionship (*ṣuḥba*) between Usāma b. Munqidh and Ṭalāʾiʿ b. Ruzzīk. According to Usāma, "ever since I arrived in Egypt, there had been a warm friendship and intimate fellowship between me and Ibn Ruzzīk."[23] The two poets used their poetry to initiate a series of correspondences aimed at encouraging Nūr al-Dīn to unite Egypt and Syria, and advocate cooperation

22 For more information on the poet, see ʿImād al-Dīn al-Iṣfahānī, *Kharīdat al-qaṣr*, 1:173–185; Ibn Khallikān, *Wafayāt*, 2:469–473.

23 Usāma b. Munqidh, *The Book of Contemplation*, 32.

between the Egyptian and Syrian armies to liberate Jerusalem, since the unity of the regions was deemed a necessary prerequisite to the reconquest of the sacred city. Ibn Ruzzīk used Usāma b. Munqidh as a mediator between himself and Nūr al-Dīn; perhaps this indirect approach reveals his realisation that Syria itself was divided and any calls for unity with Egypt would have to be initiated with internal concord. Ibn Ruzzīk's promotion of, albeit Sunnī, unity in Syria was intended perhaps to provide a temporary buffer between the growing strength of the Franks and the dwindling power of the Fāṭimids. In any case, for his dedication to the *jihād* against the Latins he was considered by Ibn al-Qalānisī as the 'knight of Islam' and his bravery and leadership skills were also noted by Abū Shāma.[24] Ibn Ruzzīk's concerns were brought to the fore in a different area, when, in 550/1156, trouble broke out between Nūr al-Dīn and Qilij Arslān b. Mas'ūd II of Iconium (d. 588/1192). Nūr al-Dīn initially played a conciliatory role in the conflict between the sons of Qilij Arslān and the sons of Qutulmish, but Nūr al-Dīn later captured castles in territories belonging to Qilij Arslān who "considered it a detestable outrage in view of the treaty terms, truce, and marriage relations which existed between them, and wrote letters to him in a tone of censure, reprobation, intimidation, and threat."[25] Ibn Ruzzīk was troubled by the strife between the two leaders, a division that could hinder the anti-Frankish *jihād* for the liberation of Jerusalem. He addressed his poem to Qilij Arslān:

(9) There is no one in power who will remain forever.
And no one can escape the decree of God.
(10) After the enemy tasted well your expertise in the
war, they realised that it was extremely difficult and bitter.
(11) But you returned to fighting between yourselves.
And in your hearts there is animosity like the kindled fire.
(12) Is there no one among you who fears God alone, or anyone
among your people who is truly a Muslim?
(13) Come and unite, so that perhaps God will give victory to His
religion, if we both do our part in giving victory to it.
(14) And rise toward the unbelievers with resolve, the like of which
will control the countries and regions.[26] (2.2)

---

24 Ibn al-Qalānisī, *Tārīkh Dimashq*, 509; Ibn al-Qalānisī, *The Damascus Chronicle*, 323; Abū Shāma, *Kitāb al-Rawḍatayn*, 3:290.

25 Ibn al-Qalānisī, *Tārīkh Dimashq*, 511; Ibn al-Qalānisī, *The Damascus Chronicle*, 325.

26 Ibn al-Athīr, *al-Kāmil fī l-tārīkh*, 9:321.

In Ibn al-Athīr's *al-Kāmil*, the date of the entry for this poem is 560/1165. Ibn Ruzzīk, however, died in 558/1163, and this led Ibn al-Athīr to question the attribution of this poem and wonder if the antagonism, described by Ibn al-Athīr as a *fitna* between Nūr al-Dīn and Qilij Arslān, continued until the year 560/1165.[27] In any case the poem strikes a spiritual chord that questions or challenges the religious disposition of the lord of Anatolia. The penultimate line of the poem is certainly an echo of a Qur'ānic prescription, If you give victory to God, He will give victory to you (*In tanṣurullāha yanṣurkum*),[28] one that formed part of a predictable selection of Qur'ānic verses used by advocates of the anti-Frankish *jihād*.[29]

In a poem intended for Nūr al-Dīn but seemingly also directed toward Usāma, Ibn Ruzzīk demonstrated his concern about the *jihād* and the need for a cooperative effort to liberate Jerusalem.

> We are requesting you to fulfil missions, indeed you are the most appropriate for the task.
> The most important matter is the matter of *jihād* against unbelief, so listen to us because with us is the realisation.[30] (2.3)

His call to unity is furthermore realised from the following verses of another poem. Here he seeks to inspire confidence in Nūr al-Dīn by promising financial and military support for him from the Fāṭimid base in Cairo if he turns his focus toward Jerusalem.[31]

> (49) Rise now quickly; with people like you we can fulfil our aims.
> (50) Dispatch [on our behalf] our letter to Nūr al-Dīn; there should be no doubt about what is sent.
> (52) O the one who is just, and who for the religion is energetic, and who for the wars is youthful.
> (53) And who remains experienced in Islam with a resolve that removes agonies.
> (54) Tomorrow will be a difficult day for the Franks when they meet him.

27 Ibid.
28 Qur'ān, 47:7.
29 Al-Sulamī, 'Kitāb al-Jihād,' 49.
30 Ibn Ruzzīk, *Dīwān*, 103.
31 For more information on the strategic advantage of 'Egypt versus Iraq in relation to Syria' see D. Ayalon, *Outsiders in the Lands of Islam: Mamlūks, Mongols and Eunuchs* (Aldershot: Variorum, 1988), 18, 17–47.

(57) We have written to you clearly now, so how will you respond?
(58) We intend [to establish] between us a fixed date in our journey [to one another].
(59) We have innumerable soldiers that will cover even the vastest space.
(60) And we are obliged to support Syria with money that will flow like continuous rain.
(61) Or to see it like a bride; its soil reddened with the blood of the enemy.[32] (2.4)

Perhaps one would not have expected a response, given the sectarian division that strained the two communities. The Sunnī world would have looked upon the Shīʿīs with suspicion and resentment for the latter's conciliatory relationship with the Franks.[33] Neither Nūr al-Dīn nor Usāma responded; at this point in time matters were far from conducive for any political unity between the Sunnīs and Shīʿīs, but the poetry nevertheless reveals the awareness among Shīʿīs of Frankish or crusader focus on Egypt. The authorities in Egypt certainly realised the colossal effect that the loss of Egypt would mean for Islam. Not only would the Maghrib be severed from the eastern Muslim world, but the Franks might also empower the Christians of Nubia and Abyssinia. Poetry of this period quite clearly reveals the poets' belief that the unity of Egypt and Syria under Nūr al-Dīn provided a tenable opportunity to liberate Jerusalem. We may also see the poem in light of Ibn Ruzzīk's own standing; he held a Fāṭimid Shīʿī perspective and advocated the military *jihād*, so his appeals to Nūr al-Dīn were also an acknowledgement of his own lesser rank in the *jihād*. A poem composed by ʿImād al-Dīn – who worked in the chancery of Nūr al-Dīn and was arguably the most outspoken of the scholars who carried the theoretical ideas of the anti-Frankish *jihād* – praises Shīrkūh for entering Cairo and putting Shāwar to death in 564/1169.[34] The poet saw these events as a positive sign that the liberation of Jerusalem was close. While Ibn Ruzzīk was eager to witness the unity of Syria as a precursor to liberation, the unification of Damascus, Aleppo, Egypt, and Mosul brought with it a newfound and realistic

32 Ibn Ruzzīk, *Dīwān*, 65–65.

33 Ibn Taghrībirdī also questioned why al-Afḍal failed to dispatch his Egyptian army during the advance of the First Crusade –

و ما أدري ماكان السبب في عدم إخراجه مع قدرته على المال والرجال.

Ibn Taghrībirdī, *al-Nujūm*, 5:147.

34 Dajani-Shakeel, 'Some Medieval Accounts,' 103.

hope that the political situation of the Near East was now conducive to an attack on the Holy City:[35]

(1) With seriousness, and not through play, you have gained. Consider how many stages of ease have you now acquired, [that permit you] to relax!
(5) You liberated Egypt, and I hope that while you are a liberator of Egypt, you will ease the way to liberate Jerusalem.
(11) We raised our hands to God in thankfulness, since Islam will not be harmed because of you.
(12) The people of Islam complained to you that they were orphans, so you stood for them in the place of a comforting father.
(13) In every home of the Franks you will find a wailing woman;
because of what struck them they spend their nights in grief.
(14) You have saved the Muslims from the evil of Shāwar.
So consider just how much you have achieved for the party of God.
(15) He [Shāwar] is the one who made the Franks aspire to the lands of Islam, till they reached the level of confidently putting [forth] their conditions.
(25) He [Shīrkūh] returned the caliphate to the ʿAbbāsids; leave the claimant [of the caliphate] to meet the worst enemy.
(26) Do not merely cut the snake's tail and leave the snake to escape. My wish is that you also cut the head along with the tail.[36] (2.5)

The above verses, part of a longer poem, offer many interesting features. Line 1 strikes a chord similar to ideas pertaining to 'seriousness,' 'play,' and 'tiredness' in ʿImād al-Dīn's *dubayt* compositions for Nūr al-Dīn assessed earlier. The talk of a liberation (*fatḥ*) was certainly more consequential and evocative at this point in time. ʿImād al-Dīn sought to inspire a sense of vigour in Shīrkūh by reminding him of the greater liberations (*futūḥ*) necessary to free Jerusalem and that his position in Egypt needed to serve that goal. Shīrkūh's depiction as a "comforting father" who removed grievances perhaps speaks of a more general optimism in Egypt and Syria that ʿImād al-Dīn sought to describe.

We also find an allusion to a gender perspective in ʿImād al-Dīn's description of the Frankish women who were wailing because their menfolk had been

35 For more information on Shīrkūh, see Ibn Khallikān, *Wafayāt*, 2:436–439.

36 Ibn Wāṣil, *Mufarrij*, 1:165–167.

killed. The description is not altogether unusual, since women often mourned those killed in battle, but this portrayal perhaps tried to reveal an emotionally devastated society that was vulnerable to attack. In the poet's thoughts we see the gender inclusion as a negative judgement of what the chronicler and his audience believed about women and their role in the crusader campaigns. We know also from his chronicle that 'Imād al-Dīn considered notions of gender. He describes women and children at the conquest of Jerusalem as "quickly divided up among us, bringing a smile to Muslim faces at their lamentations."[37] In 'Imād al-Dīn's work we also find other references to gender that focus on the misery of Frankish women. In his description of the Third Crusade, he notes that "there were indeed women who rode into battle ... clothed only in a coat of mail. They were not recognised as women until they had been stripped of their arms ... consider how men and women led them into error."[38] Alternatively, this may be a criticism of the Franks' lack of manliness; they needed women to fight in their battles, and it may also hint at male weakness – they were unable to protect their women.

The terms party of God (*ḥizb Allāh*) in verse 14, and party of unbelief (*ḥizb al-kufr*) are demarcations that have a Qur'ānic origin and are used here to reflect an unequivocal dichotomy between the belief and purpose of the Muslims and that of Christians – notwithstanding their crusading role; essentially it is their religious leaning that places them in the bounds of the description.[39] The crusades aggravated the Christians' unbelief, while Shīrkūh's defence of the *ḥizb Allāh* only augmented his positive reputation.

In the poem Shāwar's killing was justified because of his alliance with the Franks; the poem serves as a warning to other rulers. 'Imād al-Dīn reassures Shīrkūh that his efforts would not go to waste in the hereafter, since he earned himself a place in God's favour with his commitment to the *jihād* and specifically because of his conquest of Egypt. In 'Imād al-Dīn's eyes, it would do Shīrkūh even more good to continue his *jihād* until Jerusalem is liberated. In light of the poet's talk of dynastic expansion, its rationale was the defeat of the crusaders, and in that case it was warranted. In light of this we can detect the historian's own thoughts. Cahen notes that people like 'Imād al-Dīn

> probably regarded history as a part of a literature and wanted to use it as a means of displaying their virtuosity. However, this aspect should not

---

37 See Y. Friedman, 'Captivity and Ransom: The Experience of Women,' in *Gendering the Crusades*, ed. S. B. Edgington and S. Lambert (Cardif: University of Wales Press, 2001), 126.

38 'Imād al-Dīn al-Iṣfahānī, *al-Fatḥ al-qussī*, 347–349.

39 Qur'ān 5:56, 58:22.

> be exaggerated. Apart from the fact that they were few in number, they never used their literary acrobatics, at least before the Mamlūk era, to mask or falsify the hard facts which were the subject of their expositions.[40]

ʿImād al-Dīn concluded his poem by hearkening back to the legitimate authority of the Sunnī caliphate. Shīrkūh's actions reinforced the power and legitimacy of the Sunnī caliph at the expense of the Fāṭimid caliphate. Although it was the death of the young caliph al-ʿĀḍid (d. 567/1171) that marked the end of the Fāṭimid dynasty, Shīrkūh's invasion with Ṣalāḥ al-Dīn and the unification of Syria meant that the Fāṭimid caliphate was effectively out of the frame. ʿImād al-Dīn's concluding verse seems to reinforce this; the killing of Shāwar did not dismantle Fāṭimid authority, instead the Fāṭimid caliph should also be killed. That the caliph did not reciprocate the loyalty shown to him by the Ayyūbid leaders is not of absolute consequence; it was the care that Ṣalāḥ al-Dīn took to ensure caliphal approval for his actions that served his interest in the long run.

As outlined in an earlier section, al-Sulamī's *Kitāb al-Jihād* text made clear the responsibility of the caliph in authorising and managing the *jihād*. The resolute approaches of Nūr al-Dīn and Ṣalāḥ al-Dīn in ensuring that the authority of the ʿAbbāsid caliph was reaffirmed was essential for their *jihād* because it was only through the caliph that Sunnī Islam could be strengthened, the authority of the Fāṭimids could be weakened, and the political unity of Islam could be established. Following Nūr al-Dīn's defeat and capture of Count Joscelin II of Edessa in 545/1150, Ibn al-Munīr praised Nūr al-Dīn in this manner:

> (23) The caliph slept but the army rose up quickly to protect his position in government.[41] (2.6)

We must recall that during this time the caliphs were an important fixture in the political structure of Islamic society. In spite of the caliph's apparent inertia, Nūr al-Dīn and Ṣalāḥ al-Dīn's display of fealty was symbolic inasmuch as it bolstered the caliph's credibility and the position of the ʿAbbāsid dynasty. When the Fāṭimid caliphate fell, ʿImād al-Dīn composed a *qaṣīda* congratulating Nūr al-Dīn and the ʿAbbāsid caliphs of Baghdad:

40 C. Cahen, 'History and Historians: the Post-classical Period,' in *Religion, Learning and Science in the 'Abbasid Period*, ed. M. J. L. Young, J. D. Latham, R. B. Serjeant (Cambridge and New York: Cambridge University Press, 1990), 207.

41 Abū Shāma, *Kitāb al-Rawḍatayn*, 1:251.

(1) We proclaimed al-Mustaḍīʿ in Egypt [delivered the Friday sermon in his name], to the deputy of the Chosen One [Prophet Muḥammad], the *Imām* of the era.
(2) We hindered support for al-ʿĀḍid, the powerless one in the palace.
(3) We spread the flag of Banū ʿAbbās, so the faces of victory rejoiced
(4) We left the claimant crying for perdition[42] while he is in disgrace under rocks and soil.
(5) The pulpits of the religion [mosques] rejoiced because of the sermon for the Hāshimī in the land of Egypt.
(6) For us the blessing of God increased till it could not be contained or counted.
(18) No one can become the *Imām* except by legitimate right, just as no one can obtain a beautiful girl except with a dowry.[43] (2.7)

Some historians have adopted a cynical attitude toward Nūr al-Dīn, citing Ibn Ruzzīk's reproach of Nūr al-Dīn sometime after 649/1154 for not fighting the Franks, contrary to the desire of the poets.[44] Ibn Ruzzīk's position, however, must also be measured in light of the potential threat the Franks posed to Egypt. During Fāṭimid rule, Egypt enjoyed a high level of prosperity and the threat to the Fāṭimids was all too clear. Even William of Tyre, in his account of the caliph's reception of the Frankish ambassador Hugh of Caesarea, was clearly impressed by the sumptuousness offered by the caliph; "de statu et magnificentia et inmensitate divitiarum et glorie multiplicitate comperimus …"[45] It was the rise of Amalric coupled with divisions in the Fāṭimid ruling classes that turned Frankish and Sunnī Muslim interest toward Egypt. The crusaders had taken Jerusalem from the Fāṭimids in 492/1099, the Fāṭimids had lost their empire in the Maghrib and had no real chance of controlling any of the Hijaz, and they were blamed for the excesses of the of the Nizārī Ismāʿīlīs who had fled to Alamūt; together these factors allowed both Christian and Muslim forces to believe that if they focused their efforts, they could sieze control of the dying regime.

Following the conquest of Egypt, the idea of restoring and rejuvenating the Muslim community became a salient theme in the poetry. In a poem composed by ʿImād al-Dīn al-Iṣfahānī following the death of the Egyptian caliph al-ʿĀḍid, he said that the "era of its Pharaoh had come to an end and tomorrow

42 *Yadʿū thubūrā* – "Soon will he cry for perdition," Qurʾān, 84:11.
43 See Abū Shāma, *Kitāb al-Rawḍatayn*, 2:133–134.
44 Hillenbrand, *The Crusades*, 138–139.
45 Philip D. Handyside, *The Old French William of Tyre* (Leiden and Boston: Brill, 2015), 29.

Yūsuf would be the ruler."[46] The antithesis of 'Pharaoh' and 'Yūsuf,' is a play on Pharoah and the Qur'ānic Yūsuf (Joseph) who are compared to the Fāṭimid caliph (as the new Pharoah) and Ṣalāḥ al-Dīn (whose name is Yūsuf) as the new Joseph. It draws on the polarities between al-ʿĀḍid, an illegitimate Fāṭimid Shīʿī, and the legitimate Sunnī ascendancy to power. ʿImād al-Dīn's poem in fact draws on several contrasting motifs to dispel doubts about the political turn of events in Egypt. The following examples show the juxtaposition of positive and negative themes and motifs. In verse 5 'truth' and 'falsehood' is contrasted – 'when the flag of the ʿAbbāsids was raised in truth, then falsehood was silenced.' In verse 6 it is '*tawḥīd*' and '*shirk*'; in verses 7 and 8, 'darkness' and 'light'; and in verse 12 the antithesis of 'guidance' is described as 'unbelief.' The question of legitimacy was paramount in the poet's words. As an ideal ruler Nūr al-Dīn had the moral right and duty to subdue rulers who did not fulfil the requirements of the *sharīʿa* – this included *jihād* against enemies of the faith. The poem sets Ṣalāḥ al-Dīn in a framework of divine providence. By delegitimising the enemy, Ṣalāḥ al-Dīn gained divine favour and moral superiority. The poet outlines Ṣalāḥ al-Dīn's ascendancy to the governorship of Egypt, as the renewal and rejuvenation of worldly authority at the hands of the Ayyūbid ruler, who was given divine approval, as connoted in verse 3 through a predictable play on the Qur'ānic Joseph (Yūsuf). The restoration theme of the poem is corroborated by the symbolism in the line and the incident in which Joseph was called 'truthful' in *Sūra Yūsuf* (12:46) preceding his release from prison, and that in which Jacob received Joseph's shirt and regained his sight (12:96). In the Qur'ānic narrative about Joseph, he comes to find favour and freedom with the minister-in-charge, and his father's eyesight is restored after a period of blindness. Verses 1 and 2 consolidate the same theme. Paronomasia is clear in verse 1 as the idea of *ṣulḥ* (meaning to restore, rectify, or reconcile) is a play on '*ṣalāḥ*' in 'Ṣalāḥ al-Dīn' (Ṣalāḥ al-Dīn); in the second line *salām* (peace) has a metonymical purpose, standing for the general spread of peace in Egypt. For the scholarly class of listeners these contextual Qur'ānic allusions must have seemed and felt highly relevant.

(1) Ṣalāḥ al-Dīn you have rectified the world of the wretched, which could not sleep except with vigilance.
(2) You sent your salutation of peace to all of us, but your generosity was extended, especially to me.

46 Abū Shāma, *Kitāb al-Rawḍatayn*, 2:127.

(3) And you were like Joseph the truthful when Jacob received his shirt.[47] (2.8)

In light of the poetic image created for Ṣalāḥ al-Dīn and the way he might have been viewed by his supporters, the use of the appellation 'Yūsuf' (Joseph) is the most compelling. Ṣalāḥ al-Dīn's reorganisation of the administration of Egypt after the death of al-ʿĀḍid might have been seen in a similar light to that of the Qur'ānic Yūsuf's position of authority in Egypt.[48] Although we know of no clear references that depict Ṣalāḥ al-Dīn as the 'Mahdī,' and perhaps these do not exist given that the stipulations in the *ḥadīth* would render him illegible for the position, nevertheless, the image-making of a pious ruler (through association with the Qur'ānic Yūsuf, the Prophet's companions, and the 'prophetic era') presented him in Mahdī-type eschatological terms which might have been seen as a means of legitimising his rule.[49]

In this chapter I have shown that one of the most significant political consequences of the crusades was the long-term unification of Egypt and Syria under a single ruler. The language of realpolitik in the poetry reveals the strength of political alliances. The case of Ibn Ruzzīk and his vehement petition for an alliance with Damascus reveals his own and the Fāṭimids' desire to see protection of Fāṭimid rule. But it also speaks of mounting fears in Egypt of a crusader attack, given the Fāṭimid caliphate's dwindling power. Examples of religious imagery and symbolism further underscore the need to probe deeper into poetry to better understand the range of sentiments and diverse factors at play during these years.

---

47 Ibid., 2:84.

48 Hannes Möhring, 'Zwischen Joseph-Legende und Mahdī-Erwartung: Erfolge und ziele Sultan Saladins im spegel zeitgenossischer dichtung und weissagung,' in *War and Society in the Eastern Mediterranean 7th–15th Centuries*, ed. Y. Lev (Leiden: Brill, 1997), 187–188; see al-Qur'ān, 12:54–56.

49 The fact that Constantinople was still in Christian hands was an obvious sticking point for those who might have seen Ṣalāḥ al-Dīn in such a light. Hannes Möhring, 'Zwischen Joseph-Legende,' 222. See W. Madelung, 'al-Mahdī,' *EI*², 5:1230–1238. See also Eddé, *Saladin*, 219–222.

CHAPTER 8

Shattered Dreams: Jerusalem, the *Umma*, and New Enemies

In this chapter the first poem I present was composed by the Andalusian poet ʿAbd al-Munʿim al-Jilyānī for Ṣalāḥ al-Dīn's son ʿUthmān b. al-Malik al-Nāṣir Yūsuf b. Ayyūb (d. 595/1198). The poem is a posthumous commemoration of Ṣalāḥ al-Dīn's qualities which made possible his succession of victories. The poet reminds us that ʿUthmān b. al-Malik al-Nāṣir was entrusted to continue to embody these attributes; his rule was meant to be a continuation of the glorious era of the days of Nūr al-Dīn. The second poem, composed by Muḥammad al-Mujāwir, reveals the emotions associated with the *faḍāʾil* poetry that came to the fore following al-Muʿaẓẓam's razing of the walls of Jerusalem in 616/1219. The considerable attention placed on the functions of al-Aqṣā Mosque and the Dome of the Rock reveal how contemporary poets perceived of the city's newfound Islamic character.

Post-Reconquest Poetry

In 590/1194 ʿAbd al-Munʿim al-Jilyānī composed the following poem in praise of ʿUthmān b. al-Malik al-Nāṣir Yūsuf b. Ayyūb, the second son of Ṣalāḥ al-Dīn and ruler of the Ayyūbid Empire from 589/1193 to 594/1198. The poem, composed sometime during his reign is elaborately entitled, 'The honoured description for one with prudence of knowledge and exemplary politics' and begins with these words:

(1) With determination (*ʿazāʾim*) he reached the high station,
not with the use of swords or spears.

The opening line of al-Jilyānī's poem relates to an important theme, one which was celebrated in al-Mutanabbī's *qaṣīda* for Sayf al-Dawla after the battle of al-Ḥadath in 343/954–55 and cited earlier, "With the worth of men of resolve are resolutions in accordance" relates to the idea of one's *ʿazm* (resolve), and to Abū Tammām's opening verse in his equally famous *qaṣīda* in praise of al-Muʿtaṣim's conquest of Amorium in 223/838, "The sword is truer in tidings

 | DOI 10.1163/9789004345225_009

than the written word." Al-Jilyānī's poem sets its own standard however, and is not entirely bound by either. It agrees with al-Mutanabbī's reflection on determination and challenges that of Abū Tammām by casting Ṣalāḥ al-Dīn in his own distinct and worthy light. He is not to be remembered simply by the sword which won him eminence but by more comprehensive attributes that cast him as a noble Islamic leader whose qualities were permeated with Islamic standards of piety.

(1) The kingdom is claimed if determination accompanies it; its conquest came and the people are proof of it.
(2) So honesty in speech and action is the base,
for every one of his matters there is an improvement in the people.
(3) The kingdom is taken either willingly or by force
And determination, and generosity, and fearless pursuit are its price
(4) Indeed activity is the essence of life which increases one's rank,
And the lazy are not counted among the living
(5) The politics of the kingdom is weighty, and none can establish it
Except the resilient who has excellent conduct on his scale [i.e., on his side].

By epitomising qualities such as 'honesty,' 'determination,' 'generosity,' 'fearless pursuit,' 'excellence,' 'forbearance,' and 'kindness' it serves to legitimise his victories and casts away any doubts of critics; these attributes were also intended for al-Malik al-ʿAzīz and as an appraisal of the Ayyūbids. The poet reinforces the idea that Ṣalāḥ al-Dīn's posthumous memory must entail the rudimentary traits like honesty (*ṣidq*) and generosity (*karm*) that Islam's earlier victors were remembered for, his success in winning military victories, but also his actualisation of a comprehensive triumph for Islam and the restoration of the sacred order of things.

(1) The kingdom has a secrecy like the secrecy of prophethood
In choosing from people what not everyone will be given
(2) With one who filled the earth with its wideness (*tumlaʾ al-arḍ bima rahubat*)
So human and jinn obey him
(3) The specialisation from the God of the throne shows in this part what all who fail to understand are blind of.
(4) No one can motivate the people of the earth by himself
Except if he has been favoured by God, the Most High.

(5) For God you are king, the pillar of the religion who shook the country
The way the branches of a tree are shaken.[1] (2.9)

In these verses al-Jilyānī makes a key point: since Ṣalāḥ al-Dīn was chosen by God to fulfil His purpose, he served a divine intent; God's 'choice' and 'specialisation' clearly are not confined to Ṣalāḥ al-Dīn but were used to sanction al-Malik al-ʿAzīz ʿUthmān's own claims to authority, wherein his kingship became an extension of his father's legacy. The outlook is identical to what is found in Ibn Jubayr's long poem – 'And (God) specified you for this task' (verse 16) and is one that runs as an undercurrent in al-Sulamī's *Kitāb al-Jihād* for the Muslims of Syria.[2] The poem bears a thematic resemblance to Abū ʿAlī l-Ḥasan b. ʿAlī l-Juwaynī's post-reconquest poem cited earlier. The themes of (a) heavenly support for Ṣalāḥ al-Dīn – "The one whom God gives all virtue is deserving of it" (al-Jilyānī) is akin to "The armies of heaven are support for this king" (al-Juwaynī); (b) The relationship between conquest or kingdom and prophethood – "This conquest is like the conquests of the prophets" (al-Jilyānī) is akin to "The kingdom has a secrecy like the secrecy of prophethood" (al-Juwaynī); and (c) The motifs of the blindness and ignorance of other Muslim rulers – "For ninety years the lands of God cried out, but Muslim leaders were deaf and blind" (al-Jilyānī) is similar to "The specialisation from the God of the throne shows in this part what all who fail to understand are blind of" (al-Juwaynī). Since the audience of these poets included other skilled poets, scribes, and

1 Al-Jilyānī, *Dīwān al-tadbīj*, 114.

2 Al-Sulamī uses the idea of the select 'victorious group (*ṭāʾifa*)' to bring out the merits of Syria; "You should know as well, may God have mercy on you, that your Prophet (peace of God be upon him) promised a *ṭāʾifa* from his nation with victory against their enemies, and he made them from the people of Syria, therefore specialise for that task from among them, so that perhaps you will be those unique people, and not anyone else other than you." Al-Sulamī concludes that the *aḥadīth* specify such people from Jerusalem and its surroundings, "and in this is the evidence that it will return to the Muslims and the *ṭāʾifa* will be in it." Al-Sulamī further cites another tradition: "The prominence of the people of the West will be manifest to the Day of Rising," and "The people of the West will remain manifest upon the truth until the coming of the Hour." Al-Sulamī's repetition of this tradition and its variants was intended to show its authenticity and importance, and reflects the urgency of the *ḥadīth*'s meaning for al-Sulamī. The tradition also allows for a fusion of the revival of *jihād* and the liberation of Jerusalem, as two central *jihād* objectives of Nūr al-Dīn and later Ṣalāḥ al-Dīn. Al-Sulamī, 'Kitāb al-Jihād,' 50–54.

theologians, poets were keen to show their talent to criticise and amend the verses of other poets. The poet

> assumed their knowledge of themes and motifs, enabling them to identify how much of a line or hemistich came from an existing verse and how he enhanced it by giving it a new form and meaning. The *sariqa* 'theft' or *akhdh* 'taking over,' as well as *talmīḥ* 'allusion' and *taḍmīn* 'quotation' by which modern poets referred to each other and the ancients formed an integral part of Abbasid poetry, designed for an audience steeped in the classical tradition. Borrowing was then not frowned upon in general, but depended in each case on how elegantly a poet appropriated and recast a *sariqa* in his own verse. The double resonance of a borrowed phrase or motif in a verse rather enhanced it for an educated listener.[3]

By associating Ṣalāḥ al-Dīn with Nūr al-Dīn, the achievements of the former are given added validity. Al-Jilyānī describes Ṣalāḥ al-Dīn's continuation of his predecessor's anti-Frankish commitment:

> So Yūsuf expelled you, humiliated from the land, by force
> And will continue and his anger will not leave anyone of you (31)
> And how many of your kings were perplexed by the feats of Ṣalāḥ al-Dīn
> Perhaps the conquest motivated him to continue (33)
> He followed the steps of Nūr al-Dīn, our time did not deviate from that
> Things progress, the epoch passed completely (38).[4] (2.10)

Poets like Ibn al-Munīr praised Nūr al-Dīn for 'repeating the prophetic victories' and his reputation as a devout Sunnī ruler, committed to an extensive building programme of *madrasas* and Sufi lodges, the restoration of mosques, and his focus on seeing a unified Sunnī Syria as a strategic bulwark against crusader threats directed toward the liberation of Jerusalem did much to set him up as a paragon and as one of the great Muslim rulers of Syria. The poem, however, masks the disquieting relations between the two rulers before Nūr al-Dīn's death on 15 May 569/1174. The Zangid ruler was impatient at Ṣalāḥ al-Dīn's seeming reluctance to send subsidies and accounts of the financial resources of Egypt. Moreover, Ibn al-Athīr, loyal to the Zangid House, notes that Nūr al-Dīn had prepared his troops to take Egypt from Ṣalāḥ al-Dīn, information corroborated

3 Beatrice Gruendler, *Medieval Arabic Praise Poetry: Ibn al-Rūmī and the Patron's Redemption* (London: Routledge, 2003), 6.

4 Al-Jilyānī, *Dīwān al-tadbīj*, 92.

by Ibn Shaddād, who relates to his patron the news that Nūr al-Dīn would attack him in Egypt. While some advised in favour of resisting Nūr al-Dīn, Ibn Shaddad presents Ṣalāḥ al-Dīn in approving terms, saying "I have disagreed with them, urging that it was not right to say anything of that sort."[5] The poets's words, however, 'He followed the steps of Nūr al-Dīn, our time did not deviate from that' (38) resembles the sentiments put forward by Abū Shāma who sought to reconcile the two leaders because he saw both as worthy advocates of the *jihād* and vitality of Islam. In his account of Nūr al-Dīn's death Abū Shāma follows Ibn al-Athīr's remarks about the troubled relations between the two and adds that

> if Nūr al-Dīn had known what God had reserved for him through Ṣalāḥ al-Dīn, [in terms] of glorious conquests, it would have comforted him; indeed Ṣalāḥ al-Dīn built on the foundations laid by Nūr al-Dīn with respect to *jihād* against the polytheists, and he stood for that in the most complete and perfect way. May God have mercy on them both.[6]

The poet further draws on the affinity between Ṣalāḥ al-Dīn's victory and that of the Prophet Muḥammad and his communty. Ibn al-Athīr was keen to present Nūr al-Dīn as a model ruler unlike any before him since the *khulafā' al-rāshidūn* (rightly-guided caliphs) in the early days of Islamic governance. The ruler's commissioning of the construction of a *minbar* to be placed in al-Aqṣā Mosque after the anticipated reconquest of Jerusalem sought to inspire a strategy in which the conquest of the Holy City, made possible with a unified Muslim Syria and supported with wealth and resources from a newly captured and now Sunnī Egypt, was a compelling political and religious agenda. Nūr al-Dīn's admiring biographers and trusted elites would naturally elevate his personal attributes, an approach intended to highlight his religious publicity which would elicit support from the civilian and religious elite. As seen from his *dubayt*s and other examples of poetry, Nūr al-Dīn was depicted as a selfless *jihād* fighter, uninterested in the luxuries of the world.

The Andalusian poet al-Jilyānī was, at the same time, keen to remind us that Ṣalāḥ al-Dīn purified himself "from the (trappings of the) world and its adornment."[7] The kingly attributes of the sultan were further intended to underscore the imperfections and wickedness of the crusaders. By remaining committed to a unified Syria and a Sunnī Egypt, a religiosity illustrated by his

5 Ibn Shaddād, *The Rare and Excellent History of Saladin*, 49.

6 Abū Shāma, *Kitāb al-Rawḍatayn*, 1:203–204.

7 Ibid., 3:261.

biographers, poets, and other patrons, Ṣalāḥ al-Dīn is presented as a worthy successor to his illustrious predecessor. The continuation of Nūr al-Dīn's focus on *jihād* was cumulatively seen as a support for Islam, notwithstanding tensions between the Zangids and Ayyūbids. Here Nūr al-Dīn's legacy is shown to offer future continuity of the religion under divine protection; his pietistic virtues and military commitments were believed to be a cause for the renewal of the community.

> Damascus has taken its attributes from Yūsuf which are
> Being forgiving and brave, and protecting one's subjects (40)
> So Yūsuf, between kingship and religion, stood up
> with his sword with the *sharīʿa* ruling his homeland [Damascus]. (47)[8]
> (2.11)

Dismantling the Walls

In 614/1217 the Fifth Crusade was launched and Frankish forces arrived at Acre. After setting out for Jerusalem, in 615/1218 they turned their attention to the port of Damietta and attacked the city in May of that year. This was a prelude to their attempt to recapture Jerusalem. In August al-Malik al-ʿĀdil set off for Damietta, but died en route, leaving the territories of the Ayyūbid house divided between his three sons, al-Kāmil Muḥammad, al-Muʿaẓẓam ʿĪsā, and al-Ashraf Mūsā (d. 635/1237). Together they put up a united front and lent military support to counter the crusader threat. In 616/1219, when the crusaders were laying siege to Damietta, as part of his effort to assist al-Kāmil against the Franks, al-Muʿaẓẓam ʿĪsā destroyed the fortifications around Jerusalem, the citadel of Jerusalem and other buildings to render the city unprotected and preempt the crusaders' use of them. The feelings it produced were intense. Some detail of these events is provided in Ibn al-Nabīh's poem, written in celebration of al-Ashraf's decision to set out to Damietta and meet with al-Malik al-Kāmil, which was a cause of great public jubilation.

Despite the delight generated by the brotherly union, the dismantling of Jerusalem's fortifications produced an outpouring of outrage and intense dismay. Sibṭ b. al-Jawzī explicated the panic among the city's inhabitants in his description: "the *qiyāma* [lit., resurrection] was established in all the lands of Islam" and "a chaos occurred like that of the *yawm al-qiyāma* [day of

8 Al-Jilyānī, *Dīwān al-tadbīj*, 92–93.

resurrection]."[9] Abū Shāma also described the sense of shock at the events, relating that young men, women, and the elderly gathered in al-Aqṣā Mosque and the Dome of the Rock and shaved their hair as a form of collective penitence; this went on until the mosques were full of their hair (see Sibṭ b. al-Jawzī's description, discussed in chapter 4).[10] Abū Shāma also cites a poem composed by the *qāḍī* (judge) of al-Ṭūr, Majd al-Dīn Muḥammad b. ʿAbdallāh al-Ḥanafī:

(2) The rest of my tears overflow because of what is set to occur in the coming time
(5) If souls could ransom themselves then I would surely ransom myself and this is the thought of every Muslim.[11] (2.12)

Similar sentiments of dismay were brought together in a poem composed by Shihāb al-Dīn b. al-Mujāwir (d. 643/1245). The poem describes anguish about the fate of Jerusalem and, particularly, al-Aqṣā Mosque. There is no sense of outrage directed at al-Muʿaẓẓam himself – this may suggest a recognition of the difficult decision made by al-Muʿaẓẓam and the greater threat facing the *umma* if the crusaders remained in Egypt and, even more disconcertingly, if the crusaders regained control of Jerusalem or – worse still – if the crusaders took control of both.

(1) O eyes! Do not dry from tears; I pray with tears in my eyes throughout the day.
(2) So that the downpour of tears might extinguish the embers in my heart.
(3) And O heart! Increase the fire [of grief] whenever it weakens; with remembrance it will generate grief.
(4) And O mouth! Speak of my distresses for perhaps it will soothe me from hardships.
(5) [Speak for] al-Aqṣā whose rank is illustrious, for the place which is intended for prayers and salutations.
(6) [Speak for] the abode of kings, and revelation, and guidance, for the location of the *abdāl* ['substitutes']
(7) [Cry for] the place of ascension and the Rock which boasts [its position] above the other rocks on earth.

9 Sibṭ b. al-Jawzī, *Mirʾāt al-zamān*, part 2, 8:654, 601.
10 Abū Shāma, *Kitāb al-Rawḍatayn*, 5:175.
11 Ibid., 5:175.

(8) [Cry for] the first *qibla* toward which the creation faced in prayer from [all] different directions.
(9) [Cry for] the best of buildings, and the most honoured of inhabitants and the most noble building [built] by the best of builders.
(10) And there remains in it the sanctuary of prophets. In its hope worshippers mourn.
(11) The blessed al-Aqṣā Mosque which has raised pillars and high balconies has disappeared.
(12) Although it was a place of goodness and piety, of beneficence and closeness [to God]; it has now disappeared.
(13) Coming to it was every dishevelled, humble, pious, and [those who] retreated [for worship].
(14) [Al-Aqṣā] is empty of prayers performed by those who are not bored, but those who recite its verses and chapters with pleasure.
(15) It is empty of the yearning of penitents and their grief and [they are] between [being] wailers and those who simply cry.
(16) The whole country in its entirety should cry for Jerusalem and announce its grief and sadness because of its captivity.
(17) Mecca should cry for it, because [Jerusalem] is its sister and it should plead [to God] in ʿArafat
(18) Ṭayba [Medina] should cry for what happened in Jerusalem and explain [its suffering] to the best of houses [the Kaʿba].
(21) They have destroyed the glory of righteousness [*ṣalāḥ*] when it [Jerusalem] was destroyed, and this glory was exalted and high.[12] (2.13)

The poem is an illustration of the religious sensibilities that suffered because of al-Muʿaẓẓam's decision to destroy the walls of Jerusalem. It is essential to note that al-Aqṣā Mosque was one of those structures that was not targeted; rather it appears that it was the potential loss of the Holy City that provoked

12 Abū Shāma, *Kitāb al-Rawḍatayn*, 4:196–197. An example of the effective use of Muslim orators and poets to rouse public emotion can be gauged following Frederick II's taking of Jerusalem in 627/1229 subsequent to his negotiations with al-Malik al-Kāmil. In spite of the sultan's ensuring that al-Aqṣa and the Dome of the Rock mosques would remain in Muslim control, it was seen as an affront to Ṣalāḥ al-Dīn's reconquest in 583/1187 and a crisis for Islam. Ibn Wāṣil includes in his description of the events a poem composed and read publicly by Shams al-Dīn Yūsuf, the nephew of Ibn al-Jawzī, during a speech he delivered in the Umayyad Mosque. The two lines he cites are near identical to lines cited above by Muḥammad al-Mujāwir in his 616/1219 poem. In 637/1239, the treaty between Frederick II and the sultan of Egypt came to an end, and the city of Jerusalem, in Christian hands for a decade, was once again taken by Muslims. Ibn Wāṣil, *Mufarrij*, 4:246.

outrage. The poem, however, is probably most emotive with respect to *faḍāʾil al-Quds* motifs from the poetry of this period. It shows how the symbolic nature of Jerusalem gave contemporary poets new aspects to focus on.

Here the poetic practice of nostalgia is dominated by the tone of anguish and stressed with lines of anaphora. The poem, which is composed of twenty-seven verses, can be divided into the following parts: (1) Its opening verses draw on the general state of grief that the poet describes following the razing of the walls, with descriptions of 'my eyes' (*aʿyunī*), 'downpour of tears' (*suyūl al-damʿ*), and embers (*jamarāt*). (2) It then begins a sequence of emotive entreaties, familiar in *rithāʾ* (elegy) poetry. The heart and tongue are called upon to complain and vent their anger, 'And O heart ... And O tongue ...' with the 'embers' in verse 2 and 'fire' in line 3 emphasising the outrage in the opening lines. (3) The next five lines draw on religious sites in Jerusalem, beginning predictably with al-Aqṣā Mosque, which is mentioned twice in the poem. The city's sanctity rests on the two mosques; Muḥammad al-Mujāwir realised the strong need to invoke the kind of *faḍāʾil* features that were prominent in the decades preceding the 583/1187 reconquest. The suggestion is that Frankish control of Jerusalem would see the loss of these two mosques. Notwithstanding the danger facing the Muslim world, the poem serves no real practical purpose as far as mobilising the population into action; the lament seems primarily intended to appeal to a communal religious solidarity.

The religious motifs of the poem are significant; they stress heightened sentiments of 'loss' (*khalā*) in verses 14 and 15, which precede exhortations to weep for the sanctuaries, and the sacred sites of Mecca and Medina should weep for Jerusalem (verses 16–18). The poem also highlights the religious character of the city as shaped by the reconquest; allusions to pilgrimage, asceticism, and the prominence of the Qurʾān and prayer collectively reveal the features of the city that provided a sense of religious stability for the Muslim population. The notion of pilgrimage would appear to be prominent in the poem (verse 13). The poem stresses that current events will hinder opportunities for the pilgrimage and, in a way comparable to sentiments expressed to rouse the Christians of western Europe to embark on the First Crusade, it reminds penitents that they will be denied the apposite location for pilgrimage and penitence. This point is strengthened with a description of a union of Mecca and Jerusalem, intended to stress the importance of such journeys. As Akkach remarks, "When the three most sacred centers, Mecca, Medina, and Jerusalem, are projected together a hierarchy of holiness is always evident."[13] Also important is the poet's mentioning of al-Aqṣā as a "location of the *abdāl* [substitutes]" in verse 6. The belief in and ideas surrounding the *abdāl* are popular in Sufi thought. A

13 Akkach, *Cosmology and Architecture*, 167.

tradition favoured by Sufis that brings to light the spiritual standing of Syria in the popular perception of its inhabitants can be found in the *faḍā'il* text of the Shāfi'ī Abū Sa'd 'Abd al-Karīm b. Muḥammad al-Sam'ānī (d. 562/1166).[14] The author was originally from Khurasan but after performing the *ḥajj* he settled in Damascus. Al-Sam'ānī's short text (just 42 reports) is largely eschatological in tone and reveals a perspective of the region shaped by the crusader presence:

> On an occasion when the people of Egypt reviled the people of Syria, 'Awf b. Mālik said: O people of Egypt, I am 'Awf b. Mālik, do not revile the people of Shām for I heard the Messenger of God – may the peace of God be upon him – say: "In them are the *abdāl* and with them you are given victory."[15]

Further to the discourse centred on the enigmatic *abdāl* is Ibn al-Ḥawrānī's description in his pilgrimage text, *al-Ishārāt ilā amākin al-ziyārāt*, composed during the tenth/sixteenth century. The text draws on Qur'ānic "verses and traditions on the merits of Syria" which deal mostly with end time features of the region; it includes the *ḥadīth* about the existence of a victorious party – said to be in Syria, the Muslim battalion in Damascus during end time wars, and the esoteric presence of the *abdāl* personages – "Damascus is the city that contains the most *abdāl* and ascetics."[16] While the spiritual focus of the *abdāl* is clear, it is the belief that "victory is given because of them (their saintly presence)" that makes their inclusion in books of *faḍā'il* and in the poetry of this period particularly revealing of the spiritual place accorded to the region of Syria, specifically to Damascus and Jerusalem, and fused with this are allusions indicating that chosen participants will continue the *jihād* in the region in the end days.

Such features not only highlight the continuation of the poetic themes that emerged in the latter half of the sixth/twelfth century to inspire a yearning for the holy city, but are a good contrast to sentiments expressed in the early poetry of Ibn al-Khayyāṭ and al-Abīwardī after the First Crusade. The focus on descriptions of 'prayer,' 'penitence,' and 'worship' in the poem written in 616/1219 highlights how Muslims used their sacred spaces and further speaks of Ṣalāḥ al-Dīn's enclosure of the city with a palpably Islamic character.

14 See Ibn Khallikān, *Wafayāt*, 3:191–195.

15 Al-Sam'ānī, 'Faḍā'il al-Shām,' in *Faḍā'il al-Shām*, ed. Abū 'Abd al-Rahmān 'Ādil b. Sa'd (Beirut: Dār al-Kutub al-'Ilmiyya, 2001), 137.

16 Meri, *The Cult of Saints*, 81; Ibn al-Ḥawrānī, *al-Ishārāt ilā amākin al-ziyārāt*, ed. B. A. Al-Jabi (Damascus: Maktabat al-Ghazālī, 1981), 10.

Conclusion

The loss of Jerusalem in 492/1099 inspired *jihād* poetry that was unprecedented in its multiplicity of themes. In the chapters of this book I have demonstrated the great range of ideas, and political and religious sentiments that informed the anti-Frankish *jihād* in the sixth/twelfth and seventh/thirteenth centuries. The poetry served to strengthen the Muslim resolve against the Franks and tied in with other religious texts, such as books of *faḍā'il*, *jihād* sermons, and inscriptions. I argued that old ideas were augmented with a particular and distinct religious focus during the crusades. The early poetry of al-Abīwardī and Ibn al-Khayyāṭ, for example, reveals a lay response that focused on internal problems and illuminated the great indignation caused by the overturning of the sacred order. One comes to see that the *jihād* poetry was functional, in that it could be recited at key historical moments; it served to bolster and 'Islamicise' the reputation of a patron; to outline and reinforce the struggle between Islam and Christianity; and to motivate believers to partake in armed conflict. Its imagery was largely derivative, though some themes were unknown to earlier poets, such as the description of a humiliated Jerusalem, the sight of Frankish women worshipping, the joining of 'grieving' sanctities, or the call to 'rescue' Jesus. From all the types of literature that were employed for the anti-Frankish *jihād*, poetry was the most rousing literary vehicle and the most closely connected to the *jihād* rulers; it drew on the public image they wanted to project to their subjects. The poetry in this period was more than an art form. The political commentary running through the poet's verses was integral to reinforcing the place of Islam, its sacred destinations, its enemies, and its champions during a period of spiritual and physical upheaval.

Christianity and its symbolism, the crusaders' ambitions, and Muslims vying for the personage of Jesus Christ, or as the poets were keen to stress – 'ibn Maryam' (son of Mary) were key, new features of *jihād* propaganda. Such themes, and several others – most prominently the sanctity of Jerusalem – resulted from the impact of the crusades on the Muslim world. We can appreciate the evolution of new trends and themes to inspire the liberation of the Holy Land, to discern fresh nuances, finer considerations, and, of particular importance, to assess the way poetry sought to influence the political policies of Nūr al-Dīn and Ṣalāḥ al-Dīn by highlighting concerns, fears, and hopes that generally reflected the Muslim population of the region. Though poetry is vital to our understanding of the way the ideals and sensibilities of Nūr al-Dīn and Ṣalāḥ al-Dīn were shaped, it is essential to question whether the ideas of the *jihād* that were disseminated in the crusader period had a generally universal

 | DOI 10.1163/9789004345225_010

and stereotypical content, or whether their most characteristic elements were applicable to this unique set of circumstances. During these times the *jihād* became a popular instrument of resistance among jurists. Theoretical knowledge, however, required application and could be adapted to the pressing relevance of *jihād* propaganda.

It is important not to overlook the simple competitive spirit of poets and preachers in an age in which eloquence determined respect, credibility, and wealth. It was thus in this regard that notables and the *ʿulamāʾ* were influenced by the skilful propaganda of Nūr al-Dīn and Ṣalāḥ al-Dīn to act; the religious poetry was a salient feature of this propaganda. The late Palestinian critic Jabra I. Jabra (1919–94) drew on more recent conflict in the Holy Land and noted:

> Poetry might be condemned as too weak a toy against guns, but in actual fact it was often as good as dynamite. It gave point to a whole nation's suffering and wrath. It crystallised political positions in telling verses which, memorised by old and young, stiffened popular resistance and provided rallying slogans.[1]

Whereas al-Sulamī's early *jihād* text is valuable as a response not only to the crusader occupation and expansion but also to internal problems in the house of Islam, namely divisions and avarice, then so too we must see the early poetry of the learned class of the sixth/twelfth century and its evocative lines as a significant response to the same concerns.[2] In the early years, from 494/1101 to 495/1102, the lands of Syria, Iraq, and Khurasan were troubled by internal rivalries, wars, and mutual fears.[3] In spite of these rivalries among the military class, we can see the lay population, whose views were sometimes echoed by poets, in a different light. Although the formalism and sometimes the artificiality of expression is discernible in court poetry, at other times the veritable sense of the expressions come through, particularly during times of increased apprehension.

In our assessment of the early resistance to the crusaders we must draw a distinction between the Muslim ruling elite and the lay populations of the Islamic Near East. The approach taken by some historians has resulted in a neglect of the ideas contained in poetry and an underappreciation of other political factors extant in the Muslim Near East that hindered the possibility

1 J. I. Jabra, 'The Rebels, the Committed and the Others: Transitions in Modern Arabic Poetry Today,' *Middle East Forum* 43 (1967), 20.

2 Al-Sulamī, 'Kitāb al-Jihād,' 45.

3 Ibn al-Qalānisī, *The Damascus Chronicle*, 46–59.

of a strong and united Muslim response. One example is the observation of Goitein and Grabar: "The often-noted astounding fact that the conquest of Jerusalem by the Crusaders and its conversion into an exclusively Christian city did not arouse any strong Muslim reaction for decades also indicates that the veneration for the Holy City had not yet become a spiritual force in Islam."[4] Elisséeff's observation, however, is more realistic. He argues that

> forgetting the obligation of the *Jihād* was not a new phenomenon in the Muslim world. It had been spreading ever since the end of the ninth (third H.) century when the caliphate abandoned its *ṣayfiyya*, summer raids along the northern borders (*ʿawāṣim*). The phenomenon seems to have been part of the gradual decline in the religious and moral conscience which occurred in the Muslim world at this time.[5]

Therefore, the indifference that we may impute to the peoples of Syria may stem from the disquieting political state of affairs before and during the First Crusade. Yet incapacity does not of course imply apathy.[6] Al-Sulamī, as Dajani-Shakeel notes, may be credited for "laying the theoretical foundations" of the Muslim resistance and "sowing the seeds of national and religious renaissance" that was carried on from generation to generation, finally culminating in the reconquest of Jerusalem.[7] Al-Sulamī's genuine anxiety became the concern of a broad movement of scholars, some of whom were Syrian, Egyptian, Baghdadi, Palestinian, Andalusian, and even non-Arab, such as the ever-important ʿImād al-Dīn al-Iṣfahānī. The legalistic and theological concerns of scholars in response to the crusader occupation of Muslim lands were complemented by the more fluid approach of dozens of poets. Some of these were employed, some were scholars, some were *khaṭīb*s, some were Sufi ascetics, some were even Shīʿīs like Ṭalāʾiʿ b. Ruzzīk and Ibn al-Munīr al-Ṭarābulsī.

The creation of an environment that fostered religious learning and had an identifiable and tangible end, centred on liberation, unity, and religious purification – perhaps more so in the minds of its designers – allowed the key idea of the sanctity and liberation of Jerusalem, with all its strands, both religious and secular, military and piety driven, to become an inherited responsibility. In the creation of this psychological climate, therefore, various forms of literature

4 S. D. Goitein and O. Grabar, 'Jerusalem,' in *Historic Cities of the Islamic World*, ed. C. E. Bosworth (Leiden: Brill, 2007), 238.

5 Elisséeff, 'The Reaction of the Syrian Muslims,' 162.

6 See Hillenbrand, *The Crusades*, 108–112.

7 Dajani-Shakeel, 'Some Medieval Accounts,' 103.

were employed and, as Elisséeff notes, "firstly, came poetry."[8] Court poets like ʿImād al-Dīn al-Iṣfahānī were utilised by caliphs and governors to compose panegyrics to promote their regimes. These poets reiterated the centrality of Islam's holy places in the ambitions of their patrons, and through their own perceptions pertaining to the developing ethos of their era their words allowed the conflict against the Franks to be seen as seminal. Composing verse for the purpose of inciting others to the *jihād* or satirising the enemy could fit well into a religious framework, but laudatory sentiments, though great in rousing emotions, needed some kind of validation such as the intertwining of Qurʾānic imagery into the verses and the intermittent praise of God. Szombathy notes the juxtaposition one might find in the themes of some poems, wherein a reflection of guilt ensues for a poet when he composes a light-hearted poem, thereafter requiring the subsequent composition of a more religiously acceptable and rigid poem, seen as a kind of reparation.[9] We wonder then if Ibn al-Qaysarānī's shift from poetic focus speaks of this kind of pattern that was familiar to medieval Arabic poets.

We also see how poets sought to present their time as one of untold opportunity, in a new epoch, near the events of the end of time. The poetry, in addition to providing important outlooks on Muslim sentiments, hopes, and fears, allows us to learn more about literary history during the period. Such attitudes, popular with al-Jilyānī, were a subject of other material, including a letter written by al-Qāḍī l-Fāḍil expounding his eschatological fears following Reynald de Châtillon's Red Sea incursion; Ibn al-Zakī's reference to the 'end of days' in his Friday sermon at al-Aqṣā was made in reference to the significance of the reconquest.

The study compared the lines of the Syrian panegyrist Ibn al-Munīr (d. 548/1153) and those of Ibn al-Qaysarānī. While most of Ibn al-Munīr's poetry celebrates the victories of Nūr al-Dīn and Ṣalāḥ al-Dīn, he also wrote some interesting verses about the Franks. He seems to have been the only poet to use the description *banāt al-aṣfar* (lit., 'yellow women') in relation to Frankish women as a spoil of war, though the term is not altogether uncommon in medieval Muslim literature; and he brought the very telling *masīḥ* and *Aḥmad* together in one of his poems. Ibn al-Qaysarānī's 'gendered' poetry could be a true reflection of his emotions, but it may also simply be an example of the poet's originality – he composed risky lines, crossed boundaries, and described what many others had not. By examining Ibn al-Qaysarānī's poem we ascer-

8 Elisséeff, 'The Reaction of the Syrian Muslims,' 170.

9 Z. Szombathy, 'Freedom of Expression and Censorship in Medieval Arabic Literature,' *Journal of Arabic and Islamic Studies* 7 (2007), 6.

tain whether it is consistent with his more oft-repeated sentiments, or whether there are other ways of interpreting his lines.

In spite of the theological disparity between the two communities, tensions were not perpetual. At the shrine of Saidnaya, twelve miles north of Damascus, there were cases of communal prayer involving Christians, Muslims, Nestorians, and Melkites, who gathered for prayer and healing in the thousands. Furthermore, the Church of the Holy Nativity at Bethlehem also attracted Muslim pilgrims, a fact recognised by al-Kāmil, who, when negotiating the holy places with Frederick II in 626/1229, stipulated that Muslims should not be denied free access to the site.[10] These and other examples shed light on a nuance in relationships between groups of people we might normally expect to be antagonistic toward each other.

Furthermore, travel and trade continued between Muslims and Franks, armistice agreements were conducted to end fighting, limited truces were often signed, and even some degree of fraternisation between the two camps existed.[11] Trade in fact allowed for close interaction between Muslims and Christians. Both Christian and Muslim merchants found usefulness in each other, and profit from trade was a compelling motivator that encouraged people to form civil relationships even amidst the backdrop of violence. Ibn Jubayr was particularly expressive about this phenomenon. He noted the peacefulness in which merchants conducted their trade, their respect for the payment of taxes and mutual accord:

> One of the astonishing things that is talked of is that though the fires of discord burn between the two parties, Muslim and Christian, two armies of them may meet and dispose themselves in battle array, and yet Muslim

10 Bernard Hamilton, 'Our Lady of Saidnaya: An Orthodox Shrine Revered by Muslims and Knights Templar at the Time of the Crusades,' *Studies in Church History 36: The Holy Land, Holy Lands and Christian History*, ed. R. N. Swanson (Woodbridge: Boydell Press, 2000), 209–210.

11 Ibn Shaddād reports a telling account in this regard in relation to the fighting around Acre in September 1189 (585): 'The evening of that day a major battle took place between the enemy and our people in the city, in which a great number were killed on both sides. Similar conflicts went on for a long time and not a day passed without wounding, killing, capturing and plundering. They got to know one another, in that both sides would converse and leave fighting. At times some people would sing and others dance, so familiar had they become over time, and then after a while they would revert to fighting.' Ibn Shaddād, *The Rare and Excellent History of Saladin*, 100–101. See Yehoshua Frenkel, 'Muslim Responses to the Frankish Dominion in the Near East (1098–1291),' in *The Crusades and the Near East: Cultural Histories*, ed. Conor Kostick (London: Routledge, 2011), 27–54.

> and Christian travellers will come and go between them without interference … The soldiers engage themselves in their war, while the people are at peace and the world goes to him who conquers.[12]

The cultural interactions between Christians and Muslims also highlight the danger of making too strong a case for anti-Frankish *jihād* motives; it is impossible, for example, to assess what percentage of the population was inspired by eschatological readings of their own history; one cannot reconstruct Muslim public opinion and the fact that cross-cultural coexistence existed means that the image of the 'Other' was shaped by many different factors, including pragmatic ones.

Often the battle narrative in the poetry was conventional – God's approval for the *jihād*; the army setting out; the clashing of swords; the dead lying on the battlefield/consumed by the Muslim attack; the promise of victory bearing true. Although recurring trends of glorified patrons combating infidels or impious rivals appear in the poetry of this period, one must consider the way in which images of the Christian Other differed, the way in which an image of a Frankish Christian could be fused with fascinations and consideration, as in the case of Usāma b. Munqidh, or from Ibn Jubayr in his description of a Frankish wedding. This was distinct from the way they would consider a battling crusader; poets allow us to see how Frankish women could be both spoils of war (as Banāt al-Aṣfar) and beautiful worshippers; how churches could at once be *qumāma* and centres of defilement and at other times be places of reverence and worship; how poets carefully trod around religious sensitivities with Jesus as the Messiah (*masīḥ*), while they seemingly paid homage to symbols of worship in the churches of Antioch, a city which in other descriptions was a centre of corruption and disbelief. The differential nature of themes and images of the crusades disallows an oversimplification of the undercurrents of the conflict. While poets did the bidding of their patrons we see independent sentiments by 'unaffiliated' poets whose words are unique in so much as poetic convention mandated originality as a criterion for acceptance and popularity.

How does this poetry sit outside the frame of generic *jihād* poetry? Both al-Abiwardī and Ibn al-Khayyāṭ focus their early sentiments on internal blame; Ibn al-Qaysarānī wrote quite a bit about Frankish women. Though we might ascribe *jihād* sentiments to much of the poetry, some poetry ties in with other religious undercurrents like spirituality (for example, on the *jihād al-nafs*) cited in Ibn Kathīr's poem to Nūr al-Dīn ('O Nūr al-Dīn what would you say …'); Ibn Jubayr's verses were written to compel Ṣalāḥ al-Dīn to maintain social justice

12 Ibn Jubayr, *Travels*, 300–301; Ibn Jubayr, *Tadhkira*, 224.

in Alexandria, sentiments that might suggest an individual motivation based on his recent experience to ease the way for pilgrims. These factors enable us to gauge both the multiplicity of themes and motivations. The evidence supports the necessity of a closer study of sources that have been deemed of little worth in terms of providing 'historical truth.' Poetry has been proven to shed light on the spectrum of religiosity that informed the anti-Frankish Muslim *jihād* and the dynamic religious propaganda. It served as an important cultural expression which allows us to sketch the mental structures of those involved in the anti-Frankish *jihād*. The central message for congregations who gathered to listen to poetry celebrating the victory of Ṣalāḥ al-Dīn was re-assuring; critics and supporters alike were reminded that success was possible and doubts about the promise of God to the Muslim nation were dispelled. The poets served to ratify the ascendancy of their victors. The incorporation of Islamic themes, particularly through Qur'ānic allusions, served a clear purpose. The poetry contains numerous subtleties and nuances and though this might encumber the palpable meaning of the verses, it allows for wider scopes in meaning and imagery. As Semah describes,

> The alertness and ability of the audience to decipher innuendos and to complete meanings that were not, or not yet completed, obviously determine in large measure the nature of audience response. On the one hand, its success depends on the degree of the audience's sensitivity and familiarity with the art of poetry.[13]

Was the *jihād* against the crusaders considered to be of greater merit than other *jihād*s because of the sacred designation of Jerusalem and Syria? Muslim perception of their era changed over the course of the sixth/twelfth century, when significant events such as the fall of the Fāṭimid Empire, the unification of Muslim lands, and the crusader defeats at Ḥaṭṭīn and Jerusalem inspired an effort by the military and religious classes to develop a new ideology of *jihād*. This, combined with the unification of lands with sacred religious designations, such as Jerusalem and Damascus, or areas of prophesied future conquest like Jerusalem and Constantinople, allows us to infer the special merit associated with the reconquest. These include the unprecedented succession of events that preceded the reconquest and their religio-historical bearing; the eschatological *jihād*-based significance of Jerusalem, Damascus, and Constantinople, and the developing influence and social acceptability of Sufism and the role

13 D. Semah, 'Poetry and its Audience According to Medieval Arab Poeticians,' *IOS* XI, ed. S. Somekh (Leiden: Brill, 1991), 92.

it played in creating or cementing an ascetic-warrior ethos. It seems, therefore, that the general air of piety prevalent in sixth-/twelfth- and seventh-/thirteenth-century Syria was given a new edge and focus with the Frankish occupation of Jerusalem.

And finally, to borrow Robert Irwin's phrase, this book complements studies that seek to "recreate the Einfühlung of the Muslim counter-crusade"[14] by relying on a variety of sources, with the intention of interpreting them in the parameters of medieval Islamic consciousness. Notwithstanding the sometimes excessive attention paid to the consequences of the crusades, it demonstrates that aside from the political revival of *jihād* in the sixth/twelfth century, the *zeitgeist*, the 'spirit of the time' at a popular level, coloured by various strands of political and religious belief and practice, fundamentally shaped Muslim attitudes toward their enemies.

14 Irwin, 'Orientalism and the Early Development of Crusader Studies,' 2:229.

Appendix: Arabic Poems

(1.1)
بشطّي نهر دَاريّاً   أمورٌ ما تواتينا
وأقوام رَأَوا سَفكَ الدّ(م)   ما فِي جِلِقٍ دينا
أَتَانَا مئتا أَلفٍ   عديدًا أو يزيدونا
فبعضهمُ مِن أَندَلُسٍ   وبعضٌ من فِلَسطينا
ومن عكَّا ومن صورٍ   ومن صَيدا وتِبنِينا
إِذا أبصرتَهُم أَبصَر   تَ أقوامًا مجانينا
ولكن حرّقوا فِي عا   جلِ الحال البساتينا
وجازوا المَرجَ والتعدي   لَ أَيضًا والمِيادينا
تخالهمُ - وقَد ركبوا   فطائرها - حراذينا
وبين خيامهم ضمُّوا الـ   ـخنازر والقرابينا
وراياتٍ وصُلبانًا   علَى مسجدِ خاتونا
وقُلنا إذ رَأيناهُم   لعلَّ اللهَ يكفينا
سَمَالهُم مُعِينٌ قد   أعَانَ الخَلقَ والدِّينا
وفتيانٌ تخالهمُ   لدى الهيجا شَياطِينا
فولَّوا يطلبونَ المر   جَ من شرقِيّ جِسرِنا
ولكن غادروا إليا   سَ تحت التُّربِ مدفونا
وشيخًا فِندَلاويًا   فقيهًا يعضُدُ الدِّينا
وفتيانًا تفانَوا من   دمشقَ نحو سَبعينا
ومنهم مئتا عِلجٍ   وخيلٍ نحو تسعينا
وباقيهم إِلَ الآنَ   مِنَ القَتلِ يفرُّونا

 | DOI 10.1163/9789004345225_011

(1.2) ولكن غادروا القسيس تحت الارض مدفونا

(1.3) أَتَهوِيمَةٌ فِي ظِلّ أَمنٍ وَ غِبطَتِن، وَ عيشٍ كَنُوَّارِ الخَمِيلَةِ نَاعِمِ
وَكَيفَ تَنَام العينُ مِلءَ جُفُونُهَا، عَلَى هَفَوَاتٍ أَيقَظَت كُلَّ نَائِمِ

(1.4) إن اكبر الكبائر عندي قتل حسناء غضّة عُطبول
كتب القتل و القتال علينا وعلى المحصنات جر الذيول

(1.5) وَكَم مِن دِمَاءَ قَد أَبيَحَت، وَ مِن دُمّى تَوَارَى حَيَاءً حُسنُهَا بالمعَاصِم

(1.6) فكم من فتاة بهم أصبحت تدق من الخوف نحرا وخدا
و أم عواتق ما إن عرفن حرا ولا ذقن في الليل بردا
تكاد عليهن من خيفة تذوب وتتلف حزنا ووجدا
فحاموا على دينكم والحريم محاماة من لا يراى الموت فقدا

(1.7) وكيف تنام العين ملء جفونها على هفوات أيقظت كل نائم

(1.8) و كيف تنامون عن أعين وترتم فأسهرتموهن حقدا
وشر الضغائن ما أقبلت لديه الضغائن بالكفر تحدا

(1.9) ففَلَن تَعدَمُوا فِي انتِشَارِ الأُمُورِ أَخا تُدرَاءٍ حازِمَ الرَّأيِ جَلدا

(1.10) يَكَادُ لَهُنَّ المُستَجِنَّ بطيبةٍ يُنَادِي بِئَاعلَى الصُّوت يَا آلَ هَاشِم

(1.11) فَئِيهَا، بَنِي الإِسلاَم، إنّ وَرَاءَكُم — وَقَائِع يُلحِقنَ الذُّرَى بِالمنَاسِمِ

(1.12) فَأَصبَحَ أبقَى مِنَ الفَرقَدَينِ — ذِكرًا وَأَسنى مِن الشَّمسِ مَجدَا
لَعلَّكُمُ أَن تُعِيدُوا مِنَ المَآثِرِ — وَالمَجدِ مَا كَانَ أَبدا

(1.13) أَحَلّ الكُفر بِالإِسلاَمِ ضَيمًا — يَطُولُ علَيهِ الدِينُ النَّجِيب
فَحَقٌّ ضَائِعٌ وَحِمًى مُبَاحٌ — وَسَيفٌ قَاطِعٌ وَدَمٌّ صَبِيب
وَكَم مِن مُسلِمٍ أمسَى سَلِيبًا — وَمُسلِمَةٍ لَهَا حَرَمٌ سَلِيب

(1.14) مَن قاتلَ الإِفرنجَ ديناَ غيرهُ — والخيلُ مثلُ السَّيلِ عند المَشهَدِ
حتَى لوى الإِسلامَ تحتَ لوائه — وغدا بحمدِ مِن شريعةِ أحمدِ

(1.15) نَزَعتَ لباسَ الكُفرِ عن قُدسِ أَرضِها — أَلبستَهَا الدِّين الذي كَشَفَ اللَّبسا

(1.16) وعادَت ببيتِ الله أحكامُ دينه — فلا بطركا أبقيتَ فيها ولا قَسَّما

(1.17) وَكَم مِن مَسجِدٍ جَعلُوهُ دَيَّرًا — علَى مِحرَابِهِ نُصِب الصَلِيب
دَمُ الخِنزِيرِ فِيهِ لَهُم خَلُوقٌ — وَتَحرِيقُ المَصَاحِف فِيهِ طِيب

(1.18) أُمُورٌ لُو تَعمَلَهُنَّ طِفلٌ — لَطفّل فِي عوَارِضِهِ المَشِيبُ

(1.19) أَتُسبَى المُسلِمَاتُ بِكلّ ثَغر — وَعيشُ المُسلِمِين إِذًا يطِيب
أَمَا لِلّه والإِسلام حَقٌّ — يُدَافِعُ عنه شُبَّانٌ وَ شِيب
فَقُل لِذوِى البصَائِرِ حَيثُ كَانُوا — أَجِيبُوا اللهَ وَيحَكُم أَجِيبُوا

(1.20) أقاتل حتى لا أرى لي مقاتلاً وأنجو إذا غُمّ الجبان من الكرب

(1.21) القوم أمثالكم لهم شعر في الرأس لا ينشررون إن قتلوا

(1.22) إن اكبر الكبائر عندي قتل حسناء غضّة عُطبول
كتب القتل و القتال علينا و على المحصنات جر الذيُول

(1.23) ابني إن اباك يوما هالك فاحفظ يَومًا رياسا وتقلبا
و إذا تكون كتيبة فاستقدمن إن المقدم لا يكون الالخيبا
تلق المنية او تمت من طعنة والموت آت من نأي و تجنبا

(1.24) ابو ان يفروا والقنا في نحورهم و لم يرتقبوا من خشية الموت سلم
و لو انهم فرّوا لكانوا أععزة ولكن رأوا صبرًا على الموت أكرما

(1.25) إذا مَا دمشقُ ملّكك عِنانهَا تيقّنَ مَن فِي إيليا اَنّه الذَّبحُ

(1.26) و أُقسِمُ مَا ذاقَ اليهودُ بإيليا و مَوضَعُها من بختَنصَّرَ أسوَدُ

(1.27) تَنَصَّرتَ أمّاً بل تمجّست والدًا و عمّاً فَعِرقُ الكُفرِ فيك مردّ

(1.28) يَا نُورَ دين الله وَابنَ عمادِه والكوثَرَ بن الكوثر بن الكَوثَرِ
صفّر بحدِّ السَّيفِ دار أَشائِبِ عَقَلُوا جيادَكَ عن بناتِ الأَصفَرِ

(1.29) وجاهَدَ في الله حقَّ الجها دِ مُحتسِبٌ بَالعُلا قافِلُ
فإن يكُ فتحُ الرُّها لُجَّةً فساحِلُها القُدسُ والسَّاحِلُ

(1.30) فتملَّ فَتحك واقصدِ الفتح الذَى   بحصوله لفُتوحك الإِتمامُ

(1.31) نهوضاَ إلى القُدسِ يشفي الغليل   بفتح الفتوح و ماذا عسيرُ
سَلِ الله تسهيل صَعب الخُطو   ب فهو على كلِّ شئ قديرُ

(1.32) إذا صَفِرَت من آل الأصفر ساحةُ ال   مقدّس ضاهت فَتحَ أُمّ القرَى قِدما

(1.33) الله أكبر أرضُ القُدسِ قد صَفِرَت   من آل الأصفر إذ حينٌ به حانوا
أسباطُ يوسف من مصرٍ أتَوا ولهم   من غيرِ تيهٍ بها سَلوى وأمنانُ

(1.34) راياتُه صُفرًا يَردنَ وتنثني   حُمرًا تمجُّ نجيعَ اَل الأَصفَرِ
لِمَ لم تَدِن شُوسُ الملوكِ له وقد   ملك السّوَاحل فِي ثلَاثة أَشهرِ

(1.35) بني أَصفرٍ ألقُوا السلاَحَ و وحّدوا   والا دهاكم مَن سَبَاكم بداره

(1.36) ويحَ الفِرَنجَةَ بل ويل امِّهم أوَ ما   فيهم لبيبُ علَى العِلات يعتبرُ
فكم نَثَرتَهمُ ضَربَاَ إذا انتظموا   وكم نَظَمتَهُمُ طَعناَ إذا انتثَروا
كم قد سَقَيتَهُمُ ذُلاَ فلا عَجَبُ   إن عَربَدُا سَفَهاَ فالقومُ قدّ سَكِروا
إن يمّوك فلا بِدعُ لجهلهمُ   تَسعَى إلى الأسدِ في غاباتها الحُمُرُ

فخَّامِ عن حَوطَةِ البَيتِ المقدَّسِ لا   خوفُ وحاشاك من خَوفٍ ولا ضَرَرُ
هو الشّريفُ وقد ناداك مُعتَصِماَ   فما على مجدِهِ من بَعدِها حَذَرُ

(1.37) بِفَتحِهِ القُدسَ للإسلاَم قد فُتِحَت   فِي قَمعِ طاغيةِ الإِشراكِ أَبوابُ

ففي مواقفةِ البيتِ المُقَدّس لنا   بيتِ الحَرَامِ لنَـا تِيـهٌ وإعجَابُ
وَالصَّخرَةُ الحَجَـرُ المَلثُومِ جانبـه   كلهما عتمارلا الخَلقِ مِحرَابُ
نفَى من القُدسِ صُلبانًا كما نُفِيَت   من بيتِ مكـّة أزلاَمٌ وأنصابُ

(1.38) فإن أظلم الإسلامُ أشرقَ منك ما   أجالَ بـه شمسا فـذابَ إرتِكامُهُ

(1.39) والإفرِنجُ من أسرى وموتى ويُوسفٌ   أجـال عليهـم حـدًّا وارٍ ضِرَامُـهُ

(1.40) غـدَاة طَحاَ بالمشركين اقتحامُـهُ   أخو دُلجٍ مُستنقِـذُ القـدسِ ثـاَرُهُ

(1.41) وقـامَ صَلاحُ الدِّينِ بالشِّركِ فاتكا   وأطواقُ أعنـاقِ المُلوكِ شِـفارُهُ

(1.42) حـتَى يوحِّد أهلُ الشِّـرك قاطبة   ويرَهَـب القَولَ بالثّـالوثِ رُهبانُ

(1.43) رَأيتُ فيه عظيمَ الكُفرِ مُحتَقرًا   مُعَفَّرًا خَـدُّهُ وَالأَنفُ قد تَعَسـا

(1.44) مَن سَيفُه في دِمَاءِ القَومِ مُنغَمِسٌ   من كلِّ من لم يَزَل في الكُفرِ مُنغَمِسَا

(1.45) وَبيتُ كُفرِهُمُ مِن خُبثِهِم كُنِسَا

(1.46) متواضعـًا للّهُ جَـلَّ جـلاَلُه   وبِكَ اضمَحَلَّت سَـطوَةُ المُتكبِّر

(1.47) جَلت عَزَمَـاتُك الفَتحَ المُبِينَـا   فقـد قَرَّت عُـيونُ المُؤمنِينَـا

(1.48) يقـاتِلُ كـلُّ ذي مُـلكٍ ريـاءً   و أنتَ تقـاتِلُ الأعـداءَ دينـا

(1.49) وهانَ بك الصَّليبُ وكَان قِدمًا   يَعُـزُّ عـلَى العواليَ أَنْ يَهُونا

(1.50) فيَـا اللهُ كـم سَرَّت قلوبـًا   ويَـا اللهُ كـم أَبكَت عُيونَـا

(1.51) فَقَلبُ القُدسِ مسرورٌ

(1.52) وَفَتحُكُم حَلَبـا بالسَّيفِ في صَفَر   مُبَشِّر بفـتحِ القُدسِ في رَجَبِ

(1.53) وكعادَةِ البيتِ المقدَّسِ يحَزُنُ الـ   بيـتُ الحَـرَامُ عليـه بل عَرَفاتُـهُ

(1.54) يا بَهجةَ القُدس إن أضحى به عَلَمُ الـ   إسلام من بَعدِ طيٍّ وهو مُنتَشِرُ
يا نورَ مَسجِدِهِ الأقصى وقد رُفِعَت   بعد الصَّليب بـه الآياتُ والسُّوَرُ

(1.55) خلا مِن صلاة لا يَمَلُّ مُقيمُها   تُوَشَّحُ بالآيـاتِ والسُّوَرَاتِ

(1.56) لو أنَّ ذا الفَـتحَ في عَصرِ النَّبِيِّ لقد   تَنَـزَّلت فيـه آيـات و قُرآنُ

(1.57) أنت أَحيَيته وقد كَان مَيتًا   ثـم أَعتقتَه وقد كَان قِنَّـا
شَـاق جبريلَ بيتُه بيت جبريـ   ـلَ فوَافَى إليـه شوقًا وحَنَّـا

(1.58) جُندُ السَّماءِ لهذا المَلكِ أَعوَانُ   مَن شَكَّ فيهم فهذا الفَتحُ بُرهَانُ
هذي الفُتوحُ فتوحُ الأنبياءِ وما   لها سوى الشُّكرِ بالأفعال أثمانُ
تسعون عاما بلادُ اللهِ تَصرخُ والـ   إسلامَ نُصَّارُه صُمٌّ وعُميانُ

(1.59) لو كان في عَصرِ النبيّ لأُنزِلَت   في ذِكرِهِ من ذِكرِهِ آياتُهُ

(1.60) ومن كان أملاكُ السّمواتِ جندَه   فأيةُ أرضٍ لم ترضها جيادُهُ
ولله عزم ماءُ سيحان وِردُهُ   وروضة قُسطَنطِينَةِ مُستراده

(1.61) وَأيسوفِيا ترجوك مثلَ قِيامة   فذا الفتحُ يعلو العَالمين جِهارُهُ

(1.62) اطلّت علَى افقك الزاهر   سعودٌ مِن الفلك الدائر
فَأَبشِر فانّ رقاب العِدَى   تُمَدّ الَى سَيفك البائر
وَ عمّا قليل يحلّ الرّدى   بكيدهم الناكث الغادر
وخصبُ الورى يوم يُسقَى الثرى   سحائبَ من دمها الهامر
فكم لك من فتكة فيهمُ   حكت فتكةَ الاسد الخادر
كسرتَ صليبهم عنوةً   فلله درُّك من كاسر
وغيّرتَ آثَارهم كلَّها   فليس لها الدهرَ من جابر
وامضيتَ جِدّك في غزوهم   فتعسًا لجَدّهم العاثر
فادبر ملكُهم باشآمِ   وولّى كَأَمسهم الدابر
جنودك بالرعب منصورة   فناجز متى شئتَ أو صابر
فكلّهم غارق هالك   بتيّار عسكرك الزاخر
ثأرتَ لدين الهدى في العدَى   فآثرك الله من ثائر
إله الورى فسمّاك بالملك   الناصرو رِمتَ بنص
وتُسهِر جفنَاك في حقّ مَن   سيُرضِيك في جفنك الساهر
فتاحتَ المقدّس من أَرضه   فعادت إلَ وصفها الطاهر
وجئتَ إلَ قُدسه المُرتَضَى   فخلّصتَه من رَّسمه الداثر
لكم ذخر الله هَذِي الفتُوح   من الزمن الاوّل الغابر
وخصّك من بعد ما زرتَه   بها لاصطناعك في الآخر

مُحبّتُكم أُلقيت في النفوسِ   بذكرٍ لَّكم في الورى طائر
فكم لهمُ عند ذكر الملوك   بمثلك من مَّثَلٍ سائر
رفعتَ مغارم أرضِ للحجاز   بانعامك الشامل الغامر
(وآمنت أكناف تلك البلاد   فهان السبيل على العابر
وسُحب أياديك فيّاضة   على وارد وعلى صادر)
فكم لك باشرق من حامد   وكم لك في الغرب من شاكر
وكم بالدعاء لكم كلّ عام   بمكّة من مّعلِن جاهر
وكم بقيت حبسة في الظلوم   وتلك الذخيرة في الذاكر
يعنّت حجّاج بيت الله   ويسطو بهم سطوةَ الجائر
ويَكشِف عمّا بايديهمُ   وناهيك من مّوقف صاغر
وقد أُوقِفوا بعد ما كُشِفوا   كأنّهم في يد الآسر
ويُلزِمهم حلفا باطلا   وعُقبَى اليمين على الفاجر
وإن عرضت بينهم حرمة   فليس لهَا عنه من ساتر
أَليس يخاف غدًا عرضه   على الملك القادر القاهر
وليس على حُرَم المسلمين   بتلك المشاهد من غَائِر
ولَا حاضر نافعٌ زجرُه   فيَا ذلّة الحاضر الزاجر
ألَا ناصح مُبلِغ نُصحَه   إلى الملك الناصر الظاهر
ظلوم تضمّن مال الزكاة   لقد تعست صفقةُ الخاسر
يُسِرّ الخيانة في باطن   ويُبدِى النصيحة في الظاهر
فاوقع به حادث انّه   يقبّح أحدوثة الذاكر
فما للمناكر من زاجر   سواك وبالعُرف من آمر
وحاشاك ان لّمَ تُزِل رسمها   فما لك في الناس من عاذر
ورفعُك امثالها مُوسِع   رداء فخارك من ناشر
وآثرك العِزّ تبغَى بهَا   وتلك المآثر للآثر

نذرتُ النصيحة في حقّكم وحقّ نوفاءُ على الناذر
وحبُّك أنطقني بالقريض ومَا ابتغى صِلَةَ الشاعر
ولَا كان فيما مَضَى مكسبَى وبِئس البضاعة للتاجر
اذا الشِعر صار شعار الفتَى فناهيك من لّقب شاهر
وإن كان نظمِي له نَاذرا فقد قيل لَا حُكمَ للناذر
ولكنّها خطرات الهوى تعزّ فتغلب بالخطر
وامّا وقد زار تلك العُلَا فقد فاز بالشرَف الباهر
وان كان منك قبول له فتلك الكرامةُ للزائر
ويكفيك سمعُك من سامِع ويكفيك للحظُك للناظر
ويزهَى على الرّوض غِبّ الحَيَا بما حاز من ذلك العاطر

(1.63) قل للفرنسيس إذا جئته مقال صدق من قؤول فصيح
آجرك الله على ما جرى من قتل عبّاد يسوع المسيح

وقفك الله إلى مثلها لعل عيسى منكم يستريح
إن كان باباكم بذا راضيًا فربّ غش قد أتى من نصيح

(1.64) قل للفرنسين إنّ كلاًّ له من المسلمين شاكر
لأنّهُ محسنٌ إلينا بقَودِه نحونا العساكر
ساق إلى مصر ما اقتَناهُ أمةُ عيسى من الذخائر

ورامَ باباهُمُ أُمورًا فأخلفت ظَنَّهُ المَقادر
وأذهل القومَ هولُ حربٍ تشخصُ من خوفهِ النواظر
لم تَعمَ أبصارهم ولكن قد عميت منهم البصائر

ويستريحُ المسيحُ منهم — من كلّ علجٍ وكلّ كافرِ

(1.65) يُرَجُّون ميلادَ ابن مريمَ نُصرةً — ولم يُغنِ عند القوم عنهُ ولادُه
ولا مِنبرَ إلا ترنَّحَ عُودُه — ولا مُصحَف إلا أنار مِدَادُهُ
إلى أينَ يا أسرى الضَّلالةِ بعدها — لقد ذَلَّ غاويكُم وعزَّ رشادُهُ
وقل لملوك الكُفرِ تُسلِمُ بعدها — ممالكَها إن البلادَ بلادُهُ
ومن كان أملاكُ السَّمواتِ جندَه — فأيةُ أرضٍ لم ترضها جيادُهُ
ولله عزم ماءُ سيحانَ وِردُهُ — وروضة قُسطَنطِينَةِ مُستراده

(1.66) يا مُنقِذَ القُدس مِن أيدي جَبابِرَة — قد أقسموا بذراع الرَّبِّ تدخله
فأكذبوا كِذبَهم في وَصفِ رَبِّهِم — وَصُدِّقَ الوَعدُ مأموناً تحوُّلُهُ
أَما رَأيتَ إبنَ أيوبَ إستقلَّ بما — يُعيي الزَّمانَ وأهليه تَحَمُّلُهُ
هاجَ الفرنجُ وقد خاروا لفتكته — فاستنفروا كلَّ مرهوبٍ تَغَلغُلُهُ
لما سَبَى القُدسَ قالوا كيف نتركها — والرَّبُّ في حفرةٍ منها نُمَثِّلُهُ
فكم مليكٍ لهم شَقَّ البحار سُرَى — لينصروا القَبرَ والأقدارُ تخذُلُهُ
وكم تَرَحَّلَ منهم فَيلَق بفلا — إلى الخوامعِ ألقاه تَرَحُّلُهُ
استَصرَخُوا الأَهلَ والعَدوى تمزِّقُهم — واستكثروا المال والهيجا تُنَفِّلُهُ
سَيف أمام فِلَسطِينِ بَرَى أُمَماً — خَلفَ البحارِ لقد أمهاه صَيقَلُهُ
كم قد أعَدُّوا وكم قد فُلَّ جَمعُهُمُ — من غيرِ ضَربٍ ولا طَعنٍ يُزَيِّلُهُ
وإنما اسمُ صلاحِ الدين يُذكَرُ في — جَيشِ العَدُوِّ فَيَسبيهم تَخَيُّلُهُ

(1.67) قل مَا تشاء فقولك المقبول — وعليك بعد الخالق التعويل
واستبشر القرآن حين نصرته — وبكى لفقد رجاله الانجيل

(1.68) أَمَّا وقد قصدَ الغزَاةَ وهنَّتِ القربَ النصول
وبكت به أُمُّ الصليبِ وشدوُ صَارمه الصليلُ
وبدت له أَرض الشآ مِ تهونُ إِذ كَانت تهول

(1.69) فَسِر وافتَحِ القُدسَ واسفك به دماء متَى تُجرِها يَنظُفِ
وَأهدِ إلى الإِسبِتارِ التَّبَار وهُدَّ السُّقوفَ على الأُسقُفِ
وخَلِّص من الكُفرِ تلك البلاد يُخَلِّصك الله في المَوقِفِ

(1.70) كأنَّما ساحتُه جَنَّة أجرت بها راحتُه كَوثَرا
جِهادُ ليل في نهار فَفُز إذ كنتَ فيه الأصبرَ الأشكرا
أبقاكَ للدُّنيا وللدِّين مَن خَلَّاك في ليلهما نَيِّرا
حتَى ترى عيسى من القُدسِ قد لجا إلى سيفِك مُستَنصرا

(1.71) قد أَنصَفَ التَّوحِيدَ من تثليثهم وَأقَامَ في الإِنجيل حَدَّ المُصحَفِ

(1.72) نزلت وسطه الخنازير والخمر وبارى الناقوس فيها الصليب
لو رآه المسيح لم يرض فعلاً زعموا أنه له منسوب
أبعد الناس عن عبادة ربِّ الناس قوم إلههم مصلوب

(1.73) للغَزوِ نشاطي وإِليه طَرَبِي مالي في العيش غَيرَه من أَرَبِ
بالجدِّ وبالجهاد نُجحُ الطَّلَبِ والرَّاحة مُستَودَعَة في التَّعَبِ

(1.74) اللّهم إنَّ العيشَ عيشُ الآخِرة فغفِر للأنصار والمهاجرة
نحن الّذين بايعُ محمّد على الجِهاد ما بَقينا ابدا

(1.75) لا راحة في العيش سوى أن أغزو ... سَيفِي طَرَبا إلى الطُّلى يهتزُّ
في ذُلِّ ذوي الكُفرِ يكونُ العِزُّ ... والقُدرَةُ في غيرِ جهاد عَجزُ

(1.76) أقسمتُ سوى الجهاد مالي أَرَب ... والرّاحةُ في سواه عندي تَعَبُ
إلا بالجدِّ لا يُنالُ الطَّلبُ ... والعَيشُ بلا جِدِّ جهاد لَعِبُ

(1.77) السيف أصدق أنباءُ من الكتب ... في حده الحب بين الجد والّعب

(1.78) يا عابدَ الحرمين لو أبصرتَنا ... لعلمتَ أنّكَ في العبادةِ تلعبُ
مَنْ كانَ يخضبُ خدَّه بدموعِه ... فنحورنُا بدمائِنا تَتَخَضَبُ
أوكان يتعبُ خيله في باطل ... فخيولنا يوم الصبيحة تتعبُ
ريحُ العبيرِ لكم ونحنُ عبيرُنا ... رَهْجُ السنابكِ والغبارُ الأطيبُ

(1.79) ذو الجِهَادَينِ مِن عدوٍّ ونَفسٍ ... فهو طول الحياةِ في هَيجاءِ

(1.80) ولكم مَكَرٍ قُمتَ فيه مُعلّما ... أَرضى إلهكَ وَلمسيحَ وَأَحمَدا

(1.81) يا شَمسُ لا كَسفٌ ولاَ تَكدَارُ ... ولاَ خَلَت من نُورِكَ الأَنوَارُ
البَدرُ مَنقوصٌ و أَنتَ كَامِلٌ ... لك السّرَايَا وله السّرَارُ
برؤك لِلإِسلاَم من أدوائه ... بُرء و في أعدائه بَوَارُ
مَا أَنتَ إِلاَّ السّيفُ صدَّ صدأً ... عن مَتنِهِ مَضرَبُه البَتَّارُ
لوكَنَ محمولاً أَذى عن مُنفِسٍ ... لَحَمَلَتهُ دُونَكَ الأَبصَارُ
ولو فَدَت أَرضٌ سماءَ سَاقت الـ ... ـملوكَ في فدائِكَ الأَمصَارُ

أَنتَ غيَاثُ مَحلَهم إِن أَجدبوا — وخيرهُم إِن ذُكر الخِيَارُ
وفي سريرِ الملك منهَا ملكٌ — اللهُ في سَرَّائه أسرَارُ
خَيرُ ملوكِ الأَرضِ جَدًّا وأَبَا — إِن هَزَّ عِطفَي مَاجدٍ نِجَارُ
مَدَّ علَى الدّين رِوَاقَ دولَةٍ — تنَازعت أَسمَارهَا السُّمَّارُ
علّت بنَايَاه وحلّت يدَه — فهي عليه السُّور وَلسِّوارُ
محمودٌ المحمودُ عصرُ ملكه — فلِلحَيا مِن مُزنِهِ اعتِصارُ
يا نورَ دينٍ أَظلَمَت آفاقُه — لَو لَم تبلَّج هذه الآثارُ
اللهُ أَيَّامُك مَا تخطُّه — بالمِسك من إِسفارِها الأَسفارُ
سَلِمت لِلإِسلاَمِ ترعى سَرحهُ — إِذا ونَى رُعَاتُه وجارُوا
شكوتَ فَالدُّنيَا على سُكَّانها — قرارةٌ جانبَها القَرَارُ
لا عَدِمت منك الأَماني ريّها — معطَى مِن الإِقبال مَا يختارُ
مَا سمح الدَّهرُ بأن تبقى لنا — فكلُّ جُرحٍ مَسَّنا جُبَارُ

(1.82) أنهيت عن شرب الخمور وأنت في — كاس المظالم طائش مخمور
عطلت كاسات المدام تعففا — وعليك كاسات الحرام تدور
ماذا تقول إذا تقلت إلَى البلى — فردا وجاءك منكر ونكير
ماذا تقول إذا وقفت بموقف — فردا ذليلا والحساب عسير
وتعلقت فيك الخصوم وأنت في — يوم الحساب مسلسل مجروم
وتفرقت عنك الجنود وأنت في — ضيق القبور موسد مقبور
ووددت أنك ما وتيت ولاية — يوما ولا قال الأنام أمير
وبقيت بعد العز رهن حفيرة — في عالم الموتى وأنت حقير
وحشرت عريانا حزينا باكيا — قلقا وما لك في الأنام مجير
أرضيت أن تحيا وقلبك دارس — عافَى الخراب وجسمك المعمور

أرضيت أن يحظى سواك بقربه | أبـدا وأنت معـذب مهجور
مهـد لنفـسك حجـة تجو بهـا | يوم المعاد ويوم تبـدو العور

(1.83) إن يمترَ الشُكّاك فيك فئتك الـ | ـمهـديُّ مطفئُ جَمرَةِ الدَّجّـالِ

(1.84) بَـدرٌ لأربعَ عَشرَةَ اقتـبسَ السَّـنا | من خمسَ عَشرَةَ سورة الأنفـالِ

(1.85) قـد جاء نَصرُ الله وَالفَـتحُ الذي | وُعِـدَ الرّسُولُ فسبّحوا وَاستَغفِرُوا
فُتِحَ الشّآم و طهِّرَ القُدسُ الذي | هو في القيـامة لِلأنام المَحشَرُ
واسـتَنقَذَ البيتَ المطَهَّر عَـنوَةً | من كلِّ ذي نَجِسٍ بكلِّ مُطَهَّرِ
وَارَيتَهُم لَمّا التقى الجـمعان بـالـ | بيت المقـدَّس هَولَ يومِ المحشرِ
ورَدَدتَ دينَ الله بعد قطوبـه | بالمسجـد الاقصى بوجـهٍ مُسـفِرِ

(1.86) دِ ميـاطُ طُورٌ ونـارالحرب موقَـدَةٌ | وَأنت موسى وهـذا اليوم مِقاتُ
أَلقِ العَصَـا تتلقّف كلَّ ما صَنعوا | ولا تَخَف ما حبـالُ القوم حَيّـاتُ

(1.87) سَـل البيتَ المقـدَّس عنـه يُخـ | ـبر بسورة فِتحِـهِ لَمّا تَلاهـا
محـا الناقوسَ والصُّلبـانَ عنـه | وأثبـتَ «هل أتى» فيها و «طاهـا

(1.88) إنَّ ظني والظن مثل سهام الرمي | منها المخطي ومنها المصيب
إنَّ هذا الان غدت ساحة القدس | ومـا للاسـلام فيـها نصيب

(1.89) والاسـبتار إلَى الدّاويـة التـأموا | كَأَنَّهُم سُدُّ يأجوج إذا اشـتجروا

(1.90) مَرَّ يومٌ مِنَ الزَّمـانِ عَجيبُ   كـاد يُبدي فيه السُّرورَ الجمادُ
إذ أتى الحاجِبُ الأَجَلُّ بأسرى   قَرنتَهُم فِي طيِّها الأَصفـادُ
بجمـالٍ كـأنَّهنَّ جبـالٌ   وعُـلوجٍ كـأنَّهُم أَطوَادُ
قُـلتُ بعـد التَّكبيرِ لمَّا تبَـدَّى   هـكذا هكذا يكونُ الجِهَادُ
حَبَّـذا لؤلؤٌ يَصِيدُ الأعـادي   وسِواهُ من اللآلي يُصَادُ

(1.91) الا هـكذا في الله تمضي العزائمُ   وتمضي لدى الحرب السيوف الصوارمُ

(1.92) ففي مواقفةِ البيتِ المُقَدّس لد   بيـتِ الحَرَامِ لنَـا تِيـهٌ وإِعجَابُ

(1.93) سِرتُ وَخَلَّفتُ فِي دِيَارِهِم   قلبًا اتمنيتُ أَنّـه بَصَـيرُ
وَلَم ازَلُ اغبُطُ المقيمَ بهم للقُرب   حتَّى غبطَتُ من أَسَـرُوا

(1.94) كم بلكنـائس من مبتلّة   مثـل المهـاة يزينـها الحفر
من كل سـاجدة لصورتها   لو ألصقت سجدت لها الصور
غرس الحيـاء بصحن وجنتها   وردًا سقى أغصَانـه النظـر
وتكلّمت فيهـا الجفون فـلو   حَاورتهـا لأجابك الحور

(1.95) كم لي بأنطاكية من هوى   لا أنثي عنـه بتعفيف
من كل بيضـاء مسـيحية   ما عنـدها البـدر بموصوف
فـالعين خوف العـين مصروفة   عنها ومـا القـلب بمصروف

(1.96) أَيهَا المَالكُ الذي الزم النّـا ... سَ سلوكَ المحجة البيضاء
قـد فَضَحتَ الملوكَ بالعَدلِ لمّا ... سِرتَ في النّاس سيرةَ الخُلَفاءِ

(1.97) لقـد فَتَنَتني فرنجيـة ... نسيمُ العبـير بها يَعبَقُ
ففي ثوبهـا غُصُن ناعـمٌ ... وفي تاجها قمرٌ مُشرِقُ
وإن تك في عينها زُرقة ... فإنّ سِنان القنا أَزرق

(1.98) وما أسدتم على أعداء دولتكم ... هـذا التأسـد إلا بعـد ما كلبوا

(1.99) لقـد قمتَ في نصـر النبي وآله ... مقـامًا على الرحمن قد حقّ أَجرُهُ
سرى ملك الإِفرنج ينصـرُ جمعهم ... فمَا ضرّهم في نصـرة الحقّ كفرُهُ

(2.0) أقمتَ عَـمُودَ الدينِ حين أمالَهُ ... لطـاغي الفرنج الغُتمِ بني سعدِ
وَجاهَدتَ حِزبَ الكُفرِ حتّى رَدَدتَهُم ... خـزايا عليهم خيبةُ الذُّلِ والرَّدِ

(2.1) يا رب، إني أرى مصرًا قد انتبهت ... لها عين الأعادي بعد رقدتها
فاجعـل بها ملة الإِسلام باقيـة ... واحرس عقود الهدى من حل عقدتها
وهب لنـا منك عونـًا نستجير بـه ... من فتنة يتلظى جمر وقدتها

(2.2) ومَا أحَدٌ في المُلكِ يَبقى مُخَلَّدًا ... ومَـا أحـدٌ ممّا قضَى الله يَسلَمُ
أمن بعد ما ذاق العِدى طعمَ حزبكم [بفيهم وكانت] وَهيَ صَابٌ وعلقمُ ر
رَجعتم إلى حُكمِ التّنافُسِ بَينكم ... وَفيكم منَ الشّحناء نارٌ تَضَرّمُ
أَما عندكم مَن يَتّقي الله وَحدَهُ ... أما في رَعاياكم منَ النّاسِ مُسلمُ
تَعـالَوا لعـلّ الله يَنصُـرُ دينَهُ ... إذا ما نصَرنا الدّينَ نحنُ وَأَنتُم
ونَنهض نحوَ الكـافِرينَ بعزمَـةٍ ... بأمثـالِها تُحوَى البـلادُ وتُقسَمُ

(2.3) ونـاجيك بالمهمات إذ أنت بالقـائها اليك خـليق
وأهـم الأمور أمر جهاد الكفـر فاسـمع فعنـدنا التحقيق

(2.4) فانهض الآن مسرعًا فبأمثالك مـا زال يدرك المطلوب
والق عنّا رسالة عند نور الدين مـا في القـائها مـا يريب

أيها العـادل الذي هو للدين شـباب وللحـروب شيب
والذي لم يزل قديمًا عن الاسلام بالعـزم منـه تجـلى الكروب
وغـدا منه للفـرنج إذا لاقوه يوم من الزمـان عصيب

إن يرم نزف حقدهم فلأشطان قنـاة في كل قلب قليب
غيرنا من يقول ما ليس يمضيه بفعـل وغيرك المكذوب
قـد كتبنا إليك فأوضح لنـا الآن بماذا عن الكتـاب تجيب
قصـدنا أن يكون منّا ومنكم أجـل في مسيرنا مضروب
فلدينا من العساكر ما ضاق بأدنـاهم الفضـاء الرحيب
وعلينا أن يستهل على الشام مكان الغيوث مـال صبيب
أو تـراها مثـل العروس تـراها كلّه من دم العدا مخضوب

(2.5) بالجدِّ أدركتَ ما أدركتَ لا اللعبِ كم راحةٍ جُنيت من دوحة التعب

فتحتَ مصرَ، وأرجو أن تصيرَ بها مُيَسّرًا فتحَ بيتِ القُدسِ عن كَثَبِ

لقد رَفعنا إلى الرحمن أيدينـاَ في شُكرِنا ما به الإسلامَ عَنك حُبِي
يشكو إليك بنو الإِسلامِ يُتمَهُمُ فقُمتَ فيهم مقامَ الوالدِ الحَدِبِ

في كل دارٍ من الإفرنج نادبةٌ   بما دهاهم، فقد باتوا على نَدَبِ
من شرِّ شاور أنقذتَ العبادَ، فكم   وكم قصيتَ لحزبِ الله من أرَبِ
هو الذي أطمعَ الأفرنج في بلد الـ   إسلامِ حتّى سعوا للقصدِ والطّلَبِ
رُدَّ الخلافةَ عباسية، ودَعِ الـ   ـدَّعيَّ فيها يصادف شرَّ مُنقلَبِ
لا تَقطَعَن ذَنَبَ الأفعى وتُرسِلها،   فالحزمُ عندي: قَطعُ الرأسِ والذّنبِ

(2.6) نامَ الخليفةُ واستطار لذَبّه   عن سُدَّتيه واستُطير رُقادُه

(2.7) قد خطبنا للمستضيء بمصرِ   نائب المصطفى إمامِ العَصرِ
و خَذَلنا لنُصرةِ العَضُدِ العا   ضدَ والقاصرَ الذي بالقَصرِ

وأشَعنا بها شعارَ بني العبّـ   ـاس فاستبشَرَت وُجوه النّصرِ
وتَرَكنا الدَّعيَّ يدعو ثُبُوراً   وهو بالذُّلِّ تَحتَ حَجرٍ وحَصرِ
وتباهَت منابرُ الدّينِ بالخُط   بة للهاشميِّ في أرضِ مِصرِ
ولدَينا تضاعفَت نِعَمُ اللّـ   ـهِ وجَلّت عن كلِّ عَدٍّ وحَصرِ
ما يُقامُ الإمامُ إلا بحقٍّ   ما تُحازُ الحسناءُ إلا بمهرِ

(2.8) صلاحَ الدين قد أصلحتَ دُنيا   شقيٍّ لم يَبِت إلّا حريصا
وأرسلت السلامَ لنا عموماً   وجُودُك جاءني وحدي خُصوصا
فكنتَ كيوسُفَ الصِّدّيقِ لمّا   تلقّى منه يعقوبُ القَميصَا

(2.9) هي العزائمُ لا بيضٌ وخرصانُ   بها استباحَ العُلى الأيقاظُ أوصانوا
المُلكُ دعوى إذا ما العزمُ صدّقها   أنت فتوحٌ لها في الخَلقِ برهانُ
فالصِّدقُ في القولِ والأفعالِ قاعدةٌ   لكلِّ أمرٍ له في النّاسِ بُنيانُ

المُلكُ يُبتاعُ طوعًا أو كراهيةً   والعَزمُ والجُود والإقدامُ أثمانُ
إنّ النّشاط حياةٌ ضوعِفت رُتَبًا   وليس يحسَبُ في الأحياءِ كسلانُ
سِياسةُ المُلك وزنٌ لا يقومُ به   إلاقويٌّ خ الاِحسانُ ميزانُ
مَن يُؤتِهِ اللهُ كلَّ الفضل يَسمُ له   فخالقُ الكلِّ بالكلّي منّانُ
للمُلكِ سرٌّ كما سرُّ النُّبُوّة في   تخصيص عبدٍ بما لم يُؤتَ إنسانُ
يواحدٍ تُملأُ الدنيا بما رَحُبَت   فيَستقيمُ إليه الإنسُ والجانُ
عنايةٌ من إله العرش مُظهِرةٌ   في الجزء ما الكُلُّ عن معناه عُميَانُ
مَاحرّكَ الشخصُ أهلَ الأرض مُنفردًا   إلاّ وفي المَلاء الأعلى له شَانُ
الله أنتَ عمادَ الدين من ملكٍ   هزّ البلادَ كمَا تهتزُّ أَغصَانُ

(2.10) فيوسفُ أجلاكم من الأرضِ عنوة   ويُجلي فما يُبقي عليكم نِفارُهُ

وكم واجمٍ من رَوعِه في ملوككم   عسى الفتحُ إبداءَ بهم مُستَثارُهُ

تجلّى بنورِ الدِّين ما تاهَ عصرُنا   به نامياً كهلَ التّمامِ وَقارُهُ

(2.11) دمشقُ لها منه شَمائلُ يوسفٍ   سماحًا وإقداما حمى مُستجَارُهُ

فيوسفُ بين المُلك الدّين واقفٌ   بسيفٍ وشرعٍ دائرٍ حيثُ دارُهُ

(2.12) ففاضت دموع العين مني صبابة   على ما مضى من عصرنا المتقدم

فلو كان يفدي بالنفوس فديته   بنفسي وهذا الظن في كل مسلم

(2.13) أَعَينيَ لا ترقى من العَبَرَاتِ　　صِلي في البُكا الآصالَ بالبُكُراتِ

لَعَلَّ سيولَ الدَّمعِ يُطفِئُ فَيضها　　تَوقُّدَ ما في القَلبِ مَن جَمَرَاتِ

ويا قَلبُ أسعِر نارَ وجدِك كلّما　　خَبَت بادِّكارٍ يَبعَثُ الحَسَرَاتِ

ويا فَم بُحْ بالشَّجوِ منك لَعَلَّه　　يروِّحُ ما ألقَى مِنَ الكُرُبات

على المَسجِدِ الأقصى الذي جلّ قدرُه　　على مَوطِنِ الإخبَاتِ والصَّلَواتِ

على مَنزِلِ الأَملاك والوحي والهُدَى　　على مَشهَدِ الأَبدال والبَدَلات

على سُلَّمِ المِعراج والصَّخرة التي　　أنافَت بما في الأَرض مِن صَخَرَاتِ

على القِبلَةِ الأُولى التي اتَّجهَت لها　　صلاةُ البَرَايا في اختلافِ جهاتِ

على خيرِ معمورٍ وأكرَمِ عامرٍ　　وأَشرَفِ مَبنِيّ لخيرِ بُنَاةِ

وما زالَ فيه للنَّبيين مَعبَدٌ　　يُوالونَ في أرجائِهِ السَّجَداتِ

عَفَا المَسجِدُ الأَقصَى المُبَارَكُ حَولَه الرّ(م) فِيعُ العمادِ لعالي الشُّرُفاتِ

عَفَا بعد ما قد كان للخير مَوسِمًا　　و للبِرِّ والإِحسانِ والقُرُباتِ

يُوافي إليه كلُّ أشعَثَ قانِتٍ　　لمولاه بَرٍّ دائمِ الخَلَواتِ

خلا مِن صلاة لا يَمَلُّ مُقيمُها　　تُوَشَّحُ بالآياتِ والسُّوَراتِ

خَلاَ مِن حنينِ التّائبين وحزنهم　　فَمِن بينِ نُوَّاحٍ وبينِ بُكَاةِ

لِتبكِ علَى القدس البلادُ بِأسرِهَا　　وتعلنُ بالأَحزانِ وَالتّرَحَاتِ

لِتبكِ عليها مكّةُ فَهي أختُها　　وتشكو الذي لاقت إِلَى عَرَفَاتِ

لِتَبكِ علَى مَا حلَّ بالقُدسِ طَيبَةٌ　　وتَشرَحُهُ في أكرَمِ الحُجُرَاتِ

لَقَد أَشمَتُوا عكّا وصورَ بهدمها　　ويا طَالما غادَتهُمَا بشَمَاتِ

لقد شَتَّتُوا عنهَا جماعة أهلها　　وكلُّ اجتمَاعٍ مُؤذِن بشَتَاتِ

وقد هَدّموا مجدَ الصَّلاحِ بهدمِها　　وقد كان مجدًا بَاذِخَ الغُرُفَاتِ

Bibliography

Primary Sources

ʿAbd al-Raḥmān b. Isḥāq b. Shīth al-Qunawī. *Miftāḥ al-maqāṣid wa-miṣbāḥ al-marāṣid fī ziyārat bayt al-maqdis* (M/S copying department, 1963, no. 46304/514, a collection from *Miftāḥ al-maqāṣid*).

ʿAbd al-Raḥmān b. Isḥāq b. Shīth al-Qunawī. 'Miftāḥ al-maqāṣid wa-miṣbāḥ al-marāṣid fī ziyārat bayt al-maqdis,' in *Faḍāʾil bayt al-maqdis fī makhṭūṭāt ʿArabiyya qadīma*, edited by Maḥmūd Ibrāhīm, 266–267. Kuwait: Maʿhad al-Makhṭūṭāt al-ʿArabiyya, al-Munaẓẓama al-ʿArabiyya lil-Tarbiyya wa-l-Thaqāfa wa-l-ʿUlūm, 1985.

Abū l-Fidā. *al-Mukhtaṣar fī akhbār al-bashr: tārīkh Abī l-Fidā*. Vol. 1. Cairo, 19–.

Abū Ḥayyān al-Andalusī. *al-Baḥr al-muḥīṭ*. Vol. 7. Cairo: Maktaba al-Saʿāda, 1910.

Abū Shāma. *al-Dhayl ʿalā l-rawḍatayn*. Edited by Ibrāhīm Shams al-Dīn. Beirut: Dār al-Kutub al-ʿIlmiyya, 2002.

Abū Shāma. *Kitāb al-Rawḍatayn fī akhbār al-dawlatayn al-nūriyya wa-l-ṣalāḥiyya*. Edited by Ibrāhīm Shams al-Dīn. 4 vols. Beirut: Dār al-Kutub al-ʿIlmiyya, 2002.

Abū Tammām. *Dīwān Abī Tammām*. Edited by M. A. Azzam. Cairo: Dār al-Maʿārif, 1951.

al-ʿAẓīm Ābādī. *ʿAwn al-maʿbūd: Sharḥ Sunan Abī Dāwūd*. Vol. 7. Cairo, 2001.

al-Bayḍāwī. *Tafsīr al-Bayḍāwī*. Vol. 1. Beirut: Dār al-Kutub al-ʿIlmiyya, 2001.

Bernard of Clairvaux. 'Epistolae,' in *Sancti Bernardi Opera* (no. 363), edited by J. Leclercq and H. Rochais. Vol. 8, 311–317. Rome, 1955–77.

David, C. W. (ed. and trans.). *De Expugnatione Lyxbonensi: The Conquest of Lisbon*. New York: Columbia University Press, 2001.

al-Dhahabī. *Siyar aʿlām al-nubalāʾ*. Vol. 12. Cairo: Maktaba al-Ṣafāʾ, 2003.

Guibert of Nogent. *Dei Gesta Per Francos*, edited by Robert B. C. Huygens, Corpus Christianorum, Continuatio Mediaevalis 127A. Turnhout, 1996.

al-Ḥanbalī, Ibn al-ʿImād (ʿAbd al-Ḥayy b. Aḥmad). *Shadharāt al-dhahab fī akhbār man dhahab*. Cairo, 1931–32.

Ibn Abī l-Wafāʾ al-Maqdisī. *Īqāẓ al-ghāfil bi-sīrat al-Malik al-ʿĀdil Nūr al-Dīn al-Shahīd*. Beirut: al-Maktabat al-ʿAṣriyya, 2006.

Ibn al-ʿAdīm. *Zubdat al-ḥalab fī tārīkh Ḥalab*. Edited by Sami al-Dahan. Damascus: al-Maʿhad al-Faransī bi-Dimashq lil-Dirāsāt al-ʿArabiyya, 1955.

Ibn ʿAsākir. *Tārīkh Madinat Dimashq*. Edited by Muḥibb al-Dīn al-ʿAmrawī. Vol. 1. Beirut: Dār al-Fikr, 1995.

Ibn al-Athīr. *al-Kāmil fī l-tārīkh*. Edited by ʿUmar ʿAbd al-Salām al-Tadmurī. Vol. 9. Beirut: Dār al-Kutub al-ʿArabī, 2006.

Ibn al-Athīr. *al-Tārīkh al-bāhir fī l-dawla al-Atābikiyya*. Cairo: Dār al-Kutub al-Ḥadītha, 1963.

Ibn al-Ḥawrānī. *al-Ishārāt ilā amākin al-ziyārāt*. Edited by B. A. al-Jābī. Damascus: Maktabat al-Ghazālī, 1981.

Ibn al-Jawzī. *Faḍā'il al-Quds*. Edited by Jibra'il S. Jabbūr. Beirut: Dār al-Afaq al-Jadīda, 1979.

Ibn al-Jawzī. *al-Muntaẓam fī tārīkh al-mulūk wa-l-umam*. Vol. 9. Hyderabad: Maṭbaʿat Dā'irat al-Maʿārif al-ʿUthmāniyya, 1940.

Ibn al-Jawzī. *Ṣayd al-khāṭir*. Cairo, 1999.

Ibn al-Jawzī. *al-Shifā' fī mawāʿiẓ al-mulūk wa-l-khulafā'*. Edited by Fu'ād ʿAbd al-Munʿim Aḥmad. Mecca, 1991.

Ibn Jubayr. *Tadhkira al-akhbār ʿan ittifāqāt al-asfār*. Edited by ʿAlī Aḥmad Kanʿān. Beirut, 2001.

Ibn Jubayr. *Rihla*. Edited by W. Wright. Leiden, 1907.

Ibn Kathīr. *al-Bidāya wa-l-nihāya*. Vols. 12 and 13. Cairo: Dār al-Taqwa, 2004.

Ibn Kathīr. 'Kitāb al-ijtihād fī ṭalab al-jihād,' in *Arbaʿa kutub fī l-jihād min ʿaṣr al-ḥurūb al-ṣalībiyya*, edited by Suhayl Zakkār, 413–436. Damascus: Dār al-Takwīn, 2007.

Ibn Kathīr. *al-Sīrat al-Nabawiyya*. Vol. 2. Edited by Muṣṭafā ʿAbd al-Wāḥid. Beirut: Dār al-Iḥyā' al-Turāth al-ʿArabiyya, n.d.

Ibn Kathīr. *Tafsīr al-Qur'ān al-ʿaẓīm*. Beirut: Dār al-Maʿrifa, 2003.

Ibn al-Khayyāṭ. *Dīwān ibn al-Khayyāṭ*. Edited by Khalil Mardam Bek. Beirut: Dār Ṣādir, 1994.

Ibn al-Mubārak. *Kitab al-Jihād*. Beirut: Dār al-Nūr, 1971.

Ibn al-Mubārak. *Kitāb al-Zuhd wa-yalīhi kitāb al-raqā'iq*. Beirut: Dār al-Kutub al-ʿIlmiyya, 2004.

Ibn Muʿmar, Jamīl. *Dīwān Jamīl Buthaynah: Jamīl b. Muʿmar*. Edited by Fawzī ʿAṭawī. Beirut: Dār Saʿb, 1980.

Ibn al-Murajja. *Faḍā'il bayt al-maqdis*. Beirut, 2002.

Ibn Qāḍī Shuhbah. *al-Kawākib al-durriyya fī l-sīrat al-nūriyya*. Beirut: Dār al-Kitāb al-Jadīd, 1971.

Ibn al-Qalānisī. *Tārīkh Dimashq* 360–555 H. Edited by S. Zakkār. Damascus, 1983.

Ibn al-Qaysarānī. *Dīwān Muḥammad b. Naṣr b. Ṣaghīr al-Qaysarānī*. Manuscript no. 1484. Cairo: Dār al-Kutub al-Miṣriyya.

Ibn al-Qayyim al-Jawziyya. *Zād al-maʿād fī hady khayr al-ʿibād*. Vol. 3, edited by Muṣṭafa ʿAbd al-Qādir ʿAṭā. Beirut: Dār al-Kutub al-ʿIlmiyya, 1998.

Ibn Qudāma al-Maqdisī. *al-Kāfi fī fiqh al-Imām Aḥmad b. Ḥanbal*. Beirut: Dār Ibn Ḥazm, 2003.

Ibn Qutayba. *ʿUyūn al-akhbār*. Vol. 2. Cairo, 1973.

Ibn Rajab al-Ḥanbalī. *Faḍl al-ʿilm al-salaf aʿlā ʿilm al-khalaf*. Edited by Muḥammad Nāṣir al-ʿAjamī. Beirut: Dār al-Bashā'ir al-Islāmiyya, 2003.

Ibn Ruzzīk. *Dīwān Ṭalāʾiʿ Ibn Ruzzīk*. Najaf: al-Maktabat al-Ahliyya, 1964.

Ibn Sanāʾ al-Mulk. *Dīwān ibn Sanāʾ al-Mulk*. Vol. 2. Edited by Muḥammad Ibrāhīm Naṣr. Cairo: Wizārat al-Thaqāfa, 1969.

Ibn Shaddād. 'Kitāb Faḍāʾil al-Jihād,' in *Arbaʿa kutub fī l-jihād min ʿasr al-ḥurūb al-Ṣalībiyya*. Edited by Suhayl Zakkār, 183–273. Damascus: Dār al-Takwīn, 2007.

Ibn Shaddād. *Min kitāb al-nawādir al-sulṭāniyya wa-l-maḥāsin al-yūsufiyya*, edited by Muḥammad Darwīsh. Damascus: Dār al-Takwīn, 1979.

Ibn Taghrībirdī. *al-Nujūm al-zāhira fī mulūk Miṣr wa-l-Qāhira*. Vol. 5. Cairo: Dār al-Kutub wa-l-Wathāʾiq al-Qawmiyya, 2005.

Ibn Taymīyya. *al-Jawāb al-ṣaḥīḥ li-man baddala dīn al-Masīḥ*, edited by ʿAlī b. Ḥasan b. Nāṣir, ʿAbd al-ʿAzīz b. Ibrāhīm al-ʿAskar, and Ḥamdān b. Muḥammad al-Ḥamdān. 6 vols. Riyadh: Dār al-ʿĀṣima, 1993/4.

Ibn Ṭūlūn. *al-Qalāʾid al-jawhariyya fī tārīkh al-Ṣāliḥiyya*. Part 2. Edited by Muḥammad Aḥmad Daḥmān. Damascus, 1980.

Ibn Wāṣil. *Mufarrij al-kurūb fī akhbār Banī Ayyūb*. Vols. 1–2. Edited by Jamāl al-Dīn al-Shayyāl. Cairo: Dār al-Kutub, 1953.

Ibn Wāṣil. *Mufarrij al-kurūb fī akhbār Banī Ayyūb*. Vol. 4. Edited by Ḥusayn Muḥammad Rabiʿ. Cairo: Dār al-Kutub, 1977.

ʿImād al-Dīn al-Iṣfahānī. *al-Fatḥ al-qussī fī l-fatḥ al-qudsī*. Edited by Muḥammad Ṣubḥ. Cairo: al-Dār al-Qawmiyya lil-Ṭibāʿa wa-l-Nashr, 1965.

ʿImād al-Dīn al-Iṣfahānī. *Kharīdat al-qaṣr wa-jarīdat al-ʿaṣr: qism shuʿarāʾ al-Shām*. Vol. 1. Edited by Shukrī Fayṣal. Damascus: Dār al-Kutub wa-l-Wathāʾiq al-Qawmiyya, 1955.

al-Isnawī, Jamāl al-Dīn ʿAbd al-Raḥīm. *Ṭabaqāt al-Shāfiʿiyya*. Beirut, 1987.

al-Jilyānī al-Andalusī, ʿAbd al-Muʿnim. *Dīwān al-tadbīj*. Edited by Kamāl Abū Dīb. Beirut: Dār al-Sāqī, 2010.

al-Khaṭīb al-Baghdādī. *al-Jāmiʿ li-akhlāq al-rāwī wa-adāb al-sāmiʿ*. Beirut: Dār al-Kutub al-ʿIlmīyya, 2003.

al-Kutubī. *Fawāt al-wafayāt wa-l-dhayl ʿalayhā*. Vol. 1. Edited by Iḥsān ʿAbbās. Beirut: Dār Ṣādir, 1973.

al-Mundhirī. *Summarized Ṣaḥīh Muslim*. Vol. 1. Riyadh: Darussalam Publishers, 2000.

al-Mutanabbī. *Dīwān al-Mutanabbī*. Beirut: Dār Bayrūt lil-Ṭibāʿa wa-l-Nashr, 1975.

al-Nuʿaymī. *al-Dāris fī tārīkh al-madāris*. Vols. 1 and 2. Damascus: al-Majmaʿ al-ʿIlmī l-ʿArabī bi-Dimashq, 1951.

al-Nuwayrī. *Nihāyat al-arab fī funūn al-adab*. Vol. 6. Cairo: Dār al-Kutub, 1925.

Otto of Freising. *Ottonis et Rahewini Gesta Friderici I. imperatoris*. Edited by G. Waitz. Hanover: Hannverae et Lipsiae: Impensis Biblipoli Hahniani, 1912.

Qāḍī l-Fāḍil. *Dīwān al-Qāḍī l-Fāḍil*. Cairo: Dār al-Maʿrifa, 1961.

al-Qurṭubī. *Mukhtaṣar tafsīr al-Qurṭubī*. Vol. 1. Beirut: Dār al-Kutub al-ʿIlmiyya, 2001.

al-Rabāʿī. 'Faḍāʾil al-Shām wa-Faḍl Dimashq,' in *Faḍāʾil al-Shām*, edited by Abī ʿAbd al-Raḥmān ʿĀdil b. Saʿd, 47–116. Beirut: Dār al-Kutub al-ʿIlmiyya, 2001.

al-Rāzī. *Tafsīr al-kabīr*. Vol. 10, part 20. Beirut: Dār al-Kutub al-ʿIlmiyya, 2004.

Recueil des historiens des croisades. 16 vols. Paris: Imprimerie royale, 1841–1906.

al-Samʿānī. 'Faḍāʾil al-Shām,' in *Faḍāʾil al-Shām*, edited by Abī ʿAbd al-Raḥmān ʿĀdil b. Saʿd, 119–149. Beirut: Dār al-Kutub al-ʿIlmiyya, 2001.

Sibṭ ibn al-Jawzī. *Mirʾāt al-zamān fī tārīkh al-aʿyān*. Vol. 8, parts 1 and 2. Hyderabad, 1952.

al-Sulamī. 'Kitāb al-Jihād,' in *Arbaʿa kutub fī l-jihād min ʿasr al-ḥurūb al-ṣalībiyya*, edited by Suhayl Zakkār, 41–165. Damascus: Dār al-Takwīn, 2007.

al-Ṭabarī. *Tafsīr al-Ṭabarī*. Vol. 5. Edited by Hānī l-Ḥajj, ʿImād Zakī l-Barūdī, and Khayrī Saʿīd. Cairo: Dār al-Tawfiqiyya li-Ṭibāʿa, 2004.

al-Ṭabarsī, Abū ʿAlī. *Majmaʿ al-bayān fī tafsīr al-Qurʾān*. Beirut: Dār Maktabat al-Ḥayāt, 1961.

al-Wāqidī. *Kitāb al-Maghāzī*. Edited by Marsden Jones. Beirut: ʿAlam al-Kutub, 2006.

al-Wāsiṭī. *Faḍāʾil al-bayt al-muqaddas*. Edited by Isaac Hasson. Jerusalem: Hebrew University of Jerusalem, 1979.

William of Tyre. *Guillaume de Tyr, Chronique, Édition critique, Corpus Christianorum Continuatio Mediaevalis* LXIII. Edited by R. B. C. Huygens, H. E. Mayer, and G. Rösch. 2 vols. Turnhout: Brepols, 1986.

Primary Sources in Translation

al-Bukhārī. *Summarized Ṣaḥīh al-Bukhāri*. Translated by Muḥsin Khān. Riyadh: Maktaba Dar-us-Salam, 1994.

Christie, N. *The Book of the Jihad of ʿAli ibn Tahir al-Sulami (d. 1106): Text, Translation and Commentary*. Farnham: Ashgate, 2015.

Gabrieli, F. *Arab Historians of the Crusades* [*Storici Arabi delle Crociate*]. Berkeley and Los Angeles: University of California Press, 1969.

al-Ghazālī. *Naṣīḥat al-mulūk* (Ghazālī's Book of Counsel for Kings). Translated by F. R. C. Bagley. Edited by Jalāl Humāʾī and H. D. Isaacs. London: Oxford University Press, 1964.

al-Ghazālī. *Revival of Religious Learnings: Imam Ghazzali's Ihya Ulum-id-Din*. Translated by Fazl-ul-Karim. 4 vols. in 2. Karachi: Darul-Ishaat, 1993.

al-Harawī. *A Lonely Wayfarer's Guide to Pilgrimage* [*Kitāb al-Ishārāt ilā maʿrifat al-ziyārāt*]. Translated by Josef W. Meri. Princeton, NJ: Darwin Press, 2004.

Ibn al-Athīr. *The Chronicle of Ibn al-Athīr for the Crusading Period from al-Kāmil fīʾl-Tārīkh*, parts 1–3. Aldershot: Ashgate, 2006–08.

Ibn al-Jawzī. *Kitāb al-Quṣṣās wa-l-mudhakkirīn*. Translated by Merlin S. Swartz. Beirut: Dār al-Mashriq, 1986.

Ibn Jubayr. *The Travels of Ibn Jubayr*. Translated by Roland Broadhurst. London: J. Cape, 1952.

Ibn Kathīr. *Book of the End: Great Trials and Tribulations*. Translated by Faisal Shafiq. Edited by ʿAbd al-Aḥad. London: Darussalam Publishers, 2006.

Ibn Kathīr. *Tafsīr ibn Kathīr* (Abridged). Vol. 2. Edited by Safiur-Rahmān al-Mubārakpuri. Riyadh: Darussalam, 2000.

Ibn Khallikān. *Wafayāt al-aʿyān wa-anbāʾ abnaʾ al-zamān*. Vols. 1–7 translated by M. de Slane. Edited by S. Moinul Haq. New Delhi: Kitab Bhavan, 1996.

Ibn al-Qalānisī. *The Damascus Chronicle of the Crusades*. Translated by H. A. R. Gibb. New York: Dover Publications, 2002.

Ibn Shaddād, Bahāʾ al-Dīn. *The Rare and Excellent History of Saladin*. Translated by D. S. Richards. Aldershot: Ashgate, 2002.

Ibn Taymiyya. *The Decisive Criterion between the Friends of Allāh and the Friends of Shayṭān*. Translated by Abū Rumaysah. Birmingham: Daar Us-Sunnah Publishers, 2006.

al-Maqrīzī. *A History of the Ayyūbid Sulṭāns of Egypt*. Translated by R. J. C. Broadhurst. Boston: Twayne Publishers, 1980.

Meisami, J. S. (trans. and ed.). *The Sea of Precious Virtues* (*Baḥr al-Fawāʾid*): *A Medieval Islamic Mirror for Princes*. Salt Lake City: University of Utah Press, 1991.

al-Muqaddasī. *Aḥsan al-taqāsīm fī maʿrifat al-aqālīm* (The Best Divisions for Knowledge of the Regions). Translated by Basil Anthony Collins. Reading: Garnet Publishing, 1994.

Nāṣir-i Khusraw. *Book of Travels*. Edited and translated by Wheeler M. Thackston Jr. Costa Mesa, CA: Mazda Publishers, 2001.

Peters, E. (ed.). *The First Crusade : the Chronicle of Fulcher of Chartres and other Source Materials*, 2nd edition University of Pennsylvania Press: Philadelphia, Pennsylvania, 1998.

Usāma ibn Munqidh. *An Arab-Syrian Gentleman and Warrior in the Period of the Crusades*. Translated by P. K. Hitti. New York: Columbia University Press, 2000.

Usāma ibn Munqidh. *The Book of Contemplation: Islam and the Crusades*. Translated by P. M. Cobb. London: Penguin Classics, 2008.

Usāma ibn Munqidh. *Kitāb al-Iʿtibār*. Edited by Philip K. Hitti. Princeton, NJ: Princeton University Press, 1930.

al-Wāqidī. *The Islamic Conquest of Syria*. Translated by Sulayman al-Kindi. London: Ta-Ha Publishers, 2005.

Secondary Material

ʿAbd al-Mahdī, ʿA. J. Husain. *Bayt al-maqdis fī adab al-ḥurūb al-ṣalībiyya*. Amman: Dār al-Bashīr, 1989.

ʿAbd al-Mahdī, ʿA. J. Husain. *al-Madāris fī bayt al-maqdis fī l-ʿaṣrayn al-Ayyūbī wa-l-Mamlūkī*. Vol. 1. Amman: Maktabat al-Aqṣā, 1981.

Abel, A. 'Changements politiques et littérature eschatologique dans le monde musulman.' *SI* 2 (1954), 23–43.

Adra, N. 'Dance and Glance: Visualizing Tribal Identity in Highland Yemen.' *Visual Anthropology* 11:1–2 (1998), 55–102.

Afsaruddin, A. *Excellence and Precedence: Medieval Islamic Discourse on Legitimate Leadership*. Leiden: E.J. Brill, 2002.

Agha, S. S. 'Of Verse, Poetry, Great Poetry, and History,' in *Poetry and History: The Value of Poetry in Reconstructing Arab History*, edited by R. Baalbaki, S. S. Agha, and T. Khalidi, 1–35. Beirut: American University of Beirut Press, 2011.

Ahmad, Hilmy. 'Abū Shāma.' *EI*², 1:150–151.

Aḥmad, M. H. M. 'Some Notes on Arabic Historiography during the Zengid and Ayyūbid Periods (521/1127–648/1250),' in *Historians of the Middle East*, edited by Bernard Lewis and P. M. Holt, 79–97. New York: Oxford University Press, 1962.

Akkach, S. *Cosmology and Architecture in Premodern Islam: An Architectural Reading of Mystical Ideas*. Albany: State University of New York Press, 2005.

al-Albānī, Nāṣir al-Dīn. *Silsilat al-aḥādīth al-ṣaḥīḥa*. Vol. 2. Beirut, 1985.

Ali, S. A. *Arabic Literary Salons in the Islamic Middle Ages: Poetry, Public Performance, and the Presentation of the Past*. Notre Dame, IN: University of Notre Dame Press 2010.

Allen, R. *An Introduction to Arabic Literature*. Cambridge: Cambridge University Press, 2000.

Angold, M. *The Byzantine Empire, 1025–1204: A Political History*. London: Longman, 1997.

Arberry, A. J. *Arabic Poetry: A Primer for Students*. Cambridge: Cambridge University Press, 1965.

Arberry, A. J. *Kings and Beggars: The First Two Chapters of Sadi's Gulistan*. London: Luzac & Co., 1945.

al-Asali, K. J. 'Kutub al-qarn al-khāmis al-hijrī fī faḍā'il bayt al-maqdis' [The Books of the fifth century hijrī on the merits of Jerusalem: A study and bibliography]. *Risalat al-Maktaba* 16 (1981), 5–13.

Atiya, A. *Crusade, Commerce and Culture*. London: Oxford University Press, 1962.

Ayalon, D. *Outsiders in the Lands of Islam: Mamlūks, Mongols and Eunuchs*. Aldershot: Variorum, 1988.

Azzam, A. R. *Saladin*. London: Pearson, 2009.

Badawī, A. A. *al-Ḥayāt al-adabiyya fī ʿaṣr al-ḥurūb al-ṣalībiyya bi-Miṣr wa-l-Shām*. Cairo: Dār Nahdat Miṣr, 1979.

Badawi, M. M. *A Critical Introduction to Modern Arabic Poetry*. Cambridge: Cambridge University Press, 1975.

Badawi, M. M. 'The Function of Rhetoric in Medieval Arabic Poetry: Abū Tammam's Ode on Amorium.' *Journal of Arabic Literature* 9 (1978), 43–56.

al-Bakrī, A. ʿU. *Jughrāfiyāt al-Andalus wa-Uruba min kitāb mamālik li Abī ʿUbayd al-Bakrī*. Edited by A. al-Ḥajj. Baghdad, 1968.

Bashear, S. 'Muslim Apocalypses and the Hour: A Case-Study in Traditional Reinterpretation.' *IOS* 13, edited by Joel L. Kraemer, 75–99. Leiden: Brill, 1993.

Bauer, T. 'The Arabic Ghazal: Formal and Thematic Aspects of a Problematic Genre,' in *Ghazal as World Literature II: From a Literary Genre to a Great Tradition: The Ottoman Ghazel in Context*, edited by Angelika Neuwirth, Michael Hess, Judith Pfeiffer, and Borte Sagaster, 3–13. Beirut and Würzburg: Ergon, 2006.

Bellver, J. 'Ibn Barraǧān and Ibn 'Arabī on the Prediction of the Capture of Jerusalem in 583/1187 by Saladin.' *Arabica* 61 (2014), 252–286.

Berkey, J. P. *Popular Preaching and Religious Authority in the Medieval Islamic Near East*. Seattle and London: University of Washington Press, 2001.

Bloom, J. M. 'Jerusalem in Medieval Islamic Literature,' in *City of the Great King: Jerusalem from David to the Present*, edited by Nitza Rosovsky, 205–217. Cambridge, MA and London: Harvard University Press, 1996.

Bosworth, C. E. 'Ibn 'Asākir,' *Encyclopedia of Arabic Literature*. Vol. 1, edited by J. S. Meisami and P. Starkey. London: Routledge, 1998.

Bosworth, C. E. 'Review: Amikam Elad, Medieval Jerusalem and Islamic Worship: Holy Places, Ceremonies, Pilgrimage.' *BSOAS* 60 (1997), 132–133.

Bowering, G. and Y. Casewit (eds.). *A Qur'an Commentary by Ibn Barrjan of Seville (d. 536/1141)*: *Idah al-Hikma bi-Ahkam al-'Ibra* (Wisdom Deciphered, the Unseen Discovered). Texts and Studies on the Qur'an. Leiden: Brill, 2015.

Braginsky, V. I. *The Comparative Study of Traditional Asian Literatures*. Richmond: Curzon, 2001.

Bray, J. 'Poetry, Arabic,' in *Medieval Islamic Civilization: An Encyclopedia*. Vol. 2, edited by Josef W. Meri and Jere L. Bacharach, 616–617. New York: Routledge, 2006.

Brett, M. 'The Fāṭimids and the Counter-Crusade, 1099–1171,' in *Egypt and Syria in the Fāṭimid, Ayyūbid and Mamlūk Eras: Proceedings of the 11th, 12th and 13th International Colloquium organised at the Katholieke Universiteit in Leuven in May 2002, 2003 and 2004*, edited by U. Vermeulen and K. D. Hustler, 15–26. Leuven: Peeters, 2007.

Brundage, J. A. 'Humbert of Romans and the Legitimacy of Crusader Conquests,' in *The Horns of Ḥaṭṭīn*, edited by B. Z. Kedar, 302–313. London: Variorum, 1992.

Cahen, C. 'Ayyūbids.' *EI*², 1:796–807.

Cahen, C. 'History and Historians: The Post-Classical Period,' in *Religion, Learning and Science in the 'Abbasid Period*, edited by M. J. L. Young, J. D. Latham, and R. B. Serjeant, 188–232. Cambridge and New York: Cambridge University Press, 1990.

Cahen, C. 'Ibn al-Ḳalānisī.' *EI*², 3:815.

Cahen, C. 'Sibṭ.' *EI*², 3:752–753.

Cantarino, V. *Arabic Poets in the Golden Age*. Studies in Arabic Literature 4. Leiden: E.J. Brill, 1975.

Casanova, P. *Mohammed et la fin du monde*. Paris: P. Geuthner, 1911–24.

Caton, S. C. *'Peaks of Yemen I Summon': Poetry as Cultural Practice in a North Yemeni Tribe*. London: University of California Press, 1990.

Chamberlain, M. 'The Crusader Era and the Ayyūbid Dynasty,' in *The Cambridge History of Egypt*. Vol. 1: *Islamic Egypt 640–1517*, edited by C. F. Petry, 211–241. Cambridge: Cambridge University Press, 1998.

Chamberlain, M. *Knowledge and Social Practice in Medieval Damascus, 1190–1350*. Cambridge: Cambridge University Press, 2002.

Christie, N. 'Crusade Literature: 9th to 15th Century,' in *Encyclopedia of Women and Islamic Cultures*. Vol. 1: *Methodologies, Paradigms and Sources*, edited by S. Joseph et al., 16–21. Leiden: Brill, 2003.

Christie, N. 'Ibn al-Qalānisī,' in *Medieval Muslim Historians and the Franks in the Levant*, edited by Alex Mallett, 7–28. Leiden: Brill, 2014.

Christie, N. 'Jerusalem in the Kitāb al-Jihād of 'Alī ibn Ṭāhir al-Sulamī.' *Medieval Encounters* 13, no. 2 (2007), 209–221.

Christie, N. 'Motivating Listeners in the *Kitāb al-Jihād* of 'Alī ibn Ṭāhir al-Sulamī (d. 1106).' *Crusades* 6 (2007), 1–14.

Christie, N. *Muslims and Crusaders: Christianity's Wars in the Middle East, 1095–1382, from the Islamic Sources*. Abingdon: Routledge, 2014.

Cobb, P. M. *The Race for Paradise: An Islamic History of the Crusades*. Oxford: Oxford University Press, 2014.

Cobb, P. M, 'Virtual Sacrality: Making Muslim Syria Sacred Before the Crusades,' in *Medieval Encounters: Jewish, Christian and Muslim Culture in Conference and Dialogue* 8, 39–55. Leiden: Brill, 2002.

Cobb, P. M. *White Banners: Contention in 'Abbasid Syria*, 750–880. Albany: State University of New York Press, 2001.

Constable, G. 'The Historiography of the Crusades,' in *The Crusades from the Perspective of Byzantium and the Muslim World*, edited by A. E. Laiou and R. P. Mottahedeh, 1–22. Washington, DC: Harvard University Press, 2001.

Cook, D. *Martyrdom in Islam*. Cambridge: Cambridge University Press, 2007.

Cook, D. 'Muslim Apocalyptic and Jihād.' *JSAI* 20 (1996), 66–104.

Cook, M. *Commanding Right and Forbidding Wrong in Islamic Thought*. Cambridge: Cambridge University Press, 2000.

Dajani-Shakeel, H. 'Diplomatic Relations between Muslim and Frankish Rulers,' in *Crusaders and Muslims in Twelfth-Century Syria*, edited by M. Shatzmiller, 190–215. Leiden: Brill, 1993.

Dajani-Shakeel, H. 'Displacement of the Palestinians during the Crusades.' *Muslim World* 68, no. 3 (1978), 158–162.

Dajani-Shakeel, H. 'Egypt and the Egyptians: A Focal Point in the Policies and Literature of al-Qāḍī al-Fāḍil.' *Journal of Near Eastern Studies* 36 (1977), 25–38.

Dajani-Shakeel, H. 'Jerusalem and the First Crusade,' in *Jerusalem's Heritage: Essays in Memory of Kāmil Jamil Asali*, edited by Ṣāliḥ Ḥamārina, 39–55. Amman: al-Jāmiʿa al-Urduniyya, 1996.

Dajani-Shakeel, H. '*Jihād* in Twelfth-Century Arabic Poetry: A Moral and Religious Force to Counter the Crusades.' *Muslim World* 66 (1976), 96–113.

Dajani-Shakeel, H. 'A Reassessment of Some Medieval and Modern Perceptions of the Counter-Crusade,' in *The Jihād and its Times*, edited by Hadia Dajani-Shakeel and Ronald A. Messier, 41–70. Ann Arbor, MI: University of Michigan, 1991.

Dajani-Shakeel, H. 'Some Medieval Accounts of Saladin's Recovery of Jerusalem (Al-Quds),' in *Studia Palaestina: Studies in honour of Constantine K. Zurayk*, edited by H. Nashabe, 83–113. Beirut, 1988.

Dodd, E. C. and S. Khairallah. 'The Dome of the Rock,' in *The Image of the Word: A Study of Quranic Verses in Islamic Architecture*, edited by E. C. Dodd and S. Khairallah, vol. 1, 19–26. Beirut: American University Press, 1981.

Duri, A. A. 'Jerusalem in the Early Islamic Period 7th–11th Centuries AD,' in *Jerusalem in History*, edited by K. J. Asali, 105–129. Essex: Scorpion Publishing, 1989.

Dyer, Rebecca. 'Poetry of Politics and Mourning: Mahmoud Darwish's Genre-Transforming Tribute to Edward W. Said.' *Remapping Genre* 122, no. 5 (Oct. 2007), 1447–1462.

Eddé, A. M. *Saladin*. Paris: Flammarion, 2008.

Ehrenkreutz, A. S. *Saladin*. Albany: State University of New York Press, 1972.

El-Awaisi, A. F. 'The Significance of Jerusalem in Islam: An Islamic Reference.' *Journal of Islamic Jerusalem Studies* 1 (1998), 47–71.

El-Cheikh, N. M. 'Byzantine Leaders in Arabic-Muslim Texts,' in *Elites Old and New in the Byzantine and Early Islamic Near East: Papers of the Sixth Workshop of Late Antiquity and Early Islam*, edited by J. Haldon and L. I. Conrad, 109–132. Princeton, NJ: Darwin Press. 2004.

El-Cheikh, N. M. *Byzantium Viewed by the Arabs*. London: Harvard Middle Eastern Monographs XXXVI, 2005.

El-Hibri, T. *Reinterpreting Islamic Historiography: Harun al-Rashid and the Narrative of the ʿAbbāsid Caliphate*. Cambridge: Cambridge University Press, 2002.

El-Shayyal, G. 'Ibn Shaddād.' *EI*², 3:933–934.

El-Shayyal, G. 'Ibn Wāṣil.' *EI*², 3:967.

Elad, A. 'The History and Topography of Jerusalem during the Early Islamic Period: The Historical Value of Faḍā'il al-Quds Literature: A Reconsideration.' *JSAI* 14 (1991), 41–70.

Elad, A. *Medieval Jerusalem and Islamic Worship, Holy Ceremonies, Pilgrimage*. Leiden, E.J. Brill, 1995.

Elad, A. 'Pilgrims and Pilgrimage to Hebron (al-Khalīl) During the Early Muslim Period,' in *Pilgrims and Travelers to the Holy Land*, edited by B. F. le Beau and Menachem Mor, 21–62. Omaha, NE: Creighton University Press, 1996.

Eliade, M. *The Sacred and the Profane: The Nature of Religion*. Translated by Willard R. Trask. New York: Harper & Row, 1961.

Elisséeff, N. *Nūr ad-Dīn un grand prince musulman de Syrie au temps des croisades (511–569H./1118–1174)*. Vol. 3. Damascus: Institut Francais de Damas, 1967.

Elisséeff, N. 'The Reaction of the Syrian Muslims after the Foundation of the First Latin Kingdom of Jerusalem,' in *Crusaders and Muslims in Twelfth-Century* Syria, edited by Maya Shatzmiller, 162–172. Leiden: Brill, 1993.

Ephrat, D. and M. D. Kabha. 'Muslim Reactions to the Frankish Presence in Bilād al-Shām: Intensifying Religious Fidelity within the Masses.' *Al-Masāq* 15 (2003), 47–58.

Fahd, T. 'Malḥama.' *EI*², 4:247.

Faris, N. A. 'Arab Culture in the Twelfth-Century,' in *A History of the Crusades*. Vol. 5: *The Impact of the Crusades on the Near East*, edited by Kenneth Meyer Setton, Norman P. Zacour, and Harry W. Hazard, 3–32. Madison: University of Wisconsin Press, 1969–89.

Folda, J. *Crusader Art in the Holy Land: From the Third Crusade to the Fall of Acre, 1187–1291*. Cambridge: Cambridge University Press, 2005.

Frenkel, Y. 'Muslim Responses to the Frankish Dominion in the Near East, 1098–1291,' in *The Crusades and the Near East: Cultural Histories*, edited by C. Kostick, 27–54. London: Routledge, 2011.

Frenkel, Y. 'Political and Social Aspects of Islamic Religious Endowments ("awqāf"): Saladin in Cairo (1169– 73) and Jerusalem (1187–93).' *BSOAS* 62 (1999), 1–20.

Frenkel, Y. 'The Qur'ān versus the Cross in the Wake of the Crusade: The Social Function of Dreams and Symbols in Encounters and Conflict (Damascus, July 1148).' *Quaderni di Studi Arabi* 20–21 (2002–03), 105–132.

Friedman, Y. 'Captivity and Ransom: The Experience of Women,' in *Gendering the Crusades*, edited by Susan B. Edgington and Sarah Lambert, 121–139. Cardiff: University of Wales Press, 2001.

Fück, J. W. 'Ibn Khallikān.' *EI*², 3:832–833.

Gabrieli, F. 'Religious Poetry in Early Islam,' in *Arabic Poetry: Theory and Development*, edited by G. E. von Grunebaum, 5–17. Wiesbaden: Otto Harrassowitz, 1973.

Garulo, Teresa. 'Women in Medieval Classical Arabic Poetry,' in *Writing the Feminine: Women in Arab Sources*, edited by Manuela Marín and Randi Deguilhem, 25–40. London: I. B. Tauris, 2002.

Gelder, G. J. van. *Classical Arabic Literature: A Library of Arabic Literature Anthology*. New York: New York University Press, 2013.

Gelder, G. J. van. 'Mirror for Princes or Vizor for Viziers: The Twelfth-Century Arabic Popular Encyclopedia Mufid al-'ulum and its Relationship with the Anonymous Persian *Bahr al-fawa'id*.' *BSOAS* 64, no. 3 (2001), 313–338.

Gibb, H. A. R. 'Al-Barq al-Shāmī: The History of Saladin by the Katib 'Imād al-Dīn al-Iṣfahānī.' *Wiener Zeitschrift für die Kunde des Morgenlandes* 52 (1953–55), 93–115.

Gilbert, J. E. 'Institutionalization of Muslim Scholarship and Professionalization of the 'Ulamā' in Medieval Damascus.' *SI* 52 (1980), 105–134.

Goitein S. D. and O. Grabar. 'Jerusalem,' in *Historic Cities of the Islamic World*, edited by Clifford Edmund Bosworth, 224–256. Leiden: Brill, 2007.

Grabar, O. *The Dome of the Rock*. London: Thames and Hudson, 1996.

Grabar, O. 'al-Ḳuds.' *EI*², 5:322–344.

Grabar, O. 'The Umayyad Dome of the Rock in Jerusalem.' *Ars Orientalis* 3 (1959), 33–62.

Grossman, A. 'Jerusalem in Jewish Apocalyptic Literature,' in *The History of Jerusalem: The Early Muslim Period 638–1099*, edited by Joshua Prawer and Haggai Ben-Shammai, 295–310. New York: New York University Press, 1996.

Gruendler, B. *Medieval Arabic Praise Poetry: Ibn al-Rūmī and the Patron's Redemption.* London: Routledge, 2003.

Grunebaum, G. E. von. 'The Sacred Character of Islamic Cities,' in *Mélanges Taha Husain*, edited by 'A. al-Badawī, 25–37. Cairo: Dār al-Ma'ārif, 1962.

Grunebaum, G. E. von. 'The Spirit of Islam as Shown in its Literature,' in *Themes in Medieval Arabic Literature*, edited by Gustave E. von Grunebaum, 101–119. London: Variorum Reprints, 1981.

Guillaume, A. 'Where was al-Masjid al-Aqsa?' *Al-Andalus* 18 (1953), 323–336.

Hamblin, W. 'To Wage *Jihād* or Not: Fāṭimid Egypt During the Early Crusades,' in *The Jihād and Its Times*, edited by Hadia Dajani-Shakeel and Ronald A. Messers, 31–39. Ann Arbor: University of Michigan Press, 1991.

Hamilton, B. 'The Elephant of Christ: Reynald of Chatillon,' in *Studies in Church History 15: Religious Motivation*, edited by D. Baker, 97–108. Oxford: Basil Blackwell, 1978.

Hamilton, B. 'Our Lady of Saidnaya: An Orthodox Shrine Revered by Muslims and Knights Templar at the Time of the Crusades,' in *Studies in Church History 36: The Holy Land, Holy Lands and Christian History*, edited by R. N. Swanson, 207–215. Woodbridge: Boydell Press, 2000.

Hamori, A. 'Love Poetry (*Ghazal*),' in *Abbasid Belles Lettres*, edited by J. Ashtiany, T. M. Johnstone, J. D. Latham, and R. B. Serjeant, 202–218. Cambridge: Cambridge University Press, 1990.

Hamza, 'Abd al-Laṭīf. *Adab al-ḥurūb al-ṣalībiyya*. Cairo, 1949.

Handyside, P. D. *The Old French William of Tyre*. Leiden and Boston: Brill, 2015.

Harris, J. *Byzantium and the Crusades*. London: Hambledon, 2003.

al-Harthi, J. M. 'I Have Never Touched Her: The Body in al-Ghazal al-'Udhrī.' PhD thesis, University of Edinburgh, 2010.

Hashmi, S. H. 'Political Boundaries and Moral Communities: An Islamic Perspective,' in *States, Nations and Borders: The Ethics of Making Boundaries*, edited by Allen Buchanan and Margaret Moore. Cambridge, 2003.

Hasson, I. 'Muslim Literature in Praise of Jerusalem: Faḍā'il Bayt al-Maqdis,' in *The Jerusalem Cathedra: Studies in the History, Archaeology, Geography and Ethnography of the Land of Israel*. Vol. 1, edited by Lee I. Levine, 168–184. Jerusalem: Yad Izhak Ben Zvi Institute, 1981.

Heidemann, S. 'Economic Growth and Currency in Ayyubid Palestine,' in *Ayyubid Jerusalem: The Holy City in Context 1187–1250*, edited by R. Hillenbrand and S. Auld, 276–300. London: al Tajir World of Islam Trust, 2009.

Heinrichs, W. 'The Meaning of Mutanabbī,' in *Poetry and Prophecy: The Beginnings of a Literary Tradition*, edited by James L. Kugel, 120–139. New York: Cornell University Press, 1990.

Hermes, Nizar F. 'The Byzantines in Medieval Arabic Poetry: Abū Firas' *Al-Rumiyyat* and the Poetic Responses of al-Qaffal and Ibn Hazm to Nicephorus Phocas' *al-Qaṣīda al-Arminiyya al-Mal'una* (The Armenian Cursed Ode),' in *BYZANTINA ΣΥΜΜΕΙΚΤΑ* 19 (2009), 35–61.

Hermes, Nizar F. *The [European] Other in Medieval Arabic Literature and Culture: Ninth-Twelfth Century AD*. New York: Palgrave Macmillan, 2012.

Hillenbrand, Carole. '"Abominable Acts": The Career of Zengi,' in *The Second Crusade*, edited by J. P. Phillips and M. Hoch, 111–132. Manchester: Manchester University Press, 2001.

Hillenbrand, Carole. *The Crusades: Islamic Perspectives*. Edinburgh: Edinburgh University Press, 1999.

Hillenbrand, Carole. 'Ibn al-Qaysarānī,' in *Encyclopedia of Arabic Literature*, vol. 1, edited by J. S. Meisami and P. Starkey. London: Routledge, 1998.

Hillenbrand, Carole. 'The Imprisonment of Reynald of Chattilon,' in *Texts, Documents and Artefacts: Islamic Studies in Honour of D. S. Richards*, edited by C. F. Robinson, 79–102. Leiden: Brill, 2003.

Hillenbrand, Carole. 'Jihad Poetry in the Age of the Crusades,' in *Crusades – Medieval Worlds in Conflict*, edited by Thomas Madden, James Naus, and Vincent Ryan, 9–23. Aldershot: Ashgate, 2010.

Hillenbrand, Carole. 'Jihad Propaganda in Syria from the Time of the First Crusade until the Death of Zengi: The Evidence of Monumental Inscriptions,' in *The Frankish Wars and Their Influence on Palestine*, edited by K. Athamina and R. Heacock, 60–69. Birzeit: Birzeit University Publications, 1994.

Hillenbrand, Carole. 'A Little-Known Mirror for Princes of al-Ghazali,' in *Words, Texts and Concepts Cruising the Mediterranean Sea*, edited by R. Arnzen and J. Thielmann, 593–601. Leuven: Peeters, 2004.

Hillenbrand, Carole. *Turkish Myth and Muslim Symbol: The Battle of Manzikert*. Edinburgh: Edinburgh University Press, 2007.

Hillenbrand, R. and S. Auld. *Ayyubid Jerusalem: The Holy City in Context 1187–1250*. London: al-Tajir Trust, 2009.

Hillenbrand, R. 'The Legacy of the Dome of the Rock,' in *Studies in Medieval Islamic Architecture*. Vol. 1, 1–19. London: Pindar Press, 2001.

Hillenbrand, R. 'Qur'ānic Epigraphy in Medieval Islamic Architecture,' in *Studies in Medieval Islamic Architecture*. Vol. 1, 308–327. London: Pindar Press, 2001.

Hilmy, M. and M. Aḥmad. 'Abū Shāma, 'Abd al-Rahmān (1203–1268),' in *Encyclopaedic Historiography of the Muslim World*, edited by N. K. Singh and A. Samiuddin, 17–18. Delhi: Global Vision Publishing House, 2003.

Hirschler, K. 'Ibn Wāṣil: An Ayyubid Perspective on Frankish Lordships and Crusades,' in *Medieval Muslim Historians and the Franks in the Levant*, edited by Alex Mallett, 136–160. Leiden: Brill, 2014.

Hirschler, K. 'The Jerusalem Conquest of 492/1099 in the Medieval Arabic Historiography of the Crusades: From Regional Plurality to Islamic Narrative.' *Crusades* 13 (2014), 37–76.

Hirschler, K. *Medieval Arabic Historiography*. London: Routledge, 2006.

Hirschler, K. 'Narrating the Past: Social Contexts and Literary Structures of Arabic.' PhD thesis, School of Oriental and African Studies, 2003.

Hirschler, K. 'Social Contexts of Medieval Arabic Historical Writing: Court Scholars Versus Ideal/Withdrawn Scholars – Ibn Wāṣil and Abu Šāma,' in *Egypt and Syria in the Fatimid, Ayyubid and Mamluk Eras IV*, edited by U. Vermeulen and J. Van Steenbergen, 311–331. Leuven: Peeters, 2005.

Hitti, P. K. *History of the Arabs*. New York: Macmillan, 1958.

Hitti, P. K. 'The Impact of the Crusades on the Near East,' in *A History of the Crusades*. Vol. 5, edited by K. M. Setton, N. P. Zacour, and H. W. Hazard, 33–58. Madison, WI and London: University of Wisconsin Press, 1985.

Hodgson, N. 'The Role of Kerbogha's Mother in the *Gesta Francorum* and Selected Chronicles of the First Crusade,' in *Gendering the Crusades*, edited by Susan B. Edgington and Sarah Lambert, 163–176. Cardiff: University of Wales Press, 2001.

Holt, P. M. 'Saladin and His Admirers: A Biographical Re-assessment.' *BSOAS* 46 (1983), 235–239.

Hoyland, R. *Seeing Islam as Others Saw It: A Survey and Evaluation of Christian, Jewish and Zoroastrian Writings on Early Islam*. Princeton, NJ: Darwin Press, 1997.

Humphreys, R. S. 'Politics and Architectural Patronage in Ayyūbid Syria,' in *The Islamic World from Classical to Modern Times: Essays in Honor of Bernard Lewis*, edited by C. E. Bosworth, C. Issawi, R. Savory, and A. L. Udovitch, 151–174. New Jersey: Darwin Press, 1989.

Humphreys, R. S. 'Women as Patrons of Religious Architecture in Ayyubid Damascus,' in *Muqarnas XI: An Annual on Islamic Art and Architecture*, 35–54. Leiden: E. J. Brill, 1994.

Ibrāhīm, M. *Faḍā'il bayt al-maqdis fī makhṭūṭāt 'arabiyya qadīma* [The virtues of Jerusalem in old Arabic manuscripts]. Kuwait, 1985.

Ibrāhīm, M. 'Filasṭīn fī l-adab al-'arabī zamān al-ḥurūb al-ṣalībiyya,' in *al-Sirā l-Islāmī l-Faranjī a'lā Filasṭīn fī l-qurūn al-wusṭā*, edited by H. Dajani-Shakeel and B. Dajani, 341–395. Beirut, 1994.

Ibrāhīm, M. *Ṣida al-ghazwu al-salībīyy fī shiʿr ibn al-Qaysarānī*. Amman: Dār al-Bashīr, 1988.

Irwin, R. *The Arabian Nights: A Companion*. London: Tauris Parke, 2005.

Irwin, R. 'The Arabists and Crusader Studies in the Twentieth Century,' in *Cultural Encounters during the Crusades*, edited by K. V. Jensen, K. Salomen, and H. Vogt, 283–298. Odense: University Press of Southern Denmark, 2013.

Irwin, R. 'Islam and the Crusades,' in *The Oxford Illustrated History of the Crusades*, edited by Jonathan Riley-Smith, 217–259. Oxford: Oxford University Press, 1995.

Irwin, R. 'Orientalism and the Early Development of Crusader Studies,' in *The Experience of Crusading: Defining the Crusader Kingdom*. Vol. 2, edited by Peter W. Edbury and Jonathan P. Phillips, 214–230. Cambridge: Cambridge University Press, 2003.

Irwin, R. 'Usamah ibn Munqidh: An Arab-Syrian Gentleman at the Time of the Crusades Reconsidered,' in *The Crusades and their Sources: Essays Presented to Bernard Hamilton*, edited by J. France and W. G. Zajac. Aldershot: Ashgate, 1998.

Issawi, C. 'Al-Mutanabbī in Egypt (957–962),' in *Medieval and Middle Eastern Studies: In Honor of Aziz Suryal Atiya*, edited by S. A. Hanna, 236–239. Leiden: E.J. Brill, 1972.

Jabra, J. I. 'The Rebels, the Committed and the Others: Transitions in Modern Arabic Poetry Today.' *Middle East Forum* 43 (1967), 19–32.

Jackson, D. E. P. '1193–1993. An Appreciation of the Career of Saladin,' in *Egypt and Syria in the Fāṭimid, Ayyūbid and Mamlūk Eras: Proceedings of the 1st, 2nd and 3rd International Colloquium Organised at the Katholieke Universiteit Leuven in May 1992, 1993 and 1994*, edited by U. Vermeulen and D. De Smet, 219–228. Leuven: Peeters, 1995.

Jacobi, R. 'Time and Reality in Nasīb and *Ghazal*.' *Journal of Arabic Literature 16* (1985), 1–17.

Jacobson, R. 'Linguistics and Poetics' in *Style and Language*, edited by Thomas Sebeok, 350–377. Cambridge, MA: MIT Press, 1960.

Jarrar, S. 'Suq al-Maʿrifa: An Ayyubid Hanbalite Shrine in al-Haram al-Sharif,' in *Muqarnas XV: An Annual on the Visual Culture of the Islamic World*, edited by Gülru Necipoglu, 71–100. Leiden, E. J. Brill: 1998.

Jotischky, A. 'Ethnographic Attitudes in the Crusader States: The Franks and the Indigenous Orthodox People,' in *East and West in the Crusader States: Context, Contacts, Confrontations III*, Orientalia Lovaniensia Analecta 125, edited by Krijnie Ciggaar and Herman Teule, 1–20. Leuven: Peeters, 2003.

Juynboll, G. H. *Muslim Tradition: Studies in Chronology, Provenance and Authorship of Early ḥadīth*. Cambridge: Cambridge University Press, 1983.

Kedar, B. 'The Jerusalem Massacre of July 1099 in the Western Historiography of the Crusades.' *Crusades* 3 (2004), 15–75.

Khadduri, M. *The Islamic Concept of Justice*. Baltimore, MD: Johns Hopkins University Press, 1984.

Khalidi, T. *Arabic Historical Thought in the Classical Period.* Cambridge: Cambridge University Press, 1994.

Kister, M. J. 'A Comment on the Antiquity of Traditions Praising Jerusalem,' in *The Jerusalem Cathedra*. Vol. 1, 185–186. Jerusalem, 1981.

Klausner, C. L. *The Seljuk Vezirate, a Study of Civil Administration, 1055–1194*. Cambridge, MA: Harvard University Press, 1973.

Lane, E. W. *An Arabic-English Lexicon*. Beirut: Librairie du Liban, 1968.

Laoust, H. 'Ibn al-Djawzī.' *EI*², 3:751–752.

Laoust, H. 'Ibn Kathīr.' *EI*², 3:817–818.

Lapidus, I. M. *A History of Islamic Societies*. Cambridge: Cambridge University Press, 2002.

Lapidus, I. M. 'Review of "Saladin" by Andrew S. Ehrenkreutz.' *JAOS* 94 (1974), 240–241.

Larkin, M. 'Al-Mutanabbī, Abū'l-Ṭayyib Aḥmad ibn al-Ḥusayn al-Ju'fi,' in *Medieval Islamic Civilization*, edited by Josef W. Meri, 542–544. Abingdon: Taylor & Francis, 2006.

Latiff, O. 'Qur'anic Imagery, Jesus and the Creation of a Pious-Warrior Ethos in the Muslim Poetry of the Anti-Frankish Jihad' in *Cultural Encounters during the Crusades*, eds. K. V. Jensen, K. Salomen and H. Vogt, 135–151. Odense: University Press of Southern Denmark, 2013.

Le Strange, G. *Palestine under the Moslems*. London: Palestine Exploration Fund, 1890.

Leiser, G. 'The Crusader Raid in the Red Sea in 578/1182–83.' *Journal of the American Research Center in Egypt* 14 (1977), 87–100.

Leiser, G. 'The *Madrasa* and the Islamization of the Middle East: The Case of Egypt.' *Journal of the American Research Center in Egypt* 22 (1985), 29–47.

Lev, Y. *Saladin in Egypt*. Leiden: Brill, 1999.

Lint, T. M. van. 'Seeking Meaning in Catastrophe: Nerses Snorhali's *Lament on Edessa*,' in *East and West in the Crusader States: Context – Contacts – Confrontations*, edited by Krijnie Ciggaar and Herman Teule, 29–105. Leuven: Peeters, 1999.

Little, D. P. 'Review: Amikam Elad, Medieval Jerusalem and Islamic Worship: Holy Places, Ceremonies, Pilgrimage.' *JAOS* 116 (1996), 338–339.

Livne-Kafri, O. 'Jerusalem in Early Islam: The Eschatological Aspect.' *Arabica* 53 (2006), 382–403.

Livne-Kafri, O. 'Jerusalem: The Navel of the Earth in Muslim Tradition.' *Der Islam* 84 (2007), 46–72.

Lyons, M. C. and D. E. P. Jackson. *Saladin: The Politics of the Holy War.* Cambridge: Cambridge University Press, 1982.

MacEvitt, C. *The Crusades and the Christian World of the East: Rough Tolerance*. Philadelphia: University of Pennsylvania Press, 2008.

Madelung, W. 'Has the *Hijra* Come to an End?' *Revue des études islamiques* 54 (1986), 225–237.

Madelung, W. 'Al-Mahdī.' *EI*², 5:1230–1238.

Mahamid, H. '"Franks" Effect on Islamic Spirit, Religious and Cultural Characters in Medieval Syria.' *Nebula*, 4.1 (2007), 166–183.

Makdisi, G. 'The Significance of the Sunni Schools of Law in Islamic Religious History.' *IJMES* 10 (1979), 1–8.

Mallett, A. (ed.), *Medieval Muslim Historians and the Franks in the Levant*. Leiden: Brill, 2014.

Mallett, A. 'The "Other" in the Crusading Period: Walter the Chancellor's Presentation of Najm al-Dīn Il-Ghāzī.' *Al-Masāq* 22 (2010), 113–128.

Mallett, A. 'Sibṭ Ibn al-Jawzī,' in *Medieval Muslim Historians and the Franks in the Levant*, 84–108. Leiden: Brill, 2014.

Mallett, A. 'A Trip Down the Red Sea with Reynald of Châtillon.' *Journal of the Royal Asiatic Society* 18 (2008), 141–153.

Mason, H. *Two Statesmen of Medieval Islam: Vizir Ibn Hubayra (499–560 AH 1105–1165 AD) and Caliph an-Nāṣir li Din Allāh (553–622 AH/1158–1225 AD)*. Paris: Mouton, 1972.

Matthews, Charles. *Palestine-Mohammedan Holy Land*. London, 1949.

Meisami, J. S. 'Ghazal,' in *Encyclopedia of Arabic Literature*. Vol. 1, edited by J. S. Meisami and P. Starkey, 249–250. London: Routledge, 1998.

Meisami, J. S. 'Madiḥ, Madḥ,' in *Encyclopedia of Arabic Literature*. Vol. 2, edited by J. S. Meisami and P. Starkey, 482–484. London: Routledge, 1998.

Meri, J. W. *The Cult of Saints among Muslims and Jews in Medieval Syria*. Oxford and New York: Oxford University Press, 2002.

Meri, J. W (ed.), *Medieval Islamic Civilization: An Encyclopedia*. Vol. 1. Abingdon: Routledge, 2006.

Meri, J. W and J. L. Bacharach (eds.) *Medieval Islamic Civilization: An Encyclopedia*. Vol. 2. New York: Routledge, 2006.

Meri, J. W and J. L. Bacharach (eds.). 'Re-Appropriating Sacred Space: Medieval Jews and Muslims seeking Elijah and al-Khaḍir,' in *Medieval Encounters: Jewish, Christian and Muslim Culture in Confluence and Dialogue*, vol. 5, 237–264. Leiden: Brill, 1999.

Milwright, M. 'Reynald of Chatillon and the Red Sea Expedition,' in *Noble Ideas and Bloody Realities: Warfare in the Middle Ages*, edited by Niall Christie and Maya Yazigi, 235–257. Leiden: Brill, 2006.

Möhring, H. *Saladin: The Sultan and His Times, 1138–1193*. Translated by D. S. Bachrach. Baltimore: Johns Hopkins University Press, 2008.

Möhring, H. 'Zwischen Joseph-Legende und Mahdī-Erwartung: Erfolge und ziele Sultan Saladins im spegel zeitgenossischer dichtung und weissagung,' in *War and Society in the Eastern Mediterranean 7th–15th Centuries*, edited by Y. Lev, 177–223. Leiden: Brill, 1997.

Morris, C. *The Sepulchre of Christ and the Medieval West: From the Beginning to 1600*. Oxford: Oxford University Press, 2005.

Mottahedeh, R. P. and R. al-Sayyid. '*The Idea of the Jihād in Islam before the Crusades*,' in *The Crusades from the Perspective of Byzantium and the Muslim World*, eds. Angeliki E. Laiou and R. P. Mottahedeh (Washington, DC: Dumbarton Oaks, 2001).

Mourad, S. A. 'Ibn 'Asakir,' in *Medieval Islamic Civilization: An Encyclopedia*, edited by J. W. Meri, vol. 1, 351–352. Abingdon: Routledge, 2006.

Mourad, S. A. and J. E. Lindsay. *The Intensification and Reorientation of Sunni Jihad Ideology in the Crusader Period: Ibn 'Asākir of Damascus (1105–1176) and His Age, with an Edition and Translation of Ibn 'Asākir's* 'The Forty Hadiths for Inciting Jihad.' Leiden: Brill, 2013.

Mourad, S. A. and J. E. Lindsay. 'The Symbolism of Jerusalem in Early Islam,' in *Jerusalem: Idea and Reality*, edited by Tamar Mayer and Suleiman Ali Mourad, 86–102. New York: Routledge, 2008.

Mouton, J.-M. *Damas et sa principaute: sous les Saljoukides et les Bourides 468–549/1076–1154*. Cairo: Institut Français d'Archéologie Orientale, 1994.

Murray, A. 'Ethnic Identity in the Crusader States,' in *Concepts of National Identity in the Middle Ages*, edited by Simon Forde, Alan V. Murray, and Lesley Johnson, 59–73. Leeds: Leeds Texts and Monographs 14, 1995.

Netton, I. R. 'Ibn Jubayr: Penitent Pilgrim and Obervant,' in *Seek Knowledge: Thought and Travel in the House of Islam*, 95–102. Richmond: Curzon Press, 1996.

Neuwirth, A. 'The Spiritual Meaning of Jerusalem in Islam,' in *City of the Great King: Jerusalem from David to the Present*, edited by Nitza Rosovsky, 93–116. Cambridge and London: Harvard University Press, 1996.

Nicholson, H. J. 'Muslim Reaction to the Crusades,' in *Palgrave Advances in the Crusades*, edited by Helen J. Nicholson, 269–288. Basingstoke: Palgrave Macmillan, 2005.

Nicholson, R. A. *A Literary History of the Arabs*. Cambridge: Cambridge University Press, 1930.

Ouyang, W. *Literary Criticism in Medieval Arabic-Islamic Culture: The Making of a Tradition*. Edinburgh: Edinburgh University Press, 1997.

Partner, P. 'Holy War, Crusade and *Jihād*: An Attempt to Define Some Problems,' in *Autour de la première croisade*, edited by Michael Balard, 333–343. Paris: Publications de la Sorbonne, 1996.

Phillips, J. *The Crusades 1095–1204*. Abingdon: Routledge, 2014.

Phillips, J. *The Second Crusade: Extending the Frontiers of Christendom*. New Haven and London: Yale University Press, 2007.

Phillips, J. 'The Travels of Ibn Jubayr and his View of Saladin,' in *Cultural Encounters during the Crusades*, edited by K. V. Jensen, K. Salomen, and H. Vogt, 75–90. Odense: University Press of Southern Denmark, 2013.

Pinault, D. 'Images of Christ in Arabic Literature.' *Die Welt des Islams* 27 (1987), 103–125.

Preminger, A. and T. V. F. Brogan (eds.). *The New Princeton Encyclopedia of Poetry and Poetics*. Princeton, NJ: Princeton University Press, 1993.

Purkis, W. 'Elite and Popular Perceptions of *imitatio Christi* in Twelfth-Century Crusade Spirituality,' in *Elite and Popular Religion*, Studies in Church History 42, edited by K. Cooper and J. Gregory, 54–64. Woodbridge: Ecclesiastical History Society, 2006.

Rabbat, N. 'The Ideological Significance of the *dār al-ʿadl* in the Medieval Islamic Orient.' *IJMES* 27 (1995), 3–28.

Rabbat, N. 'The Meaning of the Umayyad Dome of the Rock.' *Muqarnas* 6 (1989), 12–21.

Rabbat, N. 'The Visual Milieu of the Counter-Crusade in Syria and Egypt,' in *The Crusades: Other Experiences, Alternate Perspectives: Selected Proceedings from the 32nd Annual CEMERS Conference*, edited by Khalīl I. Semaan, 71–81. New York: Global Academic Publishing, 2003.

Raby, J. 'Nur al-Din, the Qastal shuʿaybiyya, and the "Classical Revival."' *Muqarnas* 21, *Essays in Honor of J. M. Rogers* (2004), 289–310.

Reynolds, D. F. (ed.), *Interpreting the Self: Autobiography in the Arabic Literary Tradition*. Berkeley: University of California Press, 2001.

Richards, D. S. 'Ibn Wasil, Historian of the Ayyubids,' in *Ayyubid Jerusalem*, edited by R. Hillenbrand and S. Auld, 456–459. London: al-Tajir Trust, 2009.

Richards, D. S. "Imād al-Dīn al-Iṣfahānī: Administrator, Litterateur and Historian,' in *Crusaders and Muslims in Twelfth-Century Syria*, edited by M. Shatzmiller, 133–146. Leiden: Brill, 1993.

Richter-Bernburg, L. "Imād al-Dīn al-Iṣfahānī,' in *Medieval Muslim Historians and the Franks in the Levant*, edited by Alex Mallett, 29–51. Leiden: Brill, 2014.

Riley-Smith, Jonathan. *The First Crusaders 1095–1131*. Cambridge: Cambridge University Press, 1998.

Riley-Smith, Jonathan and Louise Riley-Smith. *The Crusades: Idea and Reality 1095–1274*. London: Edward Arnold, 1981.

Robinson, C. F. *Islamic Historiography*. Cambridge: Cambridge University Press, 2003.

Rosenthal, F. *A History of Muslim Historiography*. Leiden: Brill, 1968.

Rosenthal, F. 'Political Justice and the Just Ruler.' *IOS* 10 (1980), 92–101.

Rubin, U. 'Al-Sāʿa' ["the Hour"]. *EI*^{2}, 8:656–657.

Runciman, S. *A History of the Crusades*. 3 vols. Cambridge: Cambridge University Press, 1951–54.

Sadan, J. 'Maidens' Hair and Starry Skies: Imagery System and *maʿānī* guides: The Practical Side of Arabic Poetics as Demonstrated in Two Manuscripts.' *IOS* XI, edited by S. Somekh, 57–88. Leiden: Brill, 1991.

Safwat, A. Z. *Jamharat khuṭab al-ʿarab fī ʿuṣūr al-ʿarabiyya al-zāhira*. Vol. 1. Beirut: al-Maktabat al-ʿIlmiyya, 1933.

Satō, T. *State and Rural Society in Medieval Islam: Sulṭāns, Muqtaʿs, and Fallahun*. Leiden: Brill, 1997.

Seidensticker, T. 'Sarī al-Raffāʾ,' in *Encyclopedia of Arabic Literature*. Vol. 2, edited by J. S. Meisami and P. Starkey, 690. London: Routledge, 1998.

Semah, D. 'Poetry and its Audience According to Medieval Arab Poeticians.' *IOS* XI, edited by S. Somekh, 91–106. Leiden: Brill, 1991.

Sharlet, J. *Patronage and Poetry in the Islamic World: Social Mobility and Status in the Medieval Middle East and Central Asia*. London: I. B. Tauris, 2011.

Singer, L. (ed.), *The Minbar of Saladin*. London: Thames and Hudson, 2008.

Sivan, E. 'The Beginning of the Faḍā'il al-Quds Literature.' *IOS* 1 (1971), 263–72.

Sivan, E. 'Le caractère sacré de Jérusalem dans l'Islam aux XIIe–XIIIe siècles.' *SI* 27 (1967), 149–182.

Sivan, E. *L'Islam et la croisade: idéologie et propagande dans les réactions musulmanes aux croisades*. Paris: Adrien Maisonneuve, 1968.

Smoor, P. 'Al-Mahdi's Tears: Impressions of Fāṭimid Court Poetry,' in *Egypt and Syria in the Fāṭimid, Ayyūbid, and Mamlūk Eras: Proceedings of the 4th and 5th International Colloquium Organized at the Katholieke Universiteit Leuven in May 1995 and 1996*, edited by U. Vermeulen and D. De Smet, 131–170. Leuven, 1998.

Smoor, P. "Umāra's Poetical Views of Shāwar, Ḍirghām, Shīrkūh and Saladin as Viziers of the Fāṭimid Caliphs,' in *Culture and Memory in Medieval Islam: Essays in Honor of Wilfred Madelung*, edited by Farhad Daftary and Josef W. Meri, 410–432. London: I. B. Tauris, 2003.

Sperl, S. *Mannerism in Arabic Poetry: A Structural Analysis of Selected Texts (3rd Century AH/9th Century AD–5th Century AH/11th Century AD)*. Cambridge: Cambridge University Press, 2004.

Stewart, Devin J. 'The Doctorate of Islamic Law in Mamluk Egypt and Syria,' in *Law and Education in Medieval Islam*, edited by Joseph Lowry, Devin Stewart, and Shawkat Toorawa, 45–90. Cambridge: E. J. W. Gibb Memorial Trust, 2004.

Stewart, Devin J. 'The Maqāmāt of Aḥmad b. Abī Bakr b. Aḥmad al-Rāzī al-Ḥanafī and the Ideology of the Counter-Crusade in Twelfth-Century Syria.' *Middle Eastern Literatures* 11, no. 2 (2008), 211–232.

Stewart, Devin J. 'Review of Michael Chamberlain, Knowledge and Social Practice in Medieval Damascus, 1190–1350.' *Comparative Education Review* 50.3 (August 2006), 531–533.

Stewart, Devin J. 'The Students' Representative in the Law Colleges of Fourteenth-Century Damascus.' *Islamic Law and Society* 15.2 (2008), 185–218.

Stewart, Frank Henderson. *Honor*. Chicago: University of Chicago Press, 1994.

Stoetzer, W. 'Rubāʿi.' *EI*², 8:578–585.

Sumi, A. M. *Description in Classical Arabic Poetry: Waṣf, Ekphrasis, and Interparts Theory*. Leiden: Brill, 2004.

Szombathy, Z. 'Freedom of Expression and Censorship in Medieval Arabic Literature.' *Journal of Arabic and Islamic Studies* 7 (2007), 2–24.

Tabbaa, Y. *Constructions of Power and Piety in Medieval Aleppo*. University Park: Pennsylvania State University Press, 1997.

Tabbaa, Y. 'Monuments with a Message: Propagation of *Jihād* under Nūr al-Dīn (1146–1174),' in *The Meeting of Two Worlds: Cultural Exchange between East and West during the Period of the Crusades*, edited by Vladimir P. Goss, 223–240. Ann Arbor, MI: Medieval Institute Publications, 1986.

Tabbaa, Y. *The Transformation of Islamic Art during the Sunni Revival*. Seattle and London, University of Washington Press, 2001.

Talhami, G. H. 'The Modern History of Jerusalem: Academic Myths and Propaganda.' *Middle East Policy Council* 7 (Feb. 2000), 113–129.

Talmon-Heller, D. *Islamic Piety in Medieval Syria: Mosques, Cemeteries and Sermons under the Zangids and Ayyūbids (1146–1260)*. Boston: Brill, 2007.

Talmon-Heller, D. 'Islamic Preaching in Syria during the Counter-Crusade (Twelfth-Thirteenth Centuries),' in *In Laudem Hierosolymitani: Studies in Crusades and Medieval Culture in Honour of Benjamin Z. Kedar*, edited by Iris Shagrir, Ronnie Ellenblum, and Jonathan Riley-Smith, 61–76. Aldershot: Routledge, 2007.

Talmon-Heller, D. 'Muslim Martyrdom and Quest for Martyrdom in the Crusading Period.' *Al-Masāq* 14, no. 2 (September 2002), 131–139.

Taylor, C. *In the Vicinity of the Righteous: Ziyara and the Veneration of Muslim Saints in Late Medieval Egypt*. Leiden: Brill, 1999.

al-Tel, O. I. *The First Islamic Conquest of Aelia (Islamic Jerusalem): Critical Analytical Study of the Early Islamic Historical Narratives and Sources*. Dundee: Al-Maktoum Institute Academic Press, 2003.

Tibawi, A. L. *Jerusalem: Its Place in Islam and Arab History*. Beirut: Institute for Palestine Studies, 1969.

Tibawi, A. L. 'Origin and Character of *al-madrasah*.' BSOAS 25 (1962), 225–238.

Tourneau, R. le. (trans.) *Damas de 1075 à 1154*. Damascus: Institut Français de Damas, 1952.

Tramontini, L. 'Poetry Post-Sayyāb: Designing the Truth in Iraqi War Poetry of the 1980s,' in *Poetry and History: The Value of Poetry in Reconstructing Arab History*, edited by R. Baalbaki, S. S. Agha, and T. Khalidi, 289–312. Beirut: American University of Beirut Press, 2011.

Tyerman, C. *God's War: A New History of the Crusades*. London: Penguin, 2006.

Wansbrough, J. *Quranic Studies*. Oxford: Oxford University Press, 1977.

Watt, W. M. *The Faith and Practice of al-Ghazālī*. Oxford: Oneworld Publications, 1953.

Watt, W. M. 'Al-Ghazālī.' *EI*², 2:1038–1041.

Werthmuller, K. J. *Coptic Identity and Ayyubid Politics in Egypt 1218–1250*. Cairo: American University of Cairo Press, 2010.

Wiet, G. 'Baybars I.' *EI*², 1:1124–1126.

Wilfong, T. G. 'The Non-Muslim Communities: Christian Communities,' in *The Cambridge History of Egypt*, edited by M. W. Daly and Carl F. Petry, 175–197. Cambridge: Cambridge University Press, 1998.

Zakkār, S. (ed.) *Arbaʿa kutub fī l-jihād min ʿaṣr al-ḥurūb al-ṣalībiyya*. Damascus: Dār al-Takwīn, 2007.

Zwartjes, O. *Love Songs from al-Andalus: History, Structure, and Meaning of the Kharja*. Leiden: Brill, 1997.

Zwettler, M. *The Oral Tradition of Classical Arabic Poetry: Its Character and Implication*. Columbia: Ohio State University Press 1978.

Index of Names and Places

'Abd al-Dawla (d. 502/1109) 70, 71
'Abd al-Ghanī b. Surūr al-Maqdisī 21 n.50
'Abd al-Mahdī, *Bayt al-maqdis fī adab al-ḥurūb al-Ṣalībiyya* 52
'Abd al-Malik b. Marwān (d. 86/705) (Umayyad caliph) 35, 170, 174 n.120
'Abd al-Qādir al-Jilānī (d. 561/1165) 14, 21 n.50, 28, 151
'Abd al-Raḥīm b. Shīth al-Qurashī 174 n.120
  Miftāḥ al-maqāṣid wa-miṣbāḥ al-marāṣid fī ziyārat bayt al-maqdis 173
'Abd al-Raḥmān b. Isḥāq b. Shīth 'al-Qunawī', *Miftāḥ al-maqāṣid wa-miṣbāḥ al-marāṣid fī ziyārat bayt al-maqdis* 174 n.120
Abī 'Abdallāh b. 'Alī b. Mihrān (Shaykh) 134
al-Abīwardī, Abū l-Muẓaffar (d. 507/1113) 3, 49, 51, 67–72, 78, 218, 219, 224
Abraham (Prophet) 95, 114, 179
Abū 'Alī l-Ṭabarsī (d. 548/1153) 105
Abū l-'Atāhiyya (d. 211/826) 160–161
Abū Bakr al-Ṣiddīq (d. 13/634) 111, 113
Abū l-Faḍl b. al-Khashshāb (d. 519/1125) 60–61
Abū l-Fatḥ Banjīr al-Ashtarī (d. 579/1183) 161–162
Abū Firās al-Ḥamdānī (d. 357/968) 164
Abū l-Ḥakam al-Andalusī 61–62
Abū Ḥāmid Muḥammad al-Shahrazūrī (d. 586/1190) 163
Abū l-Ḥasan 'Alī b. Muḥammad al-Raba'ī (d. 444/1052)
  Faḍā'il al-Shām wa-faḍl Dimashq 8
Abū Ḥayyān al-Andalusī (d. 745/1344) 105
Abū-l Ḥasan al-Ghadayrī 25
Abū l-Ma'ālī l-Musharraf b. al-Murajja 107
  Faḍā'il al-Quds wa-l-Shām 178
Abū l-Najīb al-Suhrawardī 28
Abū l-Qāsim al-Fārisī 79
Abū Shāma, 'Abd al-Raḥman b. Ismā'īl (d. 655/1268) 43, 45, 61, 63, 84, 104–105, 134, 152, 173, 200, 213, 215
  Kitāb al-Rawḍatayn 15–16, 87, 176, 179
  'Uyūn al-rawḍatayn 16
Abū Tammām (d. 232/845) 92 n.62, 93, 154, 182, 209
  Ḥamāsa 40
Abu 'Ubayda 111
Abyssinia 202
Acre 12, 14, 63, 91, 214, 223 n.11
  bishops of 104
  capture of (497/1104) 14
al-'Āḍid (d. 567/1171) 176, 197 n.17, 205–208
al-'Ādil 180–181
Agha, Saleh Said 43
Aḥmad b. Abī Bakr al-Rāzī l-Ḥanafī
  Maqāmāt 163
Akkach, Samer 33, 110, 217
Alamūt 206
Aleppo 12, 14, 22, 24, 82, 104–105, 171, 178 n.129, 202
  Shī'ī mosques in 25
Alexandria 24, 33, 34 n.89, 99, 121, 123, 125, 225
  sack of (1365) 14
  state of affairs in 127–128
Alexius II (Emperor) 119
'Alī b. Abī Ṭālib (d. 40/661) 60, 111, 113
Alp Arslān (d. 465/1072) 72
Alp Qutlugh Jabūghā Ulugh Atābak 10
Amalric, King of Jerusalem 195–196, 198–199, 206
Amorium 92 n.62
  conquest/siege of (223/838) 77, 154, 182, 209
  personified 93
Anatolia 73
al-Andalus 15, 63, 111, 116–117
Andronicus 119
Antioch 92, 138, 148, 183–184, 186, 190
  churches of 224
'Aqaba 180
al-Aqṣā Mosque 2 n.2, 3, 8, 19, 32, 37 n.95, 38, 75, 88, 93–94, 98, 99, 101, 106–107, 109–110, 112, 147, 168, 172, 178, 209, 213, 215–217, 222
  sanctity of 83, 108
Āq Sunqur Aḥmadīlī 10
Arabian Peninsula (Jazira) 100, 199
'Arafat 216
al-'Arqala Ḥassān (d. 591/1195) 74
Arslān Aba b. Āq Sunqur 150 n.56

Ascalon 33, 69, 177
  siege of 38
al-Ashraf Mūsā (d. 635/1237) 214
ʿAwf b. Mālik 218
Ayyūb, Najm al-Dīn 151

Baalbek 86–87
Badawī, Aḥmad Aḥmad 100
  al-Ḥayāt al-adabiyya fī ʿaṣr al-ḥurūb al-ṣalībiyya bi-Miṣr wa-l-Shām 52
Badr, battle of (2/624) 114, 198
Badr al-Dīn Luʾluʾ (r. 619–57/1222–59) 12
Badr al-Jamālī (d. 487/1094) 4 n.6, 193, 196
Baghdad 3, 12, 15, 19, 35, 67, 151, 179
Baḥr al-fawāʾid (anon.) 10, 17, 71, 74, 120, 150 n.56, 151, 161
Balak (Artuqid prince) 138
Balat, battle of ('Battle of the Field of Blood') (513/1119) 60–61, 138, 149
Baldric of Dol 162
Baldwin I 2 n.1, 138 n.23
Baldwin IV 91
Bānyās 61
  battle of (559/1164) 164–166, 172
Barkiyāruq, Rukn al-Dīn (487–498/1094–1105) (sultan) 67–68
Bauer, T., 185
Baybars (r. 658–676/1260–77) 131
al-Bayt al-Ḥarām [noble sanctuary] 94, 108, 183
Bayt al-Maqdis [Jerusalem] 108, 112, 174
Bernard of Clairvaux (Abbot) 4 n.8
Bilād al-Shām (Greater Syria) 34, 36, 58
Black Stone 94
Byzantium 89, 115, 117, 119–120

Caesarea 14, 33
Cahen, Claude 49, 204
Cairo 24, 33, 174 n.120
  madrasas in 23
Caton, Steven 52, 192
Chamberlain, M. 97
Christie, N. 51
Cobb, P. M. 8, 32, 192 n.2
  The Race for Paradise: An Islamic History of the Crusades 49
Constable, G. 48
Constantinople 116, 134, 208 n.49
  eschatological role of 120
  future conquest of 99, 115, 118–120, 225
  and Jerusalem 34–35
Cook, D. 114

Dajani-Shakeel, Hadia 2 n.1, 50–51, 54, 68 n.3, 155 n.66, 221
Damascus 14–15, 19, 22–24, 28, 121, 151, 214, 218
  alliance with Egypt 199, 202
  as bastion of Islamic resistance 34
  defence of 61, 63–64
  description of 12
  religious community of 85
  sanctity of 33, 225
  siege of (543/1148) 4, 61, 74, 82, 95, 140 n.27
  as spiritual center/substitute for Jerusalem 34, 106, 129
  virtues/merits of 34 n.90, 36
Damietta 132, 169, 197, 214
  captured (616/1219) 168
  victory (618/1221) 170 n.108
Dār al-Ḥadīth (*madrasa* in Damascus) 33
Darwish, Mahmoud 53
Dirgham 195
Dome of the Rock 19, 31, 35, 94, 105–106, 147, 170, 182, 209, 215
  cosmological role of 110
Duri, ʿAbdul Aziz 32

Eddé, A. M. 73
Edessa, fall/conquest of (538/1144) 4, 58, 61, 67, 81–82, 86, 88, 98, 116, 133–135, 138–139, 148–149, 198
Egypt 12, 89, 100, 103, 121, 143, 163, 178–180, 201 n.31
  crusader interest in 197–199, 202, 206
  disunity in 199
  faḍāʾil (merits) of 169
  and Fāṭimids 19
  fears in 208
  financial resources of 212
  independence/autonomy 194–195
  Oriental Christians in 141
  sanctity of 33
  Sunnī 213
  unity with Syria 192, 199, 202, 208

El-Hibri, T. 46
Ehrenkreutz, Andrew 26
Elad, Amikam 31
El Cheikh, Nadia Maria 161 n.82
Elisséeff, N. 36, 47, 51, 221–222
Ephrat 37

Faris, Nabih Amin 162
Fariskur, battle of (Muḥarram 648/April 1250) 130, 145
Farrūkshāh 178
al-Findalāwī, Yūsuf (d. 543/1148) 60, 63, 65–66
as *ḥujjat al-Islām* 62
martyrdom of 61–62, 64
Fityān al-Shāghūrī (d. 615/1218) 90, 103–104, 167
Frederick Barbarossa of Germany (r. 1152–90) 92
Frederick II 216 n.12, 223
crusade of 13
took Jerusalem (626/1229) 109
Fucher of Chartres 148
al-Fuḍayl b. ʿIyāḍ (d. 187/803) 154

Gabrieli, F. 16, 48, 87
Garulo, Teresa 42 n.6
al-Ghazālī, Abū Ḥāmid (d. 505/1111) 14, 21 n.53, 39
Iḥyāʾ ʿulūm al-dīn (Revival of the Religious Sciences) 27
Kīmiyā 160 n.79
as *mujaddid* (lit., renewer) 29
Naṣīḥat al-mulūk 27–28, 157, 161
Gibb, Sir Hamilton 26, 49
Gilbert of Aalst 5
Goitein, S. D. 8 n.20, 221
Grabar, O. 221
Guibert of Nogent 7, 162
Guy de Lusignan, King of Jerusalem 103

al-Ḥadath, battle of (343/954–55) 79, 182, 209
Hagia Sophia 116
al-Ḥalḥūlī, ʿAbd al-Raḥmān al-Ḥalḥūlī 62, 65
Hama 13, 131
Hamblin, W. 196
Hamori, A. 187

Ḥaramayn (two sanctuaries) 182
al-Harawī, ʿAlī b. Abī Bakr 137 n.18
al-Harawī, Zayn al-Dīn Abū Saʿd 67
al-Ḥārith b. al-Ṣamma 59
al-Harthi, J. M. 187
Ḥaṭṭīn, battle of (583/1187) 13, 49, 103–104, 225
Hawran 84
Hijaz 123, 126, 174 n.120, 180 n.135, 206
Hillenbrand, Carole 50, 54, 138, 142–143
The Crusades: Islamic Perspectives 49
Hirschler, K. 2 n.2, 45–46
Hitti, P. K. 37, 41, 49, 192 n.2
Hodgson, N. 162
Holy City 99, 126, 135, 138, 203, 213, 216, 221
See also Jerusalem
dismantling the walls of 197
sanctification of 171
Holy Land 32, 112, 123. *See also* Palestine
Holy Nativity at Bethlehem, Church of 223
Holy Sepulchre 4 n.8, 6 n.13, 137–138, 146
Hugh of Caesarea 206
Humbert of Romans (d. 1277) 131 n.4
Humphreys, Stephen 24
Ḥusām al-Dīn Luʾluʾ 181–182

Ibn Abī Ṭayy (d. 633/1233) 15
Ibn al-ʿAdīm 60, 149
Ibn al-Afḍal, Abū ʿAlī (d. 515/1121) 193, 196, 202 n.33
Ibn al-ʿArabī, Muḥyī l-Dīn (d. 638/1240) 28
Ibn ʿAsākir, Thiqat al-Dīn Abū l-Qāsim ʿAlī b. al-Ḥasan (d. 571/1175) 6, 33, 36, 38, 150 n.55
Arbaʿūn fī l-ijtihād fī iqāmat al-jihād 177
Faḍl ʿAsqalān 177
Tārīkh madinat Dimashq 10, 62
Ibn al-Athīr, ʿAlī ʿIzz al-Dīn (d. 630/1233) 15, 62, 72, 92, 97, 135, 156, 166, 198, 212–213
al-Kāmil fī l-tārīkh 12, 49, 134, 201
Ibn Barrajān, Abū l-Ḥakam al-Maghribī 19, 105–106
Ibn Bassam 163–164
Ibn al-Dharawī 181–182
Ibn al-Firkāḥ, Burhān al-Dīn (d. 729/1329)
Kitāb Bāʿith al-nufūs 178
Ibn al-Ḥawrānī, *al-Ishārāt ilā amākin al-ziyārāt* 218

Ibn al-Hubayra (d. 560/1165) 22
Ibn Isḥāq 59
Ibn Jahbal = Majd al-Dīn b. Jahbal al-Shāfiʿī 104–105
Ibn al-Jawzī, Abū l-Faraj 17, 66, 107, 216 n.12
Faḍāʾil al-Quds 36, 174 n.120
Kitāb al-Quṣṣās wa-l-mudhakkirīn 44 n.11
Ibn Jubayr, Abū l-Ḥusayn Muḥammad b. Aḥmad (d. 613/1217) 91, 95 n.69, 99, 122, 124–128, 156 n.72, 166, 174 n.120, 179, 211, 223–224
Riḥla 11–12, 58, 96 n.72, 119, 121, 127, 188
Ibn Kathīr, ʿImād al-Dīn Ismāʿīl b. ʿUmar (d. 774/1373) 43, 159, 161–162, 224
al-Bidāya wa-l-nihāya 14
al-Ijtihād fī ṭalab al-jihād 14, 105
Tafsīr al-Qurʾān al-ʿaẓīm 14
Ibn Khallikān (d. 681/1282) 83, 86, 194 n.6
Wafayāt al-aʿyān wa-anbā abnāʾ al-zamān 13
Ibn al-Khayyāṭ, Aḥmad b. Muḥammad (d. 517/1123) 3, 49, 51, 68–69, 71–72, 78, 84, 93, 127, 218, 219, 224
Ibn Mamātī, Asʿad (d. 605/1209) 100, 139, 171
Ibn Maṭrūḥ (d. 649/1251) 130–131
Ibn al-Mubārak, ʿAbdallāh b. al-Mubārak (d. 181/797) 36, 154–155
Kitāb al-Jihād 38, 155
Kitāb al-Zuhd 155
Ibn al-Mujāwir, Yūsuf b. al-Ḥusayn (d. 600/1204) 146
Ibn al-Munīr al-Ṭarābulsī (d. 548/1153) 82–86, 144–145, 157–159, 166, 172, 186, 205, 212, 221–222
maqāmāt of 164–165
Ibn Munqidh, Abū l-Ḥasan 38
Ibn al-Nabīh (d. 619/1222) 168, 214
Ibn al-Qalānisī (d. 555/1160) 15, 62, 64, 84, 149, 196, 200
Dhayl Tārīkh Dimashq 49
Ibn al-Qaysarānī, Abū ʿAbdallāh Muḥammad al-Ḥalabī (d. 547–48/1153–54) 14, 82–83, 86, 88, 98, 104, 116, 133–134, 161, 222, 224
and gender/Frankish women 51, 142, 183–187, 189–190, 222, 224
Ibn Qudāma al-Maqdisī (d. 620/1223)
al-Kāfī fī fiqh al-Imām Aḥmad b. Ḥanbal 109
Ibn Rajab al-Ḥanbalī (d. 795/1393)
Faḍl al-ʿilm al-salaf ʿalā ʿilm al-khalaf 96
Ibn Rashīq (d. 471/1078) 190
Ibn Ruzzīk, Malik al-Ṣāliḥ Ṭalāʾiʿ (d. 556/1161) (Fāṭimid vizier) 146–147, 176, 182, 192–193, 199–202, 206, 208, 221
Ibn al-Sāʿātī (d. 604/1209) 103–104
Ibn Sanāʾ al-Mulk (d. 608/1211) 49, 111, 171
Ibn Shaddād, Bahāʾ al-Dīn (d. 631/1234) 15, 106, 213, 223 n.11
al-Nawādir al-sulṭāniyya wa-l-maḥāsin al-Yūsufiyya 12, 49
Ibn Taghrībirdī 67, 73, 78, 127, 202 n.33
Ibn Taymiyya (d. 728/1328) 56 n.3
Ibn Ṭūlūn, mosque of 174 n.120
Ibn ʿUnayn (d. 630/1233) 15, 51
Ibn Wāṣil, Jamāl al-Dīn Muḥammad (d. 697/1298) 45, 118, 131–132, 179, 181, 216 n.12
Mufarrij al-kurūb fī akhbār Banī Ayyūb 13
Ibn al-Zakī, Muḥyī l-Dīn (d. 598/1202) 101, 105–106, 172, 222
sermon of, as *khaṭīb* in al-Aqṣā Mosque 19, 112–114
Ibn Zubayr 80
Ibrāhīm, Maḥmūd 8, 174 n.120
Īl-Ghāzī 60–61, 138, 148–149
ʿImād al-Dīn al-Iṣfahānī (d. 579/1201) 20, 40, 50, 74–75, 89, 94–95, 100, 116, 139–140, 145, 173, 182, 190, 198, 202–207, 221–222
al-Barq al-Shāmī 11, 15, 38, 115, 179
al-Fatḥ al-qussī fī l-fatḥ al-qudsī 11, 15
Kharīdat al-qaṣr wa-jarīdat al-ʿaṣr 11
on liberation of Jerusalem 86–88, 137–138, 140–141, 166
and Nūr al-Dīn 102, 151–153, 163, 203, 205
poems about Ḥaṭṭīn 103
poems for Ṣalāḥ al-Dīn 74, 93, 108, 110, 115, 166
ʿImād al-Dīn Zangī (r. 521–41/1127–46) 4, 10, 14, 82, 98, 116, 133–134, 138, 187
patronage of 14
Imruʾ l-Qays, *Muʿallaqa* 186
Inab, battle of (544/1149) 88
Innocent IV (Pope) 131
Iraq 13, 103, 116, 220
Irwin, R. 16, 42, 51, 57, 173, 192 n.2, 226
Isaac II (Emperor) 119

Jabra, Jabra I. (1919–94) 220
Jackson, D. E. P. 26
    Saladin: The Politics of Holy War 51
Jacob (Prophet) 207–208
Jamāl al-Dīn al-Iṣfahānī 86
Jarrar, Sabri 37 n.95
al-Jawwānī (d. 587/1192) 167
Jerusalem 2, 4–5, 8 n.20, 12, 29–30, 33, 67, 69–70, 115, 151, 168, 170, 174, 182–183, 216 n.12, 218
    capture of (492/1099) 9, 72, 82, 91, 97, 112, 142
    conquered by ʿUmar and Ṣalāḥ al-Dīn 170
    and Constantinople 34–35, 118, 120
    defence of 93, 174 n.120
    destruction of walls of 169, 214, 216
    eschatological significance of/in end times 35, 110, 178
    expulsion of crusaders from 147, 176
    faḍāʾil al-Quds 29–30, 32
    fate of 215–216
    image/perception of 36
    importance of, to Christians 137–138
    Islamic character of/'Islamised' 37, 108, 209
    and *jihād* 116, 173
    Latin Kingdom of 1, 26
    majesty of 92
    merits/virtues of 8, 113, 178
    and monotheistic religions 4–5
    occupation of 23, 34, 36, 83, 176, 177, 180, 226
    personified 93, 104, 219
    purification of 89, 146, 167
    reconquest/liberation of 4, 11, 13, 19, 24, 35, 67, 86–88, 90, 94, 97–98, 99–100, 103, 117–120, 121 n.71, 123, 137, 139, 192, 200–203, 211 n.2, 213, 221
    role/importance of 3–4, 31, 35, 39, 73, 83, 135
    sanctity/sacred space of 4, 6, 8 n.20, 32–33, 75, 99, 108, 126, 172, 219, 225
    symbolic nature of 217
    united with Mecca 94–95, 107, 217
    yearning for 30, 51
Jesus (ʿĪsā) Christ 4, 7, 126, 144, 148
    appropriation of, by Muslims 96, 129, 144–145, 146, 157
    Christian ascriptions of 129–131, 134, 149
    Christian faith in/devotion to 90, 141
    as ibn Maryam (son of Mary) 104, 134, 157, 165, 219
    image of 145, 183
    as Messiah (*masīḥ*) 224
    nation of 132
    rescued by Muslims 144, 157, 219
    second coming of 173
    and Shīʿīs 144
al-Jilyānī, ʿAbd al-Munʿim b. ʿUmar b. ʿAbdallāh al-Jilyānī l-Ghassānī l-Andalūsī (d. 602/1205–06) 89, 93, 101–102, 110–111, 116, 129, 135–136, 145, 173, 176–177, 209–213, 222
    Dīwān al-tadbīj 14–15
Jordan 8
Joscelin II of Edessa (Count) 205
Joseph (Prophet Yūsuf) 101, 111, 207–208
al-Juwaynī, Abū ʿAlī l-Ḥasan b. ʿAlī (d. 586/1190) 99 n.1, 110, 113, 115, 211
Juynboll, G. H. A. 31

Kabha 37
al-Kāmil (son of Shāwar) 195, 197, 223
al-Kāmil Muḥammad 214
Kedar, B. 2 n.2
Kerak 178
Khātun, Masjid/Mosque of 63
Khurasan 19, 218, 220
Kister, M. J. 31, 32–33
Kufa 12

Lane-Poole, Stanley 26
Lapidus, Ira 26
Lisbon, capture of (541/1147) 156 n.70
Livne-Kafri 32
Louis IX (d. 1270) 130–132
    crusade of, to Egypt 13
Lydda, bishops of 104
Lyons, Malcolm 26
    Saladin: The Politics of Holy War 51

MacEvitt, C. 143
Madrasa al-Ḥallāwiyya (Aleppo) 25
Maghrib 202, 206
Majd al-Dīn Muḥammad b. ʿAbdallāh al-Ḥanafī 215
Makdisi, G. 24

al-Malik al-ʿĀdil 214
al-Malik al-Ashraf (d. 693/1293) 168, 169
al-Malik al-Kāmil 168, 170 n.108, 216 n.12
al-Malik al-Muʿaẓẓam 169, 173
al-Malik al-Ṣāliḥ Ayyūb 130
al-Malik al-Ẓāhir al-Ghāzī (d. 613/1216) 22, 28, 171
Mallett, Alex 8 n.21, 148, 180 n.135
Manfred of Sicily (r. 1258–66) (King) 131
Manzikert, battle of (463/1071) 50, 72 n.12, 73
al-Maqrīzī Aḥmad b. ʿAlī (d. 845/1442) 170 n.108
Marāgha 10
Marj 63
Mary (mother of Jesus) 184, 187
Masjid al-Nabī (Prophet's mosque) 106
Mayer, Hans Eberhard 48
Mecca 3, 8, 12, 35, 86, 94, 122–123, 126, 154–155, 178–179, 180 n.135, 216–217
  conquest of, by Prophet (8/630) 89, 167 n.99
  sanctity of 33, 93
Medina 3, 8, 35, 86, 178, 179 n.131, 180 n.135, 217
  Ṭayba 216
Meisami, J. S. 10, 185
Milwright, Marcus 178 n.129
Moses (Prophet Mūsā) 169–171
  -Pharaoh dichotomy 170
Mosul 10, 12, 26, 58, 86
  unification of 202
Mount Sinai 169
Mourad, S. 31
al-Muʿaẓẓam ʿĪsā (d. 624/1227) 77, 97, 197, 209, 214
  and destruction of walls of Jerusalem 215–216
Muḥammad (Prophet) 35, 71, 95, 110–111, 114–115, 135, 145–146, 149, 153, 156–157, 170–171, 180, 182, 213
  bravery of 59
  Farewell Sermon of (10/632) 68
  as model 72
  night journey and ascension (*al-isrāʾ wa-l-miʿrāj*) 3, 88
  place of his family 195
  visitations from 179 n.131
Muḥammad b. Malikshāh, Ghiyāth al-Dunyā wa-l-Dīn 28, 74
Muʿīn al-Dīn Unur 62–63, 166
al-Mujāwir, Yaʿqub b. Muḥammad (d. 643/1245) 109, 209, 216 n.12, 217
Mujīr al-Dīn (r. 534–549/1140–54) 82, 84–85
Mujīr al-Dīn Abaq (d. 565/1169) 74
al-Muqaddasī 34 n.89, 168 n.104
  Aḥsan al-taqāsīm fī maʿrifat al-aqālīm 35
Muqātil (d. 150/767) 32
al-Muqtafī (ʿAbbāsid caliph) 22
Murray, A. 148
al-Mustaḍīʾ bi-Amr Allāh = al-Ḥassān al-Mustaḍīʾ b. Yūsuf al-Mustanjid (536–75/1142–80) (ʿAbbāsid caliph) 118, 206
al-Mustanjid (ʿAbbāsid caliph) 22
al-Mustaẓhir bi-Llāh (487–512/1094–1118) (ʿAbbāsid caliph) 3, 67–68
al-Mutanabbī (d. 354/965) 79, 89, 155 n.66, 182, 197 n.17, 209–210
  Dīwān 40, 159 n.78
al-Muʿtaṣim (d. 227/842) (caliph) 77, 92–93, 154, 182, 209

Nablus 97, 108
Nāṣir-i Khusraw 7
al-Nāṣir li-Dīn Allāh (r. 575–622/1180–1225) (caliph) 93, 108
Nawf al-Bakkālī 35
Nicholson, Helen J. 51
Niẓām al-Mulk 39, 57
Nubia 202
Nūr al-Dīn (d. 569/1174) (son of ʿImād al-Dīn Zangī) 4, 10, 22, 47, 62, 75, 82–85, 100, 102, 111, 120, 129, 140, 150, 155, 157, 162, 176, 181, 187, 195, 202, 209, 212–213
  and ʿAbbāsid caliph 205
  attributes of 156, 164, 166
  commitment/focus on *jihād* 10, 32, 158, 177
  educational ambitions 130
  endowment programmes of 19, 24
  eschatological role of 165
  historians on 206, 214
  image of 18, 36, 152, 159, 163, 213–214
  as pious fighter 18, 20, 151–152, 163, 183, 213–214
  and poetry 50, 219

propaganda campaigns of 114, 220
and Qilij Arslān II 201
and spirituality/piety 20–21, 84, 86, 152, 156, 161, 179 n.131, 183
and unification of Egypt and Syria 199–200
victories/achievements of 88, 154, 158, 222

Palestine 6–8, 31, 63, 67, 137, 163
under Franks 12
Oriental Christians in 141
Partner, Peter 55
Peter Tudebode 162
Pharaoh 5, 136, 169, 206–207
Philip II Augustus of France (r. 1180–1223) 92
Phillips, J. 51

al-Qāḍī l-Fāḍil = ʿAbd al-Raḥīm b. ʿAlī l-Baysānī 20, 28, 40, 51, 86, 100, 179–181, 192–196, 199, 222
Qāḍisiyya, battle of (15/636) 57
al-Qāsim (d. 600/1203) (son of Ibn ʿAsākir) 177
al-Jāmiʿ al-mustaqṣā fī faḍāʾil al-masjid al-Aqṣā 178
Qastal al-Shuʿaybiyya (Aleppo) 25
al-Qaynī, Quṭba b. al-Khaḍrāʾ 80–81
Qilij Arslān b. Masʿūd II of Iconium (d. 588/1192) 119, 200–201
Qubbat al-Miʿrāj (596–597/1200–01) 37 n.95
al-Qurṭubī (d. 671/1273) 8 n.20, 43
Quṭb al-Dīn Mawdūd 86
Qutulmish 200

Rabbat, Nasser 32, 48
al-Ramlī (d. 300/912) 31–32
al-Rashīd b. Nābulsī 91, 93, 108
Raymond, Prince of Antioch 88
al-Rāzī 8 n.20
Recueil des Historiens des Croisades 16, 48
Red Sea 136, 178, 180 n.135, 222
Resurrection, Church of (Kanīsat al-Qiyāma) 116, 137
Reynald of Châtillon 178, 180 n.135, 222
Richard I of England (r. 1189–99) 92
Richards, D. S. 49
Robert of Rheims 4 n.8
Robert the Monk 162
Roger II (of Sicily) 135
Roger of Antioch 61
Rome 34
Rosenthal, F. 43–45
al-Rukn b. Jahbal al-ʿAdl 104
Runciman, S. 141

Sadan, Joseph 189
Saʿd b. Abī Waqqāṣ 57
al-Ṣafadī 197 n.17
al-Saʿīd, Ḥamīd 53
Saidnaya, shrine of 223
Ṣalāḥ al-Dīn (d. 613/1216) 10, 26, 28, 74–75, 86, 93, 100, 103, 110–111, 113, 125–126, 128, 140, 145, 180–181, 194, 196, 205, 212
appellation/title of 93, 108
attributes of 12, 103, 136, 209
career of 12–13, 26–27
as champion/defender of Islam 116, 126, 180
colour and symbolism of 90
commitment to *jihād* 102, 104, 146
endowment programmes of 19–20, 23–24
image of 18, 36, 49–50, 100–101, 112
jihād programmes of 32, 163
and Joseph/Yūsuf 207–208
and justice/corruption 121–122
likened to ʿUmar b. al-Khaṭṭāb 170
memory/legacy of 210–211
piety of 127, 172
and poetry 110, 139, 219
propaganda campaigns of 114, 195, 220
reconquest of Jerusalem (583/1187) 11, 67, 125, 127, 135
and Sufis 20–21
victories/achievements of 99, 137, 157, 176–177, 212–213, 222, 225
al-Ṣaliḥiyya (Sufi hospice in Jerusalem) 19
al-Samʿānī, Abū Saʿd ʿAbd al-Karīm b. Muḥammad (d. 562/1166) 8 n.19, 218
Sayf al-Dawla al-Ḥamdānī (d. 356/967) 79, 89, 155 n.66, 164, 182, 209
Sayf al-Dīn Ghāzī 62
Sayf al-Dīn Manjak (d. 776/1374) (Mamlūk *amīr*) 14

Sayḥān, waters of 134
Semah, D. 225
al-Shāfiʿī (d. 204/820) 56
Shams al-Dīn Yūsuf 216 n.12
Shāwar (d. 564/1169) 192, 194–196, 202–203
and Amalric 198–199
execution of 204–205
Shihāb al-Dīn b. al-Mujāwir (d. 643/1245) 215
Shīrkūh, Asad al-Dīn (d. 564/1169) 151, 192, 194–196, 202–205
Shuʿayb (prophet) 177
Shuʿayb b. al-Ḥusayn b. Aḥmad al-Andalusī 25
Sibṭ b. al-Jawzī, Abū l-Muẓaffar (d. 654/1256) 64, 77, 95–97, 140 n.27, 173, 179, 214–215
Mirʾāt al-zamān fī tārīkh al-aʿyān 13
Sicily 9, 12, 80, 119, 131–132, 135
ruler of 147
Sidon 63
Sivan, Emmanuel 30–31, 144–145
Smoor, P. 75–76, 144, 197 n.17
Solomon. *See* Sulaymān
Spain 9, 12, 80
Sperl, S. 193
St. Anne, Church of 24
Stewart, D. 163
Sufyān al-Thawrī 18
Suhrawardī, Shihāb al-Dīn Yaḥyā b. Ḥabash (d. 587/1191) 28
al-Ṣūʾigh, Yūsuf 53
al-Sulamī, ʿAlī b. Ṭāhir (d. 499–500/1106) 12, 27, 56, 69, 80–81, 91, 117–118, 220–221
jihād treatises 36, 50
Kitab al-Jihād 2–3, 9, 51, 57, 59, 65, 78, 98, 205, 211
Sulaymān (Prophet Solomon) 156, 174 n.120
Sumi, Akiko Motoyoshi 128
al-Suyūṭī, Jalāl al-Dīn (d. 911/1505) 33
Tuḥfat al-muhtadīn bi-akhbār al-mujaddidīn 29
Syria (Shām, Greater Syria) 6–8, 13, 67, 70, 73, 100, 103, 116, 122, 163, 167, 174–175, 177, 202, 220
disunity in 199
and Egypt 178, 199
faḍāʾil of 32
merits/virtues of 93, 211 n.2, 218, 225
Oriental Christians in 141
spiritual standing of 218, 225
unification of 205, 212
unity with Egypt 192, 202, 208
Szombathy, Z. 222

al-Ṭabarī (d. 310/923) 43
Tabuk, military expedition of 56 n.3
Talhami, Ghada Hashem 31
Ṭaqī l-Dīn (nephew of Ṣalāḥ al-Dīn) 104
Taymāʾ 178
Tefillat Rabbi Shimʿon ben Yohai [Prayer of Rabbi Simeon ben Yohai] 5
Temple (in Jerusalem) 8 n.20
Tibawi, A. L. 8 n.20, 19, 131
Tiberias 103
Tibnin 63, 91
Tramontini, L. 53
Trench, Battle of the (5/627) 153
Ṭughtikin 2 n.1, 138
al-Ṭūr (Mount Sinai) 169, 215
Tyre 12, 63, 188

Uḥud, battle of (4/625) 59, 64, 168
ʿUmāra al-Yamanī (d. 571/1175) 193, 197, 199
ʿUmar b. al-Khaṭṭāb (r. 13–23/634–644) 57, 111, 113, 123, 126, 157, 176
conversion to Islam 171
and initial conquest of Jerusalem 112
and Ṣalāḥ al-Dīn 170
Umayyad Mosque (Masjid al-Umawī, Damascus) 9, 14, 106, 151 n.58, 166, 216 n.12
Ummaya b. Khalaf 59
Urban II (Pope) 4 n.8, 7
Usāma b. Munqidh (d. 588/1188) 38, 147, 176, 192–193, 196, 199–202, 224
Dīwān 40
Kitāb al-Iʿtibār 10–11, 43, 49
ʿUthmān b. ʿAffān (d. 35/656) 95–96, 111, 113, 117
ʿUthmān b. al-Malik al-Nāṣir Yūsuf b. Ayyūb (d. 595/1198) (son of Ṣalāḥ al-Dīn) 209–211

al-Wahrānī 51
Walter the Chancellor 148
Wansbrough, J. 8 n.20

Wasit 35
al-Wāsiṭī, Abū Bakr Muḥammad 32, 107
Faḍā'il al-bayt al-muqaddas 38
Werthmuller, K. J. 143
Wilfong, T. G. 143
William of Tyre 148, 206
Wright, W. 121 n.71

Yāqūt al-Hamawī 15
Yemen 52
poetry in 192
Yüzendag, Amnet 50

Zubayr [b. al-ʿAwwām] 60

Index of Subjects

ʿAbbāsids (of Baghdad) 25, 189, 203
 caliphs 22, 71, 100, 113, 205
 loyalty to 22, 100
 poetry of 212
abdāl (substitutes) 150 n.55, 161, 215, 217–218
accountability
 to God 78, 140, 160
adab 43
adhān (call to prayer) 106, 146
admonitions/chastisement 38, 53, 68, 71, 161
advice 80, 124, 128, 176
adviser(s) 100, 124, 127
advisory (*naṣīḥa*) texts 17
aesthetics 191
afterlife 140. *See also* hereafter
agency 143
alcohol 109, 147
 wine 159
Alexander 177
alliances 85, 195, 208. *See also* unification/union
 Egypt and Damascus 199
 Shāwar and Amalric 198–199
allusions 42, 176, 197, 212, 218
 Qurʾānic 111, 165, 167–168, 183, 207, 225
Almohads (al-Muwaḥḥidūn) 121, 174 n.120
Almoravids (al-Murābiṭūn) 121
amīr (leader) 160–161
anaphora 217
Anatolians 121
anecdotes 10, 15, 17, 59, 64, 82, 97, 120, 134–135, 148, 150 n.56, 157, 161–162
angels 114, 150 n.55, 160–161
anguish 215, 217
animals
 deer (*mahāt*) 185
 dogs 120, 193
 donkeys 92, 96
 lions 92, 164–165, 193
 pigs/swine 63, 76, 91, 109, 120, 147
 snakes 203
Anṣār (lit., 'Helpers') 153
Antichrist 7
 and Dajjāl 144, 165, 172
anti-Christian
 motives 109
 rhetoric 114
 sentiment 24, 143
anti-crusader texts 16, 155 n.66, 163
anti-Frankish
 commitment 212
 feeling 183
 jihād 1, 27, 29, 31, 37, 48, 49, 51, 54, 55, 57, 106, 113, 117, 129–130, 138, 142, 145, 150 n.56, 152, 163, 200–202, 219, 224–225
  poetry/literature 2, 17, 65, 72, 142, 147
 motive 109
 stance 60
antithesis 75, 95, 101, 126, 128, 159, 168, 207
 clarity (*bayyināt*) *vs.* concealment (*tukhfī*) 75
 gathered, *vs.* divided 92
 misguidance (*ḍalāla*) *vs.* guidance (*rashād*) 134
 pure *vs.* impure 168
 removal (*nazaʿa*) *vs.* clothing or covering (*labasa*) 75
 rest (*rāḥa*) *vs.* effort (*jidd*)/weariness (*taʿab*) 152, 154
 serious *vs.* playful 153–154, 203
 uncovering *vs.* revealing (*kashafa*) 75
anxiety 29, 173, 221. *See also* fear(s)
apathy 2, 27, 67, 70, 71, 91, 221
apocalypse/apocalyptic 7, 113, 120, 126, 173
 and battle/Armageddon (*malḥama*) 117
 *ḥadīth*s/traditions 34, 114, 117
 literature 5
apocalypticism 44, 118
apostasy 189
appellations 86, 90, 93, 156 n.72, 164, 208. *See also* title, al-Malik al-Nāṣir
appropriation
 of Jesus, by Muslims 96, 129, 144–145
 of Shīʿī sites of worship 25
Arabic
 grammar 37
 literature 16
 medieval historiography 46
 poetry 1, 125, 139, 162
 sources, translations of 48
 writing 45
Arab/Israeli conflict 30

Arabs 41, 71, 129
architecture 53, 110
armistice agreements 223. *See also* alliances
army(ies) 21, 56–57, 87, 111, 113, 136, 159, 162, 165, 168, 176, 223–224
  cooperation of Egyptian and Syrian 199–200
  of God/heaven 113, 116, 211
arrogance 103, 134
ascension, of Prophet 37 n.95, 114, 215
  and night journey (*al-isrā' wa-l-mi'rāj*) 88
asceticism/ascetic 2 n.2, 28, 51, 61, 65, 100, 151, 155–156, 217–218
  jurists 14
  poetry of (*zuhdiyya*) 160
  Sufis 221
  and warrior ethos 226
assimilation/acclimitisation 91, 188
audience(s) 157, 169, 176, 189, 194, 199, 204
  language of 163
  of poets 41–42, 71, 77, 87, 101, 111, 141, 156–158, 163, 167, 169, 172–173, 183, 199, 211–212, 225
authenticity 19, 44 n.11
  of traditions 38, 211 n.2
authority 17, 21, 23, 74, 86, 132, 166, 170, 193, 207–208, 211. *See also* legitimacy
  of 'Abbāsid caliph 4, 100, 205
  of Fāṭimids 205
  Frankish 188
  legal/sacred (*shar'ī*) 75
  political 10, 17, 28, 40, 162, 193
  of Qur'ān 85
  religious 55
Ayyūbids 17–18, 23, 25, 90, 111, 135, 144, 151, 192, 209–210, 214
  and civilian elites 11, 20
  era/period 51, 142
  Kurdish 162
  leaders/rulers 100, 136, 205, 207
  rule/dynasty 13, 15, 101, 112, 163, 195, 214
  and Sufis/endowments 20–21

Banū 'Abbās 206
Banū Aṣfar (pale-faced ones) 34, 89–90, 115, 145
Banāt al-Aṣfar ('pale-faced women') 85, 186, 222
Banū Munqidh 192 n.2
Banū Qudāma 151
battle(s) 57–58
  of Badr (2/624) 114, 198
  of Balat ('Battle of the Field of Blood') (513/1119) 60–61, 138, 149
  of Bānyās (559/1164) 164–166, 172
  epic (*malāḥim*) 177
  of Fariskur (Muḥarram 648/April 1250) 130, 145
  of al-Ḥadath (343/954–55) 79, 182, 209
  of Ḥaṭṭīn (583/1187) 13, 49, 103–104, 225
  humane (methods of fighting) 63–64
  of Inab (544/1149) 88
  of Manzikert (463/1071) 50, 72 n.12, 73
  of Qādisiyya (15/636) 57
  of the Trench (5/627) 153
  of Uḥud (4/625) 59, 64, 168
bayt Allāh (house of God) 106
beauty 184–187, 190
  worldly *vs.* transcendent 187
belief/believers 57, 62, 70, 142, 168, 219
  false, in Jesus 141
  īmān, as light 168
  of Muslims 174 n.120, 197
  in One True God 172
  vs. unbelief 170
belle-lettres 49
bells (church) 146–147, 172
benefit 19, 43–44, 128, 133
betrayal 84
Bible 65, 108–109, 130, 139, 146
  Gospel (Injīl) 109, 139, 146
biographers 12, 88, 100, 151, 213–214
biographies 12, 48
  of Prophet Muḥammad 171
bishops 104, 140–141. *See also* priests/clergy
blessedness 6, 44
blessing (*baraka*) 6, 17, 19, 206
blinded/blindness 132–133, 207, 210–211
booty 73, 136. *See also* spoil-of-war
boundaries 6, 73, 82, 222
bravery 79, 92, 152, 200, 214
  shajā'a 59, 64
brotherhood, ideals of 67
building projects. *See* construction/building projects
Buwayhids (Būyids) 162

Byzantine(s) 9, 66, 73, 79, 89, 121, 154, 155 n.66, 164
Christians 72
women 190

calamity 76, 174, 176. *See also* catastrophe
caliphate 6, 196
caliph(s) 3, 151, 188, 205, 222
ʿAbbāsids (of Baghdad) 22, 71, 100, 113, 205
and defence of Muslims 71
early Sunnī 111, 113, 213
Egyptian 206
responsibility of 205
captivity
of Amorium 93
of Holy Sepulchre 112
of Jerusalem 83, 216
catastrophe 5 n.11, 6, 132, 173, 188
celestial
and earthly realms 112
maidens 184–185
chancery 151, 168, 181, 192, 194–195, 202
chaos 40, 77, 173, 214
chastisement. *See* admonitions/chastisement
children 58, 68, 70, 74, 97, 204
good deeds of 81
Christian(s)/Christianity 1, 7, 8, 20, 23–24, 34, 72, 75, 84–85, 96–97, 103, 108, 141–144, 148, 156 n.70, 168, 171–173, 183, 204, 206, 219, 223–224
Armenians 82 n.32, 196
ascriptions/references to Jesus 129–130, 133, 144–146, 149
and battle of Balat 149
beliefs about Jesus 135, 138, 141, 165
broader military scheme of 9, 12, 80, 206
on Byzantium/Byzantines 72–73, 120
defeat of 117, 133
Egyptian Copts 23–24, 142–143
errors/deviations of 172, 204
eschatology of 6–8, 117
European/western 72, 121, 168, 180
faith/devotion of 130, 133–134, 146, 187
Frankish 129, 143, 183, 224
vs. Islam 146, 219
'jihād,' 9
local/indigenous 141–143, 184
mixing/interactions with Muslims 2, 91, 189, 223–224
mobilising/rousing 8, 217
Muslim polemics against 130
Muslims converting to 97
of Nubia and Abyssinia 202
Orthodox (Syrian, Arabic-speaking) 96
Other 224
priests/clergy 65, 103, 130, 133, 140–141
religiosity/worship of 96–97, 110
role of Jerusalem/sacred sites 4–5, 7, 135, 137–138, 221
scriptures 55, 108–109
symbols 75–76, 89, 95, 102, 104 n.14, 110, 112, 125, 147, 219 (*See also* crosses)
views on crusades 131–132
women 184, 186, 188–189
Christmas 133–134
chronicles/chroniclers 16, 19, 36, 41–43, 46–47, 53, 61–62, 87, 96, 112, 142, 151, 162, 177, 181, 204
Christian 149
Muslim 140
church(es) 184, 186, 224
of Antioch 224
disputes in 131
of the Holy Nativity at Bethlehem 223
of the Resurrection (Kanīsat al-Qiyāma) 116, 137
of St. Anne 24
cities/towns 34
civilian elite 17, 19, 192–193, 213
aʿyān 41, 58, 151
Fāṭimid 11
cleansing. *See* purification
colour imagery
blue 189
green 149
white 186–187
yellow, for Mamlūks 90
commemoration (poetry of) 50, 123, 125, 164, 172, 209
commentaries 32, 45, 61, 105–106
communal
attitudes 118
dispute 52
identity 53
prayer 106, 223
religious solidarity 217

companions (of Prophet Muḥammad) 25, 30–31, 43–44, 61, 64, 111, 114, 117, 170, 208
companionship (*ṣuḥba*) 41, 192, 199
complaint, poetic 121, 185–186, 217
conquest(s) 164, 211, 213
of all conquests (*fatḥ al-futūḥ*) 87
construction/building projects 24–25, 212
Contextual Approach 45
conventions 190
of Arabic poetry 139
theological 193
conversion 97, 171
Copts 142–143
correspondence 199. *See also* letters
poetic 192
with sultan 128
corruption 125, 224
of tax officials 126–127
cosmology/cosmological
relationship between Mecca and Jerusalem 107
role of Jerusalem 6, 110
counter-crusade 35, 55, 226
courage 59–60, 64, 193
court(s) 86, 156 n.72
ceremonies/ceremonials 22, 163
circles 47, 128
poets/poetry 40, 82, 100, 128, 139, 151, 190, 220, 222
cowardice/weakness 79, 136
credibility 26, 205, 220
creed 196
Ashʿarī 25
Islamic 90, 110
Shīʿī 194
Sunnī 23
criticisms 59, 100, 128, 131 n.4, 197, 204
cross-cultural exchange 12, 192, 224
crosses 63, 94–96, 101, 104, 109, 122, 138–139, 147, 174 n.120, 195
breaking of 126
umm al-ṣalīb (lit., 'mother of the cross') 139
crucifix 76, 172
crucifixion 104 n.16, 138, 147
crusades/crusaders 14, 34, 55, 58, 67, 76, 80, 85–86, 92, 94–95, 97, 100–102, 122, 129, 131, 138, 141, 148, 163, 171, 176, 183, 186, 188, 192, 221
ambitions/aspirations of 133–134, 219
and apocalypse/eschatology 5, 7–8, 34, 44, 118–119, 218
arrogance of 103, 134
as battle between Christians and Islam 78, 133
battle of Ḥaṭṭīn 103, 225
broader Christian aims 9, 12, 80, 206
and Byzantines 9, 72–73
constructs around 48
descriptions of 72, 76, 78, 89, 133
and Edessa 81–82
and Egypt 143, 180, 195, 197–199, 202, 208, 215
expulsion of 18, 127, 147
and *faḍāʾil* ideas/literature 30–32, 107, 115
Fifth Crusade (614–18/1217–21) 13, 168, 170 n.108, 197, 214
First Crusade (488–93/1095–99) 2–3, 12, 67, 68 n.3, 73, 81, 83–84, 93, 97, 120, 173, 217
as *ʿilj*, pl. *ūlūj* 63–64, 115, 133, 181
imagery of 79, 112, 132, 137, 168
influence/impact of 1, 49, 74, 142, 150, 171, 208, 219
and Jesus 144–146, 148–149, 157
jihād /physical response to 55, 57, 64, 66, 78, 98, 122, 125, 163, 187, 196, 225 (*See also jihād*)
loss/defeat of 64, 103, 125–127, 130, 133–134, 136, 158, 171, 204, 225
and martyrdom 58, 61
methods of fighting 63–64
Muslim reactions/attitudes to 1–2, 26–27, 36, 48–49, 68 n.3, 78, 220
and Nūr al-Dīn 82, 84–85, 154, 157, 159, 195
occupation of Jerusalem 26, 36, 66, 72, 76, 93, 105–106, 120, 180, 196, 206, 221
plans 126, 176
plan to attack Mecca and Medina 179
and poetry 40, 50–51, 70–72, 75–76, 79, 83, 92–94, 99, 101, 103, 108, 125, 127, 131, 135–137, 139, 155, 157, 163, 224
polemics against 145
presence 176, 218
religious rationale of 135–138, 140
role of Jerusalem 4, 7, 30–32

sack of Alexandria (767/1365) 14
sanctioning 132
satirising 157
scholarship on/studies 1, 51
Second Crusade (541–43/1147–48) 4, 38, 61, 63, 65–66, 81, 96 n.70, 97, 140 n.27
settlement of 74, 142
siege of Damascus 4, 61, 64, 74, 95
sources for 13
symbols of 95, 126, 158, 174 n.120
in Syria 78, 177
Third Crusade 91–92, 204
threat 18, 25, 73, 111, 146, 151, 165–166, 177, 181, 212, 214
as wicked 134, 213
and women 162, 202
cultural/religious syncretism 189
culture/cultural 27
acceptability 186
boundaries 189
encounters/interactions 186, 224
expectations 96
expressions 225

Dajjāl (Antichrist) 144, 165, 172
dār al-ʿadl ('house of justice') 22
dead 64, 160, 178 n.129, 224
celebrated, in elegies 130
resurrected 6, 35
ruins 123, 126
death 80–81, 95, 122, 126, 160, 164
in God's cause 72
defeat 27, 41, 80
of Antichrist 165
of Byzantines 73
of Franks/crusaders 26, 79, 90, 103, 125–127, 130, 133–136, 138, 149, 158, 204, 225
of Muslims 81, 205
of Pharaoh 169
of polytheism/Christianity 102, 117, 196
defence 34, 39, 56, 71, 182, 204
of Damascus 34, 61, 63
of Islam 23, 47
of Jerusalem 23, 93, 174 n.120
of Muslims 62, 65
of people/of faith 76
of weak/oppressed 70, 72
defilement 224
desecration 63, 76, 147
desperation (*iḍṭirār*) 198
determination 103, 116, 134, 182, 209–210
devotion
of Christians/Franks 90, 130, 133–134, 146, 184, 187
to *jihād* 37, 57, 65, 146, 154, 158, 181, 200, 204
of Muslims 106, 156, 159, 183
religious 47, 101, 104, 184
dhimmīs 141–143
Dhū l-Qarnayn 174 n.120, 176–177
dichotomies 103, 183, 190
Moses *vs.* Pharaoh 170
Muslims *vs.* Christians 204
dignity, of Muslims 81, 123, 155 n.66
diplomacy 51, 54, 192
and poetry 52, 199
disbelief 224. *See also* unbelief
disorder 158, 173
disunity/division 27, 91, 121, 136–137, 143, 198, 200
among Fāṭimids 206
internal 2, 220
sectarian 202
in Syria 199–200
divinations 94. *See also* omen(s); portents
divine/heavenly 156 n.70, 167, 185
approval/assistance 20, 57, 112–113, 149, 150 n.55, 168, 211
decree/providence 130, 135, 207
design 110, 167
favour 110, 145, 166, 207
intent/purpose 168, 211
order 22, 146
protection 214
punishment 101–102
signs 5
dīwān (anthology of poetry) 11, 42, 184
double entendres 42, 102, 104, 163
dreams 62, 64. *See also* sleep
dubayts (poems) 50, 152–155, 203, 213
duty, collective (*farḍ al-kifāya*) 56

earthquakes 147, 176
education 19, 44, 130
institutions of 24
elegy(ies) 20
rithāʾ/marthīya 53, 108, 115, 130, 217

eloquence 113, 220
emotions/passion 46, 54, 67, 70, 74, 97, 112, 128, 173, 209, 217, 222
end of days/end of time 7, 35, 110, 116, 172–173, 177–178, 180, 218, 222
  role of Jerusalem in 178
endowment(s) (*waqf*, pl. *awqāf*) 18–20, 24
enemy(ies) 57, 59, 71, 79, 80, 87, 102, 121–122, 137, 146, 158, 219, 222
  external 55
  of the faith/Islam 56, 176–177
  internal 163
  lampooning of, in poetry 2, 41
  'otherness' of 89
epithets 106, 148
erotic/sensual (poetry) 187, 189
eschatology/eschatological 35, 116, 119, 137, 144, 165, 172, 178, 208, 218, 222, 224–225
  Biblical/in Christianity 5–6
  expectations/fears 120, 180
  imagery 77, 173, 177
  Islamic/Qurʾānic 3, 6, 114, 117, 177
  in Judaism 6
  motifs 129, 173, 177
  and role of Jerusalem 37, 114, 225
ethics 44 n.11, 103
  of just rule 16–17
  practical 17, 28
ethnicities 111
ethos
  of era/culture 26, 222
  of *jihād* 57, 59, 82
  of piety 152
  of pious warriors 20, 129, 151, 226
euphoria 113, 119, 181
  in poetry 108
exhortation 37, 57, 72, 81, 140, 153, 161, 165, 169, 217
  assemblies of (*majālis al-waʿẓ*) 13
exoneration 41, 102, 115

faḍāʾil (merits, virtues)
  books/texts of 1, 20, 30, 34–35, 51–52, 95, 99, 107, 110, 113, 115, 173, 174 n.120, 177, 218, 219
  of Egypt 169
  literature 30–33, 36
  poetry 209
  proliferation of works on 4, 37
  al-Quds (of Jerusalem) 8, 30, 32–34, 106, 114, 135, 217
  al-Shām (of Syria) 8, 32
  studies 39
  themes 51, 183, 217
  traditions 33
  faith(s) 57, 141, 193
  champion of 157
  defence of 76, 101
  devotion to 159
  millat Aḥmad 146
  vs. unbelief 103, 177
Faranj. *See* Franks
fate 11, 80, 137, 215. *See also* predestination
Fāṭimids 4 n.6, 10, 17, 19–20, 22, 174, 181, 197 n.17, 205, 225
  caliphs/caliphate 93, 196, 205, 207
  chancery of the state (*dīwān al-inshāʾ*) 194
  and civilian elite 11
  poetry of 144, 192
  rule, protection of 208
  Shīʿīs 3, 144
  threats to 206
fealty 205. *See also* loyalty
fearlessness 135–136, 210
fear(s) 69–71, 79–81, 92–93, 122, 126, 168–169, 173–175, 177, 179–180, 197, 199, 219–220, 222
  in Egypt 208
  of God 57, 193, 200
festivals 53, 166
fighting 69, 80, 122, 159 n.78, 200, 223 n.11
  commitment to 71
  crusaders methods of 64
filth 75, 86. *See also* impurity
fitna (temptation, trial, upheaval) 58, 71, 91, 188, 190–191, 198, 201
forbearance 193, 210
formalism 47, 82, 220
Formal-Cultural Approach 45–46
fortifications/walls of Jerusalem, destruction of 77, 214
Franci 148
Franks (Faranj) 2 n.2, 11, 19, 26, 59–60, 63, 72, 87, 89–91, 98, 101, 121, 130, 140–142, 174, 180, 194, 196–198, 204, 222, 224
  attitude toward 117
  and Copts 143

Franks (Faranj) (cont.)
- descriptions of 97, 136
- and Europeans/non-Franks 141
- expulsion from Jerusalem 176
- identity of/Rūm 120
- as *ʿilj*, pl. *ūlūj* 63–64, 115, 133, 181
- Muslim alliances/treaties with 84–85, 204
- and Muslims 12, 99, 132, 186, 188
- occupation of 83, 91, 112, 147, 217, 226
- as Other 103, 115, 190, 224
- presence of 147, 187, 189
- threat of 198, 206
- women 184–190, 185, 186, 187, 188, 189, 190, 203, 204, 219, 222, 224
- women/Faranja 1, 51, 85, 183, 185, 187–190, 204

fraternisation 223
Friday
- prayer 174
- status of 38

Gabriel (angel) 111–112
gender. *See also* women
- -based poetry 142, 188, 222
- and imagery 139
- inclusion 204
- perspective 184, 203

generosity 76, 118, 207, 210
ghazal (love poems) 184–185, 189–190
- *al-ghazal al-ʿudhrī* 185, 187

Ghaznavids 25
girls 69–70, 82, 93. *See also* women
glory 125, 159 n.78, 216
God 136, 138, 145
- anger of 179
- approval of 224
- decree of 130, 200
- favour/promise of 204, 210, 225
- party of 203–204
- power of 88, 116, 119, 169, 171
- praise of 222
- trust in 156

Gog (Ya'jūj) 176–177
- and Magog 178

government/governance 10, 24, 28, 53, 195, 205, 207
- Islamic 73–74, 156, 213

governors 28, 91, 97, 178, 207, 222
graves 65, 136, 138, 150, 160, 166, 173
Greek (s) 96 n.71, 121
- of Antioch 96 n.71

grief 46, 52, 70, 82, 203, 215–217
grievances 22, 52, 203
guidance 95, 122–123, 193, 195, 198, 215
- *vs.* misguidance 103, 133–134
- *vs.* unbelief 207

ḥadīth 32–34, 43–44, 78–79, 99, 106, 114, 118, 129, 151 n.58, 153, 171, 208, 211 n.2, 218
- on apocalypse 34
- literature of 31, 39, 44, 55, 81, 177
- scholar of (*muḥaddith*) 11

ḥajj 30, 107, 150 n.55, 218. *See also* pilgrimage
Hamdanid(s) 79
Ḥanafī(s) 23
Ḥanbalī(s) 151
Hāshimī 206
heaven 37 n.95, 116, 134, 178. *See also* paradise
- army(ies) of 113, 211

hellfire 166, 178
hereafter 65, 81, 85, 123, 140, 153, 159–161, 166, 204
heresy(ies) 197 n.17
- internal 166
- Shīʿī 18, 121

hermeneutics, Qur'ānic 104, 105 n.23
heterodoxy 25
historians 19, 26, 30, 35, 43, 45, 47–48, 54, 68 n.3, 91, 204, 206, 220
historicism 163, 170
historiography 30, 42, 44–46, 49, 51, 54
history/historical 13, 15, 43–44, 47, 52, 78, 162, 170, 181, 204
- context 2, 152
- social 45
- sources 46, 49–50
- truth 1, 43, 44 n.11, 46, 47, 225
- and value of poetry 42, 50
- world/universal 12–14, 45
- writing, and rewriting 45–46, 53

holiness 7
- designation of 106
- hierarchy of 217

holy 6
  city(ies) 179–180, 218
  of holies (*quds al-quds*) 6
  men 151
  places/sites 108, 222
  war 26
  warriors 18, 149, 163, 195
honesty 210
honour 58, 65, 81, 97, 123–125, 153, 186
  ʿirḍ 68, 70, 125
hopes 4, 169, 173, 177, 180, 199, 219, 222
Hospitallers (al-Isbatār/Asbatār) 140–141, 176, 177
hostility 85, 142
Hour 211 n.2. *See also* end of days/end of time; Last Day(s)/Last Hour
  portents of 119–120
ḥujjat al-dīn ('proof of the religion') 62
humbleness 103–104
humiliation 69, 92, 123–126, 130, 133, 155 n.66, 196
  of Jerusalem 219
humility 96, 151, 156, 163, 172
hunger 188. *See also* suffering
al-ḥūr al-ʿīn (celestial maidens) 184–185, 187
hyperbole 43, 83, 87, 96, 115, 176
hypocrisy (*nifāq*) 84–86

icons 147, 174 n.120, 184, 187
ideals 44, 65, 219
  of brotherhood 67
  of courtly virtue, chivalry/bravery 40, 59–60
  Islamic/Qurʾānic 41, 193
  of *jihād* 55, 88
  pietistic/religious 46, 56
identity(ies) 51
  communal 53
  cosmopolitan Islamic 151
  social, religious 143
ideology(ies) 156, 170
  of *jihād* 23, 31, 163, 225
  of poets/poetry 1, 42, 129, 183
  of Sunnī revival 25
  of tribalism 53
ignorance 92, 211
ijāzas (certificates) 23
ijmāʿ (consensus) 75–76
ʿilj, pl. *ūlūj* 63–64, 115, 133, 181
images/imagery 42, 52, 87, 93, 112, 139–140, 155, 163, 187, 219, 224–225
  colour 90, 149, 186–187, 189
  of crusaders 224
  eschatological 77, 173, 177
  ghazal 189
  light *vs.* dark 101, 145, 168
  Qurʾānic 49, 77, 85, 101, 129, 132, 136, 166, 169, 183, 222
  religious 2, 89, 110–111, 137, 160, 208
  of sultans 101–103, 126, 145, 195
imagination 170–171
imāms 2 n.2, 106, 110, 206
  Shīʿī 144
impurity 73, 171
incentives 81, 166, 197
  financial/political 199
  religious 141
independence
  of Egypt 194, 195
  of thought 190
infatuation 184–186, 189
infidels 50, 71, 147, 150, 224
infighting 2, 71. *See also* disunity/division
injustice 21 n.53, 58, 70, 99, 123–125, 127
  and oppression (*maẓālim*) 161
inscriptions 1, 22, 25, 37 n.95, 172, 219
  Qurʾānic 170, 172
  on tombs 138
institution-building 22
internal 57
  blame 68, 224
  concord 200
  conflict 16, 71
  division 2, 219–220
  religious weakness 27, 82
  revolts 91
  schismatic disputes/heresies 163, 166, 193
  theological debates 25
interpreters 45, 163, 183
invectives 15, 85, 91
invention 189–191
inviolable/inviolability 70. *See also* sacred/sacredness
  ḥarīm/*ḥurma* 68, 125, 127
  of women 73, 123, 127

irreligiousness 84
Islamicising/Islamicisation 60, 219
Islam/Islamic 15–16, 71, 74–75, 78, 133, 142, 158, 174, 183, 203, 216 n.12. *See also* Shīʿa/Shīʿī(s); Sunnī(s)
abode of (*dār al-Islām*) 73, 105
character 94, 209, 218
vs. Christianity 146, 219
claim to Jesus 157
conversion to/embracing 90, 171
creed 90, 110, 196
defence/defenders of 22–24, 83, 126, 164, 180
early feats/heroes 71–72, 113, 151–153, 156, 167, 210
enemy(ies) of 56, 176–177, 198
government/governance 73–74, 156, 213
holy/sacred places 179, 219
ideals 193
identity 151
and Jerusalem 30–31, 34–36, 39, 82, 101, 176, 209
lands of 156, 159, 203, 214
law 26, 73–74
and loss of Egypt 202
order 74, 111, 126, 127, 158
poets as spokesmen of 41
political unity of 205
promotion of Sunnīs 25, 166
and Qur'ānic eschatology 3, 6, 114, 117, 177
renouncing 189
resistance against unbelievers 34
rhetoric 146
sciences 18, 43–45, 44 n.11, 45
and Shīʿī 25, 144
social order 127, 143
Sunnī(s) 20, 22, 76, 111
superiority of 2, 90, 99, 103, 108, 121, 130, 140–141
symbols 75–76, 90
themes 74, 225
triumph/victories of 83, 90, 95, 126, 168, 173, 210
Isrāʾīliyyāt traditions 32

Jamālī(s) 4, 193
viziers 196
jealousy/protection (*ghayra; ghāʾir*) 70, 125
jesting (*hazl*) 43, 155
jihād 1, 15, 30, 37, 47, 56 n.3, 79, 81, 87, 98, 102, 112, 129–130, 139, 143, 152–153, 159, 163, 165, 181, 201, 211 n.2, 220, 225–226
advancing/promoting 16, 72, 89, 125, 140, 187, 222
advocates of 213
anti-Frankish 1, 27, 29, 31, 37, 48–49, 51, 54–55, 57, 106, 113, 117, 129–130, 138, 142, 145, 150 n.56, 152, 163, 193, 195, 200–202, 219, 224–225
-based context 168
-based motifs/themes 49–50, 154
Christian 9
commitment/devotion to 37, 57, 65, 146, 154, 158, 181, 200, 204
defensive 64, 66
endorsing/sanctioning 196
ethos 57, 59, 82
fighters/warriors 29, 50–51, 59, 161, 183, 213
greater inner *vs.* lesser physical 27, 29, 56 n.3, 150 n.56, 156, 167
ideal 55, 88
ideology(ies) of 23, 31, 163, 225
initiatives 17, 182
leaders 10, 79
legal framework of 57
to liberate Jerusalem 99, 173
al-lisān (of the tongue) 37
military/physical 56–57, 64, 116, 156, 202
al-nafs 59, 65, 224
obligation of 29, 36, 56, 66, 80, 146, 154–155, 221
personal/public 21
poetry/literature of 2, 50, 52, 65, 67, 68 n.3, 72, 125, 130, 140, 142, 147–148, 190, 199, 219, 224
praise (poetry) of 81, 154
preaching/sermons 1, 219
programme 10, 17, 163
propaganda 4, 51, 54, 61, 196, 219–220
and Qur'ān 56
rhetoric 38, 57, 61, 164
slogans/banner of 4, 78
spirit of 67, 82, 88 n.52, 93
texts/treatises 9, 27, 36–37, 52, 69, 105, 114–115, 177
theory 35, 51, 111

traditions on 34, 211 n.2
against unbelief/polytheism 155, 201, 207, 213
vocabulary/language 61, 67, 99, 138
yearning for 36
jubilation, public 169, 214. *See also* euphoria
Judaism/Jews 5–6, 84, 141, 172
judgement, day of 6, 77, 119, 140, 160, 168, 179
descriptions of 173
jurisprudence 23, 29, 57, 75–76, 78, 85, 109, 141
Shāfiʿī 19–20
jurists 13–15, 21, 23 n.58, 25, 28–29, 56, 58, 61–63, 66, 91, 104–105, 109, 117, 120–121, 128, 134–135, 151, 161–162, 167
orthodoxy of 28
resistance among 220
justice 22, 28, 91, 121, 127, 141, 161 n.82, 174 n.120, 188
divine 156 n.70
house of (*dār al-ʿadl*) 22
rules of 160 n.79
justification 57, 64, 166
juxtapositions 64, 76–77, 80, 102–103, 122, 125–126, 128, 134, 136, 146, 154, 172, 187, 195, 207, 222

Kaʿba 35, 89, 106, 182, 216
Kawthar (fount of abundance) 85
khānqāhs 25, 51. *See also* Sufi(s)/Sufism
*khaṭīb*s (preachers) 2, 19, 24, 36–38, 61, 113, 199, 221
Khiḍr (lit., green one) 150 n.55
kingdoms 158–159, 210–211
kings/kingship 10, 28, 123, 126, 136, 161, 211, 214
Knights Templars 176

lament/lamentations 68, 70, 73, 109, 126, 147, 156 n.70, 188, 204, 217
land(s) 95
grants (*iqṭaʿ*) 20 n.48
Islamic 156, 159, 203, 214
language 42, 46, 111, 163, 167, 194
of diplomacy 54
eschatological 77
figurative 185
hegemonic use of 53
of *jihād* 61, 67
mastery of 111, 191
multiple, of army 103, 111
of poets 70, 169
of realpolitik 194, 208
religious 187
Last Day(s)/Last Hour 7, 35, 101, 107, 113, 117, 173, 178, 180. *See also* end of days/end of time; Hour
Latini 148
laudatory lines/poems 126, 165, 222. *See also* praise (poetry)
law(s)/legal 73, 85, 157, 221
Islamic/Qurʾānic 26, 73, 146
religious 74–75
Sunnī schools of 23
lay population 58, 68, 92, 220
leaders/leadership 200
Ayyūbids 100, 136, 205, 207
of *jihād* 10, 79
military 21, 92, 183, 197
Muslim 113–114
religious 21, 183
legitimacy 4, 17, 21, 38, 40, 112, 193, 207–208
of rulers 182
of Sunnī caliph 205
letters 15, 51, 62, 118, 179, 181, 195, 200–201, 222
liberation 39, 94, 221
fatḥ, futūḥ 203
of Holy Land 221
of Holy Sepulchre 137
of Jerusalem 4, 83, 86, 88, 95, 98, 100, 118, 136, 139, 176, 192, 200–203, 211 n.2, 212, 221
life 43, 86, 112, 123, 126, 146
daily 11–12
nature/essence of 65, 80, 160, 210
public 11, 23, 37
spiritual 37, 56, 95, 154
worldly 81–82, 151, 153–154, 171
light 108, 158, 185
vs. darkness 85, 101, 138, 145, 159, 168, 207
nūr 85, 159
literary
benchmarks 163
critique 46
device 33, 128, 205
features 42, 45, 52, 152
genre 31, 150 n.56

literary (cont.)
  history 222
  qualities/elements 87
  skills 151, 195
  sources 29
  vehicles 47, 219
literature 16, 219. *See also* mirrors for princes (genre)
  of anti-Frankish *jihād* 147
  apocalyptic 5
  faḍā'il (merits, virtues) 30–33, 36
  ḥadīth 31, 39, 44, 55, 81, 177
  and history 204
  Qur'ān in 166
  rabbinical 5
  religious 177
litterateur (*adīb*) 14, 40, 151
loss 1, 158, 168, 196
  of Jerusalem/Holy City 77, 216
  of sacred locations 176, 178
love 19, 185
  and religion 187
  as theme/motif 185, 189
loyalty 19, 22, 142
  to ʿAbbāsids (of Baghdad) 22, 100
  religious 71, 196
lyricists 1, 139
lyrics/lyrical 187
  mood 73
  verses 53, 146

madhhab (school of jurisprudence) 29. *See also* jurisprudence
madrasas 18–19, 38–39, 51, 57, 111, 170, 212
  building programme of 166 (*See also* construction/building projects)
  in Damascus 23
  and defence of Islam 24
  in Fustat 23
  Ḥanafī 25
magic 41, 174 n.120
magnanimity 28, 151
Mahdī 144, 165, 172, 208
Majūs (fire worshipper/Zoroastrian) 84
Mālikī(s) 23
  madhhab 61
Mamlūk(s) 13, 51, 111, 142–143, 181
martyrs/martyrdom 51, 62, 65, 98, 151
  pursuit of (*ṭalab al-shahāda*) 55, 58–59, 61–62, 66, 79, 81, 117, 150 n.56
  status of 62, 65
  tropes 80
massacres 2 n.2, 36, 73
maxims 10, 17. *See also* anecdotes
meanings 190, 212, 225
  syntactic (*maʿānī*) 185, 189
mediation 192
mediators 52, 200
Melkites 223
memory(ies) 155
  collective 53, 73, 94, 114
merchants 141, 178, 223
merits 8. *See also faḍā'il;* virtues
  of Egypt 169
  of Jerusalem 1, 30, 32, 35–36, 95, 113, 178
  of Mecca 95
  of Syria 1, 211 n.2, 218
messengers 95, 114, 148. *See also* prophets
Messiah (*masīḥ*) 96, 133, 144, 147, 157, 222, 224
metaphor 77, 137, 185
metonym 134, 207
migration 18, 69, 178
military 117, 141, 169, 173, 197, 201
  alliances 84
  broader Christian schemes 9, 12, 80, 206
  campaigns 60, 156
  class 58, 66, 100, 220, 225
  encounters 58
  jihād/struggle 56, 156, 157, 202
  leaders 21, 92, 183, 197
  orders (Hospitallers) 141, 177
  victory(ies) 210
minarets 22, 170
minbar (pulpit) 133–134, 144–145, 213
  in al-Aqṣā Mosque 100
miracles 119, 134, 149, 150 n.56, 170, 180
  and victories 117
mirrors for princes (genre) 10, 21 n.53, 27, 74, 160 n.79
misfortune 91, 102, 176
misguidance 103, 138
  vs. guidance 103, 133–134
modesty 184

monasteries 76. *See also* church(es)
Mongols 142–143, 150, 169
 invasion of (658/1260) 18
 threat of 197
monotheism 89–90, 136, 146
 vs. polytheism 95, 103
 victory over polytheism 99
monuments 122, 126. *See also* inscriptions
moon 158, 185–186, 189
 motif of 165
mosques 34, 38, 63, 76, 108, 166, 170, 215
 Frankish occupation of 147
 restoration of 212
 sanctity of al-Aqṣā Mosque 83, 107–108
 Shīʿī 25
 space of 106
motifs 76, 101, 126, 158, 160, 166, 177, 185–187, 207, 212, 217
 day, *vs.* night 145
 eschatological 129, 173, 177
 of finality 167
 foul, *vs.* pure 76
 of ghazal (love poems) 189
 jihād-based 154
 light 145
 moon (*badr*) 165
 positive *vs.* negative 207
 religious 94–95, 129, 189, 217
 of war 137
Muhājirīn (emigrants) 153
mujaddid (lit., renewer) 29
mujāhid 56 n.3, 61, 88, 117, 138, 152, 179 n.131, 199
Munkar and Nakīr 160. *See also* angels
Muslim(s) 12, 63–64, 66, 70–71, 90, 93, 112, 117, 119, 123, 135, 148–149, 161, 170, 203, 206, 221, 223
 alliances/treaties with Franks 84–85, 204
 appropriation of/attachment to Jesus 96, 129, 144–146, 157, 165
 belief of 136, 174 n.120, 197
 and Byzantium/Byzantines 117, 120
 cause of defeat 81, 176
 and Christians 2, 5, 91, 96, 129, 168, 186, 189, 204, 223–224
 community 58, 65, 68, 206
 consciousness/self-perceptions 18, 87
 converting to Christianity 97
 and crusaders 27, 49, 90, 95, 147, 183
 defence of 62, 65
 devotion of 93, 106, 156, 159, 183
 dignity of 81, 123, 155 n.66
 early community of/predecessors 56, 129
 early victories/feats of 114, 197
 fears 88 n.52, 168
 and Franks 11–12, 87, 90, 99, 132, 186, 188, 219
 infighting of (i.e., *vs.* Muslims) 27, 71, 84, 102
 on Jerusalem 30
 leaders/rulers 113–115, 211–212
 nation 70 (*See also umma*)
 as 'Other' 148, 186
 population 198–199
 prisoners 91, 188 (*See also* prisoners)
 reactions/responses and attitudes 1–3, 26–27, 30, 36, 48–49, 55, 67, 68 n.3, 78, 196, 220–221
 of Syria 74, 82, 171
 unity 3, 26, 83, 221
 weakness of 9, 68, 71, 82, 84–85, 98, 111, 120, 198
 women 68, 73, 77, 91, 127

nafs (soul) 156
 jihād al- 59, 65, 224
narrative(s) 15, 77, 80, 148
 apocalyptic 120
 of battle 168, 224
 Qurʾānic 168–169, 171, 207–208
nāṣir (victor) 93, 126
nation 139
 of Jesus/cross 132, 139
 Muslim/of Prophet 70–71, 120, 174 n.120, 198, 211 n.2, 225
 of unbelief 72
Nestorians 223
night journey, and ascension (*al-isrāʾ wa-l-miʿrāj*) (of the Prophet) 3, 88
Normans 135
nostalgia 217
notables 15, 17, 220. *See also* civilian elite

oaths, false 123. *See also* pledge (*bayʿa*)
obligation/obligatory 30, 37, 72, 77, 88, 124, 155
collective (*farḍ al-kifāya*) 56, 68
individual (*farḍ al-ʿayn*) 56, 66, 78
of *jihād* 29, 36, 56, 66, 80, 146, 154–155, 221
for men, *vs.* women 80
of poets 125
to recapture Jerusalem 83, 140
occupation 2–3
of crusaders/Franks 30, 83, 91, 105, 112, 118, 120, 147, 217, 226
of Jerusalem 26, 34, 36, 66, 72, 76, 83, 93, 105–106, 110, 112, 120, 177, 180, 196, 206, 221, 226
of mosques 147
of Syria 78
omen(s) 174 n.120. *See also* portents
oneness (of God)(*tawḥīd*) 114, 130, 146
vs. shirk 207
opportunists 18, 56, 100
oppression 58, 81, 127, 159
and injustice (*maẓālim*) 161
oratory/oratorical 71, 128
order 173
divine/heavenly 22, 146
Islamic 74, 111, 126–127, 158
natural 146, 168
political 74
sacred 75, 210, 219
social 40, 57, 70, 74, 127
orthodoxy 19, 22, 29, 145
defence of 23
of jurists 28
Sunnī 12, 197 n.17
Other/otherness 89, 103, 186, 190
of Christians/Franks 103, 115, 130, 190, 224
of Muslims 148, 186

paganism/pagan(s) 8, 89, 148
panegyrics 34, 47, 50, 74, 128, 181, 222
madīḥ 115, 127–128
nasīb 128
qaṣīda (ode) 130, 193
panic 77, 173, 214
paradise 22, 34, 57, 59, 61, 107, 144–145. *See also* heaven
paronomasia 207
patience 57, 81, 193
patriarchs 75. *See also* priests/clergy
patron(s)/patronage 10, 12, 14, 17–18, 23, 38, 46–48, 79, 98, 100, 128, 176, 196
of architecture 25, 171
religious 18, 29
reputation of 29, 219
peace 83, 108, 137, 207, 223–224
brokers, poets as 192
state of (*ṭumaʾnīna*) 154
pen 87, 195
penitence 96, 215, 217–218
Christian practice of 97
penitents 216
people of the book (*ahl al-kitāb*) 94, 130, 141, 146
deviations of 172
people of the house (*ahl al-bayt;* household of the Prophet) 194
perdition 44 n.10, 206
personification 134
of Amorium 93
of Jerusalem 93, 104
piety 20–21, 29, 44, 47, 57, 65, 97, 100, 122, 133, 151–152, 154, 156, 162, 179 n.131, 181, 210, 216, 226
of rulers 4, 127, 172, 179 n.131
of Sufis 149
and warrior ethos 20, 129, 151, 226
pigs. *See* animals
pilgrimage 12, 31, 33, 107, 155, 178 n.129, 217–218
of Christians 6 n.13
routes 179
ziyāra 3, 155
pilgrims 121–123, 126–128, 225
iḥrām (garb of) 107
Muslims to Christian sites 223
pledge (*bayʿa*) 153
plunder 73, 127, 178, 181, 223 n.11
poetry/poetic 1, 15–17, 19, 29, 33, 36, 41–43, 48, 49, 53, 64, 77, 88, 91, 95, 98, 108, 111–112, 124, 134, 151, 157, 165–166, 177, 183, 185, 192, 197 n.17, 198, 222, 224. *See also* panegyrics
ʿAbbāsid 212
analyses of 46–47
anthology of (*dīwān*) 11, 42, 184

anti-Frankish 2, 17, 65, 72, 142, 147
Arabic 1, 125, 139, 162
of asceticism (*zuhdiyya*) 160
audiences for 141, 167, 183
celebratory 41, 49, 113, 128, 157, 167, 172, 225
commemorative 50, 164, 172, 209
complaint 121, 185–186, 217
congratulatory 67, 116, 126–127, 177
conventions 139, 145, 224
court 82, 100, 139, 220, 222
and crusades/crusaders 40, 50–51, 70–72, 75–76, 79, 83, 92–94, 97, 99, 101, 103, 108, 125, 127, 131, 135–137, 139, 155, 157, 163, 224
devices 212
and diplomacy 52, 192, 199
dubayts 50, 152–155, 203, 213
duels 52
early 78, 81, 89
erotic/sensual 187, 189
faḍāʾil (merits, virtues) 209
Fāṭimid 144, 192
of First Crusade 120, 127
form 185
gendered 142, 188, 222
genius 190
ghazal (love poems) 184–185, 189–190
on Ḥaṭṭīn 103
and history 42–43, 49–50, 52, 78, 87
as ideological and political vehicle 1
ideology(ies) of 1, 42, 129, 183
imagery in 89, 111
of Iraqi and Lebanese war 53
jāhilī (pre-Islamic) 40
and *jihād* 2, 52, 65, 67, 72, 81, 130, 140, 142, 147–148, 154, 190, 199, 219, 224
lampoon (*hijāʾ*) 2, 41, 83, 115, 130
as literary vehicle 47, 219
and literature of *jihād* 2, 50, 52, 65, 67, 68 n.3, 72, 125, 130, 140, 142, 147–148, 199, 219, 224
of longing/yearning (*ḥanīnī*) 82, 86, 185
muwashshaḥ 111
non-Arabic words in 176
as political 50, 53
position of/role of 41, 49, 50, 54
praise/laudatory (*madīḥ*) 15, 128, 165, 209 (*See also* praise (poetry))
Qurʾān references in 101–102, 201
recitation of 67, 163
religious 16, 72, 220, 225
to rouse popular support 195
satire 144
of social unease/division 121
as source of information 50, 53
spiritual aspects of 129, 201
structure of 124
study of 11, 52
theft (*sariqa*) 19, 212
themes 2, 27–28, 41, 46, 52–53, 68 n.3, 81, 83, 103, 108, 116, 125, 129, 169, 185–186, 192, 206, 211–212, 218, 219, 222 (*See also* motifs)
translations 42, 47
use of quotations (*taḍmīn*) 212
veneration expressed in 62, 93
vocabulary of 111, 173
poets 1, 9, 19, 23, 36, 40, 64, 71, 92, 98–99, 110, 112, 142, 151, 176, 211–212, 220
advisory 125
audiences of 41–42, 71, 77, 87, 101, 111, 141, 156–158, 163, 167, 169, 172–173, 183, 199, 211–212, 225
on Christianity 142
court 40, 82, 100, 128, 139, 151, 190, 220, 222
function of 41
invectives of 85
language of 70, 169
love (*ḥubb*) 19
power of 40, 193, 195
sentiments of 47, 69, 71, 79, 86, 115, 127–128, 140, 145, 152, 160, 166, 182, 186, 199, 217–218, 222, 224–225
significance of 16
as spokesmen of Islam 41
status of 40, 111, 139, 145, 146
subjects of 184
Sunnī, of Syria 193
Yemeni 192
polemics 90, 108, 130, 136, 145, 147
anti-Shīʿī 25
of Muslims, against Christianity 130
politics/political 11, 74, 140, 173, 194, 196, 199, 213, 226
alliances 208
authority 10, 17, 28, 40, 162, 193

politics/political (cont.)
disunity 143, 199
milieu/state of affairs 143, 221
patronage 29
and poetry 50, 53, 219
policies 160, 219
power 26, 112, 193
rivalries/squabbles 3, 84–85, 97–98, 193
unity 26, 192, 197, 202, 205
weakness, of Muslims 9, 198
polytheism/polytheists 83, 89–90, 94–95, 98–99, 101–102
shirk 94–95, 102, 198
pope 81, 132, 134
portents 119, 150, 179
portrait, literary 128
portrayal (of traits) 185–186
power 119, 164, 179, 188, 194
of caliphs 77, 193, 196, 205, 207
of Christians 23–24, 143
of Fāṭimids 193, 196, 197 n.17, 200, 208
of God 88, 116, 119, 169, 171
holders 15
of literary word/poets 40, 193, 195
miraculous 21, 114
political 26, 112, 193
of sultans 22, 116
temporal 161
praise (poetry) 41, 86, 115–116, 122–123, 128, 133, 154, 171, 182, 185, 193, 197 n.17, 199, 202, 209
of God 114, 167, 222
hyperbolic 176
of *jihād* 81, 154
madīḥ; madḥ 125, 128, 130
for Nūr al-Dīn 20, 187, 205, 212
for Ṣalāḥ al-Dīn 15, 74, 113, 127, 139, 181
prayer(s) 94–95, 106, 123, 162, 166, 215, 217–218
communal 223
direction of 216
preachers/preaching 18, 36, 110, 112–113, 149. *See also khaṭībs*
competitive spirit of 220
jihād 38
predecessors (early Muslims) 56, 129, 151
feats of 111
religiosity of 183
salaf 96
predestination 80, 130
predetermination/fate 43, 119
priests/clergy 75, 97, 102–103, 140
prisoners 91, 123, 133, 148–149, 180–181, 188
proof (*ḥujja*) 62
propaganda 1, 31, 37, 47, 51, 64, 106, 113, 152, 220, 225
anti-crusader 163
jihād 4, 51, 54, 61, 196, 219–220
of Nūr al-Dīn 114, 220
religious 163, 225
of Ṣalāḥ al-Dīn (d. 613/1216) 114, 195, 220
prophecy 104, 114–115, 177
prophethood 210, 211
prophets 32, 95, 111, 113, 149, 170–171, 177, 179, 216
propriety 184
prose 16, 42, 46–47, 53–54, 80, 88
rhymed 42, 78, 87–88, 116, 137–138
prosimetrum 78
prostration 187
public
exhortation 37
jihād 21
jubilation 169, 214
life 11, 23, 37
readings 18, 23, 36, 38, 106
punishment 166, 198
divine 101–102
purification 86, 94, 101, 147, 167–168, 213
of Jerusalem/Holy Land 123, 125, 145–146, 168
of occupied land 140
religious 143, 221
purity 75, 186

qāḍīs 151, 215
qaṣīda (ode) 40, 53, 79, 115, 128, 130, 151, 182, 185, 193, 197 n.17, 209
congratulatory 205
panegyric 130, 193
traditional 160
qibla 216
ahl al-qibla (Muslims) 179
quatrains (*rubāʿī*) 152
Qurʾān/Qurʾānic 32, 43–44, 55, 57, 64–65, 70, 76–77, 81, 85, 96 n.70, 109–110, 114, 139, 166, 204
allusions 111, 165, 167–168, 183, 207, 225
and Dhū l-Qarnayn 174 n.120
on end times/eschatology 114, 177, 218

hermeneutics 104, 105 n.23
ideals 41
imagery 49, 52, 77, 85, 101, 129, 132, 136, 166, 169, 183, 222
inscriptions 25, 170, 172
on Jerusalem 36
and *jihād* 56
and Joseph 207–208
laws/injunctions 18, 141, 146
in literature 166
muṣḥaf 133–134, 146
narratives and parables 126, 168–169, 207–208
and oneness (*tawḥīd*) 130
prominence/importance of 108, 166–167, 170, 183, 217
prophets 177
reciters/recitations 18, 21, 30, 106, 109, 146, 166–167
references in poetry 101–102, 201
superiority of 96, 109
Sūra al-Tīn (The Fig) 33
Sūra Rūm 105
Sūra Ṣaff 157
Sūra Ṭā-hā 170–172
Sūrat al-Anbiyā' (The Prophets) 172
Sūrat al-Anfāl 165
Sūrat al-Fatḥ 172
Sūrat al-Insān 172
Sūrat Rūm 121
Sūra Yūsuf 207
themes in 78, 171
vocabulary of 85, 169
and Yūsuf (Joseph) 207

raids (*ghazwa*) 152
summer (*ṣayfiyya*) 36, 154, 221
rationale 113, 204. *See also* justification
for crusades 137
religious 135, 182
realpolitik 192
language of 194, 208
reckoning, day of (*yawm al-ḥisāb*) 160. *See also* judgement, day of
reconquest (of Jerusalem) (583/1187) 11, 35, 37, 67, 74–75, 86–87, 97, 99, 103, 108, 110, 113, 115, 117–118, 121, 123, 167, 213, 221
rectification 60, 97, 197
redemption 5, 144
reflection 43, 171, 182, 189, 222
reforms 57, 162, 180
refugees 83, 100, 128
religion/religious 1, 3, 33, 40, 44 n.11, 45, 55, 73, 85, 104, 107, 112, 114, 117, 122, 127, 132, 145–146, 151, 154, 158–159, 168, 173, 174 n.120, 187, 196, 198, 213, 219
agendas/policy 26, 142, 213
ascriptions 133
authority 55
awakening 51
belief/practice 26, 226
boundaries 161, 190
character of Jerusalem 217
classes 2 n.2, 3, 18, 20, 21, 60, 66, 73–74, 100, 150, 165, 183, 213, 225
commitment/devotion to 47, 101, 104, 184
conscience 189, 221
contention/differences 139, 142
cosmology 6
ideals 56
imagery 72 n.12, 110–111, 137, 160, 208
institutions 18, 20, 22, 51
laws of 74–75
laxity/weakness 27, 36, 159
literature 177
loyalty 71, 196, 217
milieu/context 17, 26, 55, 140, 143
orthodoxy 145 (*See also* orthodoxy)
patronage 18, 29
poetry 72, 220
principles 28, 146, 148
propaganda 163, 225
rationale behind crusades 64, 135, 182
scholars 2 n.2, 19, 64, 66, 193
sciences 18, 43
sensibilities 74, 78, 194, 197, 216
sentiments 57, 159, 162, 173, 219, 224
sites 93, 217
superiority of 129, 140, 183
symbolism 32, 140
terminology/language 52, 145, 187
themes/motifs 94–95, 99, 129, 189, 217
transgressions 138
warnings 140–141
religiosity 17, 29, 43, 63, 72, 99, 140, 156 n.70, 159, 173, 213, 225
Christian 96
of Hospitallers 141
of predecessors 183

reputation 38, 61, 64, 92, 204
of Nūr al-Dīn 86, 151, 183, 212
of patrons 29, 219
of Ṣalāh al-Dīn 100, 121, 180
resistance 36, 57, 60
Islamic/Muslim 34, 66, 221
popular 220
resolve 79, 92, 169, 182, 200, 209
respect 38 n.101, 220, 223
resurrection 7, 35, 84, 161, 167
day of (*yawm al-qiyāma*) 35, 77, 116, 137, 173, 214–215
of Jesus 4
revelation(s) 109, 111, 114, 166
place/abode of 94, 215
reverence 104, 126, 184, 224
for Jesus 144, 148
for sacred space 36
reward 33, 65–66, 86, 107, 114, 123, 144, 166, 194
financial/monetary 124, 127
rhetoric(al) 37, 43, 47, 83, 87, 90, 113
anti-Christian 114
devices 95, 163, 190
images 128
Islamic 146
jihād 38, 57, 61, 164
rhyme(d) 41–42, 53, 152, 172
prose 42, 78, 87–88, 116, 137–138
righteousness 161, 216
rivals/rivalry 3, 16, 26, 98, 100, 192–193, 220, 224
dynastic 173
faith 24, 97
of Jesus *vs.* Muḥammad 145
between Shāwar and Shīrkūh 194
Romans 121
rule/rulers 16–17, 19, 22, 23 n.58, 40–41, 57, 78, 159, 163, 166, 193, 204
Ayyūbids 100, 136, 205, 207
beliefs of 28
ideal 16, 207
just/pious 66, 164, 208
legitimacy of 182
Muslim 211–212
and saints 21
Sunnī 212
ruling class/elite 17, 22, 50, 66, 68, 206, 220
Rūm 72–73, 105, 115, 120
Rumiyya 190
rumours 58, 179

sacred/sacredness 4 n.8, 6, 69, 74–75, 82, 95, 219
designations 8, 94, 225
Jerusalem as 4–6, 8 n.20, 32–33, 36, 73, 94, 99, 108, 114, 126, 145, 200, 218, 219, 225
knowledge 38
loss/violation of 4, 82, 176, 178, 180
Mecca as 94, 182, 217
order 75, 126, 210, 219
personages 95
precincts/sites 95, 112, 141, 179–180, 219
sites, for Christians 4–5, 7, 36, 135, 137–138, 221
space 4, 36, 110, 126, 135, 218
text/scripture 165–166
sacrifice 63, 127
sacrilege 89. *See also* desecration
saints 10, 21, 161 n.85
shrines of 178 n.129
visions of 149
salaf (Muslim predecessors) 44 n.11, 96
Saljūq(s) 23, 25, 68, 162
period 10, 27–28, 39
rulers/sultans 22, 66
salvation 140, 166
sanctification (of Jerusalem) 99, 170–171
sanctity(ies) 73, 75, 110, 134, 172, 219, 221
of al-Aqṣā Mosque 83, 107–108, 147
of Bilād al-Shām region 39
of Damascus 33–34
of Islam 74
of Jerusalem 6, 8 n.20, 30, 32–33, 35, 73–75, 94, 99, 108, 172, 217, 219, 221
lost 93–94
of Mecca 33, 93
of mosques 147
of space/place 39, 68–69, 76
of tomb/grave of Jesus 138
sanctuary(ies) 107, 216–217
maqām 137
Saraceni 148
sarcasm 131
satire 134, 144, 222
of Franks/crusaders 104, 157
Sayhān, waters of 116, 134

scholars 2, 58, 93, 106, 110, 151
Arab 54
religious 193
role of 23
of *tafsīr* 45
science(s) 53, 151
of *ḥadīth* 33
Islamic 18, 43–45
scribes 100, 193–194, 211
scriptures 55, 76, 96, 115, 146, 166, 183
importance of, for Christians 108–109
second coming (of Jesus) 126, 173
sectarian (division/discord) 173, 196, 202
secular 221
agendas 18
influences 1
motives 20, 55
self-accountability 161
self-rectification 97, 197
sentiments 1, 57, 106, 112, 121, 125, 135, 154, 162, 180, 182, 199, 208, 213, 222–223, 225
of crusaders 137, 174 n.120
of dismay 215
of grief/loss 82, 217
pietistic 122, 151, 169
of poets 47, 69, 71, 79, 86, 115, 127–128, 140, 145, 152, 160, 166, 182, 186, 199, 217–218, 222, 224–225
political 219
religious 57, 85, 112, 145, 159, 162, 168, 173, 219
sermon(s) 1, 33, 60, 114, 172, 206
and end of time references 222
of Ibn al-Zakī 113
sexual
immorality 190
violations 68
Shāfiʿī(s) 23, 56
shahīd (witness/martyr) 65. *See also* martyrs
shame 127
ḥayāʾ, 68–69
sharīʿa 73, 75, 100, 207, 214
shaykhs, status of 23
Shīʿa/Shīʿī(s) 24, 34, 57, 100, 111, 145, 193–195, 199, 207, 221
in Aleppo 25
countering/suppressing 18, 23
heresy/unorthodoxies 18, 121, 196
Nizārī Ismāʿīlīs 206
Rāfiḍī(s) 83
response to crusaders 196
sites of worship 25
and Sunnīs 202
Twelver and Ismāʾīlī 163, 192 n.2
shrine(s) 4 n.8, 34, 178 n.129, 223
of Saidnaya 223
shyness (*ḥafr; ḥayāʾ*) 93, 184–186
signs 105, 149, 157, 174 n.120, 176, 188, 202
divine 5
of last days 113, 116, 173
sincerity 128, 136, 184
sin(s) 57, 69, 80, 107, 109, 134, 156 n.70, 160, 173
slaughter 5, 74, 83, 131
sleep 68, 70–71, 135, 207. *See also* dreams
slogans 220
jihād 4
social
acceptability 184, 190, 225
act, poetry as 50
bias 52
history 45, 48
identity 143
justice 224
memory, collective 73, 94
milieu/circles 143, 151
order 16, 40, 57, 70, 74, 127, 143
role/standing 37, 106, 128, 141, 152
unease/tumult 5, 21, 121, 198
soldiers 18, 26, 122, 134, 149, 160, 162, 199, 202, 224. *See also* army(ies); warriors
solidarity 92, 217
sorrow 52, 78, 108, 139, 156 n.70. *See also* grief
souls 56, 123, 125, 215
Source-Critical/Factual Approach 45
source(s) 1, 225
for crusades/crusaders 1, 13
history/historical 49–50
literary 29
poetry/verse as 50, 53
translations of Arabic 16, 47–49, 99
space
conceptualisation of 110
of mosques 106
sacred 4, 36, 110, 126, 135, 218
sanctity of 39, 68–69, 76

spiritual/spirituality 151–152, 161, 224
  aspects of poetry 129, 201
  center, Damascus/Syria as 34, 106, 129, 218
  connection to Jerusalem 4, 6, 37, 221
  dimension of *jihād* 21, 37, 57, 156
  focus 28, 151–152, 156, 159, 167, 218
  laxity 27
  struggle 55, 57, 150 n.56, 157–158
  and Sufism 149
spoil-of-war 85, 165, 186, 222, 224
station, of Abraham (Ibrāhīm) 95, 179
statues 94, 174 n.120
status
  of *dhimmīs* 142–143
  of Franks 194
  of Jerusalem 30
  of martyrs 62, 65
  of Nūr al-Dīn 84
  of people of the book 94, 130, 141, 146
  of poetry/poets 40, 111, 139, 145–146
  religious, of crusaders 131, 146
  of shaykhs 23
steadfastness 57, 92, 165
struggle 56
  inner/outer 57
  military 56, 156–157, 202
  physical 64, 66, 70, 98
  spiritual 55, 57, 150 n.56, 157–158
subjugation 69
  of Muslims 77, 90–91
subtleties/nuances 45–47, 76, 152, 163, 190, 219, 225
  of approach 33, 42 n.6
  of language 111
suffering 5, 67–68, 71, 81, 97, 126, 158, 216, 220
Sufi(s)/Sufism 10, 14, 19–21, 59, 161–162, 221
  growth of/influence 129, 149–151, 183, 225
  hospices (*ribāṭ; khānqāhs*) 19, 21
  lodges (*zāwiya*) 21 n.50, 134, 170, 212
  and Ṣalāḥ al-Dīn 20–21
  Suhrawardiyya order 28
  thought/outlook 28, 151, 217–218
suicide 58
sultans 16, 18, 75, 101, 121, 127, 137
  attributes/qualities of 104, 111, 213
  as exemplar 72, 115
  images/depictions of 102–103, 126, 145, 195
  justice of 28, 99, 122, 127
  legitimacy of 112, 182
  power of 116
  Saljūqs 22
sun 72, 101, 158, 187, 189
Sunnī(s) 3, 29, 39, 100, 143, 192 n.2, 193, 195, 197 n.17, 212
  caliphs/caliphate 3, 111, 113, 205
  creed/faith 23, 57
  defence of 23
  enemies of 177
  Islam 20, 22, 76, 111
  legitimacy of 207
  orthodoxy of 12, 197 n.17
  poets of Syria 193
  promotion of 25, 166
  revitalising/strengthening of 18, 23
  revival 25, 26, 27, 57, 111, 121, 183
  schools of law 23
  and Shīʿī tensions 25, 202
  unity of 200
superiority 148, 207
  of Qurʾān 96, 109
  of religion (Islam) 2, 90, 99, 103, 108, 129–130, 140–141, 183
supplications 20, 63, 126, 162
Suriani 148
swords 73, 83–84, 102–103, 122, 126, 137, 144–145, 153, 155 n.66, 158, 159 n.78, 163, 182, 195, 209–210, 214, 224
symbols/symbolism 136, 168, 170, 185, 205, 207–208, 219
  Christian 75–76, 89, 95, 102, 104 n.14, 110, 112, 125, 147, 219 (*See also* crosses)
  of crusaders 95, 126, 158, 174 n.120
  Islamic 75–76, 90
  of Jerusalem 217
  love/erotic 189
  religious 32, 140
  of worship 94, 224

taxes/taxation 91, 140, 159, 166, 173, 223
  officials 125
tears/weeping 61, 155, 184, 215, 217
tenacity 59–60, 135–136
  of the Prophet 64
Textual Approach 45–47
themes 69, 197
  ancient 193, 209
  of crusades 4 n.8, 224

of dependence/reliance 158
Islamic 74, 225
of Jerusalem 51, 219
of *jihād* 49–50, 142, 154
of lost sanctity 93
of love/longing 185, 189
of merits (*faḍāʾil*) 51, 183, 208, 217
of al-Mutanabbī 79, 209
in poetry/poetic 2, 27–28, 41, 46, 52–53, 68 n.3, 81, 83, 103, 108, 116, 125, 129, 169, 185–186, 192, 206, 211–212, 218, 219, 222 (*See also* motifs)
Qurʾānic 78, 171
religious 94–95, 99–100, 129, 183
of restoration 168, 206–207
theologians 27, 29, 101, 212
theology/theological 101, 109, 111, 130, 165, 183, 221
conventions 193
discussions 25, 78
of Shīʿīs 196
victory 134, 146
title, al-Malik al-Nāṣir 93, 107, 123–124, 126
Torah 109
trade 179, 223
tradition(s) 6, 8, 24, 30, 33, 35, 107, 117–119, 150, 186, 212, 218
apocalyptic 33–34, 114, 117
authenticity of 38, 211 n.2
Isrāʾīliyyāt 32
on *jihād* 34, 211 n.2
on martyrdom 62
on merits, virtues (*faḍāʾil*) 31 n.77, 32–34, 36, 218
oral 42
prophetic 10, 36, 43, 119, 150, 211 n.2 (*See also ḥadīth*)
transgressions 127, 136, 138, 146, 173. *See also* sin(s)
translations 49, 67, 99
of Arabic sources 16, 47–49, 99
of Latin sources 1
literal 42
travel/travellers 18–19, 21, 24, 34, 66, 99–100, 102, 123, 127, 136, 183, 223–224
accounts of 11, 34 n.90, 121–122
treachery 84, 124, 126
tribal/tribalism 53
grievances 52
loyalties 71
society, praise of 193
trinity 102, 130, 146
symbol of 95
triumphs 82, 99, 114, 126, 150, 162, 168, 210. *See also* victory(ies)
troops. *See* army(ies); soldiers
tropes 145, 187. *See also* motifs; themes
martyrdom 80
truces 178, 200, 223. *See also* alliances
truth 43, 45, 53, 93, 119, 154, 182, 190–191, 208, 211 n.2
vs. error 95
vs. falsehood 207
historical 1, 43, 44 n.11, 46–47, 225
Turci 148

ʿulamāʾ (scholars) 17–21, 23, 29, 106, 220
ʿālim 96
consensus of 76
Umayyad period 31, 185, 190
umma (nation) 28, 56–57, 111–112, 139, 163, 171, 215
blame on 68, 97
collective memory of 38, 64
of Jesus 132
weakness of 111, 198
unbelief 57, 71, 73, 75, 84, 86, 103, 134, 140
vs. belief 170
books of 109
of Christians 204
vs. faith(s) 103, 177
vs. guidance 207
jihād against 201
kufr 72, 85, 109, 141, 168, 204
party of 196, 204
unbeliever(s) 84–85, 110, 123, 133, 153, 155, 162, 164–165, 174 n.120, 197 n.17, 200
jihād against 155
rule over believers 91
unification/union 202
of Egypt and Syria 208
of Mecca and Jerusalem 217
of Muslims 225
of Syria 205, 212
unity 16, 78, 82–83, 102, 110, 122, 200–201, 221
of Egypt and Syria 192, 199, 202
of God 114 (*See also* oneness)
political 197, 202, 205
urban (milieu) 151

valour (*ḥamāsa*) 52, 64
veneration
  expressed in poetry/literature 62, 93
  of Jerusalem 3, 31, 221
  objects of 89, 101
verses. *See also* poetry/poetic; Qur'ān
  forms of (*balāh* and *zāmil*) 52
  lyrical 53, 146
  ornate/embellished 1, 128, 189
  theft of (*sariqa*) 212
victory(ies) 1, 13, 21, 72, 80, 83, 86, 88, 90, 117–118, 120, 123, 126, 134, 136, 138, 149, 164–165, 168, 172, 200, 209–210, 218, 224
  of crusaders 9
  of early Muslims 114, 197
  from God 167, 201
  for Islam/of Muslims 4, 83, 90, 95, 126, 168, 173, 176, 210
  and miracles 114, 117
  over Byzantium 115
  over Christians/crusaders 146, 154
  over unbelief/polytheism 99, 170
  poems about 103
  of Ṣalāḥ al-Dīn 177, 212–213
  theological 134, 146
  of *umma* 112
  of victories (*fatḥ al-futūḥ*) 88, 115
virgin birth 138
virtues 30, 36, 40, 64, 72, 95, 152, 186, 211. *See also faḍā'il;* merits
  of Alexandria 33
  of Jerusalem 8, 38, 95
  of Mecca 95
  religious 107, 214
  of Ṣalāḥ al-Dīn 12
  of Syria 8, 34 n.90, 93
virtuosity 204
visions 149
visitations 31, 88
  sites of (*ziyāra*) 65, 155
viziers (*wazīrs*) 13, 22, 86, 151, 176, 193, 195–196, 199

warrior(s) 34, 149, 152
  -ascetics 156, 226
  holy 18, 149, 163, 195
  for Islam 151
  jihād 29, 50, 183
  pious ethos of 20, 129, 150–151
war(s) 5, 72, 77, 132, 136, 150, 155 n.66, 169, 182, 200–201, 220, 224. *See also* prisoners
  with Byzantium 89
  of end time 218
  holy 26
  motifs of 137
  between Muslim(s) 27
  poetry of Iraq and Lebanon 53
  Qur'ān on 18, 56
  sanctioning/justifying 23
  spoils of 85, 165, 186, 222, 224
weakness 79, 130, 204
  of Muslim(s) 9, 27, 71, 82, 84–85, 98, 111, 120, 198
wealth/resources 201–202, 213, 220
  of Egypt 206, 212
wedding procession (Frankish) 188, 224
women 204
  attitude toward 162
  Banāt al-Aṣfar ('pale-faced women') 85, 186, 222
  beauty of 224
  bodies of 190
  chaste 69, 80
  and children 58, 68, 70, 74, 97, 204
  and fighting 80
  Frankish 98, 184, 187, 190, 203–204, 219, 224
    as a *fitna* 185, 188–189
    as spoil of war 186, 222, 224
  inviolability of 73–74, 123, 127
  mourners 139
  Muslim 77, 91
  worship (in churches) 184, 187, 219, 224
wonders (*'ajā'ib*) 87, 174 n.120
word-play/word associations 42, 89, 101, 103, 116, 137, 154, 158, 170
worldly
  adornment 213
  dunyā 65, 71
  life/trappings 81–82, 151–154, 213
  love of 156
  success 145
worship 51, 58, 110, 138, 154–155, 193, 198, 216, 218, 224
  acts of 28, 31, 155
  Christian 110, 130, 138, 147
  false/misdirected 98, 130, 134–135, 138

places of 141
Shīʿī sites of 25
symbols of 94, 224
of women (in churches) 184, 187, 219, 224
worshippers 2 n.2, 84, 98, 161, 198, 216, 224

yawm al-maḥshar (day of gathering) 168
yawm al-qiyāma (day of judgement/resurrection) 77, 137, 173, 214–215. *See also* judgement, day of; resurrection
yearning/longing 73, 112, 171, 216
for holy city/Jerusalem 30, 51, 218
for *jihād* 36, 73
poetry of (*ḥanīnī*) 82, 86, 185

zakāt 121, 124, 127
Zangids 15, 17, 25–26, 51, 100, 136, 144, 151, 212, 214
dynasty 12–13, 163
ziyāra (visitation) 3, 65, 155, 162

Printed in the United States
By Bookmasters